MACARTNEY
OF LISANOURE
1737–1806

Essays in Biography

Edited by

PETER ROEBUCK

Belfast
Ulster Historical Foundation

1983

ISBN 0-901905-30-5

© The Contributors, 1983.

*Printed by Graham & Sons (Printers) Ltd.,
51 Gortin Road, Omagh, Co. Tyrone BT79 7HZ.*
*Bound by Eric E. Honeyford & Sons Ltd.,
6 Bridge Street, Belfast BT1 1LU.*

THE U.H.F. HISTORICAL SERIES

1. *Ulster Emigration to Colonial America 1718-1775* by R. J. Dickson (1966: reprint, 1976).

2. *Essays in Scotch-Irish History,* edited by E. R. R. Green (1969). Essay titles and contributors are as follows:

    i 'Woodrow Wilson and his Presbyterian Inheritance' by Arthur S. Link.
    ii 'Education in the American Colonies: The Scottish Impact' by Esmond Wright.
    iii 'Ulster Emigration 1783-1815' by Maldwyn A. Jones.
    iv 'The Scotch-Irish: Their Cultural Adaptation and Heritage in the Old West' by E. Estyn Evans.
    v 'Ulster Emigrants' Letters' by E. R. R. Green.

3. *The Scottish Migration to Ulster in the Reign of James I* by M. Perceval-Maxwell (1973).

4. *Penal Era and Golden Age: Essays in Irish History, 1690-1800,* edited by Thomas Bartlett and D. W. Hayton (1979). Essay titles and contributors are as follows:

    i 'The Irish Parliament of 1692' by James I. McGuire.
    ii 'The Beginnings of the "Undertaker System" ' by David Hayton.
    iii 'The Money Bill Dispute of 1753' by Declan O'Donovan.
    iv 'The Townshend Viceroyalty, 1767-72' by Thomas Bartlett.
    v 'The Volunteers and Parliament, 1779-84' by P. D. H. Smyth.
    vi ' "The Parliamentary Traffic of this Country" ' by A. P. W. Malcomson.
    vii 'Middlemen' by David Dickson.
    viii 'Change in Ulster in the late Eighteenth Century' by W. H. Crawford.
    ix 'Irish Republicanism in England: the First Phase, 1797-9' by Marianne Elliott.

5. *Scottish Covenanters and Irish Confederates: Scottish-Irish Relations in the Mid-Seventeenth Century* by David Stevenson (1981).

6. *Macartney of Lisanoure, 1737-1806: Essays in Biography,* edited by P. Roebuck with contributions by T. J. Bartlett, J. L. Cranmer-Byng, T. G. Fraser, W. R. Fryer, E. M. Johnston, J. L. McCracken, M. Roberts and P. Roebuck (1983).

CONTENTS

PREFACE

Few of his contemporaries led a more interesting or adventurous life than George Macartney of Lisanoure. Born in 1737, he was the great-grandson of a Scottish immigrant to Ulster who had prospered from business and trading activities in post-Restoration Belfast. Following school, university and private education in Leixlip and Dublin, Macartney attended Lincoln's Inn and the Middle Temple in London during the later 1750s. Thereafter, having inherited his family's modest estate at Loughguile and Dervock in north-east Co. Antrim, he embarked on a European tour. In the course of his travels Macartney encountered the wealthy and well-connected Stephen Fox, whom he rescued from one of his disastrous bouts of gambling. The two subsequently became firm friends and it was through the patronage of Fox's father, Lord Holland, that Macartney made a brilliant start to a public career in 1764 on being appointed Britain's Envoy Extraordinary to the Court of Catherine the Great of Russia. Besides involving him in Irish affairs as Chief Secretary under Lord Townshend, later appointments took Macartney to the Caribbean as Governor of Grenada; to India as President of Fort St. George, the East India Company's establishment at Madras; to China as Britain's first Ambassador; to Verona in Italy on an unofficial mission to the exiled Louis XVIII of France; and finally to Africa as Governor of Britain's newly-acquired settlement at the Cape of Good Hope. Macartney's record as a diplomat and administrator earned him a decoration from the King of Poland, a knighthood of the Bath, successive promotions in the peerage, and membership of the Privy Council. In addition to supplementing his meagre private income, the profits of office enabled him to expand and improve his Ulster estate, to acquire further property in London and Surrey and, latterly, to amass considerable wealth. He was eventually offered a seat in the Cabinet, but declined on the grounds that his health was too uncertain for him to contemplate further public service. Nevertheless, he continued to be solicited for advice on public affairs and by the end of his life was generally regarded as one of the most successful and widely experienced Irishmen of his generation.

The purpose of this book is to provide the first comprehensive account of Macartney's extraordinary career. Besides being scattered throughout numerous collections in several repositories, the evidence relating to his activities is far from complete. Many of his files were irretrievably lost in the Caribbean, for example, and numerous private papers disappeared in the century or so after his death. Thus, earlier works by Barrow[1] and Robbins[2] remain valuable: for, although both were uncritical and incomplete, they drew on some records which are no longer extant. However, in recent decades a vast amount of additional material has been identified or become available. In addition the accumulation of other completed work has facilitated the task of placing each aspect of Macartney's career in its full historical context. It was this requirement which prompted the decision to engage in a collaborative effort. Macartney's public duties were so complex and varied that it is doubtful whether a single author could do full justice to them. Accordingly, each episode has been scrutinized by an individual specialist, while the editor has dealt with Macartney's private life and attempted to co-ordinate the whole.

This book could not have been published without generous financial assistance from the Institute of Irish Studies at Queen's University, Belfast, and Coutts Bank. This help is most gratefully acknowledged. A host of other individual acknowledgements are made at appropriate points elsewhere in this volume. We would like, however, to express our collective gratitude to those who deposited the records which we have consulted, and to the numerous librarians and archivists who have assisted us in the course of our work. Our best thanks are reserved for Mr. Brian Trainor (administrator of the Ulster Historical Foundation) and Dr. A. P. W. Malcomson, who have laboured unstintingly over many years to make the publication of this book possible; they have been our fellow contributors throughout this venture.

Peter Roebuck

Department of History
New University of Ulster

LIST OF CONTRIBUTORS

Thomas Bartlett   Lecturer in History, University College, Galway.

J. L. Cranmer-Byng   Professor of History, University of Toronto.

T. G. Fraser   Lecturer in History, New University of Ulster.

W. R. Fryer   Emeritus Professor of History, University of Nottingham.

E. M. Johnston   Professor of History, Macquarie University.

J. L. McCracken   Emeritus Professor of History, New University of Ulster.

Michael Roberts   Emeritus Professor of History, Queen's University, Belfast.

Peter Roebuck   Senior Lecturer in History, New University of Ulster.

LIST OF MAPS AND ILLUSTRATIONS

Note: The spelling of all Ulster place- and townland names has
been standardised to accord with the current usage of the
Ordnance Survey.

CHRONOLOGY OF THE LIFE OF LORD MACARTNEY

1737	Birth.
1745-50	Schooling at Leixlip.
1750-54	Undergraduate at Trinity College, Dublin.
1754-57	Dublin: Private Tuition under William Dennis.
1757-59	London: Lincoln's Inn and Middle Temple.
1759	M.A. Trinity College, Dublin.
	Inherits Loughguile and Dervock estates on death of his uncle.
1760	Embarks on European Tour.
1760-61	Meets Stephen Fox in Geneva.
1764	Knighthood.
1764-67	Envoy Extraordinary to the Court of Catherine the Great of Russia.
1767	Knighthood of the White Eagle of Poland.
1768	Marriage to Lady Jane Stuart, daughter of the Earl of Bute.
1769-72	Chief Secretary for Ireland.
1770	Begins re-building Lisanoure Castle and improving the demesne.
1772	Knighthood of the Bath.
1775-79	Governor of Grenada.
1776	Barony in the Irish Peerage.
1779	Captured by the French; shipped to France; returned to England.
	Inherits Killinchy and Porter estates on death of his father.
1780	Unofficial mission to Ireland on behalf of Lord North's government.
1781-85	President of Fort St. George, Madras.
1786	Elected to the Literary Club.
1786-87	Buys house in Curzon St. London, and property at Parkhurst in Surrey.
	Embarks on further improvements in north Antrim.
1792	Member of the Privy Council.
	Fellow of the Royal Society.
	Viscountcy in the Irish Peerage.
1792-94	Ambassador to China.
1794	Earldom in the Irish Peerage.
1795-96	Unofficial mission to King Louis XVIII in exile at Verona.
1796	Barony in the British Peerage.
1796-98	Governor of the Cape of Good Hope.
1801	Trustee of the British Museum.
1801-6	Expands and improves Loughguile estate.
	Re-builds Dervock and founds a market.
1806	Death.

CHAPTER I

EARLY YEARS 1737-64

I

When Macartney was offered the post of Envoy-Extraordinary to Russia in May 1764, he was just twenty-seven years of age. While it was not unknown for young and inexperienced individuals to obtain senior official positions, there can be little doubt that this appointment constituted a remarkable start to what was to become an extraordinary career. Macartney secured the appointment largely through the influence of Henry Fox, Lord Holland, who had known him for some three years. It was equally remarkable that someone of Holland's public stature should have been thus quickly persuaded to promote the interests of a young Irishman, so recently emerged from his native country and from a comparatively obscure and insubstantial background. Holland was deeply indebted to Macartney for having extricated his son, Stephen Fox, from one of his periodic and exceedingly costly bouts at the gaming table; but, of itself, this seems an inadequate explanation of the extent of his patronage. He must also have been greatly impressed by Macartney. Nor, apparently, was Lord Holland alone in his enthusiasm: particularly at this stage, Macartney seems to have won the respect, if not the admiration, of many of those who came into contact with him. Indeed, Macartney himself never seriously doubted his own abilities. Everyone attested to his sharp mind, his easy manners and his great charm; but his early success was also due to considerable ability and self-confidence.

It is difficult to identify the formative influences on Macartney's early behaviour and attitudes. Compared with the voluminous sources dealing with his middle and later years, the evidence relating to his childhood and youth is both uneven and sparse. There is no doubt, however, of two matters. Firstly, he came from a family which, following success in business, politics and the marriage market, enjoyed no more than solid gentry status. The bulk of his comparatively modest and scattered estate was situated at Loughguile and Dervock in north Antrim, quiet rural backwaters, far distant from the centres of power and influence in Dublin and London. Macartney was lucky to inherit even this property because, as the only son of a younger son, he was not in the direct line of succession.

Secondly, however impressive, his qualities were insufficiently underpinned by wealth. Despite the substantial loans which accompanied Holland's other support, Macartney was for long embarrassed by the dichotomy which existed between his public position and his private lack of substance. Only after many years of public service did the rewards of office substantially outweigh the expenditure associated with it.

None of this is to suggest that it was because Macartney's family and property were Irish that he was of relatively modest means; rather that his rise to office was so precipitate, and related costs so disproportionate to his earnings, as to outstrip what he had to dispose of. Indeed, by the time he came of age in 1758 Ireland had already embarked on a long period of rapid change and development. Since the Restoration the economy had participated in the general expansion of international trade and Ulster in particular had witnessed the rise of a strong domestic linen industry. Politically, however, the full, stabilising effects of the Williamite settlement of the 1690s had yet to emerge in many localities; while agriculture, by far the dominant sector of the national economy, remained frequently depressed by the poor seasons and fluctuating prices which characterised farming conditions before the 1750s. In addition, Ulster especially continued to adjust to changes in the size and distribution of its population: there had been heavy immigration during the later seventeenth century; emigration across the Atlantic, though still spasmodic, was underway; and internal migration from the east to the west of the province continued apace. By the second quarter of the eighteenth century many Ulster towns showed signs of steady development; on the other hand rural areas, particularly towards the periphery of the province, retained features of the frontier economy and society of an earlier age. Instinctively Ulstermen still looked south to Dublin for many of their needs, as indeed the young Macartney was to do before he ventured further afield. Even before then, however, he was well aware that his forebears had won respectability and much local prestige in circumstances which were a good deal less auspicious than any that he was likely to encounter. For by the mid-eighteenth century Ireland was beginning to respond more vigorously to the twin forces of population growth at home and demand for Irish goods, particularly agricultural produce, from abroad. In 1737, the year of Macartney's birth, no-one anticipated the extent of the growth and prosperity which Ireland was to experience until beyond 1806, the year of his death. Still less did anyone imagine that Ulster, the place of his birth and the site of most of his family's property and influence, would in the course of a generation or so become the most economically and socially advanced of the four Irish provinces.

II

The origin of the family's endeavours in Ireland dated back to 1649 when, at the age of twenty-three, Macartney's great-grandfather had left Auchinleck in the parish of Dundrenan, Kircudbrightshire, to emigrate to Ulster.[1] Throughout this earlier period a sparse population in relation to other resources had retarded economic development in the northern province. The official plantation scheme of the early seventeenth century failed to attract sufficient colonists of substance, creating an imbalance which was only rectified from mid-century onwards by further and much heavier immigration from northern England and lowland Scotland. By then, however, 'Black George' Macartney, as he was known (because of his swarthy appearance and to distinguish him from another, related immigrant of the same name), was well established in Belfast.[2] There is no indication of what prompted his migration from Scotland; nor of the extent of his means on arrival in Ulster, beyond the fact that he still owned a very small estate at Auchinleck.[3] Before long he was not only among the foremost public figures but also the leading merchant in south-east Co. Antrim.

Admitted to the franchise of the borough of Belfast in 1656, 'Black George' steadily accumulated a substantial leasehold estate as one of the head-tenants of the Donegall family who, then and for long afterwards, owned all the freehold in and around the town.[4] George sub-let much of this property at a profit; the rest he energetically developed on his own account. Besides building a fine house, he acquired several corn mills and a tuck mill, and established a part share in a sugar refinery; he was also instrumental in providing a market hall in the town. Above all, his commercial activities, conducted both from Belfast and through other ports up and down the Irish seaboard, were thoroughly international in scope; he even owned some of the ships in which his own and others' cargoes were carried. No less active in more public capacities, he served for several terms as Sovereign, or Mayor, of Belfast, became jointly engaged in improving the local water supply, collected the port's customs revenue, captained a troop of horse in the militia, and in 1678 was appointed Sheriff of Co. Antrim. A decade later it was he who proclaimed in Belfast the accession of William and Mary. Soon obliged to flee for safety to England, he was subsequently attainted in James II's Dublin Parliament in 1689, only to be restored following the Williamite settlement in 1691.[5] At that point, having publicly supported the victorious party and both promoted and prospered from Belfast's emergence as the chief centre and port of east Ulster, 'Black George' was clearly pre-eminent in the local business community.

It is possible to obtain only a vague impression of the extent of George Macartney's wealth at his death, which occurred shortly afterwards. However, his will[6] leaves no doubt that, along with those of many other proprietors and businessmen in Ulster, his affairs were then in a less buoyant condition than had been the case some time previously: for, amidst the threat, occurrence and aftermath of hostilities, the late 1680s and 1690s witnessed acute dislocation and recession in the Ulster economy. In addition, despite George's vigorous support of the Williamite cause, he had been accused of embezzling part of the customs revenue which he had collected, and of having made the money available to the Jacobite army — a charge which was only dismissed as groundless some three years after George's death.[7] Moreover, some of his leases from the Donegall family may have terminated with his own life, and not been renewed. Whatever the truth of these matters, George left the Auchinleck estate, together with a legacy of £600 and a life annuity of £20, to James, the eldest son of his first marriage, who had already received financial assistance from his father at the time of his own marriage. The leasehold property and other personal estate in Ulster George divided between Arthur, the younger son of his first marriage; Chichester and George, the sons of a second and final marriage; and his widow, whom he also required to make further 'bountiful' provision for his eldest son, James. Financially, the net result of the will remains uncertain, though there seems little doubt that the bulk of the commercial interests and premises were not inherited by James Macartney. Perhaps George's decision not to devise his fortune more or less intact to his eldest son and heir was dictated by caution, given the possibility of an adverse conclusion to the proceedings over the charge of embezzlement and treachery; in addition, or alternatively, he may have been motivated by the generally uncertain economic outlook. On the other hand it was quite common at that time for successful merchants to share their wealth amongst numerous survivors, particularly in cases where little or no freehold property was involved.[8] The major consequence of the will was that, while all four sons received assistance, all were required, to an extent at least, to make their own way in the world.

Although much of his career remains shrouded in mystery, not the least successful of them was young George, the future lord's grandfather. Like his elder step-brother, James (who was M.P. for Belfast in 1692 and 1695, and later a judge in the Irish Court of Common Pleas),[9] George pursued a legal career as a preliminary to entering politics. Born in 1671, he was educated at Christ Church College, Oxford and at the Middle Temple in London before being called to the Irish bar in 1700. At a by-election three years later George became M.P. for Limavady in Co. Londonderry. Thereafter he sat continuously in the Irish Parliament for over fifty-four years, initially for Limavady, briefly in 1713-14 for Donegal borough, and then for Belfast from 1715 until his death in 1757, by which time he was the longest-serving and senior member of the House of Commons.[10] Like his step-brother, George was a Whig. Though never among the front rank of Whig M.P.s, his voting record reveals him to have been a staunch party man. Indeed, in 1707, together with James Macartney, he attempted to subvert the Tory interest of the Donegall family in the borough of Belfast, an action which was condemned by friends of the Donegalls on the grounds that the Macartneys had been 'raised by a dependence [upon] and by the favour of that family'.[11] Besides indicating the strength of his own support there, George's later lengthy representation of the borough in the Irish Parliament reflected a continuing personal and family involvement in the affairs of that part of Ulster: he too served as Sovereign of Belfast; and for some time he retained leasehold interests in the area which he had inherited from his father.[12]

There is little doubt, however, that for the whole of his public life George was chiefly sustained by the landed income which he acquired through his first marriage in 1700. In more than one sense this marriage represented a major stroke of good fortune for him. Anyone who lacked freehold property was lucky to obtain it via marriage. In addition George's bride, Letitia, was the eldest daughter and co-heiress of Sir Charles Porter who, before his death in 1697, had been several times Lord Justice and latterly Lord Chancellor of Ireland. Had he lived, it is difficult to imagine that Porter, an old-fashioned high Tory, would have permitted either his daughter or his property to go to an aspiring Whig, still less to one of conspicuously insubstantial means. The Porter inheritance was a valuable one, comprising a main estate in Co. Wexford and additional land and premises in King's Co. and in the cities of Dublin and Kilkenny.[13] The Macartney family's acquisition of a permanent stake in this substantial property no doubt stemmed from the fact that the marriage produced three sons — Charles, George and Hugh — before Letitia's death in 1721. Though barren, a second marriage, to Elizabeth, daughter and co-heiress of William Dobbin, brought further additions (freehold in, and leaseholds near, Carrickfergus, Co. Antrim) to George's now sizeable landed possessions.[14]

Besides being scattered, the Porter estate was far distant from George's early home and constituency in Ulster, a disadvantage which was no doubt accentuated by the death of his first wife and his re-marriage to an Ulster woman. At some point subsequent to these events, he decided to sell the bulk of the property and to use the proceeds in purchasing a country house and estate in the north-east. By the time he had realised this ambition George was well into his sixties; by then also the economy was in the midst of an acute depression which culminated in the disastrous famines of the early 1740s.[15] It was probably these latter circumstances which made the smaller, detached portions of the Porter estate difficult to sell, though perhaps personal convenience dictated the retention of the town house in Molesworth Street, Dublin. Eventually, however, the main property in Wexford was sold, for an unknown sum, with additional resources being raised from the disposal of some of George's leasehold interests in the Belfast area. The subsequent re-investment took place in three stages. Firstly, in 1733 George bought the Loughguile estate for £5,985 from the Catholic O'Haras of Crebilly. The property consisted of some 6,146 statute acres in eight townlands, situated in three blocks, about halfway along the route from Ballymena to Ballycastle in north Antrim; and was centred on the modest country residence at Lisanoure, near the village of Loughguile in the townland of Castle Quarter. Then in 1736, for an unknown sum, George bought the chief rents of fifteen townlands in Co. Down, known collectively as the Killinchy estate, from Viscount Limerick. And finally, in 1741, he purchased the Dervock estate from the Hon. John Skeffington, son of the Earl of Massereene, for £7,205. This last property of some 2,189 statute acres (situated in two blocks) consisted of seven townlands, the central one being that of Dervock itself, a village to the north-west of the Loughguile estate, not far from the market town of Ballymoney. A comparison of the sizes and purchase prices of the two freehold properties confirms that Dervock was clearly the more valuable. Being nearer to market, it had better roads and contained some good agricultural land, whereas much of the acreage on the Loughguile estate consisted of mountain or ill-drained boggy pasture. Taken together, the purchases of these remote and scattered properties firmly established George Macartney as a landowner in the county of his birth.[16]

However, while these transactions were proceeding, George must also have been pre-occupied by his continuing lack of a grandson. Though married, neither of his two eldest sons, Charles and George, had produced a male heir by 1733, while his youngest son, Hugh, had died without issue two years previously.[17] As further years went by his hitherto successful efforts to found a landed dynasty were increasingly jeopardised by demographic failure, at least in the male line. Appropriately, the confinement whose satisfactory conclusion removed this threat took place at his newly-acquired country house at Lisanoure. On 3 May 1737 Elizabeth, wife of George's second son, George, gave birth to a son, also named George — the future Lord Macartney. It was to be of the utmost importance to the child's career that he remained not merely an only son, but also an only grandson.

III

Although the first twenty-five years of Macartney's life are, for the most part, poorly documented, it is clear that by the standards of his day he was provided with an excellent education, in the course of which he demonstrated the powerful intellect which was both to sustain him and, at times, to underlie his frustration in the years ahead. On 18 July 1745, shortly after his eighth birthday, he was enrolled at a private boarding school run by a Dr. Thompson at Leixlip, a few miles from Dublin.[18] The school was among the more superior of the numerous establishments which catered for the sons of the gentry and the professional and business classes: it appears to have been small in size, even by contemporary standards, and to have specialised in preparing its pupils for early entrance to Trinity College, Dublin. Its curriculum was dominated by the study of Classics, but the availability of tuition in French perhaps laid the basis of Macartney's subsequent linguistic prowess; there were also optional classes in 'writing' and dancing.[19]

Even at this stage there are clear signs of Macartney's precocity and of the care taken to nurture it. He arrived at Leixlip with what, for someone of his age, was an exceedingly elaborate wardrobe; among his other possessions were a 'writing book' and a few additional volumes, mostly of a religious nature.[20] He was accompanied to the school not only by his grandfather (who carefully recorded the memoranda from which these details are drawn), but also by Dr. Obins who, in the capacity of Senior Lecturer, was then responsible for the academic functioning of Trinity College.[21] Moreover, Macartney brought with him a copy of a condensed version of *The Whole Duty of Man* by the German jurist, Pufendorf, which was then one of the set books for the final year undergraduate course in Science at Trinity College. This work, which examined the ground where ethics and jurisprudence met, has since been identified as the least conservative element in Trinity's current undergraduate syllabus.[22] Other than that he stayed there for five years, nothing else is known of Macartney's period at Leixlip. In common with many of his colleagues, he left for Trinity College at a remarkably early age. Most entrants to Trinity were aged sixteen or seventeen, and some were older: but when Macartney enrolled there as a Fellow Commoner on 10 July 1750 he gave his age as fifteen, and had in fact just celebrated his thirteenth birthday.[23]

In Macartney's day the undergraduate syllabus at Trinity remained almost uniformly conservative, demanding study of a varied course in Classics, but of a much more restricted course in Logic, Ethics and Natural Science. While free to pursue additional studies, for example by attending the lectures of Professors in a variety of other disciplines, undergraduates were not required to prove their competence in other than the aforementioned subjects; nor indeed to remain in residence, even for a limited period. Instead, under the guidance of a tutor (in Macartney's case a Mr. Radcliffe[24]) they had merely to take a number of examinations held at the beginning of each term. As a Fellow Commoner, Macartney was among the more privileged undergraduates, able to dine with the Fellows and, if he so wished, to take his degree within three and a half instead of the standard four years. Despite his youth, Macartney's studies got off to an excellent start. At the end of the Michaelmas term, 1750, he was formally commended for his diligence in Greek classes and awarded a premium (a prize of £2) for one of the best performances in the ensuing examination. He was similarly commended at the close of the Hilary term, 1751, and went on to win a further premium at the Easter examination.[25] At that stage, still aged only thirteen, he was clearly regarded as one of the ablest and most conscientious students in his year.

There, however, the record of his academic performance at Trinity ceases. There were no further commendations or premiums; nor was he cautioned for poor performance. Apparently, having laid a solid foundation to his studies during his first year, he was content thereafter to do little more than was strictly required of him. The records of the College Bursar confirm this judgment.[26] Initially Macartney spent more time at home (probably his grandfather's house in Molesworth St.) than in College and worked steadily. From late January 1751, however, he appears to have been based in Trinity and to have combined a satisfactory but undistinguished academic performance with other facets of life as an undergraduate. Then from mid-1753, during the run up to his final examinations, he again withdrew to concentrate on his work. Taking advantage of the shorter course available to Fellow Commoners, he graduated early in 1754, several months before his seventeenth birthday.

Nevertheless, there is no formal record of his graduating B.A., though he *was* listed as one of four M.A. graduates on 27 February 1759.[27] Candidates for masterships did not have to be enrolled for such, unless they wished to vote in any election of a College M.P. The sole formal requirement for the award was the possession of a first degree of at least three years standing; and in practice only those in pursuit of a career in the Church stayed on at Trinity after having obtained a B.A. It is possible that, having passed the necessary examinations, Macartney qualified for the B.A. but neglected to

Map of Ireland: Major Place-Names in the Text.

graduate; and that because he was of appropriate standing he was subsequently allowed to graduate M.A. However, although it was not uncommon at that time for as many as forty B.A. candidates to graduate in a single year, only two are listed for 1754 when, according to other records, Macartney took his final examinations. [28] The more likely explanation, therefore, is that he did graduate B.A. in the spring or summer of 1754; but that, due to the negligence of the Fellow responsible for compiling the current list of graduands, no formal record of his first graduation was made. [29]

Macartney's education, however, was by no means purely formal and institutional. At some point during these years he also came under the influence of the Rev. William Dennis (son of the Archdeacon of Lismore), to whom he went for private tuition. Barrow suggests that this development took place several years previously and, indeed, it is likely that Macartney was privately tutored before proceeding to Leixlip in 1745. [30] But, if this was the case, the cleric concerned could not have been Dennis, who was only eleven years older than Macartney, and who did not himself graduate at Trinity until 1747. [31] The two probably met either while Macartney was an undergraduate or in the immediately succeeding period when he was still based in Dublin. Their relationship was important on a number of counts. Dennis was 'clever and ingenious'; was competent in Classics, Literature, Politics and Philosophy, as well as in Theology; and also possessed 'a curious collection of tracts on heraldry, genealogy and chronology' which is reputed to have laid the basis of Macartney's deep knowledge of those subjects. [32] There is some evidence to suggest that it was the perusal of this collection which led Macartney to abandon an initial plan to enter the medical profession and encouraged him to think instead of a more public career. [33] Moreover, besides being a lively and cultured man, Dennis was a long-standing and close friend of Edmund Burke, whom he had first met when they were pupils together at Shackleton's celebrated school at Ballitore in Co. Kildare. The two later shared rooms at Trinity College and were co-founders of a Debating Club which eventually became the College Historical Society. [34] Thus, when Macartney moved to London he was armed with at least one valuable introduction. Subsequently, both he and Burke expressed their gratitude to Dennis by seeking to alleviate his financial difficulties: it was through their influence that Dennis was appointed chaplain to Lord Lieutenant Townshend in 1767; and they also secured his preferment to several lucrative benefices. [35]

The precise date of Macartney's move to London remains uncertain, though it would appear to have taken place during the autumn of 1757. His intention was to enrol at an Inn of Court and in December 1757, and again in July 1758, he was described as being 'of Lincoln's Inn', from whence he later transferred to the Middle Temple.[36] Anyone wishing to be called to the Irish bar, in order to be able to practise law or as an appropriate preliminary to a public career, was still obliged to study at one of the London Inns, as indeed both Macartney's grandfather and Edmund Burke had done, also at the Middle Temple.[37] However, the timing of Macartney's decision to pursue this course of action was influenced, if not determined, by the alteration in his financial circumstances which resulted from his grandfather's death, at the advanced age of eighty-seven, in October 1757.

The main beneficiary of grandfather Macartney's will[38] was his eldest son, Charles (Macartney's uncle), who inherited the bulk of the deceased's estate, both real and personal, but who was also made responsible for the payment of his debts, funeral expenses and legacies. The only sizeable legacy was one of £1,500 to the deceased's granddaughter (Macartney's younger sister), Elizabeth, who in 1759 married Major John Belaquier. The other granddaughter (Macartney's elder sister), Letitia, had married Godfrey Echlin, a Co. Down man, in 1756; and had earlier been allocated a portion of £1,200, which remained unpaid. The deceased's surviving younger son (Macartney's father) inherited an annual rent charge of £200 — to be derived from the freehold properties in Ulster — and also the income from the fee farm rents at Killinchy. Macartney himself received an annual rent charge of £150 from the freeholds in Ulster, together with the income derived from the property in Co. Antrim and in Carrickfergus which his grandfather had inherited through his second marriage. Because the extent and value of these latter interests are unknown, it is impossible to determine the total income which thereby accrued to Macartney; but the sum allowed him to raise a mortgage for £600 in December 1757 to meet current expenses and was sufficient to justify his quitting Dublin for London.[39] Of much greater significance, however, was the fact that by the will Macartney stood to gain the bulk of the family's estate on the death of his uncle, Charles, should the latter continue to fail to produce a male heir.

Very little is known of Macartney's first sojourn in London other than that it was brief, and that it was broken by his return to Trinity College in February 1759 to graduate M.A. The early relationship which he struck up with Edmund Burke inevitably brought him into contact with others, such as Bacon, Dodwell and Will Burke, who had already set about making their way in the world of British public affairs.[40] As yet none of these men was politically influential or successful; nor is there any evidence to suggest that at this point

Macartney had any clearly defined plan as to the future course of his career. On the other hand, he quickly became reasonably well-connected and gained an entrée to a circle which, however narrowly defined, was to be of some use to him in establishing his position.

And then, towards the end of 1759 or, more probably, early in the following year, he decided to leave the Middle Temple and to embark on a Continental tour. Barrow and Robbins suggest that this decision stemmed from a singleminded determination to equip himself more adequately for a public career by examining the 'various natural resources' of certain countries in western Europe and the 'character and politics of their respective courts'.[41] As we shall see, the evidence suggests that Macartney spent much of the first part of his tour in pursuit of *intellectual* interests, and there is no indication that he specifically designed his activities abroad to cater for any more strategic purpose. Previous explanations undoubtedly smack of a rationalisation, perhaps uttered by Macartney to Barrow, which bore little relation to historical reality. Macartney merely felt it appropriate to avail himself of the European tour which contemporaries regarded as *de rigueur* for heirs, prospective or actual, of landed estates. Indeed, by that time it was not uncommon for younger sons of gentry to round off their education in this fashion. Macartney would no doubt have embarked on his travels somewhat earlier if financial circumstances had permitted. He was able to do so in 1760 because by the death of his uncle without issue in the previous year he had inherited the greater part of the family fortune.[42] Quite apart from any other consideration, this development made it less than imperative that he continue his studies in London.

Macartney's inheritance derived primarily from the terms of his grandfather's will, which had devised most of the family property to Charles Macartney for life, and then to his lawfully begotten male heirs in succession; but which, in default of such heirs, had vested the property in Macartney, Charles's nephew. On Charles's death Macartney's father lost his annual rent charge of £200 but retained for life the income from the fee farm rents at Killinchy, with reversion to Macartney. While Macartney's separate annual rent charge of £150 also ceased, he obtained the Loughguile and Dervock estates, and a house in Henry St. Dublin which his grandfather had purchased shortly before his death in 1757; he also retained the income from the remaining property in Co. Antrim and in Carrickfergus.[43] Macartney made further gains as a result of his uncle's will: but, as had happened in regard to the Killinchy estate, and as was common in cases of indirect male succession, these were subject to intermediate interests.[44] Thus, the remnants of the

Macartney aged 21, 1758-9, by R. Hunter (Robbins, *First Ambassador,* p.12).

Porter estate (in Dublin, Kilkenny and King's Co.) were vested in trustees who were required to pay life annuities of £50 and £30 respectively to two of Charles's sisters-in-law. Following the death of the latter, the property was to go to Macartney's father for life, and only thereafter to Macartney himself. Moreover, although Macartney inherited his grandfather's diamond ring, plate, books, china, pictures and much of his furniture (all previously devised to Charles), the rest of his uncle's personal estate was devoted to paying small legacies, debts and funeral expenses; then to defraying the still unpaid portions of Macartney's sisters; and finally, to the further supplementation of the income of Charles's aforementioned sisters-in-law. Not a little of Macartney's inheritance, therefore, was prospective rather than immediate.

Another striking feature of these arrangements was the treatment of Macartney's father, who was largely by-passed in favour of his only son and of various other, more distant relatives. Despite the fact that his wife had died in July 1755 and that he had not re-married,[45] he could reasonably have expected much more from both wills. While this alone may account for the apparent lack of any close relationship between Macartney and his father, the evidence hints at the existence of a wider problem of longer standing. Macartney was born at his grandfather's house at Lisanoure; and was accompanied to Leixlip in 1745 by his grandfather, not by his father.[46] The latter not only emerged rather poorly from the grandfather's will in financial terms but was also excluded from those nominated as guardians of Macartney until he came of age in 1758.[47] The second will provided Macartney's father with a stake in the residue of the Porter estate, subject nevertheless to the prior interests of others. Moreover, although Macartney's father lived on until 1779, he is mentioned again only once, and then indirectly, in the papers extant for the preceding period;[48] and apparently he left no will.[49] On the other hand a portrait of him (painted when he was sixty years of age) hung at Lisanoure for many years after his death.[50] Members of the family possibly became estranged at a much earlier date; alternatively, he may have been incapacitated in some way, mentally, physically, or both.

Thus, Macartney gained considerable personal independence following the deaths of his mother and grandfather in 1755 and 1757 respectively. However, until his uncle's death in 1759 he lacked sufficient means to pursue his growing ambitions as he would have wished: in February 1759, for example, he was obliged to extend his mortgage to a total of £1,200. However, having in the meantime attained his majority, he acquired a substantial increase in the income at his disposal as soon as his uncle died, and within a year had completely discharged the debt.[51] He ceased to be a mere annuitant and became a landed proprietor with at least a reversionary interest in property in several parts of Ireland; but, above all, with an estate in Co. Antrim over which he had immediate and absolute control. In eighteenth-century terms he had obtained the one commodity, landed property, which promised to enable him to overcome previously insurmountable restraints on his activities. Thereby, he became wealthier, both financially and in terms of the scope now available for the development of his undoubted talents. That he achieved this accidentally, through the operation of the demographic lottery, was among the greatest strokes of good fortune to befall him.

There were also, however, other, less benign aspects of Macartney's new situation. As was true of most inheritances, his brought with it duties as well as privileges. Thus, if undischarged in any other way, his sisters' portions became his responsibility as owner of the property on which they were secured. Moreover, while it undoubtedly increased the opportunities available to him, Macartney's new-found wealth was far too modest to free him completely. It encouraged and allowed him to aspire to higher things but remained insufficient to underpin success in fulfilling such aspirations. In this sense, ironically, his inheritance made the pursuit of salaried office both feasible *and* necessary.

IV

In 1766 a Church of Ireland clergyman, the Rev. William Tisdall, who lived in London, claimed that he had been of some assistance in regard to Macartney's grand tour, though he appears merely to have offered 'advice' and not to have acted as a travelling companion.[52] Macartney also sought help from 'M[r] Burk[e]' (probably either Edmund or Will), who put him in touch with Rev. Fr. Ruggiero Giuseppi Boscovich, an Italian Jesuit of the Sacred School, Turin, then temporarily resident in London.[53] No doubt because of the delay involved in settling the details of his uncle's will, Macartney did not set out for the Continent until the summer of 1760. Ignoring the conventional itinerary, which would have taken him first to the Low Countries and France, Macartney proceeded directly to Italy and Boscovich furnished him with several letters of introduction for use on his arrival there. Few details of this part of his tour have survived, but the letters which Boscovich (and later his contacts) wrote on Macartney's behalf indicate that he was anxious not merely to sightsee and enjoy himself but also, and primarily, to meet scholars and to visit a wide range of academic and ecclesiastical institutions. Though frankly designed to create the most favourable impression on their recipients, the introductions paid uniformly eloquent tribute to Macartney's erudition and intellectual curiosity, and stressed his desire to continue to further his education. If his plans came to fruition, Macartney certainly widened his mental horizons during his sojourn in Italy: for, besides seeking out individual notables in Milan and Lucca, he arranged to visit the Sacred School, the College of Nobles and the University in Turin, the Universities of Pisa and Rome, the Laurentian Library at Florence, and the Institute in Bologna.[54] The evidence suggests that he spent up to six months south of the Alps before returning northwards, to Geneva, during the winter of 1760-61; at which point he first came into contact with Stephen Fox, as a result of which the prospects, both for his tour and for his future career, were profoundly altered.

Stephen, the eldest son of Henry Fox, the future 1st Lord Holland, suffered from poor health throughout his childhood and youth. Following a serious illness, he left Eton in 1759 and proceeded abroad, accompanied by a tutor, in February 1760. By March he was based in Geneva under the care of the celebrated physician, Dr. Tronchin.[55] The circumstances in which Macartney met Fox remain somewhat obscure. Heavy reliance must be placed on the nearest contemporary account of the episode, by Farington in 1795. According to him, Macartney 'prevented' Fox from 'falling into snares laid for him by sharpers'; and soon afterwards 'communicated such information on this subject to Lord Holland ... as engaged the friendship of that nobleman, who was the first cause of Lord M[acartney]'s promotion to political situations'.[56] Farington was almost certainly wrong, however, in stating that the incident took place in Paris: separate items of evidence strongly suggest that it occurred in Geneva in the winter of 1760-61.[57] There is no reason to doubt Farington's main contentions that the encounter arose because of Fox's gross (and ultimately notorious) addiction to gambling, and that in this instance Macartney contrived to rescue him from those who sought to exploit it. Indeed, in March 1761 (perhaps in response to the suggested communication from Macartney) Fox received a stern warning from his father to beware of 'sharpers'.[58]

Thereafter, following a brief return visit to northern Italy, Macartney became a close friend of Stephen Fox and returned to England with him in July 1761. The Foxes may have known of him before his encounter with their son, for they were friendly with the senior branch of his family (who had inherited the small estate at Auchinleck but who lived in London), particularly with his cousin, Kitty Macartney; but they had never previously met Macartney himself.[59] The entire family quickly became exceedingly fond of him: he was a distinctly personable young man who, moreover, seemed able, at least occasionally, to exercise some restraining influence on the Foxes' sick and wayward eldest son. Henry Fox was particularly appreciative of this, the more so because he had previously encouraged excess in his children; and also, perhaps, because he himself was instinctively closer to his second son, Charles James, than he was to Stephen, his prospective heir. By midsummer 1761 those close to the family were beginning to gossip about Macartney's impact on the Fox household. As the Marchioness of Kildare remarked to her husband: 'you can't imagine what racket the Holland House people make with this new Mr. Macartney; he rivals Lord Shelburne, I think'.[60]

Following Stephen Fox's return to Geneva with his tutor in December 1761, Henry Fox asked Macartney to join his son as 'companion and mentor'.[61] Thereby Macartney was able to meet a much wider range of minor potentates, celebrities and people of fashion than would otherwise have been possible, though occasionally, as when Macartney went alone to see Rousseau at Neuchatel in 1762, Stephen was too lazy to share his intellectual curiosity.[62] It was almost certainly through Stephen Fox, however, that Macartney met Voltaire in the spring of 1763. Voltaire had recently settled at Ferney, near Geneva, was also attended by Dr. Tronchin, and had become acquainted with Henry Fox some years previously.[63] And although Voltaire received an endless stream of visitors, many of them young tourists, Macartney would appear to have risen to the occasion splendidly. He more than held his own in a discussion of epic poetry; persuaded Voltaire to provide him with letters of introduction to two French statesmen, the Duc de Praslin and the Duc de Richelieu, and to two *philosophes,* Helvetius and D'Alembert; and left the great man with the impression that his visitor was not only modest, learned and wise, but also extremely wealthy! Whether Macartney subsequently conducted a regular correspondence with Voltaire is uncertain, though he certainly maintained that he did so.[64]

Although, in deference to a promise made to his father, Stephen Fox temporarily repressed his passion for gambling, his other expenditure continued beyond all reasonable bounds. Henry Fox nevertheless allowed him to remain abroad with Macartney for an extended period, despite the fact that the latter's reports often made depressing reading. Henry must have derived little, if any, comfort, for instance, from the following analysis of his son's behaviour, sent from Geneva by Macartney in November 1762.

Ste[phen] continues in perfect health and perseveres with great steadiness in his resolution with regard to play. He still attends the Manege and is become a perfect lawyer. He takes pretty constantly to his exercises and with the application to letters which you recommend to him has it certainly in his power to be everything you wish him. He is beloved and esteemed by everyone, but with all his amicable qualities there is one circumstance which I can't think of without infinite concern. Tho[ugh] he has abandoned play, his passion for clothes and horses is pretty nearly equivalent. He can't deny himself anything of this kind, and as he has not even the economy of extravagance, I fear let his future fortune be ever so great, he will always be distressed in his circumstances. 'Tis indeed, Dear Sir, with uncommon pain, that I mention this to you, but you must know it in the end; and this moment Ste has received a letter from Mr. Foley desiring a draft for his balance which is near six hundred pounds, and the only articles of his expense are clothes, horses and cabriolets. I can't avoid feeling in the most sensible manner for my dear Ste on this occasion. His person I love, his friendship I value, but tho[ugh] he has in me the greatest confidence, he wants resolution to follow the plans we concert together. His intentions are the best in the world, and nothing is wanting to him but firmness enough to follow them.[65]

In May 1763 Macartney's fears were justified when Henry Fox received a list of Stephen's drafts for the preceding eighteen months which totalled nearly £7,000.[66] However, the letter also paid tribute to the confidence and intimacy which already characterised Fox's relations with Macartney, who would have avoided such a frank diagnosis had he not felt that it was expected of him, and that it would be accepted at its face value.

In the early summer of 1763 Henry Fox, by then Lord Holland, arranged a family re-union abroad. His party was met at Valenciennes by Macartney, who conducted them to a bedridden Stephen in Paris. Thereafter the Hollands, their three sons and Macartney spent some three months together in France and the Low Countries. During this period Macartney made a brief excursion to Germany with Charles James Fox, who was on vacation from Eton. The two then returned together to England in August, leaving the rest of the family to continue their tour.[67]

Following his encounter with Stephen Fox in 1761, Macartney undoubtedly seized every opportunity of consolidating his connection with the Hollands, corresponding regularly with all members of the family, but particularly with Lord Holland. During his second period abroad Stephen's letters home were few and far between, so that his parents relied heavily on Macartney for news of his progress. Moreover, when their situations were reversed from August 1763, Lord Holland looked to Macartney to keep him abreast of political developments at home. When both men were in London Macartney was a frequent guest at Holland House, where he enjoyed access not just to the Hollands but also to many other leading public figures of the day. Lord Holland soon came to appreciate his astute comments on national affairs which, while always couched in suitably deferential terms, were invariably expressed with vigour and confidence. Before long, Holland, who was publicly most unpopular and who, no doubt because of this, lacked a close, male confidant, was openly professing his enjoyment of their relationship, as well as his gratitude for Macartney's continuing interest in the concerns of both Stephen and Charles James. As early as October 1762, when Lord Holland returned to the Cabinet under Bute, Macartney felt able to request that Holland engineer a promotion to 'an old regiment' for a Mr. William Glendowell, one of Macartney's distant relatives.[68] It was but a short step from there to the point where Holland began actively to promote Macartney's own career.

Before that process could begin, however, something had to be done about Macartney's conspicuous lack of means. Again, precisely what Holland did and when remains unclear, though significantly in October 1763 Macartney informed Holland, who was then in Paris, that 'my own business will be finished in a few days'. He went on, almost equally obscurely:

> You have given me that ease of mind which I have been for some time a stranger to, and made me perfectly happy. Since my coming over [from the Continent in August] I have reason to prize the obligation still more as I fear I would not have brought my own scheme to bear without the greatest difficulty or disadvantage.[69]

At Holland's death in 1774 Macartney owed him several thousand pounds. This interest-free loan, or at least the first instalment of it, appears to have originated at this point in 1763, as Macartney sought both to discharge his existing obligations and to fulfil his rising expectations for the future.[70]

The financial predicament which confronted Macartney at this juncture certainly threatened to thwart the progress in his career which, despite a recent exit from both the Commons and the Cabinet, Lord Holland remained in a position to promote on his behalf. Following their rendezvous in France earlier that summer the two had discussed the matter and had clearly agreed on a joint course of action. It was the need to implement this agreement without delay, rather than merely to accompany Charles James Fox, that had brought Macartney back to England in August, ahead of Holland who returned in November 1763. To be effective, any plan had to bridge the gap between Macartney's modest income and his steadily rising expenditure. Although no contemporary rentals are extant, gross annual receipts from the Loughguile and Dervock estates could not have exceeded the £694 recorded some years later in 1768.[71] When the rents from the property in Carrickfergus (£10. 10s. 6d. in 1768) and from the leaseholds in Co. Antrim were added to this, Macartney's annual income remained well short of £1,000, a paltry sum for someone whose sights were now set much higher than at the outset of his overseas tour. Whether the proceeds of his uncle's personal estate had been sufficient to meet the previously unpaid portions of Macartney's sisters is uncertain. The suspicion must be that this had not proved the case, and that Macartney had thereby become liable for their discharge. A substantial loan from Holland enabled him to meet this obligation and perhaps also to lay up something for the future.

Macartney's gratitude to Holland, frequently re-iterated in subsequent correspondence, was genuine enough: if not absolutely essential, the loan placed his ambition on a more secure footing. Nevertheless, the transformation in his lifestyle which followed the forging of the Holland connection posed continuing problems, as Lord Holland himself realised only too well. In periodically referring to Macartney's need to balance his budget, his advice stemmed not from bitter experience of his sons' gross extravagance, nor from his familiarity with Macartney's personal circumstances, and still less from the realisation that he was Macartney's chief creditor. Rather, he recognised in Macartney someone who, with exceedingly limited means, was prone to live well beyond them. There was also, perhaps, a tinge of guilt: for the success of Macartney's relations with the Hollands derived, to a considerable extent, from the ease with which he had adopted the carefree manner of living which they had encouraged him to share. Stephen Fox later maintained that 'except in the article of play, I never was so extravagant as you', while Macartney himself also confessed to having developed a 'passion' for play.[72] Moreover, with his long experience of public life, Lord Holland worried that his efforts on Macartney's behalf would merely exacerbate the latter's financial predicament: the salaries attached to so many offices in no way compensated for the expenditure to which they gave rise. It was for this reason that his reaction to the offer of the Russian post was somewhat less than wholly enthusiastic; to him the key factor was that 'if you like the life, it will carry you to much higher things'.[73] Macartney on the other hand was utterly jubilant, and quickly announced himself 'determined to live for the future within my income'. [74] Many anxious years were to elapse before he achieved this objective.

V

One must beware, however, of placing undue emphasis on Macartney's inexperience and naivete at this stage in his career. While indubitably oversanguine as to his future financial prospects, he was under no illusion as to the prime source of his recent good fortune: their friendship, he told Lord Holland, was 'the happiest circumstance of my life'. [75] And yet there was more to the matter than that. Holland himself, than whom no-one was more brutally realistic about public life or less given to useless flattery, certainly viewed things somewhat differently: 'nobody of your age', he declared, 'perhaps ever went out with so high a character'. [76] In fact both compliments were valid. Without Holland's patronage Macartney may never have emerged into public life; with it, he was, by the standards of his day, by no means unworthy of his appointment.

Youth, inexperience and insufficient wealth and property were counterbalanced not just by connection but also by a range of other attributes. Compared with many of his contemporaries, Macartney was well educated, possessed of a sharp and enquiring mind, intellectual discipline and a capacity for hard work. His command of the written language, so evident to Holland (and doubtless to others too), was a singularly appropriate qualification for a public representative abroad; and was eventually to bear fruit both in the quality of his despatches and in published accounts of some of his experiences. He had a prodigious memory: for example, prior to departing for Russia, he memorised the entire corpus of the Navigation Acts to the point where he could recite any part with ease. [77] He was also widely travelled and had a fluent command of French and Italian, together with some knowledge of German. No less significant was his ability to move with easy assurance in polite society: to charm and good looks were added a taste for (and success with) older women which was the subject of frequent comment among those closest to him.[78] More pertinently, though it continued to pose private financial problems, what may aptly be described as his apprenticeship under Lord Holland had introduced him to some of the mechanics of a public career and fired an ambition to succeed therein.

With the benefit of hindsight it is clear that Macartney never enjoyed the ideal temperament for his chosen way of life — a natural impulsiveness, a tendency to arrogance, and a short temper saw to that. Nor was he physically well-tuned to the combination of drudgery and high living which went with his work. He was to succumb somewhat earlier than most to the ravages of gout, and eventually to a variety of other ailments too. For the moment, however, some of his best qualities were to the fore. One of the least formal of the several portraits of him was completed shortly after his departure for Russia. On accidentally encountering it in Reynolds' studio, Lord Holland proclaimed it 'excessively like' Macartney. [79] Compared with that executed by Hunter six years earlier, it showed a polished, eager and confident man.

CHAPTER II

RUSSIA 1764-67

I

On Macartney's return from his continental tour, the immediate object of his ambition was to secure a seat in Parliament at Westminster; and in this Lord Holland was very ready to oblige him.[1] A seat at Midhurst was expected to become vacant shortly; and Lord Holland, who had some grounds for thinking that the nomination would be at his disposal, promised to bring him in. George Grenville, however, claimed the seat for the Treasury; and after a sharp exchange of letters with Lord Holland he had his way. Fortunately for Macartney, however, Holland had a friend in the administration in the person of Lord Sandwich, the Secretary of State for the Northern Department; and it was no doubt with Sandwich's approval that he wrote to Macartney, on 22 May 1764, virtually offering him the post of Envoy-Extraordinary to the Court of St. Petersburg. No trace seems to have survived of Macartney's reply; but his circumstances were such that he could scarcely afford to hesitate. He was already heavily in debt to Lord Holland, and his prospective emoluments as minister ('£5 a day, and all other usual agrements') looked so attractive (in London) that he was encouraged to believe that he might be able to live within his income — though Lord Holland knew better. By July at latest he had made up his mind to accept; on 4 October he was appointed Envoy-Extraordinary; on 19 October he was knighted. As far as Sandwich was concerned, the sooner he set out the better; for Lord Buckinghamshire, the existing ambassador, had proved both tiresome and ineffective, and his replacement was equally desired in London and in St. Petersburg. He had, indeed, already asked for his recall; but had latterly been showing disquieting signs of a disposition to remain. Lord Sandwich was not sorry to be able to cut short these unwelcome vacillations by a curt intimation that his successor had actually been appointed. Macartney, for his part, wasted no time: on 26 October the Russia Company gave 'a grand dinner' in his honour; on 31 October he arrived at Harwich in a snowstorm; on 1 November he set sail. Travelling by the Hague, Amsterdam, Hanover and Brunswick, he made excellent time, despite the lateness of the season and the badness of the roads, arriving in Berlin on 24 November. By 29 November he was off again; by 27 December he had reached St. Petersburg. He arrived afflicted with 'a very bad cold and sore throat'; and either this, or his inexperience, may explain how it happened that at his first audience with the Empress he committed the embarrassing *gaffe* of turning up without his credentials. Certainly he seems to have taken to his bed immediately afterwards; and in bed he remained, incapacitated by a severe attack of rheumatism, for the next five weeks.

II

When Holland had written to Macartney suggesting that he might like to go to Russia, he had observed that 'there is business there, which will not be transacted with success by his Lordship [Buckinghamshire], and it is hoped may be by his successor'. There was indeed business; business which had now been pending for full three years, business more important, perhaps, than any falling to the share of any other British minister at this period: of such consequence, indeed, that it is surprising that Sandwich should have been willing, for the sake of obliging a friend and disburdening himself of Lord Buckinghamshire, to entrust it to a beginner. It consisted, on the one hand, of negotiating a treaty of commerce; and, on the other, of exploring the possibilities for a political alliance. As to which of these took priority, there had been — or at least there appeared to have been — differences of opinion between Russia and Britain: in 1763, as in 1734, it had seemed that the Russians would have preferred to postpone the commercial to the political negotiation, or at least to make the one contingent upon the other. In the face of British protests they had given way on this point, and when Macartney arrived in St. Petersburg his immediate task was to negotiate the commercial treaty: as to the alliance, he was ordered only to listen attentively to any Russian proposals, but to take no initiative himself. The difference in emphasis fairly reflected the important of the two questions. In the state of political isolation in which Great Britain found herself after the peace of 1763, an alliance with Russia was certainly desirable, and might sooner or later be inevitable; but it was not of immediate urgency; the conclusion of a commerical treaty, on the other hand, was. The old treaty of 1734 had expired in 1749, and though most of its provisions had *de facto* remained operative in the years that followed, the treaty had never been wholly satisfactory, and the Russia trade was in any case of far too great an importance to be

Macartney aged 27, 1764, on the eve of his departure for Russia: by Sir J.
Reynolds and, according to Lord Holland, 'excessively like' Macartney
(Courtauld Institute neg. B.58/317).

left much longer dependent upon the Empress's forbearance. The volume of trade between the two countries had been rising steadily since the beginning of the century: by 1764-5 it may have amounted to something over £1 million, or more than double what it had been thirty years before. At the English end, it was dominated by the merchants of the Russia Company, originally a close monopoly, but since 1698 thrown open to anyone who was prepared to pay an entrance-fee of £5; in Russia it was managed by firms or factors established in St. Petersburg, Archangel, Riga and Narva. In St. Petersburg, through which by far the largest proportion of the trade passed, there was a score or so of well-established firms, whose members lived together under the care of the British consul as a community of more or less permanent residents.

The most immediately striking feature of Anglo-Russian commerce was the invariable, and often enormous, visible adverse balance against Great Britain. Even granting the difficulties of eighteenth-century statistics, the discrepancy between imports and exports — and the tendency for that discrepancy to increase — is beyond dispute. If this was an evil, it was an evil which Britain had no choice but to endure. The trade to Russia was vital, on political and strategic grounds. The 'naval stores' which were fetched from St. Petersburg provided the cordage and sailcloth for the British navy; Riga masts were of unique excellence. From time to time it was suggested that alternative supplies might be obtained from the American colonies, that the Russian monopoly could be broken, as earlier Britain had broken the Swedish monopoly of tar; but though this was a threat which might be deployed in negotiation, both sides well knew that it was a rather empty one, at least in the foreseeable future. These were unpalatable truths; but they were sweetened by certain countervailing considerations. Even from a narrowly economic point of view, it was argued, the Russia trade was a good deal less disadvantageous than the crude statistics might suggest. The whole of the trade was carried in British ships; and British shipping was so predominant in Russian ports that the adverse balance was considerably offset by the freights they earned as carriers. The raw materials imported from Russia were manufactured in Britain, and contributed substantially to British re-exports. And since most exports to Russia were manufactured goods, while imports from that country were not, the 'balance of industry' was really in Britain's favour. Russia, moreover, offered a valued alternative to Sweden as a source of iron: the quality might be inferior to the best Swedish sorts, and the range of choice might be smaller, but at least the trade was not subjected to the stints and price-controls imposed by the Swedish Iron Office. British and Irish importers were increasingly turning to Russian iron: in the mid-'sixties Russia's share of the British market exceeded Sweden's for the first time. Lastly, the bulky nature of naval stores required a large mercantile marine for their transport, and so made the trade a 'nursery of seamen'.

If the trade between the two countries could thus be defended on the English side as not only necessary but beneficial, there was no doubt as to its advantage to Russia, and of this Russian ministers were well aware. Britain was beyond comparison Russia's largest customer. The balance of trade in Russia's favour resulted in substantial imports of specie. British capital and British credit were available to Russian enterprises; Russian noblemen looked to British loans to enable them to stave off their creditors or indulge their extravagance. The British mercantile community in St. Petersburg was more stable, more highly organized, financially stronger than that of any other nation; and for so long as trade remained mainly 'passive' the long credits and long experience of the British community were almost essential to the effective marketing of Russian exports. Considerations such as these, as well as the hope of entangling Great Britain in political commitments, had induced the Russian government, a generation ago, to agree to the Commercial Treaty of 1734; and though there had been progress — economic as well as political — since that date, they were considerations still sufficiently valid to persuade the Tsarina and her ministers that a renewal of the treaty (with some modifications) was very desirable.

The Commercial Treaty of 1734 had been concluded by Great Britain with two main objects in view. One was to secure the predominance of British exports in the Russian market, and of British merchants in the Russia trade; the other was to provide safeguards against the vexatious and often corrupt practices of Russian officials, and protection against the frauds and defaults of the sellers with whom they had to deal. The most important article in the treaty, therefore, was that which fixed the maximum duties payable on specified types of British cloth at a lower level than that applying to any of its competitors. At the same time another article, almost equally important, secured the position of the great exporting firms of St. Petersburg against possible undercutting by providing that henceforward they should pay the same export duties as the Russians. A 'most favoured nation' clause gave them further protection by ensuring that they should in no case pay a higher rate of duty than any other foreigners. Lastly, the British negotiators brought off what was considered to be a commercial *coup* by obtaining the right for British subjects to participate in the overland trade to Persia, on condition of paying a 3 per cent *ad valorem* transit duty upon the passage of their imports thence through the Russian dominions. A long string of clauses was designed to give better security to resident British merchants: they were promised protection against fraud by the general application of the 'brack' (the official quality-grading) to Russian exports; they were given some protection against the peculiarities of the Russian justice by special provision for dealing with cases in which they were concerned. The vendor who failed to deliver the goods for which payment had been made in advance could no longer cheat the merchant by retiring to the inaccessible interior; and the business archives of English firms were no longer to be liable to production to Russian officials on trivial pretexts. In theory, the agreement of 1734 was based upon the principle of reciprocity. In fact, while it gave to Great Britain many valuable and special privileges, it offered the Russians concessions that were illusory, and rights of which they were in no position to avail themselves. The assumption which underlay the whole treaty was that Russia was an economically backward and undeveloped country, with no option but to entrust her trade to a more skilful, richer and more experienced power.

In the thirty years which elapsed between the signature of the treaty of 1734 and the arrival of Macartney in St. Petersburg, this assumption, though still true, had undoubtedly been somewhat weakened. It was no longer possible to be blind to the fact that Russia had emerged as one of the great powers. Economically, too, there had been development. There were still very few Russian merchants abroad, relatively few Russian ships outside the Baltic; but it could be predicted with fair confidence that there would soon be more. Above all, the enhanced international status of the country seemed to her rulers to justify, and indeed to demand, that no future commercial agreement should be concluded upon terms as humiliating as those of 1734. Catherine herself seems to have wished to liberate trade from some of the restrictions and monopolies which had hitherto fettered it; she was concerned to increase Russia's exports; and she was doubtful of the wisdom of a policy which channelled the greater part of those exports to one single foreign market. The simple renewal of the treaty of 1734, therefore, might well be considered objectionable, not only on grounds of prestige, but on grounds of economic policy.

There had been at least one important modification of the treaty-terms already, when the Empress Elizabeth abrogated the Persian clause of the treaty in 1746. But if the Russians had reason to complain, so too had the British merchants in Russia. The treaty had not made their Russian suppliers more honest, or the Russian administration less obstructive; nor was Russian justice noticeably more speedy or less corrupt than of old. They chafed under the restrictions upon their freedom of settlement. If a merchant should happen to die in Russia, his heirs might find his estate dealt with according to the Russian laws of inheritance; if he went bankrupt, his creditors might be subjected to procedures which compared unfavourably with those which prevailed at home. The regulation which prevented any British resident from engaging in wholesale dealings with another British resident bore heavily on the man who was overstocked with one commodity but was debarred from disposing of it to a colleague who would have been glad to take it off his hands.

Thus both sides had grounds for wanting a new treaty which should correct the errors, or supply the deficiencies, of the old. The first move had come from the Russians as long ago as 1761; but by the end of 1762 negotiations had come to a dead stop. Lord Sandwich, however (who succeeded Halifax as Northern Secretary in September 1763), was becoming impatient. On 3 August 1764 he transmitted a virtual ultimatum to his ambassador: either the negotiations must be re-opened at once, or Buckinghamshire must forthwith take his departure, and leave the matter to be dealt with by his successor. The prod proved effective. On 3 January 1765, soon after Macartney arrived in St. Petersburg, the Russian minister, Baron Gross, formally presented a draft to the British government. Sandwich spent the next two months in consultation with the Board of Trade, the Russia Company, and the Advocate-General, and on 15 March he forwarded their various opinions, together with his own orders, to his new minister in St. Petersburg.

III

The Russian draft treaty reflected very clearly the desire of Catherine and her ministers to escape from a position of economic subordination which they felt to be unworthy of a great power. They did indeed take the text of 1734 as their basis; but they made changes and omissions which from the British point of view robbed that agreement of most of its value. It was not surprising, perhaps, that there should now be no question of giving British merchants access to the Persia trade. It was much more serious that they should have cut out one of the two main benefits of the treaty of 1734, by dropping the clause which guaranteed equality of export duties as between British and Russian merchants. The omission was made still more disquieting by Panin's avowal to Buckinghamshire that his government intended to give a preference to Russian merchants exporting goods in English ships, as well as in Russian. The removal of safeguards against the arbitrary sale of British property taken in execution threatened a revival of old abuses; the liability of English merchants to rates and other municipal burdens (including billeting) for houses which they rented (as against those which they owned) imposed a new obligation. Moreover, apart from the changes which affected British trade, Panin had taken the opportunity to re-draft the clauses which dealt with the right of search, blockade, and contraband, in terms which no British ministry could possibly accept. The list of goods which were to be deemed contraband remained the same as in 1734, except that at Buckinghamshire's insistence 'masts' was added to it: what was really exceptional was that, after the schedule of goods which were to be free, the Russians had inserted a formulation so wide as to make it impossible to deny to France access to many strategic commodities in the event of war.

Nevertheless, the British government had no option but to treat the Russian draft very seriously. The brief which Sandwich now transmitted to Macartney certainly did that: it was detailed, explicit and supported by full documentation. On the purely trading side, the first essential (Sandwich emphasized) was to recover and entrench England's status as most favoured nation: any additional benefits over and above that were to be regarded in the light of a bonus. That status was especially important, of course, in regard to woollens: it must if possible be buttressed by a provision that, if lower tariffs should in future be accorded to any other foreign textiles, the duties on English cloth would be reduced accordingly. On the question of equality of export dues for English and Russian merchants Sandwich was less categorical — and not very optimistic: 'it is much to be apprehended', he wrote, 'that, after thirty years advancement in commerce since the conclusion of the last treaty, this beneficial concession is more to be wished for, than expected'. But if it proved impossible to secure the restoration of this clause, Macartney was to press instead for a concession of a quite different nature: the right of British merchants resident in Russia to sell wholesale to one another. At the suggestion of the Russia Company he also advanced another new demand, for a drawback of seven-eighths of the import duty upon unsold English goods re-exported from Russia: on this, he thought, the Russians were not likely to prove intransigent. Nor did he expect much difficulty about clauses providing for the right of appeal to the College of Commerce from the decisions of local magistrates — a safeguard to which British merchants in Russia attached great importance. Finally, Macartney was told that the Russian formulation of the clauses dealing with neutral rights and contraband was 'utterly inadmissible'. His instructions ended, in words which were to have some importance later, by directing him, as soon as he should reach an agreement with the Russian commissioners, to

transmit it to me without loss of time, in order to receive His Majesty's pleasure with respect to its absolute conclusion.

Nowhere in his despatch did Sandwich commit himself to the view that, if the Russians should stand firm upon their draft, it would be better to accept it rather than lose the treaty; and as regarded the contraband clauses he cannot possibly have thought so. But as regarded the purely commercial arrangements, it is clear that both the Russia Company and the Board of Trade were so anxious for a settlement that they took the line of 'better a bad treaty than none at all'. The Russia Company had indeed failed to persuade Sandwich to give his backing to all their *desiderata*; but they wanted a treaty — any treaty — most of all. Their anxiety suggests that they were not too sanguine about the outcome of the negotiations. If so, their doubts were fully shared by Samuel Swallow, the British Consul in St. Petersburg, whom Macartney consulted about the prospects of success. Swallow was anything but optimistic: he did not expect Russia to allow British merchants to sell wholesale to each other; he did not think that the drawback on unsold goods would be obtained; he considered it unreasonable to ask that export duties be paid in roubles. And he was quite clear that, even if equality of export duties could not be secured, a treaty without that provision was better than no treaty at all.

It was thus no very promising negotiation upon which Macartney was to cut his diplomatic teeth. He came to it as a beginner, unfamiliar with the forms of diplomatic business, and unschooled in the etiquette of a great court. Of commercial and economic matters it does not appear that he had any other grasp than such as might be supplied by acting *in loco parentis* to Stephen Fox, or derived from a reading of the papers sent to him from the office. It was expected nevertheless that his arrival would give new life to the negotiation, and the event was to prove the expectation well-founded. Certainly he had the advantage of his predecessor in vigour, application and quickness of mind; his youthful energy was better able to endure the endless dancing and the innumerable *fêtes* which had taxed the portly Lord Buckinghamshire. His forthrightness, his businesslike enthusiasm, and his undeniable social talents proved more congenial to the Russians than the pompous self-sufficiency of the previous ambassador; and the need to make a success of his mission, as a necessary step to a career in politics at home, sharpened his faculties and stimulated his exertions. His friends seem to have calculated that his youth and personable appearance would commend him to the Empress; in which perhaps they were not mistaken. Until he compromised himself by his social indiscretions, he also succeeded in the important point of gaining the trust and indeed the friendship of Panin. He mixed easily in the agreeable society of the British colony in St. Petersburg, enjoying their entertainments and gaining their confidence in return; and he probably gathered useful lights from the information they were able to afford him.

It was not until 1/12 March that he was sufficiently recovered from his attack of rheumatism to write his first despatch to the office; and for more than a month thereafter he had little progress to report. He soon made up his mind that the Russian commissioners were 'equally averse to our interest, and to one another'; and he decided if possible to get the negotiation out of the hands of 'the Hydra', and to transact his business with Panin alone. By the beginning of July he had succeeded in this; and thereafter the pace became quite brisk. There was still much hard bargaining; but by 26 July/6 August he was able to inform his chief that the treaty was virtually settled; three days later he notified his intention to sign it; and on 4/15 August the Commercial Treaty was signed and sealed by all four Russian commissioners, on the one hand, and by Macartney on the other. On 8/19 August he sent it home for ratification, with a great mass of *pièces justificatives,* under cover of a despatch in which nervous anxiety fought a losing battle with self-satisfaction.

Macartney's pride in his handiwork was understandable, for the treaty was indeed a remarkable diplomatic achievement. To this the reactions of England's enemies bore witness. Macartney had in fact secured Sandwich's main objective, the restoration of Great Britain to most favoured nation status, with maximum duties for woollens fixed at the same level as in 1734. Against all expectations he had persuaded the Russians to renew the undertaking that British merchants should pay the same export dues as Russian — a privilege enjoyed by no other foreign country. Fortified by the arguments of the Advocate-General, he had secured, after a very tough struggle, the rejection of the new clauses concerning neutral rights and contraband, and restored the more generally-worded text of the former treaty, so that it was now left to the British Admiralty Courts to decide what did, and what did not, constitute munitions of war. By article XIV he obtained a concession which Sandwich and Swallow had both deemed impossible: the right of British merchants to settle in any town in the Russian Empire. That the implication of this success might not be lost upon his government, Macartney appended the typically exuberant gloss that 'it seemed that possibly one day the East India Company might once more attempt a trade to Japan; and nothing could be more easy or practicable than by means of a factory established either at Kamtchatka, or in the Curili Islands . . . but of this Your Grace [Grafton] will be a better judge than anyone . . .'. It may perhaps be doubted whether Grafton's acquaintance with Kamtchatka equipped him to make a cool appraisal of this exciting prospect; but it is at least to be hoped that he was sufficiently well-informed to be able to appreciate the importance of the concession in other respects. British merchants might now build, buy and sell houses freely, in any part of Russia. If such houses were located in St. Petersburg, Moscow or Archangel they were to be exempt from billeting and from municipal dues; though houses elsewhere remained liable, as also houses in the three specified towns which were not owned but rented: this last represented a British concession, but a concession which was greatly overbalanced by the advantages secured. A series of articles reinforced the rights and privileges of the British community, and safeguarded them against injustice: they were guaranteed the free exercise of their religion, freedom of bequest, better procedures in the event of bankruptcy, the right of appeal from local justice to the College of Commerce. They even obtained the right to pay export duties in roubles, which Swallow had considered to be an unreasonable pretension. And the old provision for the recovery of debts from Russian traders, which had been omitted in Gross's draft, was restored.

There were of course some points which Macartney failed to carry: most conspicuously, the re-opening of the Persia trade. On this, he had to be satisfied with Panin's assurance that he would be prepared to make it the subject of a separate negotiation. Nor was Macartney able to persuade Panin to permit British merchants to sell wholesale to each other. Panin took refuge behind the College of Commerce, which he said was examining the whole question, and all that Macartney could obtain was a sentence in article IV permitting such transactions in case of 'death, extraordinary need . . . or bankruptcy' — which was probably as much as Panin could have been expected to concede. He was equally unsuccessful in securing the inclusion of a drawback on unsold British goods. Panin did indeed profess himself convinced by Macartney's arguments, and promised (probably sincerely) that the College of Commerce would take the appropriate administrative action: a year later he seems in fact to have been under the impression that something had been done about it. But he would not include it in the treaty, on the ground that since Russia intended to accept the principle, and to give it general application, Great Britain must not be encouraged to think of it as a particular privilege granted to British merchants. And lastly, Macartney failed to obtain any security that the brack should be more effective than in the past.

If in some respects the treaty fell short of the British ideal, the gains enormously outweighed the failures. From the Russian point of view, certainly, the treaty showed scarcely anything to offset Macartney's successes. They had started the negotiation determined to do something to emancipate their country from economic subjection to Great Britain, and they had finished with an agreement which (save for the Persia trade) not only re-established all the old privileges of 1734, but greatly extended them. They did indeed secure a definition of the right of search which on paper safeguarded them rather better against arbitrary action by the British Navy; and they carried their point about municipal burdens on rented houses. But for the rest, Panin seems in the course of the negotiation to have come to the conclusion that Russia's interests would after all be best served by British predominance, at least for the present, and that in any case it was vain to kick against the pricks. If his realism thus provided the basis on which the treaty was built, it also produced an incidental difficulty which came very near to wrecking it. The difficulty arose in regard to article IV — that article which restored equality of export duties as between English and Russian merchants. Into the text of this article Panin had insisted on inserting a reservation which ran as follows:

> Mais alors on se reserve de la part de la Russie, en réciprocité de l'Acte de Navigation de la Grande Bretagne, la liberté de faire dans l'interieur tel arrangement particulier qu'il sera trouvé bon pour encourager et étendre la navigation Russienne.

Macartney undoubtedly realized that this reservation might be disagreeable to his government, since what was intended to give Russia liberty to favour her own mercantile marine might be interpreted as a general freedom to discriminate in favour of Russian *merchants,* notwithstanding the provisions of the rest of the treaty. In order to clear up this point, therefore, he had written to Panin requesting an explanation of the sense which the words were intended to bear; and in particular — with a prescience of trouble ahead which the event was to justify — had pressed him to delete the reference to the Navigation Act. Panin was not prepared to do this; but in his reply he gave Macartney what he probably considered to be an explicit and binding declaration about what the reservation was intended to mean:

> quoiqu'il ne me soit pas possible de vous marquer positivement l'arrangement qu'on se propose de faire pour encourager la navigation Russienne, rien n'étant encore arrêté à ce sujet, je suis cependant

authorisé par l'Impératrice ma souveraine a vous assurer que quelque
soit cet arrangement, il sera tel que les marchands Britanniques
pourront y participer et en retirer les mêmes avantages que les sujets
de l'Impératrice.

He added that his letter was written

sur l'approbation de l'Impératrice ma souveraine, et qui vous tiendra
lieu de la déclaration que vous m'avez demandé;

and he warned Macartney that this was his ultimatum: if it was
rejected, he should consider the negotiation at an end.

Whether the word 'ultimatum' was to be taken literally may well
be doubted; but however that may be, it was no part of Macartney's
duty either to accept it or to reject it. His instructions had explicitly
required him to send home an agreed draft; the decision upon that
draft was to be made by the Cabinet; Macartney had been forbidden
to sign any treaty on his own responsibility. Yet he took it upon
himself to accept Panin's declaration; and in direct disobedience to
his instructions he signed the treaty. His despatch announcing his
action betrays, by the number and length of his excuses, his uneasiness about how his conduct would be regarded by his superiors. In
some of his arguments, it may be conceded, there was considerable
force, though it is impossible to take seriously what was after all the
most important of them — the suggestion that a negotiation which
had now been dragging on for four years had suddenly become so
urgent and so critical that he could not risk the two months' delay
which would be entailed in waiting for an answer from London. But
whether his reasons were good or bad was simply irrelevant: it was
not for him to weigh the arguments; the decision did not lie in his
hands. It is not very difficult to conjecture how it was that he allowed
himself to be tempted to disobey his orders: the exhilaration induced
by reaching an agreement so much more favourable than had been
expected; the fear of losing a triumph so acceptable to his vanity;
some vague recollection of great ambassadors who had dared, in
defiance of their instructions, to seize a fleeting opportunity for their
country's good, and had earned the commendations of their superiors
for their courage — any or all of these may have moved a man who
was never deficient in self-confidence, and certainly not disposed to
underrate his own achievements.

Whatever the explanation, the consequences were deplorable,
and might easily have been disastrous. Macartney's despatch
announcing his signature of the treaty reached London on 16
September 1765. On the following day, the secretary to the Duke
of Grafton (who had succeeded Sandwich as Northern Secretary
when the Rockinghams came into office in July) wrote to Macartney
acknowledging the receipt of his treaty, 'which, it was stated, was
very agreeable to his grace, as well as to the rest of his majesty's

ministers'. Whether in so short a space of time Grafton (to say nothing of 'the rest of his majesty's ministers') had really read the treaty and appreciated its implications is perhaps a matter for legitimate doubt; but even if he had, he was soon forced to revise his views. In any event, it seems probable that it was not he, but the Lord Chancellor, Northington, who first took alarm at the possible implications of the reservation in article IV. Once they had been pointed out, the Cabinet lost no time in agreeing that the treaty could not be accepted as it stood. Merchants of the Russia Company, hastily consulted, gave it as their opinion that the reservation in article IV might make all the rest of the treaty nugatory. If ministers were thus unanimous that they could not ratify, they were nevertheless all agreed (with the exception of Northington) that they ought to avoid an outright rejection and disavowal. They felt themselves in an exceedingly awkward situation; and their anger against Macartney, whose insubordinate rashness had landed them in this predicament, was sufficiently hot to induce rumours that he was to be recalled. At last they decided that the only practicable way out of their dilemma was to demand from Russia a formal declaration, to be attached to the treaty, and to be signed by all four Russian commissioners, in the following terms:

> Nous soussignés etc. etc., pour prévenir tout sujet de contestation à l'occasion de la réserve specifiée dans le 4e article de ce Traité, qui commence par ces mots *Mais alors on se reserve* et qui finit par les mots *étendre la Navigation Russienne,* déclarerons au nom et par ordre de la dite Majesté Impériale, que, quelqu'arrangement qu'on pourra faire en conséquence de la réserve susdite, cet arrangement sera tel que les sujets Britanniques y participeront et en retireront les mêmes advantages que les sujets de la dite Majesté Impériale, et que le dit arrangement sera tel qu'il ne tendra en aucun manière à limiter ni à restreindre le commerce que les sujets de sa Majesté Britannique font actuellement avex ceux de sa Majesté Impériale, ou à en changer le cours ou la nature. Et que cette déclaration aura le même force que si elle étoit inséreé dans la Traité.

This formula Grafton now forwarded to Macartney, in a despatch which censured his proceedings with measured severity, and passed over his achievements in silence. There was not a word of appreciation of the numerous unexpected concessions which Macartney had secured; and the rigour of Grafton's castigation was not much alleviated by the professions of personal friendship with which it was accompanied. Such chastisement demanded in the recipient a large dose either of meekness or of fortitude; but Macartney, thin-skinned, brash and vainglorious, was not well provided with either. His reply made a bad business worse. 'I confess', he wrote, 'that in the vanity of my heart I had flattered myself with hopes of some small degree of applause for my conduct in the late negotiation'. No doubt it was natural that he should wish to justify his conduct; but he did not help his case by the long string of excuses which he now put forward. The string might well have been even longer, for he omitted others 'which, smarting as I am from reproof, and wounded by His Majesty's displeasure, I am as incapable of expressing as of recollecting'. It would certainly have been better if he had refrained from paying that tribute to his own zeal and abilities which Grafton had so pointedly omitted; and better still if he had forborne the petulant threat to work to rule, implicit in his assurance that henceforward he would be careful 'not to set my hand to the tittle of an iota without the most express orders and positive instructions'. The fiasco, so totally unexpected, left him angry and sore, and he was not sufficiently master of himself to be able to swallow his chagrin. He felt that he had lost face, in Europe as well as at home: in his letters to diplomatic colleagues he made rather pathetic efforts to disguise what the true position was.

Nevertheless, whatever the state of his feelings, he had to try to execute his orders; and it soon became plain that this was not going to be easy. Panin received Grafton's demand for the Declaration with anger: it was an affront to the Empress, since it implied a doubt of her good faith. To sign the Declaration would be 'un acte de dépendance marquée, qui repugneroit a la dignité de sa [Catherine's] couronne'. He was indeed willing to reiterate his former assurance word for word, in the form of a separate declaration signed by himself and the Vice-Chancellor, Golitsyn; but further than that he would not go. The affair had come to involve the dignity of his country, his Empress, and himself. Macartney could get nowhere with him. By January 1766 he was writing to Grafton, in one of those lyrical flights which occasionally diversify his despatches, that 'I think it would have been as difficult to draw the Declaration in question from this Court, as to count the billows of the Baltic, or number the trees of the forests of Onega . . . The total loss of the Treaty, and the revocation of the privileges which our merchants now enjoy, by particular indulgence, I look upon as absolutely certain'. And he continued, in his richest vein of Gothic gloom, 'dejected by disappointments, and agitated by despair, I am at a loss for expressions to paint to you the situation of my own thoughts, or the sentiments of those I am conversing with, upon this subject . . . I have nothing now before me but a most gloomy prospect unenlightened by the smallest ray of hope . . .' — which no doubt was why he allowed the concluding sentence to be sent *en clair*.

The situation was becoming critical; for Panin made it clear that if no agreement were reached shortly the Empress would issue a *ukaze* revoking the privileges which British merchants still enjoyed. It is true that this was a threat which could have no effect until the ports became ice-free, but even so it caused uncomfortable premonitory shivers to run down the backs of the merchant community. Macartney could no longer maintain a pretence that there were no difficulties: in the face of the enquiries of his diplomatic colleagues he took refuge in silence, though he permitted himself to talk a good deal about his imminent departure. However, Panin's threat to annul the privileges brought speedy reactions even from London: Macartney's despatch announcing it arrived on 18 March; and on 18 April 1766, after nine months' gestatory fumbling, Grafton at last produced a solution so simple that it had only to be stated to appear obvious. The Declaration was to be abandoned, the Russian reservation struck out; but in its place he would insert the words:

Mais alors on se réserve de la part des deux Hautes Parties contractantes la liberté de faire dans l'interieur tel arrangement particulier qu'il sera trouvé bon pour encourager leur navigation respective.

This, as Grafton rightly said, was fair, reciprocal and needed no explanation. Macartney was accordingly instructed to obtain an amendment of article IV in these terms, and was specifically ordered that no deviation whatever would be permitted from the *ipsissima verba* which Grafton had laid down.

Armed with this formula, Macartney sought an interview with Panin on 10 May. His first proposal (in accordance with his earlier instructions) was for the simple omission both of reservation and Declaration; to which Panin made no other answer than a shrug, and the comment 'tout est libre chez soi'. Adroitly seizing on this phrase, Macartney remarked that, if this was Panin's attitude, then there could be no objection to replacing the reservation by a form of words which recognized that such liberty was reciprocal.

I then took the pen out of his standish, and folding half a sheet of paper in two columns, I drew out the clause upon the first, as it stands in the Treaty, and on the opposite side I drew out the clause as I would have it stand, according to Your Grace's orders.

Panin received the new proposal not unfavourably; professed, however, that he would need to take the Empress's opinion; and the interview came to an end with Macartney convinced that his difficulties were over.

At this point it is perhaps necessary to emphasize the fact that the solution which Macartney thus propounded was not a solution of his own making. The formula was Grafton's: Macartney merely applied it. But Macartney's biographers, Barrow and Robbins, have narrated the incident as though the wording which he wrote down was a sudden personal inspiration, owing nothing to prompting from home: as though by a brilliant piece of improvisation he dextrously unravelled the knot which had entangled the negotiation for so long. This suggestion is in flat contradiction of the evidence. It seems very likely that the misrepresentation goes back to Macartney himself: the wounds to his self-esteem inflicted by successive ministers during his mission to Russia were so deep that he was ready to appropriate any incident which might supply balm to his feelings, or display him as the masterful diplomat. By simply omitting 'according to Your Grace's orders' he (or Barrow) transformed the successful carrying out of his instructions into something which looked almost like a diplomatic *coup*. And this was a pity; for his indisputable services in securing so favourable a treaty sufficiently illustrate his reputation without such additional aids.

There followed a period of some six weeks, during which Macartney waited with impatience for the official Russian reaction to his last proposal. It came at last, after the College of Commerce had made its report; and it proved to be an acceptance in substance, though not in the precise terms Grafton had prescribed. The Russians insisted on re-writing the reservation; though the changes were purely verbal, and did not affect the meaning. A letter from Panin to his minister in London explains why they were so obstinate: in general, he wrote, they resented what they considered to be the indifference of Great Britain to Russian interests in Sweden and Poland, and took this means of showing their resentment; in particular they were not prepared to permit Grafton to define the terms of a Russian obligation: 'nos engagements doivent être rédigés par nous-mêmes'. By taking this line they placed Macartney in a cruelly embarrassing position, bound as he was by his instructions not to permit the slightest variation in Grafton's terms. At last, confident that no material issue was involved, and more than ever certain that this was his last chance, he nerved himself to yield. On 20 June/2 July he disobeyed his instructions a second time, accepted Panin's text, and signed the amended treaty. And so at last the prime aim of his mission was accomplished. The commercial treaty was made; and for the next twenty years, until its expiry in 1786, British merchants could rest secure under its protection.

Since October 1765 Macartney had been subjected to a severe ordeal. Was it really necessary? Was the dispute over article IV a dispute upon a matter of any consequence? One historian, Reddaway, certainly did not think so: for him Grafton and his colleagues were 'pedants' cursed with 'perverted vision' — a judgment which may perhaps have been coloured by his apparent belief that the final solution was not Grafton's but Macartney's. Yet as far as one can see the Cabinet's objections to the original draft were not simply an expression of mere cantankerousness. Grafton made it perfectly clear that he had no objection to measures to give encouragement to Russian *shipping*. But the reservation to article IV was felt to be so vaguely worded, and so capable of elastic interpretation, that it opened the way to preferences for Russian *merchants,* in contravention of the general tenour of the treaty. There were objections, too, as Macartney had foreseen, to the allusion to the Navigation Act as though it were something which entitled the other party to a *quid pro quo:* it would be possible, Grafton argued, that other powers with whom Britain had treaties containing a most favoured nation clause might use article IV to press for fresh concessions for themselves. It was no answer to these points to urge, as Macartney urged, that the Russians were in no condition to draw any advantage from article IV. Macartney was certainly entitled to quote the rapturous applause given to his treaty by the British merchants of St. Petersburg, as more than offsetting the opinions of the Russia Company in London; but Grafton and the Board of Trade had to look beyond the Russia trade to the possible effects on relations with other countries. They could not know (as we know now) that the object of Panin's policy had ceased to be a preference for Russian merchants, and that he had decided to concentrate on the encouragement of Russian shipping; and, not knowing that, it was their duty to be careful — and it is worth pointing out that Macartney does not seem to have know it either. And the essential point about Grafton's draft, as seen from London, was its clear limitation of the right of giving preferences so that it should apply to shipping only.

If we turn now from the particular question concerning article IV, and try to assess the significance of the treaty as a whole, there can be no doubt as to the importance of Macartney's achievement. Contemporaries were well aware of it: Thulemeyer, the Prussian minister to the Hague, reported the anxiety and chagrin of the Dutch, who believed it to involve the ruin, or at least the serious curtailment, of their trade; a few years later Sabathier de Cabres was to attribute to the treaty the total ascendancy of British trading interests in Russia, and to express the view that it made any Anglo-Russian alliance superfluous. The Russia Company, and still more the British merchants in Russia, were frankly delighted. They had never quite been able to make up their minds whether they were so superior to all rivals that they could in the last resort dispense with protection, or whether they were so vulnerable that any treaty was better than none: Macartney at least relieved them from the need to settle this point. When in 1774 their agent was giving evidence to the House of Commons on the state of the Russia trade, he was able to depict the position enjoyed by his fellow-countrymen in Russia, under Macartney's treaty, in terms of splendid privilege and unshakable prestige. It is true that Russia could not be expected to acquiesce permanently in the sacrifice of her merchants to her shippers. But for twenty years to come, Macartney's treaty provided a windbreak behind which British commercial interests were enabled to strike such deep root in Russia that when at last the protective screen was cut down they were sturdy enough to survive its loss without difficulty, and to flourish thereafter with a vigour which derived from natural health rather than artificial cultivation.

Although Macartney could not foresee all this, it may be conceded that he was entitled to some self-satisfaction at his achievement: the benefits of his negotiation had been preserved, the blunder of his signature had been retrieved. Yet there was a raw egotism about the man, a repellent conceit, a tactless readiness to blow his own trumpet, which appears in his letters to his friends on the occasion, and does much to chill our sympathies. He was too ready to see himself as condemned to battle not only with the toughness of the Russian ministers, but also with the stupidity of his own government. He boasted too freely of the effect of his personal popularity with Panin: it was typical of his vanity that he should have believed Panin when he said that he had signed the treaty 'merely from personal consideration and friendship for me', and still more typical that he should have retailed this nonsense to his friends. But if there was a disagreeable stridency in his comment on his achievement, he was not suffered to be strident for long. Retribution was lying in wait for him; and before he had well finished paying tribute to his own merits he found himself fully occupied in lamenting his ill-usage.

The final version of the treaty was forwarded to England with Macartney's despatch of 23 June/4 July 1766. By the time it reached its destination, on the 26th, the Duke of Grafton had been succeeded as Northern Secretary by General Conway. It accordingly fell to Conway to acknowledge the receipt of the treaty, and to announce the government's decision upon it. This he did in his despatch of 1 August 1766. The treaty as Macartney had settled it was accepted, though not without some grumbling that he had ventured to admit a change in the wording of Grafton's reservation; but the brief despatch was couched in terms of chilling formality and grudging acknowledgment. And it ended in a bald announcement which must have struck Macartney like a thunderbolt:

> His Majesty nevertheless [!] . . . is resolved to convince the Empress the more of his cordial disposition towards Her, not only by a ready acceptance of the Treaty, in the form it is returned, but also by the appointment of a Minister in the first rank, who will shortly have his orders to repair to Petersburg. The person named is Mr. Stanley . . . who is invested with the character of ambassador extraordinary and plenipotentiary . . . I have at present nothing further in command from His Majesty to communicate to you.

'Nothing further . . . to communicate to you': neither congratulations, nor thanks; no explanation of the intention behind the new appointment; no indication whether Macartney was to consider himself superseded, recalled and disgraced; nor any hint of what his future was to be. As the final comment upon an exceptionally arduous negotiation it was, to say the least, inadequate. As an example of how to undermine a subordinate's morale, it could scarcely be improved on.

IV

This dramatic and totally unexpected development sprang from a change in British domestic politics. At the end of July 1766 Pitt had at last consented to take office; and his return meant that the most passionate believer in a Northern System was once more in power. Almost the first ministerial act for which he was responsible was to appoint Hans Stanley as Ambassador-Extraordinary to Berlin and St. Petersburg. He was to be given a special commission to conclude the Northern Alliance, and was to proceed to Petersburg by way of Berlin. Frederick the Great was to be reconciled to England by faith in Pitt's sincerity; fortified by Frederick's blessing, Stanley was to complete the negotiations for an alliance in St. Petersburg. It was all quite simple: all that was needed for a Northern System was the goodwill of Prussia, and that goodwill, it was scarcely possible to doubt, would be accorded to Pitt merely for the asking.

In the years after 1762 there was a strong feeling, widely disseminated both in England and in Russia, that the two countries were 'natural' allies. For this feeling of community of interest there was a solid material basis: the economic ties between the two countries seemed to make a political connection between them logical. They were states obviously complementary rather than competitive: between them lay no areas of friction, no disputed territorial claims, no obviously clashing interests; each could watch the progress of the other with benevolent detachment. They shared, moreover, a useful common hostility to France. At the beginning of the 'sixties', then, there was a genuine desire in both countries for an alliance, and a general expectation that an alliance would shortly be concluded. It soon appeared, however, that goodwill was not enough. Alliance meant rather different things to each of the prospective partners. For Panin, the alliance with England was to be the vital link in a northern security system which must also include Prussia. As Augustus III of Poland drew near to the end of his life, it became essential for Russia to ensure the election of an acceptable candidate to succeed him. French influence must be excluded from Poland; and to make sure of that, Prussia must be squared in advance. So too

French influence must be destroyed, if possible, in Stockholm and Copenhagen, and the two Scandinavian powers must be ranged in the 'Northern System' with England's assistance. But neither Panin nor his mistress was interested in extending hostility to France so far as to guarantee England (or even Hanover) against Choiseul's plans for revenge. English statesmen, on the other hand, looked to a Russian alliance to provide the basis for a continental league which could bring overwhelming pressure on France, if ever France should show signs of preparing to renew the struggle for empire. There was for a long time uncertainty in London whether the third element in such a league should be Austria or Prussia. But Kauntiz' Micawberish determination never to desert Choiseul effectively barred the former option, while the unappeasable rancour of Frederick simultaneously ruled out the other. Frederick would enter into no combination of which Britain was a member; he was determined, if he could, to monopolize Russian friendship for himself; and he did his best to sabotage any negotiations for an Anglo-Russian alliance.

Apart from the basic difference about the nature and purpose of any Anglo-Russian alliance, apart too from the obstacles interposed by the jealousy of Frederick the Great, there were two general considerations which were bound to cause difficulty. The first was simply the change in Russia's international position since 1742, when the last alliance with England had been concluded. English ministers found themselves confronted with a new Russia, proud, confident, exigent, touchy. The Empress and her ministers were determined that Russia's equality of status should be heavily underlined: to them it seemed that prestige was in the last resort more important than material aid. British ministers always underestimated the importance of this feeling: the very benevolence with which they regarded the rise of the Russian navy, and the encouragement which they gave to it, revealed an attitude of secure patronage and easy condescension.

The second difficulty was of a similar character, but this time on the other side. It was provided by the post-war reaction in England; a reaction compounded by war-weariness, financial exhaustion, economic crisis: with the funded Debt increased by over £66 millions, Grenvillian economies were accepted as necessary and were certainly popular. There never was a time when national opinion, as expressed by the independent country gentlemen, was less prepared to swallow the giving of subsidies in peacetime: the old Newcastle system of foreign policy, whatever its merits, was now universally condemned. It seemed poor policy to buy alliance simply for the sake of having allies: the 'overweening power of France' would always bring allies in a crisis in any case, for it threatened European countries more immediately than it threatened

Great Britain — they, by the mysterious dispensations of Providence, having been left unprovided with a 'ditch'. Hence British policy, conforming to British public opinion, had in the post-war years an air of cool detachment, of Olympian indifference, which infuriated potential friends and stung Frederick to malicious gibes. Jealousy of British economic strength, justified resentment at a naval and mercantile tyranny which seemed to threaten all trading nations, found a vent in sneers at British feebleness and decadence. Ministers found this impossible to understand, and hard to bear: three years after 1763 the world seemed to have forgotten that they had crushed the French, appropriated a vast empire, now ruled the seas, and had robustly survived the economic blizzard which followed the peace. They found it inexplicable that any nation should not regard a British alliance as a desirable object, even if Britain were not prepared to purchase it at their price. But foreign nations, who so rightly accused Great Britain of being stupid and ignorant about Europe, were themselves equally stupid and ignorant about England. They did not understand, for instance, that it was impossible to conduct a secret foreign policy, or to conceal obligations from Parliament, or to brazen it out if such engagements were discovered. They took far too much notice of English domestic politics, and often drew erroneous conclusions from their observations. It was no doubt true that Secretaries of State changed with undue rapidity in the 'sixties. It might even be true, as A.R. Vorontsov, Russian minister in London, sourly remarked, that ministers were more concerned with an election in Essex than with who was chosen King of Poland. Foreign statesmen could hardly fail to notice that young sprigs of the nobility such as Grafton or Weymouth, or older ones such as Conway, flitted in and out of the Northern Secretary's office for a month or two at a stretch, ignorant when they arrived, scarcely less ignorant when they surrendered the seals: it was a matter of lament in the diplomatic service that this should be so. British representatives abroad were often left for long periods without instructions or answers, and the instructions they did receive were often lacking in precision: Macartney's complaints on this head only show how ignorant he was of conditions in the diplomatic service.

It was against this background that the negotiations for an Anglo-Russian alliance took place. They had been initiated by Lord Buckinghamshire in December 1762, and had taken serious shape in August 1763, when the College for Foreign Affairs had produced a draft treaty which Buckinghamshire had forwarded to Sandwich for his comments. The draft clearly revealed Russia's determination to exploit her enhanced international status. There were three points about it which, in Buckinghamshire's view, were especially objectionable. In the first place, it omitted a clause which had been present in the alliance of 1742, excepting wars with Turkey from the general obligation to come to Russia's aid if she were attacked in Europe. Secondly, it included a Secret Article binding England to contribute 500,000 roubles to assist Russia's cause in Poland. And lastly, by another Secret Article, it would have pledged England to collaborate with Russia in Sweden.

All three points were unacceptable to the British government; and one of them, at least, was speedily eliminated from the discussion. A Cabinet decision of 16 September 1763 firmly rejected the idea of spending any British money in Poland. But if the case against meddling in Poland seemed irrefutable, the case against meddling in Sweden was by no means so clear. In 1764, after an interruption of diplomatic relations which had lasted no less than sixteen years, Great Britain once more accredited a minister to Stockholm, in the person of Sir John Goodricke. His mission was designed to restore the influence of England by the overthrow of the francophile party of the Hats, and their replacement by a government of the anglophile party of the Caps. In this programme Goodricke could count on the assistance of the Russian minister, Count Osterman; for an Anglo-Swedish alliance was from Russia's point of view the ideal system to replace the Hats' dependence on France. Panin accordingly cast England for the role of Sweden's ally — and paymaster. Panin was convinced that Sweden's break with France, which it was to be England's task to contrive, must necessarily be followed by a subsidy-treaty, since Sweden could not afford to sacrifice the French subsidies unless she had others to replace them. British ministers, however, though they might desire the creation of a Northern System, desired it in the name of the European Balance, as an offset against the Family Compact; and they expected other countries to adhere to it without inducements or subsidies in the name of common-sense and from considerations of self-preservation. In order to achieve the creation of such a league they were prepared to go a long way in underwriting purely selfish Russian interests. But they did not see why they should also put their hands in their pockets to pay for them.

The last obstacle to Anglo-Russian agreement, more formidable than Poland, or even than Sweden, was the intractable question of the 'Turkish clause'. The fundamental objection to the omission of the Turkish clause, from the English point of view, was that, if it were agreed to, English trade with Turkey would be prejudiced — a consideration which seemed the more important, since the trade was already hard hit by the competition of light Carcassonne fabrics. This was a valid objection if it were conceded that the Turkey trade was sufficiently important not to be sacrificed. But it was more than doubtful if this was so. Moreover, as Panin pointed out, though there was no Turkish clause in France's alliances with Austria, it could hardly be said that France's commerce had suffered in consequence. Russia's treaties with Prussia in 1764, and with Denmark in 1765, both stipulated for assistance in a Turkish war, and it would be difficult to give England easier terms without offending them. But the essential reason, underlying all these arguments, was that the omission of the Turkish clause had become a kind of talisman, a symbol of equivalence, the touchstone, by which foreign nations' attitudes to Russia were to be judged, the sign of her advance in power since 1742. British ministers never recognized the depth of Russian feeling on this point.

It had no sooner become clear that the Turkish clause was going to be a serious obstacle, than attempts were made to devise expedients to remove the difficulty: they were to continue, almost incessantly, and always fruitlessly, for the next ten years. It was all in vain: British ministers would not budge. The Russians never understood how politically impossible were the terms they were propounding: no ministry could have accepted them and survived. What would the country gentlemen have said to a Russian subsidy? Thus it happened that by February 1764 Sandwich was saying flatly that the negotiations for a Russian alliance had failed; in August he added that England would take no initiative to renew them.

V

Such, then, was the position which Macartney confronted upon his arrival in Russia. As compared with his duties in the matter of the commercial treaty, his obligations with reference to the alliance were imprecise. His instructions did indeed explicitly forbid him to take any initiative in the matter; but they also ordered him to listen to what the Russian ministers and the Empress might have to say. But this invitation to correspondence was not accompanied by any useful information as to the sentiments of the British government on such matters as Sweden, Denmark and Poland — all topics of some concern to a minister in St. Petersburg. Unlike more favoured French envoys, Macartney received no general survey of British policy, no guidance through the mazes of inter-related problems: it was tacitly assumed that common-sense and patriotism would supply without difficulty the answer to any problem he might encounter. Quite early he begged Sandwich for instructions upon the government's policy in Sweden, having found Panin's remarks on this head 'totally unintelligible'. He got no satisfaction: Sandwich told him simply that his answer to Panin had been approved, and that further instructions were unnecessary. In this situation, left to grope his way by the light of nature among many pitfalls, it would not be surprising if he made mistakes, though that was a possibility which was not sufficient to inhibit his activity. But, in fact, there was not a great deal that he could do. He could keep his ear open for hints from Panin, and be alert for any signs of a change of temperature in St. Petersburg. He could also, of course, act as a useful channel for the semi-official transmission of ideas and suggestions: between St. Petersburg and Stockholm, in particular. Macartney's cordial correspondence with Goodricke did become of considerable importance: by this means Goodricke was able to insinuate ideas to London, with Panin's blessing; while Macartney was able to send important first-hand information to Stockholm, often more reliable and always about two months quicker than the despatches which reached Goodricke from the office. Apart from this, he could devote his undoubted social talents to making useful friends. This he did with some success. The most important of them was probably Caspar von Saldern, soon to be the all-powerful Holstein agent in Denmark: Macartney seems to have been the first British minister to perceive his political usefulness and appreciate his coming importance.

All this was little enough for a pushing young man, anxious to distinguish himself in his first post, and if it had not been for the commercial negotiations Macartney might well have felt the time hang heavily on his hands. Nevertheless, in the first eighteen months or so of his residence in St. Petersburg the question of the alliance, to all appearance immovably deadlocked, did show one or two signs that progress might not be altogether impossible. One of these consisted in the mere fact of continued Anglo-Russian collaboration in Sweden. Goodricke and Osterman were able to win a succession of sweeping electoral and parliamentary victories which smashed the Hats beyond recovery, at any rate for this *riksdag,* and put Sweden firmly in the hands of the Caps. But these triumphs themselves led logically to other commitments. The destruction of French influence in Sweden must surely imply the securing of that country to the good cause by the conclusion of an Anglo-Swedish alliance. Though Sandwich set his face resolutely against any alliance which included subsidies, he was quite prepared to accept an alliance which could be obtained without them. For behind the prospect of a Swedish alliance lay the much more important possibility of expanding that alliance to include Russia.

In this situation it was almost inevitable that Macartney, inadequately briefed from home, depending for his information on Swedish affairs upon Goodricke, should have steered his course by the light of common-sense, and that common-sense should have suggested to him that the right policy for Great Britain now was to make the most of the successes which Goodricke had already won: there was no point in spending money by pennyworths, and still less in buying Swedish support and then balking at the last instalment of the purchase price. Macartney never seems to have shared Sandwich's suspicion that Russia intended to shuffle off the burden of expense in Sweden on to English shoulders. He correctly judged Russian aims in Stockholm, and he believed them to be accordant with British interests. He was sure that Russia wanted England's friendship; and he believed that co-operation in Sweden, on a basis of reciprocal confidence, 'would lay such a foundation of alliance and interest . . . as could neither be disunited by jealousy nor shaked by time'.

The difficulty was that the British government could never quite make up its mind whether a great interest was really at stake in Sweden or not; and even if ministers had been more certain about it than they were, there still remained the awkward problem of finding the money. The funds for political corruption could come only from the Civil List; and after 1760 the Civil List was notoriously inadequate to meet the legitimate demands upon it. Neither Macartney nor Goodricke realized ministers' difficulties in this matter; and they were inclined to forget that theirs were not the only countries with which a Secretary of State had to deal. Their zeal led them from time to time to commit indiscretions and exceed their instructions; but in Macartney's case some, at least, of his errors were to be ascribed to sheer lack of experience. It was mere ignorance and *naïveté* which led him, in March 1765, to commit the serious indiscretion of asking Panin 'as from his Court' just how large a subsidy from England would be required to secure Sweden. No doubt it was to be attributed to Sandwich's neglect to afford him any guidance on policy; but a more cautious and more experienced minister would never have made the enquiry 'as from his Court'. It can hardly have failed to give Panin the quite erroneous impression that the British ministers were not so adamantly opposed to subsidies as they pretended to be.

It seems likely that Macartney believed that a subsidy to Sweden ought to be paid. It is true that when he came to understand (as he very soon afterwards did) how inflexible the attitude of ministers was upon this question, he took care to declare in his despatches that he was personally opposed to it. But it is clear that he continued to discuss the question with Panin; and in October 1765 he was able to report to Grafton a conversation which on the face of it marked a decisive change in the position: Panin, he wrote, had assured him that he hoped to persuade Catherine to permit *Russia* to pay to Sweden a subsidy of 120,000 roubles a year. He had indeed also suggested that England might make a similar agreement with

Denmark; but he had not made the Swedish subsidy conditional upon this.

If Macartney's report had corresponded with the real state of the case, it might well have been a turning-point in Anglo-Russian relations. But it is clear that he had either misreported Panin, or misunderstood him. It is possible, of course, that he had been deliberately misled; but it scarcely seems very probable: all foreign ministers to Russia agreed in remarking upon Panin's strict truthfulness and plain dealing. Certainly it is inconceivable that he can have meant what Macartney represented him as saying. He was quite as determined not to pay a subsidy to Sweden as Sandwich was; and in 1766 was to tell Macartney that if Russia were at last forced to subsidize Sweden as a consequence of England's refusal to do so he would break off negotiations and never renew them again. In March 1765 Macartney had contrived to suggest to the Russians that England might after all pay subsidies, if pushed hard enough; in October he managed to imbue Grafton with the idea that the Russians might pay them themselves. There was no foundation for either notion, and the sooner each side was clear on that point, the better.

Meanwhile the purely political question of a possible Anglo-Russian alliance had (perhaps inevitably) become entangled with the matter of the commercial treaty: the difficulties about concluding the one had repercussions upon the manoeuvring for position in regard to the other. Both sides tried at various times to use the one question as a lever to accelerate the other's progress. Macartney was, of course, very well aware of the connection between his negotiation and the cordiality or coolness of Anglo-Russian co-operation in Sweden. He made no bones about avowing to Grafton that one reason which led him to sign the commercial treaty against orders was the prospect of mollifying Panin's resentment at British tight-fistedness in the matter of Swedish bribes. In November 1765 he vainly offered Panin up to 10,000 roubles for Swedish expenses, if he would sign the Declaration. He was certainly not empowered to do any such thing; but he seems to have escaped without a rebuke — perhaps because Panin rejected the offer out of hand.

Just as the negotiations for the commercial treaty entangled themselves with discussions about the policy to be pursued in Sweden, so too they became involved in the great argument over the Turkish clause. Here Macartney was undoubtedly guilty of grave indiscretions. On 19 March [OS] 1765 Golitsyn wrote to Gross that Macartney had observed, in conversation, that

we [the Russians] are justified in demanding the inclusion of Turkey, and that according to his information the Russo-Prussian and Russo-

Danish treaties did not exclude Turkey; he therefore thinks that his Court may agree, in view of the justice of the case, and so as not to give Prussia and Denmark grounds for suspicion, and also in view of our helpful attitude in the negotiation [for the commercial treaty].

Admittedly this occurred at an early stage of Macartney's mission; but on this cardinal point, at least, he can hardly have been ignorant of the attitude of his Court. Three months later, in June 1765, he repeated the offence, and this time he landed himself in trouble. In a conversation with Golitsyn he intimated that complaisance by Russia in regard to the trade treaty might well induce his government to abandon the Turkish clause. For this he had, of course, no shadow of authority. Unluckily for him, the conversation was reported by Golitsyn to Gross in London; and Gross in turn mentioned it in an interview with Grafton. Grafton, as was to be expected, lost no time in sending a rebuke to Macartney — a rebuke which (as Macartney himself admitted) was as temperate and considerate as it well could be, but nevertheless unambiguously a rebuke. Macartney now committed the further indiscretion of showing the rebuke to Panin, who had been unaware of the conversation with Golitsyn; and it seems likely that it was upon Macartney's urging that he now sent a sharp despatch to Gross, censuring him for attributing to Macartney remarks he had never made: at no time, Panin wrote, had Macartney made any effort to link the question of the Turkish clause with that of the commerical treaty, and Gross was to disavow his remarks to Grafton, and assure him that Macartney was innocent of the suggestion which had been attributed to him. But within a fortnight Panin had to eat his words. In the interim he had seen the minute of the Chancery recording Macartney's conversation with Golitsyn on 6 June, and from that minute it plainly appeared that he had said exactly what Gross had alleged that he had said. So much had to be conceded; but Panin went to great lengths to get him out of the scrape. He was sure, he wrote, that if the words had in fact been spoken, they had not been spoken ministerially (which was probably true); it seemed likely that there had been a mistake somewhere; and Gross was ordered to say that the blame for any misunderstanding lay wholly with the Russian Chancery, and to express his regret that the mistake had occurred. This was generous; but it was probably a good deal less than the truth. Though Macartney vehemently denied having said what he was alleged to have said on 6 June, and though he found it expedient at the end of August to profess that his personal opinion was in favour of insisting on the Turkish clause, it is hard to believe that he spoke the truth. It seems much more likely that he had been prepared to offer to sacrifice the Turkish clause in order to ensure the success of his commercial negotiations, and had permitted himself to use language which he must have known conflicted with the policy of his government, in the hope that once the treaty was made he would be able to disavow it if it were reported, or perhaps in the hope that it would not be reported at all.

By the summer of 1766, then, all efforts to find a way round the *impasse* in the alliance negotiations seemed to have been tried and failed: the attempt to use the commercial treaty as a bargaining counter had, if anything, worsened relations; British parsimony had spoilt, or was spoiling, the chances of an advance by way of Sweden; Russian boorishness and British idiocy were soon to lead to an open breach between Saldern and Gunning in Copenhagen. It was not what Panin had expected. The fall of the Grenville ministry in 1765 had been greeted by him as bringing the hope of better things. But his initial experience of the Rockinghams had proved sharply disappointing; and though he was prepared to attribute their intransigence to 'youth, vanity, and a pretended distrust of affairs as left to them by their predecessors', there had not subsequently been much improvement.

To Macartney, writing his despatches to the office in the spring and summer of 1766, the auguries for the alliance looked anything but promising. When he spoke to Panin of the efforts England had made in Sweden, he received replies which he took no care to soften before transmission to his chief. On one such occasion, Panin

> looked for some time very steadfastly at me, and then said, 'When I tell you that Denmark has given an hundred thousand roubles, when I tell you that I have spent half a million on this cursed Dyet, can you seriously speak to me of the efforts of Great Britain?'

Macartney proceeded to point the moral:

> All the money was absolutely thrown away, if the principal inducement to the expense was the hopes of persuading Russia by that consideration to conclude a Treaty of Alliance with us upon our terms:

neither bribes in Sweden, nor an alliance with Denmark, would budge Panin on the Turkish clause. The sooner ministers realized that negotiation with Russia was going to get more difficult, rather than easier, the sooner they made up their minds to conclude before Catherine raised her terms, the better. After eighteen months' experience of negotiation with the Russian ministers, Macartney had grasped, as his superiors had conspicuously failed to do, that behind Russian intransigence lay other than material considerations: considerations of national pride and prestige; and those feelings were as strong, and as firmly based on reality, as the very similar feelings which inspired English ministers. That Panin desired the English alliance was certain, and Macartney was correct in his assertion that

England had no better friend in St. Petersburg; but not even for the English alliance would he accept the Turkish clause — unless, indeed, British ministers made an equivalent sacrifice of principle by granting a subsidy in peacetime, either to Sweden or to Denmark, or even to Russia herself: it did not matter very much where.

The replacement of Grafton by Conway in the Northern Secretaryship, which took place on 28 May 1766, seemed for a moment to offer the chance for a fresh start. In his communications with Macartney he was much more cordial and expansive than his predecessor had ever been; he was prepared to discuss the general state of Britain's foreign relations, and even to solicit Macartney's views on them; as became an admirer of Pitt, he was an advocate of a Northern System, and sanguine of the chances of obtaining it. Macartney sensed an opportunity; on 4 July he wrote to Conway urging him to seize it. Now was the time, he suggested, for England to resume the initiative and come forward with a counter-project for the alliance: 'all that has hitherto past is mere *pour parler*'. But Macartney's suggestion was already too late at the time it reached its destination. It had been overtaken by political events in England; and those events induced Panin to think that it would be better to defer consideration of the proposal until Russia could take stock of Chatham's impending initiative.

VI

The appointment of Stanley was Chatham's personal decision. This time there was no nonsense about choosing someone who was likely to appeal to Catherine's susceptibility to charming young men: Stanley 'was a man of awkward appearance, ungracious manners, irascible temper, and eccentric habits'. The decision to send him was made in haste, without prior consultation of Chatham's colleagues. Though it was well known that Catherine objected to receiving ambassadors at her court, or to sending any, and though the acceptance of Stanley as ambassador would probably entail the appointment of a Russian ambassador to England, Chatham omitted the ordinary courtesy of giving Mussin-Pushkin notice in advance of his intentions: the first he heard about it was when he read in the newspapers that Stanley had kissed hands. Mortifying as this must have been, it was a good deal less mortifying than Macartney's experience. For as ill-luck would have it, the first intimation he received of what he could only regard as a deliberate indication of his government's lack of confidence in him came not from Conway but from Panin: it was not until a day after Panin had told him the news that Conway's despatch of 1 August arrived in St. Petersburg.

No one who had read Macartney's despatches of the previous autumn should have been greatly surprised at the way he reacted to this treatment. The disallowing of his commercial treaty had been bad enough; but this was a great deal worse. Humiliated, embittered, yet debarred by the proprieties of the service (and perhaps also by a regard for his own future) from giving free rein to his resentment, he acknowledged Conway's communication in despatches which were a nauseating blend of false humility and real boasting. At times his anger brought him perilously near to insolence, as when he wrote: 'as you have been silent . . . with regard to my destination, you'll please to inform me whether I am actually superseded'. The question was a fair one; but it might have been put with rather more amenity.

The unhappy Conway, who seems to have been genuinely taken aback by the violence of Macartney's feelings, bore all this with considerable meekness, and from time to time applied such balm as he could to his envoy's lacerated spirit. His request to be allowed to return home on leave (assuming, that is, that he had not in fact been recalled) Conway answered on the day of its arrival at the office: the request was granted, but he was ordered to stay in Russia until Stanley's arrival. Again and again Conway carefully explained that no slight had been intended, that Macartney still enjoyed the full confidence of his court, that his great services were fully appreciated. He never seems to have realized how abrupt and unexplained his original announcement of Stanley's mission had been. Macartney had not been provided at the outset, as Sir Andrew Mitchell had, with a precise statement of the purpose of Stanley's mission: it was not until 19 December that Conway produced something like an explanation, and it is apparent from the terms in which it was written that he was under the delusion that Macartney had been told all about it already. It was not until 27 March 1767 that he transmitted the information that Stanley's mission had been intended simply as a special assignment to conclude the alliance, and that it had never been the idea that he should remain as resident ambassador. If this information had been available to Macartney at the beginning, it would at least have done something to soften the blow: as it was, it came far too late.

For Macartney remained unappeased by Conway's assurances, unmollified by his dribbling explanations, and increasingly irritated at what he considered to be his tardiness in answering letters: with perverse ingenuity Conway elected to send the crucial despatch of 19 December by a private hand, with the result that it took three weeks longer than the ordinary mail to reach St. Petersburg. In these circumstances Macartney's only response to Conway's appeals was to subside into a permanent condition of petulant sulks. It was not, he explained, that he felt any resentment — as Conway (oddly enough) seemed to imagine: on the contrary, he was truly grateful for not having been actually dismissed. He tried hard to adopt a pose of philosophic resignation and stoic contempt for the blows of fortune; but his attitude was somewhat spoilt by the fact that waspishness would keep breaking through. He insisted that his credit in Russia, thanks to Stanley's nomination, had been totally destroyed; that he was considered as a man who had no longer the confidence of his court; that he could therefore be of no further service; that the duties of the post, being now purely nominal, could be perfectly well discharged by his secretary. Naturally enough, he found the prospect of waiting for Stanley extremely distasteful, and he pleaded hard to be allowed to take his leave at once if only on grounds of health:

> The vexations, disappointments and mortifications I have suffered of late, have thrown me into a severe hypochondriacal disorder.

However

> since your commands are such, I shall most certainly remain here, and drag on a miserable existence, till I am relieved by the arrival of my successor, or by a natural dissolution . . . I have too little merit to expect consideration, and know myself of too little consequence to be spared in a sacrifice, if a victim was wanting.

His temper was not improved by the fact that it was not clear how long he would have to wait for Stanley's arrival. The uncertainty made it impossible to undertake commitments in advance. In February 1767 the court was to move to Moscow: would he be justified in spending £300 on hiring a house there? Was it worth his while to go? How, if he did go, was he to transport all the old cyphers which Buckinghamshire had left behind him, and which weighed the surprising amount of between 30 and 40 stone? Apart from an order to destroy the old cyphers, he got little guidance from Conway on any of these points. For indeed the time of Stanley's departure was almost as much of a mystery to Conway as it was to Macartney.

As early as 30 July Stanley himself sensibly suggested that it would be better to reconnoitre the position in Berlin before sending him there. The suggestion was adopted; instructions were sent to Mitchell to take soundings with Frederick; and on 1 October George III decided that Stanley was not to start until Mitchell's report of Frederick's reaction had been received. It took some time before Mitchell gave his superiors what they wanted: Frederick either hedged or contrived to evade the question altogether; and Conway's irritation and impatience grew from week to week. At last, goaded by repeated instructions from London, Mitchell forced Frederick to an unambiguous declaration. It was a flat refusal: such an alliance, he said, would endanger, rather than preserve, the peace of Europe. Thus the grandiose attempt to persuade Prussia and Russia to forget their own interests for the sake of obliging Mr. Pitt was shipwrecked before it was well launched. Stanley's mission was already a fiasco. It remained only to convert it into a melancholy farce.

In view of the reaction from Berlin, it was scarcely surprising that

Stanley should have lost interest in his mission. Already in December it was rumoured in St. Petersburg that he was not coming, and that Macartney was to be raised to the rank of ambassador instead. This provoked a protest from Panin: there was a great difference between the sending of a special ambassador and the mere promotion of a man already on the spot; what had been intended as an honour paid to the Empress would be transformed into something like a slight. But in January 1767 Panin was able to inform Macartney (prematurely, as it turned out) that Stanley had resigned the appointment: his feelings at receiving this information from such a source, rather than from the office, can well be imagined. There seemed, however, to be an extraordinary lack of suitable candidates who were prepared to go. Meanwhile, the appointment came under fire in the House of Commons, where on 25 March George Grenville attacked the decision to send an ambassador as a waste of public money and a party job. The effect on the government was immediate. Two days later Conway wrote to Macartney a truly lamentable despatch. Since Stanley had never been designed to be a resident ambassador, but only to go on special mission to conclude the alliance; since the obstacle of the Turkish clause (which had been no less palpable at the time of Stanley's appointment than it was now) would make any progress on the alliance impossible; and since, finally, it was known that Catherine objected to ambassadors (an objection which they had ignored when Stanley was appointed) — Macartney was to suggest to Panin that the whole idea of an exchange of ambassadors should be dropped. To Macartney the execution of this extraordinary commission must have been felt as one humiliation the more; but fortunately he was not called upon personally to undergo it. For when the English messenger arrived with this despatch on 18 April [NS], Macartney was confined to bed with a violent cold and rheumatism; his secretary, Henry Shirley, was suffering from measles; and there was nothing for it but for him to order the messenger to hand the despatch direct to Panin. Panin, not surprisingly, was annoyed. On 10 February Count Chernyshev had been named Russian ambassador to London; a standing rule of the Empress had been broken in England's favour; and now she was coolly told that she need not have bothered. Panin waited three weeks before replying, and then, on 11 May [NS], wrote to Macartney in terms of contemptuous indifference. It was of no consequence to Russia whether there was an exchange of ambassadors or not. And if Panin could not care less about the outcome, neither could Macartney: Panin's letter was allowed to miss the post-day on 12 May, and was not sent on to London till the 19th: it did not reach Conway until 11 June. On 21 August Conway was at last able to write to Shirley to inform him officially that Stanley had declined the appointment, and that another ambassador would be sent in his place — when they could find one.

By that time Macartney had left Russia, and left it with relief. His position in the months which elapsed between Stanley's nomination and his own departure would have been trying in any event: in the circumstances Macartney found it intolerable. No guidance came to him from London as to whether he should go to Moscow or not; and in the end (economy being now no doubt an object to him) he decided on his own responsibility to stay in St. Petersburg, which meant that he was left kicking his heels in the capital with no Russian ministers to talk to, almost the sole representative of the *corps diplomatique,* miserable, furious, and above all feeling himself ridiculous. Worst of all (and this perhaps is really why he declined to spend £300 on a house in Moscow) knowing himself — for reasons to be considered in a moment — to be *persona non grata* to the Empress and Panin.

In this situation he found some relief to his feelings in transmitting to the office, and relaying to his friends, the acid comments of Panin upon British policy; and perhaps it is not uncharitable to think that he imparted an additional astringency to them before he sent them off. The proprieties might inhibit him from personally telling ministers what he thought of them and their policies; but it was some satisfaction to convey his opinions vicariously through the mouth of a foreigner. Panin, he reported, had 'of late affected to talk of our business in a jocose, if not a taunting manner'; and

> I should think a Treaty of Alliance with the Empress of Russia (during Mr. Panin's Ministry) as distant and unlikely to be brought about, as a League with Prester John, or the King of Bantam... I do really believe, that the Mufti of Constantinople might with as much probability expect a blessing from the Pope, as the Court of Great Britain flatter herself with the hopes of assistance from the Court of Berlin in any Russian negotiation... My own opinion is that this Court has long since resigned all thoughts of bringing us into the System, and therefore endeavours to compose it as well as she can without us.

At last, on 13 April [NS] 1767, he received the release for which he had been waiting. Towards the end of May he quitted St. Petersburg for ever — without the customary leaving-present, since he had not officially been recalled, though with the consolation of a jewelled snuff-box from the Empress — and on 2 June 1767 he arrived in Stockholm, where Goodricke gave him a rousing welcome. There followed three weeks of 'constant dissipation' in Goodricke's congenial company, varied by a visit to some Uppland iron-works, and by discussions with the Cap leaders.

Queen Lovisa Ulrika showed him marked attention — partly by way of snubbing Goodricke, whom she cordially disliked, but also in the hope that he might be sent back to Sweden in Goodricke's place. The Cap leaders found his political principles all that could be desired; so much so, that they commissioned him to plead their cause with Conway on his arrival in England: one may doubt if he was the most eligible advocate, in the circumstances. A few of them, noting the favour he enjoyed with the Queen, and being for one reason or another not wholly satisfied with Goodricke, conceived the idea that if they could secure him as British minister in Stockholm, he might serve as a means to draw the Queen over to their side. He thus found himself, through no fault of his own, involved in an unsavoury intrigue to displace his host. There is nothing to suggest that he gave it any encouragement: it is unlikely that the prospect of a move to Stockholm had much attraction for him.

At the end of June Macartney set sail from Göteborg; and by 18 August he had had his interview with Conway. Its temper can only be conjectured; its substance concerned the question of a subsidy for Sweden, and here he had no success. When he suggested that the Caps might be willing to take as little as half the sum which Goodricke had asked for, Conway unfeelingly replied 'that if they could accept so small a one, they might as well take none'. As Nolcken remarked, there was no escaping the fact that, however good a friend to Sweden Macartney might be, he was not *persona grata* with the ministry, either on personal or official grounds. However, he had done his best for Goodricke. When his interview with Conway was over he set out for a holiday with Lord Holland, and thereafter was lost to view for a month or two among the country houses.

The problem of finding a successor to Stanley still remained. Eligible candidates remained as shy as ever. In St. Petersburg the conviction began to gain ground in diplomatic circles that they would have Macartney back again. Early in November he was in London, talking to the Swedish minister, von Nolcken, and professing a conviction that England would have to agree to a subsidy sooner or later; but he gave no indication on that occasion as to his future prospects. On 20 November 1767, however, the long suspense was ended with his being named Ambassador to Russia. Nolcken believed that he had had no idea of it a week earlier, and that he secured the appointment, in the absence of any other suitable candidate, as a result of the influence of Lord Holland with Lord Bute. There may be something in this; but it seems likely that Macartney had already established a claim upon Lord Bute on his own account. For on 11 December Nolcken was conveying to his government the news of Macartney's engagement to Bute's daughter, Lady Jane Stuart. She was not, perhaps, conspicuous for her personal charms — George Selwyn saw her soon afterwards, and pronounced her *'laide à faire peur'* –

but for a young man at a rather critical moment of his career she was a solid, and possibly a brilliant, investment. Lady Jane, perhaps, might have hoped to do rather better; but she might easily have done a great deal worse: reports reached Lord Carlisle in Turin that she was to marry Lord March. From the point of view of British foreign policy the match was perhaps rather less satisfactory. The initial reactions to the news of Macartney's reappointment had been generally favourable among those concerned for British prestige in northern Europe: Sir John Goodricke was delighted, the Caps inspirited, the Swedish minister at St. Petersburg, Baron Ribbing, looked forward to the return of 'a whole-hearted and faithful friend, who would do everything in his power for the advantage of the country'. But the connection with Lord Bute made even well-wishers a little dubious. Seen in this light, Macartney's appointment seemed to promise, not a fresh mind and a vigorous initiative, but the continuation of the system of foreign policy which, rightly or wrongly (and almost certainly wrongly), foreign observers associated with Bute and Bedford: a system of insularity, parsimony, narrow views and faithlessness to engagements.

Even Robert Gunning in Copenhagen, who was in general sympathetic to Macartney, wrote to Goodricke that

I fear the new connection of Sir George Macartney may (from the light it is looked on by Mr. Panin) be attended with some inconveniences.

He may well have been right; but as it happened Panin's reactions to the news of Macartney's appointment were not determined by any such political considerations. That news had no sooner reached him than he wrote a personal letter to Macartney which was of such a nature as to make his acceptance of the embassy out of the question. He warned him in the strongest terms that if he came to Russia he would not be received: if he persisted in accepting the appointment the British government would be officially notified of the reasons for the Empress's objections. And he added:

C'est le comble de l'inconséquence et de l'indiscretion de sa part d'avoir sollicité ou accepté ce poste dans les circonstances où il se trouve vis-à-vis de la Cour.

What, then, were these circumstances? With what disclosures was Macartney now being threatened?

VII

It appears that he had been guilty of at least two serious personal offences. In June 1766 the Russian Master of Ceremonies had contrived to bungle the seating arrangements at a *caroussel,* so that Macartney (and also the Swedish minister) were assigned places which were lower than those to which they considered themselves entitled. Both protested; and Macartney's colleagues (including even the French Resident) thought that they were right to do so. Panin at once admitted that a mistake had been made, and sent Macartney a letter of apology. There the matter ought to have ended; but Macartney, who (in Panin's words) 'crut devoir offenser personellement' the Master of Ceremonies, took the opportunity at a dinner at the Vicomte de la Herreira's to insult him by thrusting Panin's letter under his nose, with the remark 'Voilà, Monsieur, de quoi vous apprendre votre devoir une autre fois'. This behaviour was generally condemned by the *corps diplomatique;* Panin was outraged, and wrote to Macartney saying 'qu'il ne savait pas se conduire et que le maître des cérémonies n'aurait jamais plus affaire à lui'; and when Macartney organized a horse-race in the English style at Tsarskoe Selo (at great expense), and invited the Grand Duke and most of the Court, they all pointedly stayed away. It is clear that he made himself, for some time at least, socially impossible: for some weeks he was treated by the Empress with marked coldness, and it was even supposed that Stanley's appointment (and Macartney's presumed recall) were the consequences of Russian complaints in London about his behaviour.

The affair would no doubt have blown over and been forgotten, had it not shortly been succeeded by another of a much more serious character. St. Petersburg society was well known for the laxity of its morals, and Macartney seems to have been enterprising in taking advantage of the facilities it afforded. We hear of an affair with a Mdlle. Keyshoff — 'of great family, but neither young, handsome, nor clever', whose 'only merit in my eyes was a passion which she either had, or affected to have, for me'; we hear of 'an intrigue ... that no man but myself would ever have dreamed of'. But hitherto Macartney's biographers have been discreetly silent about the affair to which Catherine took such strong exception. This was nothing less than the seduction of one of the Empress's Ladies in Waiting, Mdlle. Khitrov, who happened also (as ill-luck would have it) to be Panin's cousin. The French Resident thought poorly of the lady's personal attractions, and even worse of her moral character: in his view the whole affair was explicable only on political grounds, and Macartney was simply deploying the classic techniques of British diplomatic agents in search of information. The scandal became public when Mdlle. Khitrov was discovered to be with child. Macartney seems to have admitted responsibility; and the Empress — easy-going on morals, but not to be trifled with on etiquette — took the line that Macartney had abused the privilege of access to her Court. The Lady in Waiting was packed off home and threatened with the cloister, Macartney found it prudent to absent himself from Court and keep out of Catherine's way. The scandal blew up in November 1766; and although matters were so far patched up that he was able to appear at Court again in December, the incident does something, perhaps, to explain his lamentable letters of the autumn of that year, his protestations that he had become useless as the result of Stanley's appointment, his reluctance to follow the Court to Moscow in the following February. He was obviously nervous in case any damaging rumours should reach England, he took care to discount them in advance. At the height of the Khitrov-*fracas* he had the effrontery to write to Conway:

> This Court continues to me the highest personal regard, and has very lately given me the strongest mark of it, in an affair, which is of too private a nature to enter into in this despatch—

by which he meant, no doubt, that he had been permitted to show himself again at Court. Ministers in England certainly remained ignorant of the letter to Macartney in which Panin vetoed his return; but some knowledge of the affair must have filtered through. When a year later Macartney was named Ambassador, Conway found it expedient to write to Gunning denying that there was opposition to his return: any resentments at Macartney's intrigue with Mdlle. Khitrov were now 'quite blown over'; and as to the suggestion that his marriage was indicative of an imminent change in Britain's attitude towards Russia, it was 'as absolutely false as it is ignorant and ridiculous'.

Ignorant and ridiculous it may have been (though the French Consul in St. Petersburg informed his sovereign, as a matter of fact, that Macartney was Bute's bastard); but it was not the essence of the matter. The truth was that despite his acknowledged excellence as a man of business and his proved skill as a negotiator, Macartney had really made Russia too hot to hold him. And the memory of his conduct remained. Five years later De Visme wrote to his friend Gunning, who was then on the point of going as minister to St. Petersburg:

> that minister [Macartney] lost himself by his indiscretion. You will hear by degrees much of that matter . . .

He had indeed lost himself: the game was up. He had not hesitated, it seems, to accept the embassy, though it must have needed considerable nerve to contemplate a return to the scene of his exploits. As late as 12 January 1768 he was writing to Lord Holland, 'it gives me infinite pleasure that I am to stay abroad but two years'. But before the month was out he had married Lady Jane Stuart; and the alleged reluctance of Lord Bute to allow his daughter to travel to Russia provided a decent excuse for withdrawing.

It remained only to find some alternative employment worthy of Lord Bute's son-in-law and Lord Holland's friend, and provided if possible with emoluments to correspond. In February it was rumoured that he might go as minister to Turin; in June he was mentioned as a possible Secretary at War. At all events it was clear that something must be found for him: as George Selwyn truly said, 'he will certainly not be on the parish'. Macartney had never abandoned his parliamentary ambitions, even while he was in Russia. In a revealing letter to Lord Holland in June 1766 he had explained that though he enjoyed the career of diplomacy, the post in Russia would not suit him much longer, since there was no chance of his being raised to the rank of ambassador in view of Catherine's preference for representation at ministerial level. He expected to have finished his commercial treaty, and to be home on leave, by the end of the year: if so, that might be an opportunity to put himself in line for the succession to the embassy to Madrid. He had other plans also; for he hoped to use his leave 'to dispose of myself in the grand and most important concern in life in such a manner as to render myself and my fortunes entirely happy for the rest of my days': had he already, perhaps, his eye on Lady Jane? In the meantime, his most immediate concern was a seat in Parliament: could Holland procure him one for £2,000? As to where the money was to come from, there could be no difficulty: he would borrow it in St. Petersburg.

> Perhaps I might say without vanity that there is not an English merchant in Russia who would not warmly interest himself in everything that could contribute to my advantage.

He was interested in the possibilities at Stockbridge, a venal borough where the Fox family, at great expense, controlled one seat, and conceivably two. By August 1767 he was mentioned as a candidate for the borough at the next election. Holland was personally averse to Macartney's entering Parliament, though Lady Holland was not, and he would have liked to 'compliment the Duke of Grafton' by making a seat at Stockbridge available to the Treasury; but with his usual good-nature he agreed to bring Macartney in. It is not quite clear what prevented this arrangement from being carried out; but it seems that the expense was more than Macartney could face. A rumour reached Holland in February that he was to be ennobled as Lord Balmaine; but it proved to be no more than a rumour. In the end, the immediate difficulty was solved by Lord Bute, who persuaded his other son-in-law, Sir James Lowther, to bring in Macartney without expense as one of his members for Cockermouth. His tenure of the seat was destined to be a short one, for Sir James soon needed it for himself; and nine months after his election

Macartney found himself called upon to vacate it, though not before he had acknowledged his debt by speaking in the Commons in defence of his patron's electioneering proceedings. But it was not long before a more solid provision was made for him by quartering him on his native country; and on 1 January 1769 he began a new phase of his career when he kissed hands as Chief Secretary for Ireland.

VIII

When Macartney returned to England in August 1767 he brought with him (in addition to Catherine's snuff-box) two tangible evidences of his activity in Russia. One was the order of the White Eagle of Poland; the other was that *Account of the Russian Empire* which he subsequently published privately, and from which Barrow printed excerpts in the Appendix to his *Life.*

It is difficult to be certain of how Macartney earned his White Eagle. The reasons stated by Stanislas II, in the letter to Macartney which accompanied the insignia, were the King's 'gratitude to, and especial affection for, your nation', together with similar feelings for Macartney personally. No letters of Macartney seem to have survived which explain why Stanislas should have felt any obligation to him; and though there is a handful of letters to Macartney from Wroughton, the British minister in Warsaw, they shed little light on the problem. The only source of information seems to be the despatches of the French Resident in St. Petersburg; and from these it would appear that Macartney took an active part in trying to persuade Panin to pursue a policy of moderation in Poland. The Czartoryski had continued the Diet of 1764 as a standing Confederation, and by so doing had circumvented the *liberum veto* and made reform conceivable: it was Macartney's hope that Panin might be induced to permit the Confederation to continue. It appears that he tried to convince him that any attempt to emancipate the Dissidents would plunge Poland into civil war (as happened, in fact), and that the only hope was to purchase concessions for them by permitting some of the constitutional changes which the Czartoryski and Stanislas desired: it was even reported that Macartney had drawn up a plan of conciliation. It may not be without significance that he was in very close touch with Caspar von Saldern in the autumn of 1765 (Saldern was in fact living in his house); and it was Saldern whom Panin sent to Warsaw and Berlin, on what turned out to be a fruitless mission of conciliation, in the spring of 1766. It seems possible that Macartney used his intimacy with Saldern, and the high esteem in which he was then held by Panin, to reinforce

their already existing inclination to a 'softer' line, based on collaboration with Stanislas and his Czartoryski uncles, and a policy of
strengthening the Republic. At all events, the first offer of the White
Eagle reached Macartney in November 1765; permission to receive
it was conveyed by Grafton in March 1766; and the investiture took
place in June.

The *Account of the Russian Empire* is not quite the final report on
his mission which Macartney's instructions had ordered him to
provide; for there is virtually no attempt at an analysis of Russian
politics, and still less at an assessment of Russian politicians. What
we have is rather a broad survey of Russian society, with sections on
Population, History, Social Classes, Revenue, Trade, the Church,
and so forth. It certainly bears witness to considerable diligence in
collecting *data*; and in this the author was more enterprising, or more
successful, in some fields than in others: the length of the various
sections into which the book is divided is determined less by their
intrinsic importance than by the amount of material at his disposal.
By far the longest chapter is devoted to a detailed account of the
personnel, organization, doctrines and ritual of the Russian church;
but this, in fact, was probably the work not of Macartney, but of the
late Rev. J. G. King, chaplain to the English church in St. Petersburg.
Trade is allotted only one-third of the space devoted to ecclesiastical
affairs; but this is perhaps to be explained not by lack of information,
and still less of interest, but by the fact that the topic had been fully
covered in his despatches, and in the statistical summaries which
from time to time he enclosed with them. Since his stay in Russia
was comparatively short, and since as far as we know he never
acquired any knowledge of Russian, nor moved outside the cirlces of
court and mercantile society in St. Petersburg, his observations have
at times inevitably a somewhat conventional and second-hand
flavour. The style is artificially antithetical, and at times falls into a
tiresome sententiousness. Nor is the book devoid of signs of its
author's characteristic self-confidence: after conceding that general-
izations about national character, or the particular characteristics of
different social groups, must usually be of limited validity, he robustly
continues: 'yet I am conscious the following picture is not liable to
such an imputation'. Still, he does something to disarm the reader by
his remark that none of his own explanations of Russia's backwardness seem to him to be very convincing. His sketch of Russian
history cannot be said to add much to the sum of human knowledge,
even by the standards of the contemporary English reader; and his
views of Russian society often tend to reproduce the commonplaces
of international travel-literature: creative activity and material
progress in Russia, he tells us, are entirely dependent on foreigners,

though the Russians are docile pupils; the country is still in all essentials barbarous; the middle-class is illiterate, unenterprising and unbusinesslike; the Russian nobility's only assets are a facility in modern languages and skill at chess and billiards; the scandalous immorality of Russian court-ladies (including Mdlle. Khitrov?) is to be attributed to the corrupting influence of French governesses; and so forth. Three years before the battle of Tchesmé he laid it down as an axiom that Russia could never become a formidable naval power. But if the event made nonsense of this judgment, it was a verdict which would probably have been endorsed by those British naval officers who were best acquainted with the Russian fleet. And despite this unlucky prophecy Macartney's account has very real merits. He provided, perhaps for the first time in English, a clear and detailed anatomy of the structure of Russian government; he was informative on the confusions of Russian law; he was solid on the nature and yield of Russian revenues. And for all his gibes at Russian backwardness he did grasp the fact that an indigenous Russian culture was emerging: he was perhaps the first Englishman to see the significance of Lomonosov. Above all he realized, far better than his superiors at home, that Russia was no longer a semi-Asiatic colonial-land which other powers could ignore or cozen at their pleasure: he would have agreed with Chatham that 'there is a great Cloud of Power in the North'. To his detailed account of Russia he prefixed the emphatic reminder that:

Russia is no longer to be gazed at as a distant glimmering star, but as a great planet that has obtruded itself into our system, whose place is as yet undetermined, but whose motions must powerfully affect those of every other orb.

It was because he had learnt this lesson so well that he felt so deeply the unwisdom of English intransigence on points which seemed to him to be of comparatively subordinate importance. Earlier than anyone in London he understood how tight was the grip upon Russian policy which Frederick the Great was securing, and how hopeless were English attempts to regain his friendship. It was because he saw that grip growing stronger year by year, to Russia's discomfort and England's prejudice, that he was so anxious for his government to make concessions to Catherine while there was still time, and so obtain her alliance while she was still sufficiently free of Prussian fetters to be able to record it.

In this he failed, as all British envoys to Russia were to fail; but at least he had to his credit the solid achievement of the Commercial Treaty. And despite the painful months which preceded its conclusion, he was entitled to feel that his handling of the affair had won him the respect of Catherine and her minister. The boasts which Macartney too often made of his high favour at the Court of St. Petersburg were not all idle claims: it is clear that he soon acquired, and always retained, their respect for his abilities, and even for his character, whatever they may have thought of his manners. He had to overcome the handicaps which lack of experience imposed upon him; and in this he succeeded, thanks to his readiness to take responsibility, his willingness to work hard, his extraordinary memory (it impressed many of his contemporaries), and his sheer determination to succeed in an enterprise which was to serve as a stepping-stone to a career at home. If in the end his indiscretions, political as well as personal, lost him the friendship of Panin and the Empress, there was nevertheless a dynamic quality about him, an incisiveness in action and thought, which contrasted with the flabbiness of Buckinghamshire, and was to be pointed by the woolly verbosity of Cathcart. Even at the melancholy close of his mission it extorted Panin's respect; and it drew, from the hostile ministers of Prussia and of France, the tribute of their fear and dislike. To have excited the spleen, and escaped the contempt, of Frederick the Great — that was no bad testimonial to an English minister.

CHAPTER III

IRELAND 1769-72

I

Sir George Macartney's appointment as Chief Secretary to the Lord Lieutenant of Ireland owed something to his recent marriage to Lady Jane Stuart. The office lay within the gift of the Lord Lieutenant and luckily for Macartney the current incumbent, Lord Townshend, regarded Lady Jane's father, the Earl of Bute, as 'the first friend I ever met with in public life'.[1] Hence, a request from a Bute family member that Macartney be appointed to the vacant secretaryship was well received. Perhaps more important, the then Prime Minister, the Duke of Grafton, also wrote to Townshend strongly recommending Macartney and testifying to his abilities which he declared were 'very extraordinary'.[2] Grafton's motive was probably to pay off some political debt. Alternatively, he may have felt that something had to be done for Macartney; certainly informed opinion in London had it that Macartney was recommended for the post for no other reason than 'he was left upon their [ministers'] hands and this employment opportunity offered'.[3] Macartney's appointment as Chief Secretary was officially announced on 1 January 1769.

The office of Chief Secretary like most contemporary offices below Cabinet rank tended to vary in importance according to the character and personality of the holder and his relations with his superior, the Lord Lieutenant. Up to the time of Macartney's appointment the duties of a Chief Secretary had been primarily administrative. He handled all warrants for the payment of the civil and military establishment and issued all orders relating to the military and the treasury; all correspondence with the commissioners of the Irish revenue and board of works, and with the various members of the British government who had anything to do with Ireland, passed through his hands. Furthermore, all matters concerning the administration of justice and, as Macartney put it, 'everything that comes under the head of civil affairs' came under his control.[4] The office, in short, was the nerve centre of the Irish administration. However, from the time of Macartney's appointment a change can be observed in its function.

Hitherto, the office had been regarded as a comfortable berth for amateurs in politics. In 1762, for example, Lady Holland wished that her sister's husband, Thomas Bunbury, could be appointed Chief Secretary. As she explained, he would not have to give up his seat in the British House of Commons and furthermore 'they [Chief Secretaries] generally secure some good thing for life'.[5] For the many amateurs in politics this was the main attraction of the post. Others, who were more ambitious, saw its potential. As W. G. Hamilton, Chief Secretary to both Lord Halifax and the Earl of Northumberland in the early 1760s, pointed out to his friend John Hely-Hutchinson: 'nothing is more evident to me than that my continuance in Ireland, instead of retarding, will very essentially promote my progress in England'.[6] Hamilton sought to use the Chief Secretary's office as a position from which to build up and lead a strong parliamentary following which could monopolise the power and patronage of government. His scheme, as it turned out, came to nothing, but it is of interest in that it demonstrates that the office had wider possibilities than had previously been recognised. There is, however, no sign that later Chief Secretaries sought to follow Hamilton's example. Nonentities like Lord Beauchamp (1765-66) came and went, leaving little if any trace of their activities. Even Irishmen were not excluded from the post — in eighteenth-century Ireland usually a reliable guide to the relative importance of any position in the gift of the British government or its agents. Theophilus Jones, maliciously described as 'a young man of the lowest birth and remarkably illiterate even in a country where being illiterate is not apt to get remarked',[7] had been made Chief Secretary by Lord Bristol as recently as July 1767. His was, however, a short-lived appointment, lasting barely six weeks.

With the appointment of Lord Townshend as Lord Lieutenant in August 1767 and the ensuing struggle for control of government between Townshend and the leading political magnates in Ireland, the office of Chief Secretary underwent a significant change of function. While still substantially administrative, it became more and more important politically and increasingly the Chief Secretary was called upon to play what could be called a 'ministerial' role in Irish politics. After Macartney's time, the importance of the office ceased to vary according to the ability of the incumbent. Macartney explained the change as follows:

> When the undertakers were at the head of affairs, they arranged the business of Parliament and did not suffer the Lord Lieutenant to interfere with them on that point; but of late years, since the new system has been established, the management of the House of

Commons, and the conduct of business there, has fallen entirely to
the care of the Chief Secretary.[8]
Macartney did not approve of this change and resented having to
play a 'ministerial' role in the Irish Commons. Yet, for all that,
Macartney's tenure occupies a position of unique importance in the
history of the office for he was at once the last of the old-type Chief
Secretaries and the first of the new; the last of the amateurs and —
though he resented it — the first of the professionals. Perhaps the
major significance of his career in Ireland lies in this.

II

The political background to the Townshend viceroyalty and to
Macartney's chief secretaryship can be quickly sketched in.[9] From
1700 to 1767 the usual custom was for the Lord Lieutenant to reside
in Ireland only while the Irish Parliament was in session, i.e. for
approximately eight months every two years. In his absence three
Lords Justices were appointed to look after routine administrative
matters. This custom favoured the gradual growth of a system
whereby the Lord Lieutenant 'contracted out' the King's business to
the leading Irish politicians on his arrival in Ireland. They undertook
(hence the term 'undertakers') to see the King's business — especially
the supply or money bills — through the Irish Parliament and in
return obtained a large share of royal patronage which they
distributed among their friends to their personal advantage and the
increase of their family prestige. By the early 1760s, however,
successive British governments had become both dissatisfied and
alarmed at the way affairs were being conducted in Ireland. The
undertakers had not only become more exorbitant and imperious in
their demands but were also increasingly unable to guarantee their
control of an Irish Parliament which had become more restive. In
February 1765, therefore, the Grenville ministry decided to reform
the way Ireland was governed and at a Cabinet meeting it was
decided that future Lords Lieutenant should reside constantly in
Ireland. A resident Lord Lieutenant would abrogate the need for
Lords Justices and it was hoped that he would be able to curb the
power of the undertakers and, in general, as contemporaries put it,
bring administration back to the Castle. Apparently only one attempt
was made to implement this policy and that came to nothing.
Certainly, when Lord Townshend succeeded Lord Bristol in
August 1767 there is no evidence that any conditions were
attached to his appointment.

On his arrival in Ireland, Townshend's immediate aim was to obtain the consent of the Irish Parliament to an augmentation of the number of troops paid for by Ireland. The leading undertakers of the time, John Ponsonby, Lord Justice, Speaker of the Irish House of Commons and 'first' or Chief Commissioner of the Revenue Board; Richard, second Earl of Shannon, Master-General of the Ordnance, married to Ponsonby's daughter and, like his father-in-law, the leader of a large parliamentary connection; and other government managers such as John Hely-Hutchinson, Prime Serjeant-at-Law, and Philip Tisdall, Attorney-General, agreed to undertake the measure only if their demands for favours were met. These demands having been refused by the British ministry, they turned their parliamentary forces against Townshend's administration, and in May 1768 the augmentation proposal was rejected by the House of Commons. As a result of earlier difficulties encountered over the augmentation proposal, Townshend had already drawn up preliminary proposals for a 'new system' in Ireland. The outlines of these proposals had been laid before the Cabinet in February but there had been little reaction to them. As a result of the defeat of the 'King's favourite point', Townshend was confident that the Cabinet would be more attentive to Irish affairs and he therefore set out in detail his proposals for reforming the way Ireland was governed.

In the first place, Townshend proposed that he be considered a resident Lord Lieutenant. Only thereby could a close eye be kept on Irish government and, more important perhaps, those M.P.s who had supported government in the previous session would be reassured by his presence and by the prospect of his constant protection. Second, Townshend recommended that some people ought to be 'marked out' as objects of the King's displeasure and that, on the same principle, others should be rewarded for their conduct during the session. Finally, he proposed that the Lord Lieutenant be given full power of appointment and dismissal of all revenue officers in Ireland and that the Irish revenue board be 'new-modelled'. The independent position of the Irish revenue board and Ponsonby's control of it were, he wrote, 'the source from whence all the difficulties to the measures of the crown, the distress of successive chief governors and the dominion of party in this kingdom have flowed'. The Irish revenue board and its extensive patronage had to be brought under the control of the Lord Lieutenant.

By implementing these policies Townshend hoped to re-establish the position of English government in Ireland and the strength and power of the Lord Lieutenant. The undertakers, identifying themselves as the leaders of the Irish interest (as opposed to the English) and equating their position with that of the Protestant nation, promised bitter resistance. It was in these circumstances of all-out political warfare that the office of Chief Secretary, to which Macartney had been appointed, grew in importance. As Thomas Waite, Under-Secretary in Dublin Castle, claimed: 'there is great reputation to be gained here at present'. However Macartney seems not to have realised this or, if he did, he chose to ignore it. Despite the fact that (in his absence and through the influence of Lord Bute) he had been elected M.P. for the borough of Armagh in July 1768, the Irish chief secretaryship held no attraction for him.[10] This is to some extent understandable. Although he had not been Ambassador to Russia, nonetheless he had been *the* British representative there and, within limits, had been able to act on his own initiative. But in Ireland he would be subordinate to the Lord Lieutenant and presumably his role would be much more circumscribed. At any rate, in common with previous holders of the chief secretaryship Macartney appears to have viewed it as a useful stop-gap until something better turned up, perhaps in British politics, perhaps abroad. His plan was 'to commit him[self] in advice as seldom as possible; to obey orders and to get for himself and his old friends the best things he can', remarked Charles O'Hara who both knew and liked Macartney.[11] It was a shrewd comment from a competent observer.

III

Although Macartney's appointment dated from 1 January 1769, he did not settle in Ireland until September. During the preceding nine months, a main part of his duties was to try to obtain the Cabinet's approval of Townshend's plan. The Lord Lieutenant felt that having his Chief Secretary in England held certain advantages for the conduct of affairs in Ireland. 'I shall avail myself of your situation in England', wrote Townshend, 'and trouble you frequently'.[12] Macartney, by being at the centre of affairs in London, could possibly hasten the decision on Townshend's proposals. However, in this, Macartney met with little success. It would be unjust to attribute this to a lack of zeal for the work. British ministers had little regard for Macartney and rarely consulted him.[13] Besides, they were pre-occupied with other matters and the affairs of Ireland held no priority. Grafton found the excitement of Newmarket more congenial than the tedium of the council chamber and hardly concerned himself with state affairs.[14] When Macartney finally arrived in Ireland he had accomplished little. The Lord Lieutenant wrote bitterly:

> I presume owing as usual to dissipation . . . [the government has] . . . left things to the last moment, that is to say, the very eve of the session and at last sent over Sir George Macartney with very ample powers as to removals but no explicit declarations as to measures.[15]

Townshend realised that more than a few dismissals or one or two promotions was necessary to re-establish the strength and prestige of English government in Ireland. A 'new system' was needed but, after nine months stay in England, Macartney had left for Ireland without gaining the Cabinet's approval for such a policy.

While the Lord Lieutenant approved of Macartney's remaining in England for some time after his appointment, by June 1769 he began to feel that his Chief Secretary could be of more use to him in Ireland. On several occasions Townshend confessed to Macartney that he missed his help in dealing with Irish affairs. 'You know men and their connexions', he wrote, adding 'I have little opportunity to canvass individuals — every motion is watched, every conversation repeated'.[16] Thomas Waite was more blunt with Macartney:

> Your presence here is of infinite consequence and therefore for heavens' sake come over as soon as you can. I am very confident that your abilities and dexterity can work out our salvation . . . but a great deal of management will be necessary and of such management I know you to be a complete master . . . You cannot bring over anything of greater importance to his Exc[ellenc]y's service than yourself and the sooner that is done the better.[17]

Perhaps Townshend did not press Macartney sufficiently. In late July Macartney was staying with his father-in-law, the Earl of Bute, who had just returned to England from abroad. Townshend wrote lamely to the latter, 'I miss Sir Geo[rge] every hour, yet I will not wish to separate you immediately'.[18] It is true that Macartney continued to urge Cabinet approval of Townshend's plans and that this, in the circumstances, involved a great deal of postponement and delay. But that was not the main reason for his prolonged absence from Ireland. Macartney had stayed on in London in the hope that he would be given a better office than that of Irish Chief Secretary. During 1769 he continued to angle for the vacant post of Ambassador to Spain, a much more lucrative and prestigious post. For a time it appeared definite that he would get the job. Townshend even bade him farewell and set about looking for a successor. In the event Macartney was disappointed. Townshend then sympathised with him and promised him that if he came to Ireland he would not be the loser by it. Although Lord Frederick Campbell, Macartney's predecessor, had not wanted any reward in Ireland for his work, that in no way bound Macartney. 'No man can expect you would drudge here for nothing', wrote Townshend, and he promised to recommend strongly that 'my fellow labourer in this toilsome work' be granted a suitable reward.[19] Armed with this promise Macartney set out for Ireland in late September 1769.

In previous years the place-hunting activities of a Chief Secretary would not have merited so much attention. However, in the context of the struggle between Townshend and the Irish opposition, Macartney's activities reflected adversely on the strength of the Lord Lieutenant's administration. In April 1769 Macartney had paid a short visit to Ireland to attend Townshend's interviews with some of the leading Irish politicians currently in opposition. In particular, he had attended the interview with John Ponsonby whom he had so annoyed and exasperated that Ponsonby refused to have anything more to do with him. Ponsonby had been enraged at what he chose to describe as Macartney's 'categorical style'. Macartney had sought guarantees from Ponsonby as to his future conduct and had continued to press him on this point even though the Speaker resolutely refused to commit himself. No doubt such questioning from one whom he regarded as little more than an upstart offended the inflated pride and dignity of Ponsonby. Thereafter Macartney could be certain of a warm reception in the Irish House of Commons from Ponsonby's men. To a large extent, the battle between the undertakers and Townshend was one of confidence. Could unattached members of Parliament have confidence in the strength of Townshend's administration if, following loud threats by the Lord Lieutenant's leading opponent, his Chief Secretary resigned his office and went elsewhere? It was believed that Ponsonby had frightened Lord Bristol into resigning the lord lieutenancy; Macartney's removal elsewhere, no matter what gloss might have been put on it, would have rebounded to Ponsonby's advantage. Townshend wrote to Macartney explaining this. 'The idea of your removal to Spain has I assure you greatly shaken our credit and, as Mr. Ponsonby and his agents have so loudly proscribed you, it has given them exceeding credit for the moment'.[20] However, the table could still be turned on them. It was of vital importance, wrote Townshend, that Macartney come to Ireland to open the first session of the new Parliament in October 1769; 'their boasts and threats have been too loud and the use they have made of them too evident not to require this disappointment'.[21] Far from being the great help which many had imagined he would be in Ireland, it appeared that Macartney had only succeeded in creating further difficulties for Townshend. It was an inauspicious opening to his chief secretaryship.

In view of this, it seems strange that in the list of recommendations for peerages which Townshend sent over to Weymouth in December 1769, Macartney's name should have figured. The Lord Lieutenant explained his pretensions to the Duke of Grafton: 'if to have been indefatigable in the King's service, and much abused for it, may be deemed merit, Sir George has at least that to plead in his favour'.[22] It was true that Macartney had been 'much abused' in the King's service in Ireland. His political connections had provided the hack writers of Dublin with an easy target[23] and the fact that he was Irish-born had offered him no protection — indeed, the opposite. Soon after his appointment was announced, Waite sagely remarked to Wilmot that 'the Irish do not like that an Irishman should be first secretary and ... if they had their will, very few of their own country-men would fill the great departments here'.[24] There was, then, a prejudice against Macartney on account of his birth, his connections and his manner. His conduct during the opening session of the new Parliament did little to allay these prejudices.

IV

The new Parliament had opened in October 1769 and initially there had seemed a fair prospect that the administration would meet with some success, particularly over the augmentation proposal which, as before, was to be the main measure. Government hopes of success, however, quickly vanished. The augmentation scheme was approved by substantial majorities; but a money bill, which (in accordance with Poynings' Law) had been drawn up in the Irish Privy Council and sent over to England as one of the causes for calling the Irish Parliament, was rejected on the grounds that it 'did not take its rise in the Irish House of Commons'. This, as Townshend (and George III) realised, was a direct attack on Poynings' Law, that 'palladium of the Irish constitution', and was an affront that could not go unchallenged. Accordingly, having bided his time until the money bills (including one identical to that earlier rejected) had been given the royal assent, Townshend stepped in, protested against the Commons' action and prematurely prorogued Parliament in late December 1769; it was not to meet again until February 1771.[25]

Macartney had taken the lead in the Irish House of Commons in defending the administration's decision to send over a money bill as a cause for calling Parliament. This was all the more difficult for him as he had little experience of parliamentary debating and, worse, could expect little help from the supposed government supporters. Those who were not in active opposition contented themselves with giving merely a silent negative to opposition motions and amendments. Yet it is probable that Macartney exacerbated an already dangerous situation by the bluntness of his speech. To his credit he refused to bow before pressure, to compromise his opinions on the question of the disputed money bill. 'This m[one]y b[i]ll, sir, is a kind of fine which we pay for the renewal of p[arliamen]t', he declared to the members; and then went on to tell them that the Privy Council which drew up the bill was, 'in some respect, a branch of our legislature'. Members cried out 'No! No!' at this last remark but Macartney, undaunted, pressed on. Further tumult broke out when he accused the Speaker, John Ponsonby, of inconsistency in having years earlier agreed to a money bill as a cause for calling Parliament. Macartney was forced to withdraw this accusation. He ended on a more conciliatory note, however, telling his audience that all that was at stake over the disputed money bill was 'a point of form, a *punctilio*, a ceremony, a courtesy, which an affectionate younger sister has always paid to her elder'.[26] Such blunt speaking did not meet with a welcome reception in the House of Commons. Even Charles O'Hara, whose friendship for Macartney had cooled considerably, remarked to Edmund Burke that he 'felt for Sir George. His scrapes were many, called often to order and at last a general cry to the bar'.[27] Macartney had shown great courage in standing, almost alone, against the opposition and in making a hard-hitting speech which defended the government's position on the matter. But that apart, his speech was a singularly inappropriate one and seemed almost calculated to inflame tempers in the Commons.

Perhaps Macartney felt that such a firm declaration of support for Poynings' Law would endear him to British ministers but, if it did, they did not show their gratitude. He was not given the peerage which Townshend had recommended for him. George III had been upset at the number of peerages which the Lord Lieutenant had requested, but had absolutely refused only two — Macartney's and Clotworthy Upton's, both of whom were associated with the King's mother and Lord Bute. It was explained that these were refused because, 'without bringing the best support to your excellency's administration, [they] would raise jealousies in those who, with better pretensions in general, either are or may become friends of government'. Furthermore, the King wished to restore 'consideration and respect to the Irish peerage which had been too much neglected'.[28] Macartney pointed out that the Irish peerage was in decline and that a considerable number of peerages would become extinct with their present holders, but to no avail.[29]

It is difficult to escape the conclusion that Macartney's solicitation of a peerage was premature. It was one of the few maxims in eighteenth-century government life that rewards ought to follow service; and that service Macartney had not yet fulfilled, at least in Ireland. Apart from a courageous, if perhaps unwise, stand in the House of Commons, his chief secretaryship had been uneventful, being largely taken up with routine administrative matters. In England, he had tried to gain Cabinet approval for Townshend's plans, but then so had Lord Frederick Campbell even when no longer Chief Secretary. It is true he had come in for a lot of abuse in Ireland (and was to come in for much more on account of his speech on the money bill) but this was, after all, part and parcel of political life. Furthermore, he had, perhaps unwittingly, caused Townshend a great deal of embarrassment by his efforts to obtain a better position outside Ireland.

His projected title, Lord Belmaine, Baron of Loughguile, had a nice ring about it; no doubt he felt it would increase his chances of a plum diplomatic post, while not incapacitating him from sitting in the British House of Commons. A peerage, also, would have meant the end of his chief secretaryship. This would have pleased him for he found it uncongenial to occupy a post where he was forced to play a role as part politician, part government manager and part minister. Moreover, he had little patronage at his disposal. As Macartney explained to Wilmot:

> I shall say but one word to you on Irish politics which tho' few people will believe yet upon your honour is literally true — after the first fortnight of my residence here, I have been a mere official secretary and in no shape a minister, except in defending measures in the House of Commons which I was not suffered to guide.[30]

Macartney realised that, as Chief Secretary, difficult times for him lay ahead. What reputation there was to be gained in Ireland would have to be fought for; he would have to play second fiddle to the Lord Lieutenant; altogether it was an unpleasing prospect.

V

During 1770 Macartney continued to seek a better position outside Ireland. At the same time, however, he was concerned to fulfil his duties as Chief Secretary and to play his part in the Lord

Lieutenant's campaign against the undertakers: he believed that his ability entitled him to a more substantial position but never intentionally allowed the public service to suffer on that account. From January 1770 to February 1771 he was largely involved with the Lord Lieutenant's agent in London, Thomas Allan, in the question of the division of the Irish revenue board and on what was known as the 'rum business'. Mention has already been made of Townshend's scheme to divide the revenue board in Ireland and of the benefits he hoped would accrue to government from this. The 'rum business' he regarded as a necessary part of this plan. It involved the removal of the custom duties refunded on rum first imported into England and then re-exported to Ireland. This would have the effect of forcing Irish merchants to ship their rum cargoes directly to Ireland where they would pay full custom duties on them. It was hoped that up to £40,000 a year would be gained for the Irish hereditary revenue by this measure. There was also a strong political purpose behind the move. The revenues of Ireland came from two main sources, the hereditary, which had been granted in perpetuity to the Crown, and the additional duties, which were granted by Parliament every two years. As a result of a fall in the hereditary revenue the government in Ireland had been increasingly forced to rely for revenue on the additional duties which had, earlier on in the century, been of only marginal importance. This dependence on the additional duties had increased the importance of Parliament and had, in large measure, made necessary those 'disgraceful bargains' which government had been forced to conclude with leading Irish politicians. Townshend's plan was to increase the hereditary revenue by means of the rum duty, cut down on public works (in many cases 'private jobs') paid for out of this revenue, and root out, by re-organising the revenue board, the influence of the undertakers. Furthermore, he hoped to introduce an element of professionalism into the collection of the Irish revenue. As a result, the government, no longer so dependent on the additional duties for revenue, would be less reliant on Parliament for money; while the undertakers, no longer indispensable to government for carrying through the additional duties, and deprived of revenue patronage, would suffer a severe loss of influence. The plan was imaginative in concept and wide-ranging in its implications and its implementation brought the government some success, although not as much as had been anticipated.

Macartney had little, if anything, to do with drawing up the scheme, although he was active in trying to gain approval for it in London. He and Allan corresponded very regularly throughout 1770 and both were extremely useful agents for Townshend to have at hand. Allan was well versed in financial matters and by his ability and sound judgment gained the respect of many leading English politicians. Indeed, on several occasions, he was called into the Cabinet to discuss Irish affairs. Macartney also, no doubt because of his experience of the negotiations over the Russian commercial treaty, showed a real grasp of financial and revenue matters. Between these two — and the Lord Lieutenant — various knotty problems connected with the 'rum business' were ironed out. In this affair Macartney was particularly useful for he had contacts in London who helped put forward the Irish government's case. Wood and Bradshaw, secretaries, respectively, to Lord Weymouth and the Duke of Grafton, were on friendly terms with Macartney. Again, John Robinson, recently appointed Secretary to the Treasury, was an old acquaintance of his and Thomas Allan was able to secure an introduction to him from Macartney. Yet, for all this, progress in the matter was depressingly slow. Objections were constantly being raised. The West Indian merchants were opposed to the proposed alteration of the duty on rum. The English revenue commissioners seemed to take delight in pointing out inaccuracies and difficulties in the plan. As before, however, the main difficulty was that the British Cabinet had little interest in Ireland or Irish affairs. Allan and Macartney both agreed that 'they never think of us but when drove to it [sic] by dire necessity'.[31]

As Chief Secretary, another part of Macartney's work was concerned with the management of the House of Commons. Previously, the undertakers had had charge of this but, as they had gone into opposition, Macartney was forced to take on the task. During the intervals between sessions of Parliament, management involved wooing and winning over unattached members to the government side, trying to detach opposition members from their groups, and calculating who could safely be ignored (and who had to be supported) in recommendations for patronage at the disposal of government. It was highly skilled work, requiring patience, tact, diligence, a certain degree of ruthlessness and a great deal of knowledge of men, their connections and their interests. All these attributes Macartney, to some degree, possessed;[32] yet in his efforts at management he was hindered by the Lord Lieutenant and denied that freedom of manoeuvre so essential to the task.

Townshend was of a mercurial temperament. A bluff, hard-drinking army officer, he had little time for the niceties of management and by his outspokenness and insensitivity alienated many people. He treated his supporters as soldiers whom he could order as he pleased and too often he assumed that support, bought for the price of a deanery or an ensigncy, would prove lasting. He was a most difficult superior. Thomas Waite wrote of him:

I have been young and now am old, yet never saw I such a composition of agreeable and disagreeable, of bitter and sweet, of starts, whims, irregularity and indecisions without any ideas of time and place, now surly, now placid and gentle. Everything by fits and nothing long. There are days in which he wearies every person to death. There are others in which he blazes to such a degree and is so bright and able that you are astonished and think him the most entertaining man in the world.[33]

Townshend, moreover, wished to supervise and direct all government actions and, hence, would not permit his subordinates much freedom of action. Both Allan and Macartney agreed that 'Lord Townshend is and will be his own minister'; all that he expected of his Chief Secretary was 'an attention to the books of numbers'.[34] This lack of power hampered Macartney in his attempts to build up a majority in the House of Commons, for it was sometimes necessary to make firm promises in order to win members over. Townshend, for his part, was not only reluctant to allow Macartney much discretion in this matter, but also was reluctant to make such promises himself, at least until they were approved at ministerial level in England. 'You say you have no powers to make positive engagements', wrote Allan to Macartney in December 1770; 'how can you, when his Excell[enc]y either has not nor [sic] will not make use himself of powers to make engagements with any individual until approved of here?'[35] Management, in short, was a frustrating business for Macartney.

While carrying out his duties as Chief Secretary, Macartney had also continued to press his claims on the British ministry for a better and more lucrative position. As before, the embassy to Spain was the main attraction. Macartney's interest in this post had waned when Robert Wood, who kept him informed of the state of the embassies abroad, had told him in February 1770, that George Pitt was to go to Spain.[36] Later on in the year his interest revived when he found that no firm appointment had been made. At this time (October 1770) a dispute had broken out between Britain and Spain over the Falkland Islands and for a period there was a very strong likelihood of war. As Macartney realised, it was a situation where a great reputation could be gained, either by obtaining peace with honour or by a vigorous defence of British interests. But he was to be disappointed again. Allan reported a conversation he had had with Lord North con-

Cartoon of Lord Townshend (seated second from the right), Macartney (standing behind him) and their informal 'cabinet' of Irish advisers, reproduced in a collection of satirical letters and poems written against the Townshend administration and published under the title *Baratariana* in 1771.

cerning Macartney's future. 'He spoke of your desire to go to Spain and added he believed a man of the first rank[37] here must be sent . . . [he] spoke of you with much respect and said he knew nowhere so profitable for you as your present situation and appeared surprised when I told him there was not a sixpence to be saved in it'.[38] Financial worries and a desire to make his way in the world were the main motives for Macartney's attempt to secure the Spanish embassy. The claims of Irish hospitality and a style of living befitting his position made short work of his modest official income of £3,000 *per annum* and gave him little prospect of disentangling himself from those debts which he had already incurred.[39]

The Falkland Islands dispute with Spain, which had prompted Macartney to 'test his weight' yet again with the British ministers, also had implications for Irish politics. The threat of war necessitated the recall of the Irish Parliament in order to provide money to raise more troops. At the last moment, however, the crisis passed and war was averted. Yet Townshend was still determined to meet Parliament for he wished for a showdown with the undertakers. He believed his government would be in a very strong position because, with no substantial measures to put before Parliament, the opposition, as he put it, would 'have nothing to unite on or against'.[40] The outcome of the session which opened in February 1771 seemed to bear out Townshend's most optimistic forecasts. Ponsonby, rather than suffer the indignity of carrying an address of thanks to Townshend for continuing as Lord Lieutenant, resigned the speakership in disgust. This was hailed by Townshend as a great triumph and he paid generous tribute to Macartney's role in it: 'I think it incumbent on me in justice to Sir George Macartney to represent to your lordship [North] that the happy conclusion to which it [the session] is brought is in great measure to be ascribed to his attention and abilities'. All, continued Townshend, paid tribute to his skill in management and his ability in debating; he was, in short, 'perfectly the man of business'.[41] To Mrs. Grenville, a relative of Macartney's, he declared that Macartney had 'closed the session with *éclat* and had clearly the better of the famous Flood'.[42] Handsome compliments these, yet to his son, Lord Ferrers, Townshend wrote in quite a different vein. 'Sir George Macartney', he declared, '(who between us had as little idea of boldly meeting the Parliam[en]t as any one on this side or the other side of the water when I proposed it) has very nearly embarked me in as many difficulties for the next session as I have got over [in] this'. Townshend added darkly, 'c'est un esprit raffiné qui veut diriger le tout et qui se croit au fond de toutes choses avec une prise de tabac'.[43] Personality differences possibly contributed, but the root of the trouble lay in the fact that the Lord Lieutenant was determined to supervise and direct all government action and was quick to resent any challenge to what he regarded as his sphere of authority. A plea for mercy made by Macartney at this time on behalf of a deserter sentenced to death met with a brusque rebuff and a request by the Lord Lieutenant that he concern himself with his own affairs. Moreover, an artfully phrased motion, which referred to the money bill dispute of the previous session, had been allowed to pass unopposed by the government speakers. Ostensibly an apology, Townshend chose, probably correctly, to interpret it as a justification of the Commons' action and was incensed to see it pass. Macartney, however, was not the only one at fault in this particular matter and, indeed, may well have staved off greater trouble by acquiescing in the motion. He had certainly no wish to direct affairs but doubtless felt irritated at the restrictions placed on his conduct by the Lord Lieutenant and, to a certain extent, resented his lack of power, especially in his dealings with individual members. There appeared to be no room for both an active Lord Lieutenant and an active Chief Secretary.

'Sir George', complained Townshend, 'does not treat me with the cordiality I deserve . . . [nonetheless]. . . I shall always be his well wisher for Lord Bute and Lady Jane's sake whom I love'.[44] Townshend was as good as his word and in his patronage recommendations he put Macartney down for a pension of £2,000 *per annum*. Unfortunately, he had been authorised to spend up to £2,000 on pensions to win support and Macartney's pension, if granted, would have brought the pension list to over £4,000 for that session alone. George III refused to countenance it. Regarding the pension list, 'there are two', wrote the King, 'that can in no way be deemed essential to the conduct of affairs in Ireland, the one for £2,000 proposed for Sir George Macartney, and £500 for Major Stanton; the Lord Lieutenant's family ought to be provided for by suitable employments that may become vacant, not by pensions that lessen the hereditary revenue, of which English policy must avoid as much as possible the diminution'. North agreed with this and added the reason that a pension to Macartney would become a 'hard precedent' for every Chief Secretary thereafter.[45]

Macartney was bitterly disappointed by this refusal: a pension of £2,000 *per annum* would have alleviated his financial difficulties and, furthermore, would have been a tangible reward for his years of service — in Russia as well as in Ireland — which he felt had been ignored. He did not wish to stay in Ireland and in April 1771 had informed Lord Rochford of his great reluctance to undertake another session.[46] A pension would have permitted him to resign with honour. By late August 1771, however, he realised gloomily that there was nothing for it but to remain for another session of Parliament. Macartney described his feelings at this time in a remarkable letter to Sir Robert Wilmot:

> Instead of a journey to England I must now prepare for a journey to Dublin. I think I never went there with so much reluctance but as long as I am condemned to hold this office, I will most strictly do the duty of it — I confess to you I have long been heartily sick of it and nothing but the pressing requests, almost commands, of my friends could have engaged me to continue in it for so long. Honour and profit are usually the grand motives of political exertion. I asked for the one and did not obtain it; the other is now asked for me as you will see by the office letter. I am not very solicitous about it but if they grant it to me I shall have not great objection to give it up to them and exchange it hereafter, as you know I can't hold it beyond the term of the present Parliament; but, after the battle I have fought and the campaigns I have gone thro', I think I shall look a little ridiculous if I am the only soldier undistinguished in the distribution of rewards.[47]

A week after he wrote this letter Macartney learned that his request for a pension had been denied. In a fit of anger (or self-pity) he very nearly resigned his chief secretaryship but, as before, his friends prevailed upon him to continue.

VI

Macartney continued as Chief Secretary until November 1772 and his work and duties remained much the same as they had been previously. He kept in constant communication with Thomas Allan over the 'rum business' and the re-organisation of the Irish revenue board, and both measures, after considerable delay (and some alteration), were eventually approved by the British government. Management of the government forces also continued to occupy a great deal of his time and attention, and during the parliamentary session which began in October 1771 he acted as 'whipper-in' for the administration. During this session Macartney spoke frequently and forcibly and, although often on dubious ground and assailed on all sides, he managed to present the government case in a favourable light.[48] In some ways it was the most difficult of the three sessions of Parliament which Macartney conducted in Ireland. The division of the revenue board, which involved the creation of extra places, and the setting up of a new board of accounts aroused considerable controversy, and were too easily represented by the opposition as an exercise in corruption. Moreover, at the request, if not the command, of Lord North, a pension of £1,000 *per annum* on the Irish establishment had been granted to Jeremiah Dyson, with reversions to his three sons. Dyson was an English politician who had no connection with Ireland and his pension provided the opposition with an easy target. Opposition crystallised around these three issues and the government met with indifferent success. 'We have had some cursed rubs during this session',[49] wrote Macartney ruefully. Motions critical of the creation of new offices and of Dyson's pension were passed and, although Townshend chose to ignore them and pressed ahead with his plans, the government had received a setback and a great deal of ill-feeling had been created.

This lack of success can be blamed on supporters who, quick to take personal advantage of their situation, increasingly became exorbitant in their demands. Government 'troops', wrote Macartney, 'are stout and well-disciplined but are mere Swiss and will not fight long without being well paid'.[50] On one or two critical occasions they abstained or voted against the government in order to show their power. Townshend was, not surprisingly, disturbed at this development and, to counter it, set about trying to win over one of the leading ex-undertakers, Lord Shannon, to the government side. Macartney seems to have had misgivings about this policy; in particular, he thought Shannon's terms for coming over rather steep.[51] He had, however, little to do with it for the plan was Townshend's own. Yet with respect to Macartney's future the negotiations with Shannon were to prove highly interesting.

Townshend planned to 'catch' Shannon with a large and important office to compensate him for the one from which he had been dismissed (the master-generalship of the ordnance). Little that was worthwhile appeared until April 1771, when it was reported that the Muster-Master General, Lord Belvedere, had died. As long ago as February 1770, Townshend had promised Macartney this position should it become vacant and was still bound by this promise.[52] Macartney, however, unselfishly waived his claims to the office in order to facilitate Townshend's negotiations with Shannon. Lord North (and the King) were highly impressed at this evidence of Macartney's 'disinterestedness' and a suitable reward was soon forthcoming. In June 1771 he was made a knight of the Bath. The opposition claimed it was 'a reward for introducing an arbitrary, Scotchified government, reducing the Hibernian spirit and for bringing Ireland into a poor, weak and impoverished situation'.[53] It was, in fact, merely a modest token of George III's esteem. Later on in the year, moreover, Lord Townshend recommended Macartney for a pension of £1,500 on the Irish establishment and this was duly granted. The Lord Lieutenant told Macartney that this recommendation 'is evidence of a fixt [sic] principle I have ever borne in my mind (tho' perhaps not always justly credited) not to fail in recollection (at all times and seasons) of the friendship and affection which subsisted between my friend Lord Bute . . . [and myself]'.[54] The pension, however, was granted to Macartney, not because he was Lord Bute's son-in-law but because he had performed creditably in a very difficult situation. It was a small pension too — smaller than the one previously requested and with absentee tax deducted it would amount to scarcely £1,100 *per annum* which, given Macartney's financial difficulties, was disappointing. Moreover acceptance of a royal pension during pleasure barred one from membership of the British House of Commons under the terms of the 1707 Regency Act. Altogether Macartney certainly had grounds for feeling dissatisfied with his treatment. A modest pension and no promise of a good office were hardly adequate rewards for his service — as he frequently pointed out in letters to his friends. In June 1772 he had written: 'if I do not get something I shall have made the worst campaign ever Sec[retar]y did for I have not been able to serve either myself or my friends and am a poorer man this day than when I came over here'.[55] The pension did not improve his temper. He was soured by his treatment at the hands of British ministers and felt cheated — once more — of a just and proper reward. He left his post an embittered man. 'Sure I am', wrote Macartney, 'that no Secretary ever served government with greater fidelity to the trust than I did and no Secretary ever received so little thanks for it'.[56]

VII

Macartney had few fond memories of his time as Chief Secretary. As he wrote to a correspondent in July 1773:

My ministerial career in this country is, thank God, now at an end and as you may justly think, I have no ambition to run over it again. I entered upon it with every honest and patriotic intention which a man bound to Ireland by birth, affection and interest could possibly entertain [!] but I was unfortunate, the times and circumstances were unfavourable; I found myself obliged to do many things I did not like and to leave others undone which I wished to accomplish.[57]

Macartney had not approved of the development in function of the Chief Secretary's office during his time in Ireland and he disliked the part-administrative, part-political role he was called upon to play. As Chief Secretary in Ireland he found himself in the unenviable position of having to defend policy decisions he had little hand in making and of having to bear the brunt of the criticism of those decisions. Time and time again, he assured the Commons he was not responsible for policy. The chief secretaryship was 'an office of private trust, not public responsibility', he declared, and his duty was 'to conciliate not to conduct, to explain not to dictate, to concur not to control'. Vehemently, he asserted: 'I am no minister, I repeat it again, I am no minister. I never was in this country a minister and probably never shall [be]'.[58] Yet a 'ministerial' role, as Macartney privately admitted, was precisely what he was called upon to play, if not in policy-making, at least in its implementation and approval. This duality of function in the Chief Secretary's office — part administrative and part ministerial — caused him a great deal of concern. Before he left Ireland he recommended that, for the future, the Chief Secretary should not sit in the House of Commons and should therefore be entirely administrative in his functions. His suggestion, however, was not acted upon and his successors all took seats in the Irish Parliament and, indeed, acted a 'ministerial' part in its proceedings.

VIII

Macartney was happiest as an administrator. He may have had political ambitions at one time but he seems to have discarded them during his stay in Ireland. The Irish Parliament, he felt, was largely irrelevant to the needs of the country. He had little time for the petty squabbles and power struggles, the bickerings and disputes, that went on there. When the opposition spoke of repealing Poynings' Law, he asked candidly what advantage that would bring to the kingdom. 'Shall the poor be relieved or manufactures improved or commerce intensified? Will the Irish landlord be less severe to his miserable tenant? Will the dissenter enjoy more than toleration? Will he be relieved from a test, a load on his conscience? Will the opprest [sic] Roman Catholic be enabled to acquire fixed property or secure the little he has left?[59] An acceptance of constitutional subordination to England and a greater attention to the Irish economy and the management of the Irish revenue, he felt, would have better suited the members of Parliament. He hated waste and inefficiency and in the management of the Irish revenue he found ample cause for anger. Incompetent and corrupt officials regarded their offices as sinecures and remained uncaring about the resultant loss of revenue. He could do little about this. Waste and inefficiency — even corruption — were built into the Irish governmental system. In the Irish revenue service, appointments were made according to a person's 'weight', either locally or nationally, and considerations of expertise rarely entered in. There were few jobs Irish politicians, no matter how young or inexperienced, did not believe themselves capable of. Townshend's and Macartney's attempts to introduce a level of professionalism into the revenue service met with little success.

Macartney made himself master not only of the subject of Irish revenues but also of the whole field of Irish trade and commerce and wrote extensively and in great detail on them. In a manuscript which he sent to Lord North, he detailed the state of Irish revenue and finances with great authority. In an accompanying letter, he wrote that they were subjects which were 'likely to become every day more difficult, more interesting and more important'.[60] Part of this work was incorporated in his *An Account of Ireland in 1773,* which he had privately printed soon after he left Ireland.[61] As a concise introduction to the revenue, politics and government of Ireland, the book was first-rate and displayed to the full his wide knowledge, his 'liberal sympathies' (as they would now be called) and his diligence in collecting and organising a large amount of data. His belief in the importance of a proper understanding of Irish revenue, trade and commerce is again underlined by the fact that over one half of the book is devoted to these topics. The book seems to have been intended as a handbook for future Chief Secretaries and, if so, it admirably fulfilled its purpose.

Above all, Macartney was an imperialist. In the Irish House of Commons, he was wont to chide members for putting local before national advantage; he, on the other hand, could think imperially and would not allow national or sectional interests to stand in the way of imperial ones. That the British legislature should be supreme throughout the empire, was to him axiomatic:

> In this vast empire, on which the sun never sets and whose bounds nature has not yet ascertained, one great superintending and controlling dominion must exist somewhere, and where can that dominion reside with so much dignity, propriety and safety as in the British legislature? The inferior branches of this great body have their respective parliaments or assemblies, whilst the supreme power of Great Britain presides over the whole and like the gods of the ancient

drama, unties every knot of difficulty that demands her intervention and authority.[62]

With sentiments like these, it is not surprising that Macartney was, from an early period, a firm advocate of a legislative union between Great Britain and Ireland as the only solution to Anglo-Irish relations. Indeed in 1779 at the behest of Lord North, Macartney visited Ireland to sound out the possibilities of a union. He reported gloomily that 'the idea of an union at present would excite a rebellion', but added 'and yet, without an union how vague and loose is the connexion of Ireland with England'.[63]

Although he had met with some success in Ireland, Macartney had not enjoyed his tenure as Chief Secretary there. He was an extremely ambitious, not to say conceited, man; yet his standing in the political world had been advanced little by his stay in Ireland; and his abilities, for one reason or another, had not been fully used. He had found the political aspect of his duties irksome and had achieved little that was lasting in the one field — revenue — in which he was interested. His advocacy of Irish constitutional subordination earned him few friends in an Irish Parliament that was becoming increasingly assertive of its rights. A temperamental and erratic superior added to his difficulties. Yet, for all that, he had performed creditably in his office. Conscientious, diligent and courageous in debate, he had helped considerably in the implementation of the 'new system' for Ireland. He was the first resident Chief Secretary and under him the office increased in importance. Yet, he was never really contented at his work and constantly tried for other and better positions: financial worries, a desire to be in control, perhaps even a yearning for a quieter, easier life — all motivated him in this. At bottom, however, he felt himself destined for greater things; in his grandiose vision of the British empire, the back-stairs intrigue and petty squabbles of Irish politics had no part.

CHAPTER IV

GRENADA 1775-79

I

As Lord Townshend's tempestuous lord-lieutenancy drew to its close, Sir George Macartney's acquaintances noted with disbelief that he 'rejoices at his escape from a critical situation and talks of private life'.[1] Their cynicism was well founded as a few months later Macartney complained to the notoriously ambitious John Hely-Hutchinson that his Irish achievements had been undervalued and that Lord North appeared 'rather to underrate than justly value political services, which is a very discouraging thing to those who do them'.[2] In the two years, 1773-75, between the conclusion of his Irish chief secretaryship and his appointment as Governor of Grenada, Macartney was fully aware that he stood at a crossroads in his career. His predicament was emphasized by the brilliant failures of those closest to him, his father-in-law, Lord Bute, and his patron and mentor, Lord Holland. At the same time his frustration was increased by his dependence for future opportunities to vindicate his worth upon a minister whom he now felt did not appreciate his abilities.

The careers of the Earl of Bute and Lord Holland[3] illustrate some of the major disadvantages which confronted Macartney in these crucial years. Lord Bute had enjoyed all the advantages which royal favour and electoral influence could bestow; nevertheless, he failed to gain the parliamentary acceptance which would have enabled him to use them. Bute, like his son-in-law, was not English and did not belong to the inner circle of English political families. Henry Fox, Lord Holland, likewise enjoyed many political advantages, but he died, in July 1774, a disappointed man. Popular with his political colleagues, he had invariably supported the King's government of the day. On more than one occasion he had hovered nervously on the threshold of the highest office without ever having been invited to pass through the door. Finally, the earldom, which had rewarded the achievements of his great contemporaries, William Pitt, Earl of Chatham, and William Murray, Earl of Mansfield, and was later bestowed upon the less spectacular Charles Jenkinson, Earl of

Liverpool, had eluded him. Thus, the careers of those closest to Macartney served to illustrate the knife-edged divide which separated success and failure in eighteenth-century politics.

Macartney had neither the electoral assets of Bute nor the parliamentary gifts of Holland. As a parliamentarian in both the English and Irish Houses of Commons he had proved adequate rather than spectacular, while the able and complex character of Lord Lieutenant Townshend had hardly encouraged his subordinate to do more than display his diplomatic talents or, as one of his friends remarked, 'to commit himself in advice as seldom as possible, to obey orders';[4] and although this low profile approach had sometimes enabled him to avoid making enemies, it had also ensured that at thirty-five his potential still remained hidden while his limitations had been revealed. It was against this background that Macartney sought a third opportunity to establish his career and to ensure his future employment in high administrative or diplomatic, rather than political, office.

'Had I a seat in Parliament', Macartney had written to Lord Holland in 1766, 'might I not with more reason pretend to something better?'[5] Parliament lay at the centre of eighteenth-century public life. Parliament, apart from increasing social prestige or providing political opportunity, was the gateway to all prominent, and many mediocre, legal, administrative and diplomatic careers; in addition it offered advantages to those engaging in a wide spectrum of public activities ranging from commerce to the armed forces. In 1768 Macartney was returned for Cockermouth through the influence of his wife's brother-in-law, Sir James Lowther, and the following year he was appointed Chief Secretary to the Lord Lieutenant of Ireland. As this was an office of profit under the Crown, he was obliged to resign his seat in the British Parliament under the terms of the 1707 Regency Act. He did not seek re-election. On his return from Ireland in 1773 he was in receipt of a royal pension during pleasure, which made him ineligible for election to the Westminster Parliament, although he continued to sit for Armagh City in the Irish Parliament, which had not been included in the 'place clause' of the Regency Act. This pension placed Macartney in a dilemma. His Russian and Irish appointments had proved expensive — as had the planned improvements to his estate: consequently, he was in debt and could not afford to relinquish his pension even to obtain the parliamentary seat which was essential to his future advancement. His problem could only be solved by exchanging his pension for an equivalent sinecure, which would enable him to seek election as an established office-holder.[6] Negotiating the exchange of his pension for such a position proved to be more difficult and time-consuming than Macartney had anticipated, but he eventually achieved it and was appointed Constable for Toome Castle, Co. Londonderry — an appropriate sinecure with a salary equivalent to that of his former pension. The next problem was to find a seat which, again, was not easy as the pressure on parliamentary seats was considerable. However, Lord Bute once more exerted his influence on behalf of his son-in-law and by declaring Macartney to be a Scot ensured his election for Ayr Burghs in the general election of 1774.[7]

Macartney was a member of the British House of Commons in three consecutive Parliaments — 1768, 1774 and 1780 — but in all three his membership was short, amounting to less than three out of a parliamentary life-span of sixteen years. The necessity of these returns and the nature of the three appointments which followed them (the Irish chief secretaryship, the government of Grenada, and a similar appointment with the East India Company) all emphasize the centrality of membership of Parliament to the advancement and establishment of a public career. Even when potential seats were available, a disputed election could be very expensive and Macartney's three uncontested returns are a further illustration of the value of a well-connected marriage in providing the necessary opportunities for a career based almost entirely upon ability and ambition. In 1774-5 Macartney's parliamentary performance was, as it had been in 1768, low-key. However, it was sufficient to keep his claims before the government; for instance, in 1775 he spoke against the petition of the London merchants to have the trade embargo with the North American colonies rescinded.[8] His presence also reminded the ministry of the advisability of pleasing a well-connected and influential family. Thus, towards the end of 1775 Sir George Macartney was appointed Governor of the Caribbean island of Grenada. Six months later one of his long-time ambitions was gratified and he was elevated to the Irish peerage as Baron Macartney of Lisanoure in the County of Antrim.

II

Macartney, on accepting the government of Grenada and its dependencies, Tobago and the Grenadines, resigned his seat in Parliament. Shortly afterwards, in March 1776, he left for Grenada accompanied by Lady Jane. The Macartneys insured their books, plate, furniture and other possessions before setting sail for the Caribbean aboard a comfortable merchant ship, a mode of travel

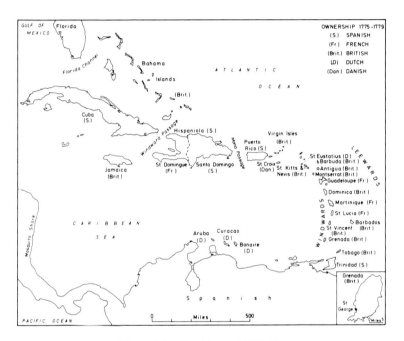

Map of the Caribbean, 1775-79.

which Macartney much preferred to the formality of a ship of the Royal Navy. After an uneventful voyage of approximately six weeks, they arrived at St George, the capital of Grenada, and Macartney reported that: 'on the 3rd of May I landed, and was immediately sworn into the government'.[9]

The government upon which Macartney now entered was more important than either its remote geographical position in the southern Caribbean or its territorial size might imply — Grenada is approximately 24 x 12 and Tobago 25 x 7½ miles at their greatest length and width, while most of the Grenadines are very small, the largest, Carriacou and Becquia, being 8 x 2½ and 7 x 2 miles respectively.[10] In 1776 Great Britain's West Indian possessions fell into four groups: Barbados, the Leeward Islands, Jamaica and the Windward Islands. Barbados and the Leeward Islands of St Kitts, Nevis, Montserrat, Anguilla and Antigua had been acquired in the early seventeenth century. Jamaica had been conquered in 1655 — an unexpected development of Cromwell's 'Western Design' — while the Windward Islands of Grenada, the Grenadines, St Vincent and Tobago were recent acquisitions having, along with Dominica (which lies to the north of the Windwards between the French islands of Martinique and Guadaloupe), been ceded at the Peace of Paris in 1763. Grenada had been a French colony with an administration responsible to the Government of Martinique;[11] Dominica and St Vincent had been officially 'neutral' islands but in fact contained fringe settlements from the French islands, in addition to some tribes of fierce Carib Indians; while Tobago — between Grenada and the Spanish island of Trinidad — was 'an absolute desert entirely covered with wood, neither inhabited nor frequented'.[12] Thus, Macartney's government was of recent origin and had many of the characteristics of a frontier colony.

In the eighteenth century the Caribbean was one of the great commercial centres of the world. The West Indian islands were the principal source of tropical agricultural products for the markets of Western Europe and North America. Consequently they occupied an important and highly valued position in the mercantilist systems of the various European powers, and their political and commercial lives were complicated both by the chessboard of European diplomacy and by the demands of local against metropolitan interests. Their importance ensured that they played a prominent part in all the major confrontations of the century, participating in the American and French revolutions as well as in the great imperial conflicts which were concluded by the 1763 Peace of Paris. Even apart from the white, negro and coloured population created by the slavery on which their agrarian economy was based, the islands, like all trading centres, attracted a floating and very varied population. Shortly after his arrival Macartney, who was a product of the European enlightenment with its cynicism as well as its speculative curiosity, commented that 'such a mixture of people will never be seen again, I believe, except in the other world in that place where we are told there is no respect of persons. However, in *this* world it affords a good deal of entertainment to us'.[13]

The larger islands, the Greater Antilles, with the exception of British Jamaica and the French colony of St Dominique in western Hispaniola, belonged to Spain, as did Trinidad, the largest island in the southern Caribbean. The Lesser Antilles, comprising the Windward and the Leeward Islands, belonged to England and France, with the exception of Danish St Croix and some of the Virgin Islands; while St Eustatius, along with Curaçao and some of the smaller islands of the Venezuelan coast, was Dutch. The terrain of these islands varied between the precipitous mountain slopes of Dominica, the volcanoes of St Vincent and Martinique, and the gently rolling country of Antigua in the Leewards or Barbados, which lay to the east of the Windward Islands in the Atlantic Ocean.

The terrain of the islands largely decided their crops, a fact which the home government was often reluctant to accept — sugar, in particular, required comparatively level ground for its labour-intensive cultivation. On his arrival Macartney was entranced by the beauty of the islands and, writing to Lady Ossory, gave the following description of Grenada:

> With regard to the face of the country it is impossible for the most lively imagination to figure anything so beautiful. It is all hill and dale or rather mountain and valley, for there are not a hundred yards of flat ground in the whole. Thro' the middle of the island runs a high rocky ridge entirely covered to the top with ever-verdant woods. This forms the background of every scene. The intermediate space down to the sea is diversified with all the variety of culture which these colonies are capable of.[14]

Macartney was equally appreciative of the other islands under his administration. Tobago was flat in the south-west, but rose gently towards the north-east where it was rugged and precipitous; the terrain of the Grenadines varied, but they all lacked water — they had no rivers and were dependent upon rain or a few brackish springs and, with a few exceptions such as Carriacou, Isle de Large, Isle de Ronde and Becquia, their soil was very poor. Becquia had a fine harbour but its inhabitants had a reputation for being wreckers. Macartney noted this activity along with the general lawlessness of many of the Grenadines, including the tendency of their inhabitants to resist forcibly any law officer who arrived to arrest them![15]

Grenada and Tobago had long been considered outside the normal pathway of the devastating hurricanes which were among the natural scourges of the islands. The hurricane season was considered to last from the end of July to the middle of October, and during August and September shipping in the area was kept to a minimum, particularly in the northern Caribbean. Hurricanes were especially dangerous in the era of wooden ships, while, in any event, the tropical seas necessitated frequent refits. The French government recalled its ships during these months as there was no naval dockyard in the French islands until one was established at St Pierre, Martinique, in 1784 — after the port had been extensively used by the Americans during the war, and its aggressive merchants had become accustomed to the profits created by a naval dockyard. The English had two dockyards: Port Royal, Jamaica, which had been established in the reign of Queen Anne, and English Harbour, Antigua, established in 1743. These stations received naval supplies from the North American colonies and they were supposed to provide a safe refuge for British ships during the hurricane season. However, on 30 August 1772 a hurricane struck English Harbour. Some idea of the devastation created by these storms in the space of a few hours can be deduced from the description of Governor Sir Ralph Payne, who wrote to Lord Dartmouth, then Secretary of State, that:

> some persons were buried in the ruins of their houses, other families who abandoned their habitations, were blown, maimed and wounded, about the fields . . . there is not a house or building in Antigua which does not bear woeful marks of the general misfortune . . . English Harbour, which has hitherto been deemed storm proof, was unable to protect that part of His Majesty's squadron which lay there . . . The Flag ship as well as the others were forced on shore.[16]

Apart from the destruction caused by hurricanes there was an abnormally high death rate in the West Indies during the eighteenth century; this was particularly true of the first half of the century and again at its close. There seems to have been — as there was in other parts of the world — a hiatus in the mortality of epidemic disease in the third quarter of the century. Thus, Macartney was fortunate in the timing of his appointment as he visited the islands at a time when the great epidemics were least in evidence; and, seeing the islands at their best, he was able to assure his English friends that 'people are sick here as they are elsewhere sometimes, but the sickness never lasts more than a few days, and I have never seen or heard of such a thing in the country as low spirits'.[17] Nevertheless, a few months later he suffered his first attack of gout, that traditional disease of the eighteenth-century establishment! Those who normally lived in temperate climates were ill-equipped for life in the tropics and lacked immunity to tropical diseases such as malaria, yellow fever and, perhaps the most feared, leprosy. A description of the vulnerability of a West Indian town to an epidemic of yellow fever was given in a despatch from Lord Lavington (formerly Sir Ralph Payne), Governor of the Leeward Islands, in 1802:

> The Church bells which announced the number of its victims were tolling almost continually from morning to night until orders were given to suspend the ceremony, in order to prevent the horror of this hourly mortality from reaching the ears of those who were labouring under the disease, but had not arrived at the last stage of it.

In a small and closed community the terrible effect of an epidemic of these proportions was magnified: 'it has', wrote Lord Lavington, 'successively swept away every white person whom I brought with me from England'.[18] Lavington was a member of a West Indian family and was perhaps more accustomed to the sudden and violent disasters which lay beneath the beautiful façade of the islands.

Climate, unsuitable diets and unreliable food supplies all contributed to this notoriously high mortality rate. Some diseases, which stemmed from a lack of hygiene, assumed more serious consequences under tropical conditions; 'belly-ache' was a common complaint. Lack of refrigeration, over-eating and the 'rum-devil' all took their toll. As might be expected, towns and concentrations of people, such as in army barracks or on board ships, were particularly vulnerable to infectious diseases, especially universal scourges like smallpox. In 1740 one writer calculated that the entire population of Jamaica died once in every seven years. In 1795, many years after he had left Grenada, Macartney read and annotated a pamphlet 'on the means of preserving health and preventing that fatal disease, the yellow fever'.[19] Macartney's immediate predecessor had died in office as did his contemporary, Governor Burt of the Leewards. Thus, the reputation for high mortality attributed to the West Indies probably caused him some concern. However, any fears that he arrived with were speedily dispersed, and his first letters expressed enthusiasm for the healthy atmosphere as well as the beautiful scenery of the island, concluding that 'all the unfavourable accounts which you have heard of the West Indies, at least of this part of them, are without foundation'.[20] Subsequently, he and Lady Macartney moved into 'an old barrack, just under the guns of the battery, about a hundred feet above the sea, very dry and breezy, and considered to be the healthiest spot in the island'; and he decided to use the £500 *per annum* which he received in lieu of a residence towards renovating it.[21]

The great sugar fortunes of the early eighteenth century had established a tradition of absenteeism among the wealthier British planters and the usual inheritance custom of primogeniture made it even more prevalent among the younger members of their families. This absenteeism had far-reaching effects on public and private life. Estates, so long as they produced a tolerable income, were left to the management of agents, managers or overseers, who were frequently responsible for more than one estate and usually had property of their own. Not only were absentees' estates often mismanaged, but money which could have been used in the social and economic development of the islands was repatriated. The labour-intensive methods of agriculture remained primitive and costly and little encouragement was given to improvements.[22] A lack of roads often prevented the development of the interior of the more recently acquired islands. Produce for export from the various plantations had usually to be conveyed by sea in small lighters which carried it from the plantations to the merchant ships anchored off the principal ports. The sugar was packed in hogsheads and tierces in the plantation factory. Thus, access to the sea was an important asset for a plantation but, at the same time, it increased its vulnerability to raids by privateers in wartime, or even to invasion by an enemy attacking in force.[23]

Absenteeism was not conducive to the development of civic pride. There were few public buildings, social or intellectual amenities, particularly in the smaller islands. There were no educational establishments of either size or repute in any of the British West Indian islands. The only possible exception was Codrington College in Barbados, but even this was very small and restricted. Consequently the children, particularly the sons, of the planters were usually educated in England which they inevitably came to regard as home. Libraries and other indications of cultural life were virtually non-existent. There were a number of newspapers published in the islands, but the standard of journalism was not high and the reports of local political infighting were not particularly edifying. With his considerable intellectual interests, Macartney undoubtedly felt this isolation acutely. 'If you saw with what avidity we seize on an old newspaper or magazine when the ships arrive . . .',[24] he wrote, and in the same letter he listed the attractions and the limitations of West Indian social activity.

Before the fire there was a Playhouse and the Leeward company visited Grenada in its turn, as regularly as the Leeward fleet used to do, but for this twelvemonth past both the players and the fleet have left us off and we have not been so gay. There are, however, balls very frequently, and notwithstanding the supposed heat of the climate people dance here all night long with as much spirit and activity as at Almacks or Cornely's. There is a good deal of small play, but no gaming, a dollar a corner is the usual whist rate, and the French play at Quadrille for sols and pistereens.

The anglophile Macartney also commented that the French women 'tho' certainly not so pretty as the English yet contrive some how or other to look infinitely prettier'![25]

The temporary nature of life in the West Indies was reflected in the flimsy and impermanent construction of the buildings in the towns. They were frequently destroyed by fire: for instance, there were two major fires in St George in the five years immediately preceding Macartney's arrival. There was a major fire in December 1771 and an itemized list placed the damages at £132,846.18.10½ currency, but this was considered an underestimate as a very few people carried a low insurance and others had private reasons for not wishing to make their losses public. On this occasion Governor Leybourne expressed concern over the haste with which the inhabitants rebuilt, commenting that it would prevent the legislature 'from taking steps to oblige the owners of each house to have partition walls of brick or stone, a measure which appears very proper in this country where the houses are little more than paper buildings'. Leybourne, who was Macartney's immediate predecessor, died in April 1775 and in the following November his fears were realised as the greater part of St George was again destroyed by fire.[26]

III

A population divided in origin, religion and outlook inevitably presented a major problem to any Governor but particularly to the administrator of an only partly developed island of recent acquisition. Possibly Macartney's origins made him more resolutely anglophile than many of his English-born contemporaries. Certainly his attitude to the 'new' or formerly French subjects of the British crown was less than sympathetic, although there is no reason to suppose that his treatment of them was other than meticulously just. He described them as follows to a private correspondent:

There still remains a considerable number of French here, but our countrymen are infinitely superior to them in wealth, ability and importance. The French not degenerate from their European relations, are lively, presumptious and vain, ever aiming at and affecting consequence, yet not much mortified if they don't obtain it; greedy of riches and not very scrupulous in the means of acquiring them, but neither dispirited by poverty nor dejected by distress. Dissipated and extravagant beyond belief, enjoying to the utmost their own fortune whilst it lasts, and when it is gone, enjoying that of others with as much relish and freedom as their own. These seem to be the most striking features of the creole French.[27]

French colonial government,[28] which many of the residents of Grenada had been accustomed to, was very different from its British counterpart, particularly in its underlying assumptions. It rested upon a separation of the ceremonial and military side of the government from the judicial and administrative: the Governor was usually a military officer and a member of the *noblesse d'epée*, while the Intendant was a lawyer and from the *noblesse de la robe*. Senior military and civil officers were sent out from France, while junior officials were appointed locally. Religion, education and social services, such as hospitals, were the preserve of the various religious orders who divided the islands between them. The only common meeting place was the militia, which comprised all white men from sixteen to sixty. The white population was much higher in the French than in the British islands. For instance, during this period, in Martinique it was about 1 : 8 while in Grenada it was approximately 1 : 27. Nevertheless, the different sections of French society tended to be more isolated: 'the French planters . . . chiefly reside upon their estates', wrote Macartney in 1777, 'keeping themselves separate from the trading part'.[29] French colonial government was bureaucratic rather than participatory; however, regulations which did not have the acceptance of the planters were unlikely to be enforced. Nevertheless, the British were surprised and a little indignant to discover that the French 'new subjects' were not particularly enthusiastic over the privilege of participation inherent in British colonial government.[30]

Unlike his French counterpart, a British Caribbean Governor combined the supreme responsibility for military affairs and defence with administrative and judicial authority. He presided over the courts of Chancery and Vice-Admiralty. In wartime the Governor issued letters of marque and commanded the militia, in addition to acting as Commander-in-Chief of such regular troops as were stationed in his government. This was a situation which could, although in Macartney's relatively small establishment it did not, create conflict with the senior professional commissioned officer on the station. However, the Governor's principal duty was to provide an acceptable link between the colony and the home government, to obtain the acquiescence of the colony to the policies of the mother country, and to advise the mother country on the state of the colony through the full and detailed despatches which he sent to the Secretary of State. Macartney was an excellent despatch writer and his clear and able expositions of a difficult situation were soon attracting favourable comment, not only from the Secretary of State, but also from the West Indian merchants, whose parliamentary influence commanded the ministers' respect, and even from the King himself.[31]

The duality of the Governor's role was emphasized by the fact that the bulk of his salary was paid partly by the colony and partly by the home government: both paid £2,500 and the remaining £1,000 came from fees and other incidentals; for instance, he received £500 *in lieu* of an official residence, but whether Macartney included this in his calculation of a salary of £6,000 *per annum* sterling is uncertain.[32] His formal despatches were filled with details of inspections of forts and military installations, but his private correspondence contained the following picture of his normal routine: 'on Tuesdays and Fridays', he wrote,' we have a sort of levée from ten till one. On the other days I pass the morning either at the Court of Ordinary, Court of Chancery, at the Council, or my secretary's office, just as the business requires my attendance. If there be none, I amuse myself'.[33]

British colonial government was proclaimed for the ceded islands on 7 October 1763. The British system had a philosophical basis in the theory of 'the rights and liberties of Englishmen', and its corollary 'the sanctity of property'. However, although Governor Melvill arrived in December 1764, the arrangements for the legislative Assembly were not completed until the beginning of 1766 and then only after considerable pressure from the new British settlers and the London merchants.[34] Practical considerations such as the religious and social tensions in post-conquest Grenada probably did not encourage a Governor to hasten towards a situation which would inevitably highlight them. The property qualification for a representative was fifty acres of freehold land held by himself or his wife; and for a voter ten freehold acres, or a town house or property of £20 *per annum* in St George, or £10 *per annum* in any of the other towns, or an income of £20 *per annum* from land or tenements. This was a very wide franchise and amounted to virtual manhood suffrage for the white community - voters had to be male, white and over twenty-one years of age. New subjects of the British crown were required to take the oaths of allegiance, abjuration and supremacy and to possess a certificate to this effect. Before he took his seat or voted in the Assembly, an elected representative had to take the oath of allegiance and subscribe to the oath against the doctrine of transubstantiation, a statement which no Roman Catholic could accept.[35]

Nevertheless, an attempt was made to modify the strict application of the religious test as it was considered important to persuade the French settlers, with their stock and slaves, to remain, both to develop the island and to prevent them from going to other islands, to their advantage and Grenada's impoverishment. However, some of the new settlers wished to drive them out in order to acquire their lands, slaves and stock; consequently a bitter conflict soon emerged, particularly between the Calvinist Scots and the Roman Catholic French. Many of the new settlers in Grenada, and particularly in Tobago, were Scottish. In fact Macartney considered that:

> Tobago seems to be one of the most extraordinary instances of British enterprise and industry. Twelve years ago it was an absolute desert entirely covered with wood neither inhabited nor frequented... Almost a third of it is now cleared. There are actually 600 whites and 12,000 negroes upon it. It produces upwards of 5,000 hogsheads of sugar at 1,500 lbs each, 30,000 lbs weight of indigo and near a million and a half of cotton... The principal planters are younger sons of gentlemen of good families in Scotland, who have undertaken their settlements upon borrowed funds, but which in a few years they will probably be able to discharge.[36]

The strong antipathy between these groups was fuelled both by material advantage and by religious zeal; it was still much in evidence when Macartney arrived. It had greatly hindered the early development of the new British colony, especially as the election of the Assembly focussed this hostility between the 'old' or British-born subjects of the crown, and the 'new' or naturalized French-speaking subjects. The British government decided that the 'new' subjects should be enfranchised simply by taking the oath of allegiance, because under the terms of the Treaty of Paris 'it did not appear to our crown lawyers to be precluded by any law of England'; and also 'that property seemed to give them a natural foundation if not an absolute right to a share in the choice of representatives, although [they] by their religion [are] themselves excluded from being such'. 'It was much hoped that so favourable and solid a privilege might tend to attach them to our constitution in preference to *one* where they had it not'; also 'it was expected that they would generally give their votes to the best and most substantial of the natural born subjects in spite of the factious pursuits of the meanest or least deserving'.[37]

The government soon had an additional need to encourage them as a moderating influence in politics for it quickly became evident that:

The Assembly . . . very early got upon the subject of their privileges, which I believe they mean to establish as largely and favourably as possible from those of every British colony of which they had any knowledge, whether in North America or in the West Indies.[38]

Partly to ameliorate this situation and partly because it was felt that their property did give them a 'natural' right to participate in the government, arrangements were made for three of the twenty-four representatives, and for two of the twelve members of the Council, to be Roman Catholics. In addition there was to be one Catholic assistant judge.

However, 'His Majesty's gracious plan for the satisfaction of His Majesty's new subjects in Grenada' created a bitter altercation between Macartney's two predecessors, Governors Melvill and Leybourne, and His Majesty's 'old' subjects. In 1767 Melvill wrote to Lord Hillsborough outlining a case in which the Returning Officer had refused to accept a candidate who did not understand 'a syllable of English'.[39] In 1771 Governor Leybourne considered that there was between the two groups 'such a thorough want of confidence, and in short so rooted an enmity, that I see but very little prospect of a reconciliation'. He suspended five members of the Council of Grenada for refusing to admit Mr de Chanteloup, a Roman Catholic. The reasons which they gave for their intransigence were, firstly, that his admission was contrary to the laws of Great Britain which were their birthright; secondly, they considered that the Roman Catholics' position could only be altered by act of Parliament and not by order in Council; and thirdly, it was contrary to His Majesty's coronation oath.[40] Some months later, in July 1772, Leybourne complained that members of the Assembly were obstructing business by the simple device of not attending, and therefore failing to meet the Assembly's quorum of eleven representatives; this he declared to be a favourite method of Mr Connor and his friends who formed the Irish faction![41]

This filibustering was made possible by the high degree of genuine absenteeism among those elected to the Assembly. Absenteeism was not only a social and an economic problem, it was also, given the participatory nature of British colonial government, a political and an administrative one which affected all levels of government. In 1772 Macartney's immediate predecessor, Governor Leybourne, apologized that:

the Assembly does not proceed with business as I could wish . . . there are so many absentees elected that it is with great difficulty that they can make a House . . . The only persons of property and experience that are elected into the Assembly are still absent; their absence is the more to be regretted as there is but one member now on the island that was ever in that capacity before.

He went on to lament 'the irregularity and confusion that must necessarily be the consequence of such inexperience'.[42]

Shortly before Macartney arrived, the situation in Grenada had improved to the point at which, after being in existence for eight years, in January 1776 the Assembly finally agreed to pass a money bill, although they accompanied it with an address in support of the Americans. However, three months later, on the outbreak of the American War, they also consented to pass a rather lukewarm address in support of the British government!.[43] Tobago had its own Assembly, which consisted of fifteen members, and when Macartney visited the island in 1777 he found 'that several of the most considerable gentlemen of Tobago were not in the Assembly, having formerly vacated their seats, which by a resolution of the House they are obliged to do in case of their going to Europe. I found also that several indigent and improper persons had been chosen in their room, who were forming cabals to obstruct the public business and throw things into confusion'.[44] The legislatures had no fixed term but could be dissolved at the discretion of the Governor, who had subsequently to explain his reasons for a dissolution (or a prorogation if he felt that that was more appropriate) to the King's ministers in London. In this case Macartney dissolved the Assembly which had been sitting for five years.

The Caribbean covered a large area and the British islands were widely spread within it. In addition, the position of the islands in relation to each other and to the prevailing winds and currents was extremely important both for defence and communications, particularly in the era of the sailing ship; for instance, in 1777 Macartney pointed out 'the uncertainty of the passage of a square-rigged vessel from the Leeward Islands to Tobago'.[45] English Harbour, at Antigua in the Leewards, was the nearest British base from which Grenada could hope for support in case of invasion or attacks from privateers. In 1777 only the presence of the government sloop had enabled the Tobago planters to 'load their crop for the market this season'.[46] This armed sloop had been provided in response to Macartney's urgent appeal for some defence against the American privateers who had been raiding his government with impunity. It was looked upon with great envy by Governor Burt[47] of the Leeward Islands, who felt that a government sloop would be more amenable to his direction than the officer commanding the squadron at English Harbour. The West Indian Governors were extremely jealous of each other and watched vigilantly for any perquisite granted to any of their colleagues by the home government.

Where a number of islands were grouped together to form a government, the Governor usually resided on the principal island, from which he visited the other islands from time to time. These were presided over by a Lieutenant-Governor, often a prominent resident of that island, who was appointed by the home government usually, but not invariably, on the recommendation of the Governor of the day. In the absence of the Governor and the Lieutenant-Governor, the government then devolved on the senior member of the Council resident upon the island. In 1767 Governor Melvill pointed this out in a letter in which he concluded that 'it is now become so much my duty to represent respectfully the distress and discouragements which have already happened and are likely rather to increase by the absence of so many officers civil and military, but more particularly by that of the King's Lieutenant-Governors'.[48] At the moment he wrote, the only Lieutenant-Governor at his post had just died. During Macartney's short administration one Lieutenant-Governor of Tobago was killed in a duel with the Collector of Customs, and his successor died after less than two years in office.[49]

The very considerable distances between the various British governments were made more so by winds and currents, so that even under normal circumstances the Governors were isolated both from each other and from the home government. In peacetime they occasionally visited each other, and in the autumn of 1777, before the American War became an international conflagration, Macartney paid a visit to Governor Hay at Barbados, whom he had known some years before.[50] Nevertheless, communications both locally and from England were a major problem. Inevitably the home government left much to the Governor's initiative: 'but I feel very painfully the disadvantage of being so remote from your Lordships' directions', wrote Governor Lyttleton of Jamaica in 1765, 'as that obliges me to act often from my own judgment and take more upon myself than I would otherwise wish to do'.[51]

Information was transmitted in a variety of ways but the official channel was via the government packet. On the first Wednesday of every month the mail was collected at the Post Office in Lombard Street, London, and from there it was despatched to Falmouth from whence the packet sailed on the following Sunday.[52] On its arrival in the Caribbean it went round the various islands, delivering and collecting despatches and other mail. Both the Governor and the Admiral had the power to delay its sailing from Jamaica and Antigua, and this possible confusion of authority gave time for some of the captains to carry out their own pursuits — they were suspected of engaging in trading on their own behalf, which was strictly illegal. When this possibility was drawn to the attention of the Post Master General, he counter-attacked by pointing out that 'none of His Majesty's Governors . . . have the privilege of sending or receiving their letters free', which apparently the complaining Governor had done!⁵³ The packet usually arrived in Grenada about forty days after leaving England. However, a three months' delay was not unknown even in peacetime, and during the American War Macartney wrote in October 1778 that 'we have received no news from America for these two months and our last letters from England are of the 9th July'.⁵⁴ As early as December 1776 he had commented on the interruption of despatches through ships being captured by American privateers.⁵⁵

The Governor was the King's representative, appointed by him on the advice of the Ministry of the day, to whom the Governor was directly accountable. In the late eighteenth century the Caribbean Governors directed their despatches to the appropriate Secretary of State; at the time of Macartney's appointment this was the Secretary of State for the American Colonies, Lord George Germain, subsequently Lord Sackville. The Governor's duties were laid down in his commission, a document which was published on his arrival in the colony. These duties were further defined and augmented in the 'secret' instructions which accompanied his commission. Although parts of this document were shown to the Council, its very existence naturally aroused the suspicions of the colonists and its real, or supposed, contents were frequently a potential, and often an actual, source of friction between the colony and the Governor.⁵⁶

The powers of the Governor were limited by the checks and balances inherent in the imperial system; for example, revenue officials were appointed by the Lords of the Treasury in London and most major appointments had to be approved in Whitehall. Many of the patentee officials delegated their duties to deputies who often performed the actual work at two or three removes from their principal; for example, Macartney found in 1777 that the position of Secretary, Registrar and Clerk of the Council of Grenada etc. had been acquired by the late Robert Wood, Under-Secretary in the Southern Department, for his brother Alexander who, 'being considerably indebted to his brother Robert, sold the office to Duncan Forbes in trust for Robert'. Robert died in 1771 and his deputy, a Mr Palairet, thereafter. In November 1775 'Mr. George Frazer came from England with a new deputation from Mrs Anne Wood, but on presenting himself to be sworn into office, a doubt arose upon the regularity or validity of his appointment'. Macartney was uncertain of the actual value of the office but thought that it could 'be farmed by a deputy for at least £2,000 sterling *per annum* secured to be paid to the principal in London'.[57] The Governor's exclusion from such lucrative patronage, and the ramifications of these appointments, seriously weakened his prestige and authority in a highly materialistic society.

However, the Governor's recommendation was an important factor in many appointments, even if it could be superseded by a direct approach to the Minister in London, usually through the candidate's influential friends. Much, therefore, depended upon the Governor's own influence and personality. One area particularly open to manipulation was membership of the Council, both with regard to initial appointments and with regard to the Governor's power to suspend recalcitrant members. In one of Macartney's earliest despatches he commented that:

> Your Lordship will probably receive many applications from gentle-men in England recommending persons here to be admitted of the Council; I flatter myself you will have the goodness to communicate them to me before any Mandamus is granted... many inconveniences have arisen from the appointment of persons as Councillors, whose characters are not perfectly understood in England.[58]

The Council consisted of a nominated body of twelve prominent residents. It had both a consultative and a legislative function: it acted both as an Advisory Council for the Governor and as an Upper House to the elected legislature. Friction between the two bodies was always a potential problem. Macartney faced it early in his government, for in April 1777 Germain wrote approvingly that 'the step you took of proroguing the Council and Assembly for three months, when you perceived a breach between them was likely to be the consequence of their continuing to sit, appears to have been very judicious'.[59]

As the members of the Council were usually chosen from among the wealthier inhabitants, absenteeism was more common among this group, while their position in the government made it a particular cause for concern. Macartney and many other Governors were frequently forced to point out that:

> Your Lordship knows that in case of death or absence of the Governor the command devolves of course not on the most loyal, or most capable, but on him who happens to be the senior member of the Council, and hence it is not impossible in times like these, when a latitude of opinion relative to the authority of Great Britain over its dependencies is entertained by many, that the administration of a remote colony might fall into very improper hands.[60]

In the 1770s there was an additional reason for concern as the inter-change of trade had made the connection between the American colonies and the West Indies a very close one. In April 1778 Macartney warned that 'numbers of people in this island have formerly lived in America, and imbibed no small portion of her levelling spirit'. Add 'Creole idolence and mischief-making',[61] suggested Macartney, and finally the presence of the French new subjects with their different attitudes to religion and government, and the situation was inherently explosive.

The intensity of religious friction is superficially surprising. British West Indian society was essentially materialistic and not usually given to religious observance, for which there was a minimal provision. Officially the British West Indies were Church of England under the pastoral care of the Bishop of London; nevertheless their entrepreneurial possibilities had attracted both Irish Catholics and Scottish Presbyterians as well as other non-conformists. These non-Anglican residents were always an element in the religious problem and sometimes a violent one. Macartney, an Irishman, was well accustomed to this problem and he handled it with considerable skill, possibly helped by his own 'enlightened' views and the external threats to the very existence of the colony. It is difficult not to conclude that, for many, privilege rather than piety was the dominant issue,[62] particularly as in the eighteenth century provision for the religious education of the large slave population was virtually non-existent.

Social and diplomatic gifts were essential for the successful conduct of an administration, and the West Indians, despite their cantankerousness, were hospitable. On their arrival the Macartneys were fêted: 'we have been received with great cordiality', wrote Macartney, 'the fruits of which I hope to see in a short time',[63] and a few weeks later he wrote to Lord George Germain:

Since my arrival here, I have used my best endeavours to discover the characters and views of the leading people and find them little different from those of our other colonies. There are a few among them of birth or education; most of them affect independence and aspire to importance. They expect great attention to their complaints and much personal civility to themselves, and if not soothed, or gratified, are apt to become troublesome at first, and often become dangerous afterwards. I have treated them all with great complaisance, some of them with a degree of confidence, and I have the satisfaction to find them much more reasonable in their sentiments, and more respectful in their language, than they were formerly supposed to be.[64]

The Macartneys made early visits to Tobago and the Grenadines and his conscientiousness and administrative ability made an early and favourable impression upon the colonists. Nevertheless, he soon found himself confronted with problems which admitted no easy solution, and shortly after the French entered the American War, he wrote to Germain expressing his concern about the fragility of the *rapport* which his diplomacy had established with the colonists.

> Your Lordship may depend upon my best endeavours to keep people in this temper but when I consider the strange discordant mass of English, Scots, Irish, French, Creoles and Americans of which this colony is composed, heated by various passions and prejudices far beyond any European idea, together with the troublesome scenes that I have passed thro', I am very far from being certain that all difficulties are over and that new ones will not arise.[65]

His government reproduced in microcosm all the problems of the British Isles aggravated by local West Indian difficulties. In addition it was still a very new British colony; one example of a difficult and delicate problem was the administration of public money, about which he commented:

> Any discretionary power, and particularly the layout of public money is a very unpleasant part of a Governor's duty ... I am under necessity of keeping a number of separate accounts with different people. It takes up a great deal of my time and is attended with infinite trouble ... I must repeat my wishes that it were in other hands. It must be lodged some-where otherwise ... mischief and confusion ... must arise in these new islands were specie is so scarce and credit so low, where sudden cases often occur, which could not have been provided for, and where the general colonial system and policy are as yet far short of that consistence and regularity which prevail in our older settlements.[66]

Macartney always had a dislike of handling public money, unusual in the eighteenth century; this may have had something to do with the career of Henry Fox, with his experience in Ireland or with the patronage which clung to the administration of eighteenth-century finance. Certainly, in his meticulous accounting for public monies he anticipated the nineteenth century and the more elaborate account-ability of public officials.

The shortage of specie was a common complaint from West Indian and other British colonial Governors. The centrifugal tendencies of the mercantilist system drew specie into the mother country. Macartney gave a number of reasons for this phenomenon, some permanent and others the temporary consequences of the American War. The causes that he listed throw an interesting side-light on the complicated economy of the southern Caribbean. They were, firstly, the clandestine trade carried in canoes and small boats between Grenada and Martinique in luxury goods, such as wine, oil, soap, silks, stockings, millinery and other articles of dress, 'the return for which is entirely made in hard money'; secondly, payments on estates bought from the former French proprietors; thirdly, ransoms for the repurchase of ships captured by privateers and taken to the French islands; fourthly, 'several planters of this colony have on account of debt and for other causes fled from hence, carried off their effects and settled in the French islands'; fifthly, there was a lack of demand for rum which was the basic cash and barter crop of the sugar islands; sixthly, and related to the latter, was the general trade disturbance created by the American War, which had also caused, seventhly, a decline in the exchange trade, whereby Portuguese gold had formerly been sent from Europe to purchase West Indian bills of exchange — the risks involved and the high rate of insurance had made this trade no longer profitable; and eighthly, the universality of debt and the need to service it — Macartney estimated the debts of the planters of Grenada, the Grenadines and Tobago at £2,000,000, and the interest on it at 15% or *c.* £300,000. 'This island', he commented, 'though *conquerored* [sic] from the French has for the most part been *purchased* from them'. He also emphasized that another drain was 'the constant absence of the great proprietors'.[67]

IV

In the eighteenth century the West Indian islands represented an area of massive capital investment and of very considerable financial complexity. This market was under the control and constant surveillance of the absentee West Indian planters and the merchant houses in London, who operated a powerful parliamentary lobby which no government or Governor could afford to ignore.[68] The strength of this lobby was illustrated in the Canada *versus* Guadaloupe debate which preceded the Peace of Paris. During the Seven Years War, Britain acquired control of all of France's West Indian colonies with the exception of the still underdeveloped St Dominique. Had she retained them at the peace, the British sugar market would have been flooded with the more economically produced French sugar, and the profits of the British planters and merchants would have been considerably reduced. The profitability of the London sugar commodity market depended upon the careful regulation of supply and demand. The monopolistic position of the West Indian planters and merchants was sustained by the British mercantilist system, which protected the less efficient production of sugar in the British colonies while further forcing up the price by burdening colonial sugar with substantial duties.[69]

However, by the middle of the century this delicate balance was under pressure. Productivity in Barbados and the Leeward Islands was declining and consequently their plantations were becoming increasingly more labour-intensive because of the need to fertilize the exhausted soil. From the seventeenth century fertilizers had been essential for sugar cultivation in Barbados, and the Leeward Islands were fully developed before the middle of the eighteenth century.[70] Thus by accepting Grenada and the undeveloped Windward Islands, the West Indian interest had hoped to stabilize their monopoly and to sustain it by gradually opening up a limited amount of new land to balance the exhausted plantations in the older West Indian colonies. Their political influence was such that they were able to secure parliamentary consent to the peace treaty, despite the anger of the London mob at the continued inflation of the price of sugar.[71] If the negotiators had decided otherwise and Great Britain had retained the French islands, she would have acquired a virtual monopoly of the West Indian sugar trade; certainly she would have been in a position to control any surplus production and thereby to have checked, or at least monitored, the illegal trade in sugar, rum and molasses carried on between the North American colonies and the French islands.[72] Thus the protection of the sugar monopoly in 1763 ultimately proved a Pyrrhic victory for the merchants as it helped to undermine the stability of the overextended British Empire.

The agricultural distribution of the British Isles and the colonies ensured a preponderance of temperate agricultural products over tropical commodities within the imperial trade system. The illicit trade between the North American colonies and the French islands was an attempt to redress this imbalance outside the perimeters of the British mercantilist system. Thus, this trade was an important factor in the American War and a major element in the Franco-American alliance. The trade provided a cause and the French islands a strategic base from which to attack some of Britain's most valued imperial assets.

The years following the Peace of Paris highlighted the complicated and shaky financial position of the British West Indian islands. Huge amounts of capital were needed to develop the ceded islands and the older colonies were already heavily in debt. At the same time increasing industrial development at home offered the investor alternative possibilities. The cost of opening up a sugar plantation was almost prohibitively expensive, particularly if a quick return was envisaged. Its dependence upon slave labour made it the most capital-intensive form of eighteenth-century agriculture.[73] In 1763 Governor George Scott explained to the Secretary of State for the Southern Department, Lord Egremont, that:

I am told that anything of a sugar plantation with the necessary works upon it will cost here from ten, to fifteen and twenty thousands pounds sterling, and that if the Grenadilles [sic] were suffered to have sugar plantations upon them, a privateer with two or three launches might ruin four or five plantations in a night's time and carry off all their slaves ... whereas the cattle and other stock upon one of those islands if they were all carried off would not amount to anything near the value of one of the sugar works with its slaves, and the cattle must be had for manufacturing the sugar and other uses.[74]

Other studies, practical and theoretical, upheld this figure; for instance Edward Long, a Jamaican planter, estimated in 1774 that the smallest scale on which a sugar plantation could be started was £4,923 currency, and that such a planter would be disadvantaged against a more affluent competitor who could afford to equip his plantation properly by laying out £14,029 currency.[75] Among the many theoretical calculations was one published in 1764 entitled: *Some observations which may contribute to afford a just idea of the nature, importance and settlement of our new West Indian colonies,* in which the writer postulated an imaginary estate of 500 acres in Tobago. He provided yearly accounts of the outlay required to make it operational within five years; this, he considered, would require a total expenditure of £20,000 sterling,[76] a sum which did not allow for the effects of disasters such as hurricanes, fires, pests, diseases, slave revolts or wars. Shortly after his arrival Macartney assessed the impact of these unpredictable variables on his government, reporting that:

There has been a combination of unfortunate circumstances, within these few years, which this island has had to struggle with. The sugar crop has in some parts suffered a good deal by the Cane Ant, and the two last seasons have been particularly unfavourable. The Scots bankruptcies in 1772, the late fire in this capital, the depredations of the Maroon negroes, the rebellion in America, on which country the people here entirely depend for lumber, livestock and provisions, all these circumstances together have contributed to retard the progress of this colony, and to prevent it from attaining that degree of prosperity and improvement which was expected and of which it is undoubtedly capable.

However, he was optimistic about the future of the colony as by the time of his arrival the bankruptcies were finding their level, the town of St George was being rebuilt, alternatives to American lumber, unavailable because of the war, were being sought in the island, and the problem of the Maroons — French negroes who escaped at the time of the conquest into the mountainous interior of the island from whence they raided the developing plantations — was being solved.

The crop promised well and it was hoped that a method of destroying the cane ants had been discovered.[77]

Despite its appearance, the sugar cane was a fragile plant, highly inflammable and vulnerable to the weather and all manner of pests and diseases. Nevertheless, as an object of universal profit the vulnerability of sugar was a unifying element in the international complexity of the West Indies. Shortly before Macartney's arrival, the Grenada legislature had passed an Act to raise £15,000 towards the public debt, and £22,000 towards the eradication of the cane ant, of which £20,000 was to reward the inventor of a 'cheap and easy manner of destroying the Sugar Ant'; the remaining £2,000 was to pay the expense of experiments and smaller rewards to those 'who throw any light upon this subject, the most devastating that ever happened upon the French or these islands. Martinico is to give £50,000 and Tobago £5,000', and Lieutenant-Governor Young continued:

> these destructive insects... carry on a very rapid desolation wherever they go both here and in Tobago. The obstacles of fire and water are nothing to them, they walk over the one as upon dry ground and attack the other with such ferocity that they extinguish it with their dead bodies... Their numbers increase most prodigiously and tho' bushels of them have been destroyed in a night their increase is such that the diminution is not observed.

In August 1776 Macartney reported that a Mr Henry Phillips had invented a powder which killed the ants on contact. Mr Phillips was unable to claim the reward before Grenada was captured by the French in 1779. Later it transpired that his invention had only a limited success as it failed to exterminate the ants which bred underground. However, he applied to the Lords of the Treasury for a reward and in 1781 the British House of Commons voted him £3,600 sterling. In the meantime the ants disappeared after an unexpected hurricane struck the island in 1780.[78]

By the time Macartney arrived in 1776, the initial stages of the settlement were over. 'Grenada', wrote Macartney shortly after he arrived, 'singly exports more produce to Great Britain and Ireland and consumes within herself more British and Irish commodities than any of our West Indian Islands, Jamaica alone excepted'.[79] Jamaica, which accounted for more than half the produce of the British West Indies, was never fully exploited. Thus, within thirteen years, Grenada had overtaken the older colonies, but this rapid development had only been possible through extensive borrowing and the restrictive obligations which it incurred. Thus Macartney found that:

> The principal estates have been purchased from the French proprietors ... the English who bought them had seldom any capital of their own

but speculated on credit; the money was advanced by the London merchants on mortgage of the estates, and on condition of having all the produce consigned to them, by which means the profit of commission and interest together sometimes amounted to near 20%; whilst the planter lay under every disadvantage for, being entirely dependent on his London creditor and obliged to remit the produce to him only, he lost both the choice of his correspondent and the chance of the market. Thus tho' the Island itself was rich the individual was poor.[80]

The sugar market[81] fluctuated very considerably and the West Indian planter, who consigned his sugars for sale on the London market, was entirely dependent upon the merchant house with whom he corresponded to see that he obtained the best price available. Assessing the commodities market could be extremely difficult and the planter who could pick and choose his agent was in a position to expect a better return than the planter whose indebtedness deprived him of any choice, although in practice families did tend to remain on the books of a particular merchant house for successive generations. Similarly the London factor was entrusted with purchasing the various necessities and luxuries which the planter required for himself, his family or the estate. In addition, he would discharge from the profits of the sugar sales monies for the education of the planter's family or to meet the annuities, dowries and other provisions charged upon the estate by the planter's predecessor. All of these services were performed on a percentage basis, usually 2½%.

The imperial expansion confirmed by the Peace of Paris placed an acute administrative and financial strain upon the government and resources of Great Britain. During the early 1770s there was a trade recession throughout Western Europe. In Britain there was a major credit crisis which produced serious problems for the two principal areas of recent imperial expansion, namely India and the West Indies. In 1772 the East India Company had to appeal to the government in order to remain solvent: its administrative structure had proved inadequate for the additional responsibilities which it had acquired in 1763. In June of the same year the Scottish banker Alexander Fordyce, who was also receiver of the land tax, went bankrupt, and Macartney was still commenting on the effects of the ensuing 'Scottish bankruptcies' some five years later.

There had been a further credit failure in 1774 when Governor Leybourne had reported that:

the distressed situation of this island, owing to the failure of credit, the low price of coffee, and the very great scarcity of money, is beyond conception... [several estates had been sold for a fraction of their value] ... these unfortunate circumstances have induced a great number of planters (all of them new subjects) to quit the island and retire with their negroes to St Lucie, where they receive protection from the French governors and these emigrations have been so frequent as to be extremely alarming, their estates and negroes being mortgaged to merchants in London for very considerable sums.[82]

This particular crisis had been principally due to an alteration in the European coffee market. In 1773 the German merchants, who had traditionally purchased much of the Grenada coffee crop, were prevented from doing so by new tariffs levied upon it by the German states, and at the same time a determined effort was being made by French and Dutch merchants to capture the German market. The planters turned to the British market which had always been small because of the preferential duties levied to favour the East India Company's tea monopoly, and these duties were now of greater importance than ever because of the Company's financial problems. The British market was flooded with the excess produce of the ceded islands; the price slumped sharply and many of the coffee planters were bankrupted. Capital-intensive sugar was the rich planter's crop; coffee, indigo, cacao and cotton were usually produced by the less affluent planters. Coffee was the major crop of Grenada under the French; for instance, in 1763 it was producing 20.4 times as much coffee as Jamaica.[83]

Traditionally, holdings in the French islands had always been smaller and the crops more diverse, thus reducing both the profits and the risks. These smaller estates and more varied crops had been encouraged by the French laws of inheritance as the French islands followed the laws and customs of Paris with their specific provision from an estate for all the children of a marriage; while the English tradition of primogeniture was customary in the British West Indies, with the usual arrangements for jointures, dowries and provision for younger sons charged against the estate which was inherited intact by the eldest son. In addition there was the need to be more self-sufficient as the French islands did not have the British North American colonies or Ireland as a dependable source of provisions; distance and climate militated against Canada — its population was small and its lands still underdeveloped. A further consideration was the mountainous terrain of the French islands, larger areas of which were unsuitable for the cultivation of sugar, while there was a heavy demand for such tropical products as coffee on the home market. Finally, the French did not have the capital resources available to the British planters to expedite their development and encourage the monoculture of sugar as was the case in the older British islands. Grenada illustrated this agricultural diversity and shortly after his arrival Macartney explained that:

Almost every estate comprehends and chequers within itself every different produce which the soil can yield. A large cane piece perhaps forms in the middle a hanging level of 50 to 60 acres. On one side rises a cotton grove; an indigo field forms the contrast on the other. Above is a coffee and a cocoa walk; below is the negro village surrounded with gardens of plantains and bananas together with pastures covered with mules, sheep, goats, oxen, etc. etc. There are also the works, the sugar mills, the coffee mills, the cotton gins, indigo vats, etc. etc. etc., all the engines, instruments and utensils necessary for the plantation.[84]

The dislocation of Grenada's economy caused by the conquest, and its slow orientation to the demands of the British market made it particularly vulnerable to the financial crises of the 1770s as both the newly established British planters and the small French planters were heavily in debt.

Arrangements did exist whereby debts could be recovered from debtors who had fled to foreign islands, but their effectiveness depended upon the willingness and the ability of the various Governors to enforce them. For example, in 1774 the London firm Chauvet and Turquand memorialized the government for assistance in recovering the £2,000 sterling which they had lent John Bernard and Margaret Brigid Girard Bernard, his wife, of Grenada, to purchase slaves for the improvement of their coffee plantation. What ensued was fairly typical: in April 1774 Mrs. Bernard 'privately' departed from Grenada, taking with her all the slaves, stock and other portable goods, for a French island, probably St. Lucie; deprived of all the slaves and equipment, the plantation became overrun with weeds and of very little value. The memorialists requested the government to intercede with the French for the payment of the debt. In August 1776 Macartney reported a similar case involving a Mr de Monchy to the Secretary of State.[85] In April 1777 Germain piously expressed the British government's attitude, commenting on the case of some French citizens who wished to recover debts owed to them in Grenada that 'the perfection of justice consists in its being speedily as well as impartially administered. And I should be sorry to afford the least pretext for foreigners to surmise that it is either denied or delayed to them in any part of His Majesty's dominions'. In fact the strictness of British law in this respect discouraged debtors from seeking refuge in British islands.[86]

The complex and indebted nature of West Indian society encouraged the litigiousness which was a feature of most British colonies. Unfortunately this did not also encourage a high level of legal training; for example, in May 1777 Macartney wrote to warn the Secretary of State that:

one Mr Arthur Pigott (who tho' not regularly bred to the law, had been admitted to practise in the courts both of Grenada and Tobago) sailed lately for England with the intention of soliciting the appointment of Attorney-General of Tobago . . . I think it my duty to inform you that the Attorney-General and Solicitor-General of Grenada are by their commission Attorney-General and Solicitor-General of Tobago also . . . as to Mr Pigott he is a very troublesome, contentious man, and extremely improper for any appointment under the crown . . . he even presumed to declare publicly his opinion that it was the interest of every colony to be upon ill terms with its Governor.[87]

The background to this story was that Mr Pigott had settled in Grenada, where he had behaved in such a way that he had found it expedient to remove himself to Tobago. The Attorney-General of Grenada was Thomas Baker, and in February 1779 he was in London and Macartney discovered that he 'was a prisoner in the King's Bench but he has now removed himself by *habeas corpus* to the Fleet and where he is likely to remain for a debt of £8,000'. Shortly afterwards Baker requested an extension of his leave of absence to settle his affairs, and a few months later Macartney wrote to Germain requesting a salary for him, 'both on account of the justice of his pretensions, and his own particular merit'![88] Many legal offices depended solely upon fees for their salaries. A few months later Baker decided that his health precluded him from returning to Grenada. In his place Macartney recommended the appointment of George Staunton, who later became Macartney's close friend and secretary.

The Stauntons were small landowners in Co. Galway, but the embarrassed state of his family-fortune had obliged George Staunton to study for a professional career. His delicate health had encouraged him to follow the path of so many of his Catholic neighbours when, during the 1750s, he studied at the universities of Toulouse, Montpellier and Paris. In 1760 he was living in London, though whether they had met before Macartney went to Grenada is uncertain. Staunton went to the West Indies in 1762 and first practised medicine in Guadaloupe, and then to Dominica where he was Secretary to the Governor. His position created envy and involved him reluctantly in duelling, which was part of eighteenth-century social and political life. However, by 1770 Staunton had accumulated sufficient capital to buy an estate in Grenada, where he adopted the legal profession. Staunton, from his background and education, had the great advantage of understanding the religious problem which, although it existed throughout the British West Indies, was particularly virulent in areas which had formerly been French and Catholic.

V

When Macartney took up his government at the beginning of the American War, he discovered that, despite their value and potential, the British islands in the southern Caribbean were defenceless and he lost no time in pointing out that 'all these deficiencies were frequently represented to the Board of Ordnance by my predecessors . . . but no answer has been returned'; and defence was a subject which he continually emphasized in his despatches. For instance, in a long despatch dated 22 October 1777, he commented that 'a British fleet alone can effectually protect it [his government] or indeed any of our West Indian possessions'; and in the following July he again pressed the point, this time detailing exactly what he had in mind.

> The principal effectual defence of these colonies against a foreign enemy must be a naval force, and as long as we have a superior squadron in these seas, there is little to be feared. When I say *in these seas,* I mean the seas round Grenada, Tobago and St Vincent, for as to the squadron at Antigua, on account of its remote station and the particular circumstances of winds and currents, we can have but little dependence upon it for protection . . . But altho' our chief reliance must be on a British fleet, it will always be prudent to station a certain number of land troops here, in order to garrison the fort and defend it against a *coup de main,* to overcome the negroes and preserve the police. There are at present five companies of foot in Grenada and two in Tobago but an entire battalion would be a proper complement.[89]

The defence of the ceded islands was vitally necessary, not only for the preservation of British investment, but even for the continuance of the mercantilist system itself by ensuring an adequate supply of tropical produce for the rapidly expanding population of the mother country. Macartney did not hesitate delicately to remind the home government of this.

> Let me mention that the old Islands (except St Kitts) are almost entirely worn out and exhausted, whilst the new islands are fresh land and uncommonly fruitful. Let me mention the vicinity of the Spanish Main and the recent establishment at Trinidada [sic], not unlikely to become troublesome and dangerous neighbours to us.[90]

Macartney's government lay between French Martinique and Spanish Trinidad. The mutual indefensibility of the islands, combined with the value and vulnerability of their produce, had led to certain conventions in the conduct of war in the Caribbean area during the eighteenth century. The American War was no exception, and in a despatch of 2 September 1778 Macartney reported that he had received:

> a proposition from the Marquis de Bouillé to restrain our respective privateers from making descents on the Islands for the purpose of

plunder and to restore mutually any negroes or effects which might be carried off in expeditions of that sort. With the unanimous advice of the Council here, I have acceded to this arrangement which I find has been usual throughout the West Indies in all former wars.[91]

Even before the French officially joined the war, the Americans had established an unofficial naval base at St Pierre in Martinique, which allowed their privateers to prey upon British shipping throughout the eastern Caribbean. In April 1777 Macartney reported that there were thirty-one American privateers based in Martinique, fifteen at sea and sixteen in port, carrying 428 guns and 2,710 men. They had taken twenty-nine ships, five carrying slaves, nineteen provisions and lumber, while another one had stores for the British forces in America, and of the remainder one ship had escaped and sailed to Antigua.[92] During these years the Americans had two resident agents in St Pierre, William Bingham and Richard Harrison. The American privateers often carried a mixture of French and American crews and Macartney reported that:

they are furnished with two sets of papers; one is a commission from the Congress, under which authority they take all our vessels which they can master, the other is a clearance from the French custom houses for the Spanish Main which they show to such of our ships as are too strong for them . . . they pass for French vessels bound on a trading voyage, and the Spanish commerce being an illicit one accounts for their being armed in a warlike manner . . . The West Indians in general, whether British, French, Dutch or Spaniards, are of a buccaneering turn.[93]

A mutual respect appears to have developed between Macartney and the Marquis de Bouillé, Governor of Martinique. Shortly after his arrival in 1777 de Bouillé, a former Governor of Guadaloupe, gave assurances that he would not support the Americans — at least not publicly, and diplomatic contacts were carried on 'with more decency and address'[94] than they had been under de Bouillé's predecessor, the Comte d'Argout, currently Governor of St Dominique. The international tangle of the Caribbean encouraged a continual traffic in rumour and speculation as well as in genuine information. This traffic increased in wartime when intelligence was an essential part of a Governor's defence. Shortly after his arrival, Macartney reported that he had 'sent a gentleman on whom I could depend to make a little tour and report to me what he saw and observed'. During wartime prisoners were usually exchanged without being repatriated and these occasions often provided opportunities to gather intelligence: in 1779 Governor Burt of the Leewards wrote that 'I might on particular occasions send a Flag of Truce as an authorised spy'.[95]

France and Spain were ruled by senior and junior branches of the

Bourbon dynasty and for most of the century a Family Compact indicated the special relationship which existed between the two countries. For instance, in October 1778 Macartney reported that French privateers in defiance of the 'convention' had removed some forty slaves from his jurisdiction, sending some to Martinique and some to Trinidad. M. de Bouillé had ensured the return of *both* groups which 'shows his weight and influence in the Spanish councils'.[96] Both Spain and France, recollecting their losses in the Seven Years' War, were sympathetic to the Americans. Spain, however, was less anxious than France to give aid to rebels in the New World, but eventually both declared war on England: France in March 1778, and Spain a year later. Spain's interest in Trinidad had been dormant until Sr. Falquez was appointed Governor in 1778, when Macartney reported that he had published:

> a proclamation . . . offering every advantage and encouragement that could be desired. In consequence of it many of the inhabitants of St Lucie, several bankrupts of this island, and various other persons of desperate fortunes, embraced the proposal, carried thither their negroes and began to form settlements and plantations.[97]

There was in the eighteenth-century Caribbean an ever moving frontier which attracted both the substantial investor and the impoverished drifter. The capital-intensive nature of tropical agriculture, particularly sugar, encouraged the British, French and Spanish governments to offer inducements to attract settlers from the established colonies to assist in the development of the new governments which emerged during the course of the century. These settlers were often a mixed asset. Frequently, in addition to being of divided loyalties, they were of a restless disposition and fugitives from debt or other anti-social activities. Nevertheless, in 1778 Macartney expressed concern about the rapid development of Trinidad, which was 'being greatly increased in its population by a very numerous *banditti* of different nations and different colours, who for debt or for crimes have fled from other colonies and found a most welcome reception from Mr Falquez'.[98] Trinidad offered a particular threat to Tobago.

Arguments based on strategic necessities were joined by those of physical geography as Macartney pointed out some of the basic problems of communications within the Caribbean. In his despatches he emphasized elements which isolated the three groups of British Caribbean possessions, explaining why it was essential in the case of Grenada that:

> they are made a distinct command from that at Antigua . . . the nature of the winds and the setting of the currents in this part of the West Indies are such that . . . none but a practical navigator or geographer on the spot

can form any just idea of them. The *Druid* sloop of war was six weeks without being able to get to Barbados from Antigua and the *Beaver* not long since made several attempts to reach Tobago but could not accomplish it.

The Leeward Islands benefited both from their position and from the naval base at English Harbour when it came to taking prizes. Macartney hinted that perhaps the islands in his government were not receiving their fair share of naval protection because:

as we lie so far to the southward and are quite out of the track of the American trading ships there are no prizes to be met with in these parts to reward the services of ships of war, and that circumstance has been hinted at by some discontented people here as a reason for our being neglected, but I should be extremely sorry to entertain even for a moment so injurious an idea.[99]

Even after the crop was safely harvested, its vulnerability continued as it had to be shipped in small lighters to the rendezvous of the merchant ships which took it to England in convoy. In wartime the convoy had an escort from the Royal Navy to protect it from hostile fleets and pirates, but the Grenada merchant ships had to sail unescorted to and from Barbados, where the men of war, which accompanied the Barbados convoy across the Atlantic, stopped. Macartney, as an inducement, hinted that the Grenadan Assembly might be persuaded to contribute towards such a project in the same manner that the Antiguan Assembly had done for English Harbour — an idea which was always attractive to the British government.[100] However, in the immediate future time was too short to allow a long and dilatory debate, essential for such a major decision, and two years later Grenada fell through lack of naval protection.

The final element in the European diplomatic jigsaw in the Caribbean was the influence of the Dutch, and to a much lesser extent of the Danes. The Spaniards and even more the French offered a direct competition in the actual production of tropical goods, but the competition offered by the Dutch and Danes was essentially commercial.[101] In 1779 there were a number of Americans residing in Dutch colonies, where 'the ships of the rebel colonies are received with open arms in all their ports, are furnished with every supply and openly conveyed by their men of war not only in the teeth of our ancient treaties, but of their own recent placards'.[102] The Dutch island of St Eustatius and, to a lesser degree, the Danish island of St Croix conducted an entrepôt trade. At the beginning of 1779 Macartney gave a very clear description of the consequences of this trade, especially in wartime.

The French Islands are mostly furnished with Irish salt-provisions from our Leeward Islands. The merchants of St Kitts and Antigua are at this moment, through the channel of St Eustatius, pouring in immense supplies of this kind to Martinique and Guadaloupe which, without such assistance, would run the risk of being literally starved... For I believe I need not mention to your Lordship that all our merchants, even of the best reputation, will not scruple to trade with our enemies, or engage in any commercial adventure, however prejudicial to the public interest, if they can derive from it any private advantage.[103]

A year later, in 1780, Great Britain declared war on Holland, largely over the trading activities of St Eustatius, whose merchants had become exceedingly wealthy in the early years of the American War by supplying munitions to the Americans and provisions to the French. As early as 1777 Macartney reported that:

The Americans on the continent are chiefly supplied in the articles of clothing and hardware with British manufactures which are sent thither through the medium of St Eustatia [sic] and Santa Cruz. Gunpowder, artillery and all kinds of naval and military supplies are furnished them by the French... it appears that the French, Dutch and Danes are prodigious gainers by this trade, whilst America itself is almost exhausted to the last farthing, having no foreign credit, and not being able to purchase a single article without ready money or an equivalent commodity.[104]

The island was completely undefended, and on 3 February 1781 made an unconditional surrender to Admiral Rodney. There followed one of the greatest bargain auctions in history, and the political storm which ensued was of equal proportions as the British merchants attempted to claim compensation for their goods confiscated in the course of their surreptitious trade with the enemy![105]

The interconnection between the Americans and the English, French and Spaniards was rather different. The West Indian islands were chronically short of lumber and provisions, and the Americans could sell these products in the British West Indies for hard currency, which they then used to trade in the French islands where tropical merchandise was cheaper, as the cost of production in the British islands was inflated by more exhausted lands, less efficient agricultural practices and heavier duties. When the war broke out, American trade with the French and the Dutch became direct and open, instead of direct and surreptitious. The British islands suffered accordingly. In December 1777 Governor Burt of the more favourably placed Leeward Islands pointed out the dangers of some of the scarcities which they were now experiencing. In the course of his despatch, he listed the goods which the West Indies had acquired from North America, writing in a private letter to Lord George Germain that:

had I not extended the liberty of importing provisions, we should in all probability have had insurrections of the slaves in every island... As all trade with America is stopped, the only method of supply we have, except from Europe, is by prizes . . . We should retain what we take; even all this will not be sufficient for us. This united with an allowance to import lumber, staves, etc., boards, oil, fish, flour, bread, pitch, tar and turpentine from Russia and they to receive rum in payment . . . besides, my Lord, Russia would take the rum which now the Dutch buy and send to North America.[106]

Their dependence upon external sources for essential supplies often created unpredictable gluts and shortages in the islands and these were emphasized in wartime. The merchants were always ready to take advantage of scarcities, and as early as November 1776 Macartney pointed out the need to regulate this tendency by allowing a Market Bill:

to establish a balance between the seller and the buyer, otherwise undue advantage will be taken by him who has what another wants, over him who wants what another has. If usury were not restrained by the laws I'm afraid it would be pretty generally practised and if the markets of Grenada are left to the mercy of the butchers the price of all articles which they deal in will rise at their discretion and become every day more exorbitant . . . Laws of this kind have long since been found necessary in our other West Indian islands.[107]

The Governor was responsible for defence and therefore he controlled the local militia. In calling up the militia, Macartney was advised to use his own judgment over the potentially dubious loyalty of the French new subjects. In December 1778 Macartney received intelligence that an invasion was imminent. He proclaimed martial law and called the militia to St George. The muster amounted to about 1,000 men and, with the addition of the regulars and some sailors, the total fighting force was about 1,300. Expenditure on military fortifications and defence was shared between the home and colonial governments. In Grenada the British government paid the militia's expenses while they were on manoeuvres, and to meet the sudden emergency the Grenada Assembly voted £1,700 currency in the hope of being reimbursed. The emergency passed, as in January 1779 the British captured the French island of St Lucie and Macartney thankfully dismissed the militia.

It became indeed high time to do so for having been so long together they were beginning to corrupt one another . . . I was not however sorry to see them assembled here as it gave me the opportunity of being perfectly acquainted with the persons and characters of all ranks of men on the island. The French of every denomiantion and colour are totally disaffected and . . . incapable of any sincere attachment to us; of our own people the leading and most respectable gentlemen profess strong principles of honour, loyalty and public spirit, but the meaner sort, composed of overseers, clerks, low planters and tradesmen, are a mere *banditti*, adverse to all order, discipline and obedience, turbulent, mutinous and impatient of any restraint whatsoever... In case of an attack on this island, my principal reliance must be upon the few regulars I have. Our French subjects are not to be trusted, and I'm afraid it is imposible to bring the militia under proper discipline and subordination.[108]

The West Indian colonies were not only vulnerable to invasion in time of war but they were continually threatened by the slave revolts, of which the heavily outnumbered white population of the West Indies lived in constant dread. Fortunately, there were no slave rebellions during Macartney's administration, but there had been one in Tobago in 1770 which Governor Melvill reported had been checked in time, though not without the loss of some slaves. Thus, calling the militia was internally dangerous as it took the white population off the plantations, but in 1778-9 Macartney was relieved to discover that:

> though the principal part of the free people of the colony are assembled here ... yet the slaves have been perfectly quiet, and no tumult or disorder has yet happened. To guard against accidents of that kind I have established four cross-patrols, which are constantly going round the island, and who regularly report the state of the country and the coast at their return.[109]

In calling out the militia Macartney had to balance the probability of being able to make a successful defence of the island against the responsibility of ensuring the departure of its produce at the earliest possible moment. Under normal circumstances the smaller early convoys sailed in April, May and June. The largest convoy usually sailed early in July and a final one with the remainder of the crop in late October or early November. In 1777 the total number of ships in the April, May, June, July and October convoys was 138.[110] In 1778 the June fleet had comprised eighteen merchant ships from Grenada, ten from Tobago and five from St Vincent, a total of thirty-three ships under the protection of the twenty-gun *Ariadne* and two sloops of war, the *Favourite* and the *Signet;* and a further fourteen ships had left at the end of July, just before the hurricane season. At that time Macartney noted that one-third of the crop was still outstanding and would be shipped after the hurricane season in November, so that the entire crop would have been accounted for in just over seventy ships. The harvest for the following year, 1779, was a good one and at the end of May 1779 Macartney told Germain that:

> the total value of our exported produce will exceed £700,000 sterling. I imagine the fleet from this island alone will consist of near 50 large topsail vessels for Great Britain and Ireland and 10 or 12 for Quebec, Halifax, New York and Savannah — and that their different loadings will amount to about half a million sterling.[111]

At the same he emphasized the shortage of ships which had been a problem in 1778. Nevertheless, in the event ninety merchant ships left Grenada, Tobago and St Vincent on 5 June 1779, instead of the forty-seven which had taken the produce of both the June and July convoys in 1778. On this occasion the ships had arrived on time. Less than a fortnight later they were loaded and Macartney reported that:

> Yesterday at noon our great merchant fleet, consisting of 150 topsails sailed from hence under convoy of the *St Albans, Centurion, Diamond, Maidstone, Aurora, Deal Castle, Supply, Favourite, Snake* and *Pelican* ships of war . . . They are all to rendezvous at St Kitts and thence to proceed on the 15 th instant with the ships of that island, Antigua and the Virgins. I suppose the whole merchant fleet for Great Britain and Ireland will consist of about 200 sail, not less in value than two million sterling to which if we add 4,000 seamen . . . the safe arrival of this convoy will be an event of immense importance as a political and a commercial object.[112]

On 5 August 1779 Germain wrote to Macartney announcing the safe arrival of the convoy;[113] but by that time Macartney was on his way to France as a prisoner of war.

On 2 July the French Admiral, the Comte d'Estaing, appeared off the coast of Grenada with twenty-five ships of the line, twelve frigates and 6,500 troops, amongst them Dillon's regiment from the Irish Brigade. Macartney played for time. 'He expected every instant', wrote Staunton, 'to see Admiral Byron and General Grant come to his relief. They knew of his danger'. In fact the danger had been so obvious that Lady Macartney had been persuaded to return home with duplicates of Macartney's personal as well as official papers; unfortunately these had been destroyed when the ship caught fire in harbour at St Kitts, and the originals were later taken by the French at the capture of Grenada. However, despite his many warnings, Macartney waited for the Navy in vain. On 4 September 1779 he wrote to Germain from La Rochelle:

> We made the best defence we could with the handful of people we had, which consisted of 101 rank and file of the 48th Regiment, 24 artillery recruits and between three and four hundred militia. We had the good fortune to repulse the enemy in their first attack but in the second they carried our lines by dint of superior numbers after a conflict of about an hour and a half, in which they had killed and wounded 300 men and upwards, which amounted to more than the whole force we had to oppose their attack, for in the preceding night we were deserted by almost all the coloured people and the greatest part of the new subjects. Being at the discretion of the enemy without means of resistance or prospect of relief, we were obliged to propose a capitulation which was

instantly and peremptorily refused by the Count d'Estaing *in toto* and in lieu of it he sent to me the most extraordinary and unexampled project that ever entered into the mind of a general or politician. This I rejected in my turn, and there being no possibility of obtaining any other, all the principal inhabitants to whom I communicated it were unanimous in preferring to surrender without any conditions at all to the one that was offered, and upon that footing the enemy are now possessed of the island . . . An assurance was given to the inhabitants of Grenada that they should retain quiet possession of their estates and that during the war they would not be obliged to carry arms against His Majesty.[114]

Despite all the attempts to safeguard property, the planters suffered considerably, as Staunton commented:

> Their properties are confirmed to them under French Laws. I mean what remains to them; for many have been totally pillaged and ruined, and I am among the chief sufferers, my plantation being close to the place of debarkation, and attracting the immediate attention of all the free booters following the fleet and army.

Nevertheless, thirty-two of the planters managed to prepare and sign an address of thanks to Macartney before he left for France on 5 July. 'Your Excellency', they wrote, 'hath to the last moment of your command and negotiations with the conquerors allied your duty to your sovereign to a true regard to the people who had been committed to your care. We wish your Excellency a safe passage to Europe and all happiness in future.'[115]

VI

The Comte d'Estaing appears to have been a less than chivalrous victor. Following the capitulation eight 'hostages' were sent from among the inhabitants to France. Macartney lost all his possessions including his papers. His plate and clothes were publicly auctioned and when he accepted an invitation to dine with his conqueror, he felt obliged to indicate the deficiencies in his wardrobe for the occasion. Macartney left the island with only the coat he had been wearing at the capitulation. D'Estaing, who had in previous wars broken his parole on two occasions, refused to parole Macartney or allow his exchange in the West Indies and sent him to France as a prisoner of war. After landing at La Rochelle Macartney was imprisoned at Limoges.[116]

George Staunton was among those chosen as a hostage and with his contacts in France he was of great assistance in negotiating Macartney's exchange for a British prisoner of war, M. de Verdière, who was in the opposite position to Macartney in that he had lost all his possessions to the British. The negotiation of an exchange rather than a parole was of importance to Macartney's future career as it made him available for consideration as Governor of Madras. Staunton subsequently became Macartney's Secretary there and the two men remained close friends for the rest of their lives. Staunton, having been educated in France, knew the country well and had the entrée into French society. Therefore, although they were hostages, he and his wife enjoyed a fairly active social life; for instance, Mrs Staunton went to Court and saw Queen Marie Antoinette.

Macartney returned to London at the beginning of November 1779 and within two days of his return Lord George Germain, the Secretary of State, wrote to Lieutenant-Governor Graham of Tobago: 'You cannot do better than follow the example of Lord Macartney . . . for no administration of government has been more meritorious than his Lordship's'.[117] Under any circumstances such praise was rare, and for it to be bestowed upon a Governor who had, for whatever reason, surrendered his government to the enemy was exceptional. Similarly, few West Indian Governors received a spontaneous address of thanks from the local inhabitants. Macartney's government of Grenada had been a triumph of diplomatic skill and administrative efficiency. Seen both as an episode in itself and as part of his career as a whole, Macartney's government marks a distinct step in the emergence of the professional colonial administrator and international diplomatist in the slowly emerging concept of 'the official servants of the Crown', the forerunners of the modern civil service. This aspect of his position received a practical acknowledgement shortly after his return when the government sent him to Ireland to report upon the difficulties which threatened to overwhelm the unfortunate viceroy, Lord Buckinghamshire.

An eighteenth-century British Caribbean Governor was confronted with a situation of incredible complexity. The Caribbean was an international chessboard in which virtually all of the major European powers held pieces. It was also subject to the legal, or usually illegal, trade of their various American colonists. Within their separate governments the British West Indian colonies presented classic examples of the duality of the British Imperial system with its belief in the rights and liberties of Englishmen and also in the rights and duties of colonists towards the mother country. The basic indebtedness, instability and underlying insecurity of West Indian society emphasized the colonists desire for protection, while their self-esteem increased their clamour for self-government. A Governor had to be skilful to handle a situation with such a quick flash-point. In this Macartney was probably helped by the imperatives of war. External dangers usually tended to unite the mother country and the colonists. Nevertheless, not all of Macartney's contemporaries managed to harness the unifying effects of common danger so effectively.

Furthermore, the West Indian islands were to the forefront of public attention; they represented a massive investment of British capital and this ensured that their Governors would be under a continual scrutiny from their creditors and particularly from the wealthy West Indian merchants in Great Britain. Ministers invariably listened to their powerful parliamentary lobby — a voice which had proved strong enough to ensure that the 1763 Peace of Paris had enshrined their interests. The West Indian economic and parliamentary influence could easily make or break an aspiring Governor. Finally there was the King. George III always took a personal interest not only in any government carried on in his name, but in the Governor who was his personal representative. His decisive views upon his servants were vital to their future careers.

Macartney's success lay in his ability to satisfy the various elements in or connected with his government. Apart from his administrative and diplomatic skills, he also displayed a capacity for leadership and hard work. Foremost among his assets was a gift for writing clear, concise and interesting letters. Through them the home government was always kept informed and, almost as importantly, felt that it was being fully appraised of situations and conditions. His despatches have a distinct professionalism which marks them out from those of his contemporaries and they probably did much to impress the Ministry of the 'meritoriousness' of his government. They may also have lessened the shock of his capitulation, for as early as 1777 the Under Secretaries were commenting to each other on 'the defenceless state of his government which is indeed a lamentable one'.[118] In these circumstances the failure of the Navy to come to his assistance may also have aroused a certain guilt. Certainly it was generally agreed that Lord Macartney had done everything that could be required of him and, when the balance sheet was drawn, he had the remarkable achievement of a personal gain in a national loss. The skills which he had displayed in the many faceted government of Grenada immeasurably strengthened, if they did not actually secure, his future prospects.[119] Moreover, his position and his fate had brought him dramatically to the forefront of public attention. He was a known public figure and as such had a potential platform from which to advance in public life.

CHAPTER V

MIDDLE YEARS 1764-80

I

The offer of the governorship of Grenada fell short of Macartney's estimate of his worth. Nevertheless, he accepted it with alacrity. For, by the mid-1770s, his career prospects, far from fulfilling earlier promise, were dangerously uncertain. His considerable achievements in Russia had been overshadowed by indiscretions; his persistent efforts to secure the ambassadorship to Spain had ended in humiliating failure; and the Irish chief secretaryship had proved both uncongenial and unrewarding. The Bute connection had been a mixed blessing since its inception, while further assistance from Holland House was unforthcoming following the death of Lord Holland in 1774. None of this persuaded Macartney to lower his sights, but it did stiffen his resolve to succeed in whatever was offered him. The appointment in Grenada, whatever its faults, had much to commend it. Undeniably, albeit rather belatedly, it vindicated Lord Holland's judgment that the Russian post would eventually carry him to 'much higher things':[1] the salary was princely compared with those attached to Macartney's previous appointments and allowed him to look forward to discharging his debts 'in a very short time' and 'as fast as I can'.[2] In addition a responsible post in the strategically sensitive Caribbean promised, and in the event provided, an opportunity for impressive conduct in unusually difficult and dramatic circumstances. On his arrival in England in November 1779 Macartney enjoyed considerable public acclaim for the first time in his career. More significant, and probably more satisfying, was the government's approbation as evidenced by Lord North's request that he undertake the delicate mission to Ireland so soon after his return.[3]

By the summer of the following year, however, Macartney's elation had given way to a mood of anxiety, bitterness and indignation. Some of those who were so carefully weighing his future potential were beginning to question his conduct in Grenada; some felt that his politics (which rarely amounted to other than unswerving support for the government of the day) were scarcely as straightforward as they appeared; and by this time also his links with the Hollands and the Butes constituted a liability rather than an asset. Writing to Lady Ossory in August 1780, Macartney stolidly maintained that 'no prejudice can be entertained of me' on any of these counts.[4]

> With regard to . . . [Grenada] . . . if I am entitled to any applause for any part of my conduct in life, I must surely deserve it from thence. As to my politics, both your Ladyship and Lord Ossory know what they are as well as I do myself. And as to my connections, I must always respect and adhere to them as a man of honour, but considered in an interested light they are not the smallest use to me. Indeed can any man of sense suppose them for a moment to be so?

Though as much given to gossip and speculation as anyone, Macartney hated the rough and tumble of party politics, particularly when, as now, he was drawn into them against his will. He felt it 'a severe trial of one's patience to be thus put between two fires without arms for defence, provisions for subsistence or hopes of relief. Yet this is exactly my situation with regard to government and opposition'.

There were also deeper reasons for Macartney's disquiet, namely his financial difficulties. In his letter to Lady Ossory he explained these as follows:

> I have now been 17 years in the service of the Crown in pretty considerable situations and am not only not possessed of a single acre that I did not inherit, but have contracted a large debt in the cause of my employment. I have an estate of above £2,400 per annum and I owe £12,000, the greatest part of which would have been discharged by this time had it not been for my losses at Grenada, which everybody, friend and enemy, knows I did what man could do to preserve.

Clearly, Macartney's early confidence that the rewards of office would outweigh the associated expenses, and that thereby his debts would be discharged and his wealth increased, had so far proved entirely misplaced. And yet, however painful to him they may have been, his remarks were by no means as frank as they appear: they were in fact a tissue of truths, half-truths and lies which, once recognised as such, are infinitely more revealing. Not only did Macartney overstate the length and continuity of his public service and falsely ascribe the whole of his financial difficulties to it alone. He also failed to acknowledge substantial purchases of property following his marriage in 1768. Even more remarkable were his gross understatement of the extent of his indebtedness and his exaggeration of the size of his landed income. In reality, through a mixture of ill luck, bad judgment and poor management, his financial situation was giving him far more serious cause for concern than he was prepared to admit. Even in sombre mood and with someone whose loyalty to him was not in doubt, Macartney preferred to keep the precise details of his personal financial circumstances to himself. Already indebted before his departure for Russia, he was still more financially embarrassed on his return. Subsequently, he embarked on an ambitious scheme of expansion and improvement of his Co. Antrim estate, and also acquired another home in London. Together with the demands made on his purse by office, marriage and title, this involved him in considerable further debt which a combination of estate income and official salaries and perquisites was quite insufficient to discharge. During the early 1770s he lived well beyond his means; although during his service in Grenada his financial problems eased, he remained unable to discharge the bulk of his debts; and on leaving the Caribbean he and his wife lost all the personal possessions which they had either carried or accumulated there. By August 1780, therefore, being again without salaried employment, Macartney was significantly worse off financially than at the outset of his career.

II

Prior to his departure for Russia in 1764 Macartney's attitude towards his financial prospects was compounded of naive optimism and unrealistic good intentions. Thus, while assuring Lord Holland that he would 'certainly keep my word with you . . . everything you mentioned upon that subject has made a strong impression upon me', he was openly dismissive of Lord Tyrawley's opinion (firmly based on previous experience of Russia) that 'I shall scarcely be able to live upon my appointments': 'I don't mind him. He, I am sure, was always more extravagant than I am'.[5] Yet in December, during his long overland journey to St. Petersburg, Macartney found it 'impossible to describe . . . the inconvenience, the expence and [the] impositions I have undergone in this expedition'.

To give you one instance of imposition for all, I was charged at Magdeburg two ducats for a pot of coffee and some bread and butter. I remonstrated loudly against such treatment and observed to the lad that I was only an envoy and not an ambassador. 'Oh Sir' (says the rascal with a most impudent smile and a low bow) 'we never make any difference'. *Ab uno disce omnes.* When I complained to the magistrate on those occasions the redress was so trifling, and the delay and trouble so great, that I at last found the surest way was to acquiesce in silence.[6]

In their different ways various members of the Holland family encouraged Macartney to beware of acquiescence. Once the negotiations for the commercial treaty were successfully completed, Lady

Caroline awarded him 'honour' and 'praise', but added: 'we only wish you a little more money'.[7] Ironically, Stephen and Charles James Fox were much less sympathetic, reminding Macartney of his natural tendency towards extravagance and particularly warning him against the 'very deep play at [St.] Petersburg'.[8] In reply they were assured that he was rid of that 'unhappy passion', though later evidence suggests that the cure was partial rather than complete.[9] Finally, Lord Holland, while always careful not to nag Macartney, emitted a steady stream of brusque and sensible advice. In June 1765, for example:

> Don't spend, upon any consideration, more than you can afford upon the public service. For one reason or another you never will be made amends for it, I promise you.[10]

And in August 1766, when Hans Stanley threatened to appear as ambassador to Russia:

> I conjure you not to look upon yourself [as] recalled if you can help it. And you might then make this an occasion of retrenching... It may be a pretence too for coming home for a time. But I beg you not to quit what you have, if you can avoid it, till you get something else.[11]

Later that same year he promised to assist Macartney in his plan to enter the English House of Commons on his return, but stated that in his opinion Macartney could 'ill afford it'.[12] Indeed, Holland persistently proclaimed his unease at the fact that Macartney had failed to find 'a way of living within your income'.[13]

Macartney's friends knew him too well to be convinced that his early encounters with the harsher realities of his new way of life would leave a lasting impression on his behaviour. None of their remarks was of any avail, if only because an unhealthy pattern of expenditure had already been established by the time their correspondence got underway. The cost and discomfort of Macartney's outward journey were such that he wished he had travelled by sea; and soon after his arrival in Russia he became committed to:

> a number of expenses which, if once entered upon, it is impossible to retrench, but which I now [1766] think it would be unnecessary to begin with. The great article... is the outset which, I promise you, if ever His Majesty honours me with an employment of this nature elsewhere, I shall most carefully guard against.[14]

The episode in Magdeburg typified Macartney's experience in Russia itself. In the absence of an ambassador (the Empress being disinclined to receive, or send, one) Macartney was commonly regarded as such; and was expected to behave accordingly, even though he was being paid only as an envoy. As predicted, his salary of under £2,000 a year proved quite insufficient to meet the demands made upon him; and, in consequence, 'I sustained my character by involving myself in a debt of £6,000'.[15] This was easily arranged for, given the nature of his official brief, Macartney enjoyed excellent relations with British merchants in Russia, who were no doubt only too glad to extend credit to one whose responsibility it was to protect their interests.

Long before he returned to England Macartney began to look to marriage as a means of rendering 'myself and my fortunes entirely happy for the rest of my days';[16] and within six months of his return he made what, from his point of view, has generally been regarded as a brilliant match. Lady Jane Stuart, whom he married in St. George's, Hanover Square, on 1 February 1768, was the second daughter of the former Prime Minister, John, third Earl of Bute, and his wife, Mary, *suo jure* Baroness Mount Stuart of Wortley. The days of Bute's greatest political influence were long past; indeed, by this time he was perhaps the most unpopular public figure in Britain. On the other hand he retained some sway (still being liked and respected, for example, by his old political collaborator, Lord Holland); socially, he was of the first rank; and, as a result of his marriage, he enjoyed enormous wealth. Contemporaries were quick to note the obvious disparity between Macartney and his bride: her family was aristocratic in both wealth and status, while he, having recently been appointed Ambassador to Russia, had 'at present a great employment' but private means that were 'but small'.[17] And yet, despite the fierce competition which characterised the marriage market, this particular match generated little fuss: it was more evenly balanced, and the mixture of motives which governed it was more complex, than has hitherto been acknowledged.

In the first place, Bute had six daughters and Lady Jane was widely regarded at the least attractive of them. On occasion her physical appearance was discussed in the most unflattering terms. As a child she had suffered from smallpox and, by 1768, was already subject to the severe deafness which blighted the whole of her adult life.[18] In contrast Macartney was freely described as an exceedingly charming and 'very pretty man'; more than a decade after the marriage Horace Walpole felt obliged to admit that he 'has always been *deservedly* a great favourite of the ladies'.[19] Secondly, Macartney derived very little financial benefit from the marriage — indeed, by giving a further boost to his expenditure, what he had earlier described as the 'grand and most important concern in life' exacerbated his financial difficulties.[20] In May 1768 Lady Jane transferred to her husband the £2,000 worth of stocks which she had obtained through a bequest from her maternal grandfather (on the strength of which Macartney opened an account at Coutts' bank in the Strand): and in November

Lord Holland lent Macartney a further £4,000;[21] but nowhere is there evidence that a marriage portion was forthcoming from the Earl of Bute. It seems that the Earl or his lawyers (or both) shared prevailing doubts in Britain as to the strength of the security which Irish property gave for the future provision of a widow's jointure and of portions for any younger sons and daughters of a marriage (in this case set at £400 a year and a total of £5,000 respectively): for, quite atypically (at least according to convention in Britain) the marriage settlement contained a detailed and comprehensive list of the townlands, acreages, tenants, tenures and rents of Macartney's estate, the whole of which was settled for these purposes.[22] Recognising Macartney's weak bargaining position, Bute apparently decided that the provision of a portion, in addition to the capital that Lady Jane had to offer, was inappropriate; and, perhaps in anticipation of further assistance from the Hollands (who were enjoying one of their periodic trips abroad), Macartney accepted this. Thus, the marriage appears to have been convenient for Lady Jane and, at least in financial terms, something less than a *coup* for Macartney. Finally, irrespective of his previous remarks on the subject, by late 1767 Macartney may have looked to an early marriage for other than financial relief. His reluctance to withdraw from the Russian ambassadorship, despite Panin's unequivocal re-iteration of the unacceptability of his appointment following the Khitrov affair, suggests that, against all the odds, Macartney hoped that marriage and further connection might yet make him welcome in St. Petersburg. With a greatly increased salary and with the benefit of previous experience of Russia, he could then afford to forego a lavish marriage settlement. Even the Hollands, with whom he corresponded regularly, apparently knew nothing of the threat to his appointment until after his resignation had been made public. And when, very shortly after his marriage, that occurred, Macartney was at least able to shelter behind the excuse that his bride's parents thought it unwise for her to travel to Russia — though acquaintances noted with surprise that he had no 'place in lieu of it'.[23]

Lord Holland's enthusiasm for the match was accompanied by further forthright advice:

> Lady Jane will assist you in being an economist. Indeed, you want assistance in that article. And, believe me, it is now most essential and most necessary. It is not enough to be frugal; be absolutely covetous.[24]

Accordingly, once he had relinquished the Russian post, Macartney avidly sought other employment and, he hoped, a lucrative salary. At first rumour had it that he might go as minister to Turin; then, in

June 1768, that he was under consideration for the post of Secretary at War. His appointment as Chief Secretary for Ireland was announced on 1 January 1769 but throughout that and the following year he continued to seek a more attractive alternative, his preference being for the Spanish ambassadorship which he had first mentioned to Holland as early as June 1766, and which at one point he was rumoured to have obtained. Thus, his growing distaste for his duties in Dublin grew out of a massive, initial lack of enthusiasm for them, and by the time he arrived in Ireland to assume his new position he was long overdue, though entirely unapologetic.[25] Yet, if it provided him with little else, the Irish chief secretaryship at least enabled him to devote more attention to the management of his property.

III

At the time of his marriage Macartney was apparently still largely unfamiliar with the estate which he had inherited following his uncle's death nine years earlier. He had returned to Dublin to graduate M.A. in February 1759[26] but there is no record of his visiting north Antrim either then or for many years thereafter. Before embarking on his European tour in 1760, he commissioned a map of the demesne at Lisanoure and a rental and tenurial survey of the Loughguile townlands;[27] and in December 1764 he asked Lord Holland to forward to Russia a copy of an 'Irish almanack', which was perhaps useful to him in connection with his property.[28] Otherwise the records are silent on the subject of his estate until after his return from Russia in 1767, when his reading included literature on agricultural improvement in Scotland, and when he arranged for both the Loughguile and Dervock properties to be surveyed and valued.[29] Subsequently, although several years residence in either Britain or Ireland encouraged, and allowed, him to become less neglectful of estate affairs, the first firm evidence of his making an 'expedition to the north' of Ireland dates from the spring or early summer of 1770, well into his period as Chief Secretary: this was certainly the first occasion on which Lady Jane visited Lisanoure.[30] By then both Macartney and his wife were ready for a break from Dublin politics. She was pregnant (but was subsequently to miscarry), while (along with his adversary) he had been wounded in a duel with Lord Mountmorres in December 1769. The prorogation of the Irish Parliament in that month, and the fact that it was not to meet again until February 1771, at last permitted him to get to grips with purely private concerns.[31]

The situation in regard to Macartney's proprietorial affairs was potentially most discouraging, especially to someone who had come to enjoy life in and around some of the grandest country houses in southern England and elsewhere. While he held the reversion to the Killinchy estate in Co. Down and to the remnants of the Porter estate in the south of Ireland, he was not entitled to receive income from those properties until after his father's death. As yet he owned property only in Co. Antrim. The size of his estate there was not inconsiderable, with over 6,000 statute acres in the vicinity of Loughguile, over 2,000 acres at or near Dervock, further holdings at Carrickfergus, and determinable leases from the Donegall family at Ballyeaston and Ballyalbinough in south Antrim.[32] However, Macartney's grandfather had entered the property market long after the basic pattern of landownership in Ulster had been established and, consequently, had been unable to accumulate a compact estate: excluding the leases under the Donegalls and the tiny plots at Carrickfergus, the estate lay in five separate locations. Moreover, both Dervock and Loughguile (particularly the latter, which was by far the larger of the two major groups of properties) were remote from the main centres of economic activity in Ulster. Much of the land consisted of ill- or undrained bog, rough pasture and mountain; many of the tenancies were held in partnership or in rundale (not necessarily a brake on good husbandry but creative of difficulties for proprietors); and, primarily because of a shortage of capital in relation to land and labour, the general economic development of the area was at a relatively early stage. Consequently, income from the estate was quite disproportionate to its size. The vast majority of the individual holdings yielded remarkably low rents; in 1768 the gross annual rental of the north Antrim properties amounted to £694 which, from a total of over 8,400 statute acres, constituted an average rent of just over 1 s. 7d. an acre, low even by the standards of peripheral areas in Ulster.[33] And, because tenants enjoyed lengthy tenures for lives, terms of years, or some combination of the two, there was for the foreseeable future little scope for rent improvement. Even a wealthy man, able to devote the bulk of his time and energy to the task, would have found the obstacles to the successful management of such an estate both numerous and intractable. Yet, despite the variety of factors beyond his immediate control, Macartney was not discouraged. Before returning to north Antrim in 1770 he had already embarked on a programme of estate expansion, which was completed in the following year. Besides more routine matters, other developments included the inauguration of an ambitious scheme for the improvement of the house and demesne at Lisanoure.

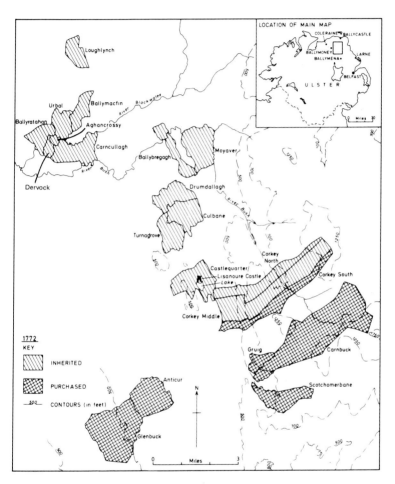

Map of the North Antrim Estate, 1772.

Particularly if they were employed in the public service, landed gentlemen required the services of both individuals and institutions in the management of their private business. Macartney was no exception. Indeed, despite the assiduity with which he supervised his personal affairs, his peripatetic way of life and the fact that his concerns spanned the Irish sea made him unusually dependent on such services. In addition to his main bank account with Coutts in London he opened a further account with the Dublin bank of Latouche;[34] and soon after assuming the Irish chief secretaryship he began to use Robert Waller, one of his juniors in the Dublin administration, to execute commissions on his behalf in the south of Ireland.[35] Although several years passed before Macartney established a satisfactory network of subordinates to cover his interests in Ulster, he secured the assistance of George Portis, a Belfast businessman, in the autumn of 1767, soon after his return from Russia. Macartney acted as one of two sureties for Portis on the latter's appointment in October 1767 to the influential and lucrative post of chief receiver and accountant to the Earl of Donegall's vast estate in south Co. Antrim and Inishowen in Co. Donegal.[36] It was probably Portis who arranged for Macartney's property to be surveyed and valued in the winter of 1767-8; and it was he who orchestrated the series of land transactions during the next three years which substantially augmented Macartney's north Antrim estate.

The purpose of these transactions, planned in the wake of Macartney's marriage and appointment to Ireland, was to enhance his status as a landed proprietor. The prestige and influence which attached to landownership derived more from the control of blocks of territory within a particular region than from the possession of sizeable but widely scattered acreages. Although only two of Macartney's purchases abutted on his existing holdings, he emerged in 1771 as a much more substantial landowner in the area around Loughguile. The first transaction — the sale for £3,000 in 1769 of the determinable leases in south Antrim which Macartney had inherited from his grandfather — raised some of the capital required for the remainder. Most of the undertenants' leases either had expired or were about to do so; thus, in terms of the market for such property, the townlands of Ballyeaston and Ballyalbinough were currently an attractive proposition. In addition, as the chief executive of the head landlord, the Earl of Donegall, Portis was in a good position to locate a buyer, Mr. John Allen, a linen draper of Rashee in Co. Antrim; more pertinently, perhaps, he was also aware of the Earl's plans to re-set part of his property on stiffer terms than had hitherto prevailed.[37]

The whole of this capital and more was immediately disbursed on two purchases of land to the south-east of Loughguile. Firstly, a local clergyman, the Rev. James Stewart, received £1,200 for a perpetuity lease of 754 statute acres at Corkey South, which lay adjacent to Macartney's property in Corkey North and Corkey Middle.[38] Secondly, a Mr. McCormick was paid £2,000 for the whole of the contiguous townlands of Gruig and Carnbuck, except for one small property, Summer Hill, which McCormick retained. These were situated some way to the south of Corkey and contained around 3,000 statute acres.[39] Then, in the following year, Macartney secured from a Mr. Gardiner a lease for three lives or thirty-one years of a parcel of land at Gallow's Hill in the townland of Lavin, which abutted on the demesne at Lisanoure and for which he subsequently paid a rent of fifteen guineas a year.[40] And finally, in May 1771, he acquired three further townlands: Scotchomerbane, whose 693 statute acres lay to the south of Carnbuck and Gruig; and Glenbuck and Anticur which lay further to the south-west, beyond the route from Ballymoney to Ballymena, and which together comprised some 2,622 statute acres. Scotchomerbane was bought from a Mr. John Crawford, though unfortunately there is no indication of its price.[41] The purchase of Glenbuck and Anticur was a rather complex trans-action with Mr. Christopher Fleming, 'commonly known as Lord Slane'. The price was £5,656, for which Macartney gave Fleming his bond; in return Fleming was allowed a perpetuity lease of between 250 and 300 acres in Anticur, where he continued to live and for which he paid Macartney £148 a year in rent.[42]

Furthermore, at some point between his marriage in 1768 and his return to Ireland early in 1770 Macartney had bought a house in Charles Street, off Berkeley Square, in London. Again, the purchase price is unknown, though in order to meet it he raised a mortgage for £2,000 from James Coutts who, with his brother, Thomas, was Macartney's London banker.[43] Despite the £4,000 loan from Lord Holland in 1768 and the money received from Allen for the Donegall leases, neither this mortgage nor the bond debt to Fleming were sufficient to cover the cost of Macartney's current activities. He borrowed a further £2,000 on a mortgage from a Mrs. Renouard.[44] Thus, only by boosting his debts by a further £7,656 was Macartney able to consolidate his estate in the north Antrim area, though in so doing he virtually doubled the acreage (though *not* the value) of his holdings there. In the midst of these developments, in March 1770, he inherited the small Scottish estate at Auchinleck in Kircudbright-shire. 'Black George' Macartney had left this to his eldest son, James, in 1691: but that branch of the family had failed in the male line during the next generation and the property was left to Macartney under the terms of an uncle's will. Currently tenanted at less than £40 a year, it provided a modest but distinct fillip to the Chief Secretary's ambition to promote his own dynastic interests.[45]

Meanwhile, less dramatic progress was being made in a number of other respects. In November 1770, through the influence of his superior, Lord Townshend, Macartney was granted, by letters patent, the right to hold a 'market... every Friday in each week forever in or at the town and lands of... Dervock'; and, in return for a fixed annual rent of 6s. 8d. to the Crown, became entitled to any market tolls he chose to levy there.[46] This development stemmed from the advice of James Sloane, the surveyor and valuer of the north Antrim properties, who in February 1768 had reported that:

> the most judicious person in the Route thinks Dervock the best situated town in the four baronies [of north Antrim] for a market, and with proper encouragement [believes it] would soon destroy Ballymoney.

Macartney was less impressed, however, with the other results of Sloane's work. The survey was brief and generalised and, apparently, unaccompanied by a map; such comments as were attached were distinctly perfunctory; and, despite the validity of Sloane's assertion that land values had 'been increasing every year since the Peace of Aix-la-Chapelle', his estimate of £2,425 for the current annual rental of Dervock and Loughguile, if newly let, was patently absurd.[47] Accordingly, once the round of land transactions was completed, Macartney arranged for each of his townlands to be freshly surveyed and mapped.[48] By mid-1772 he was armed with a much more precise description of his tenantry, their holdings, and the relative distribution of arable, pasture, mountain, moss and bog on his estate. By then also he had established a tripartite division of responsibility for the conduct of his estate affairs in north Antrim. A bailiff ran the house and demesne at Lisanoure; a steward supervised his activities and managed the rest of the estate, liaising with tenants and others who dealt with Macartney, collecting the rents, drawing up accounts, transmitting money and so on; and Richard Jackson, a newly acquired friend and colleague in the Dublin Parliament, kept an overall watching brief. This influential member of the local gentry, M.P. for Coleraine 1751-89, derived his wealth and standing from his head-tenancy of the extensive Co. Londonderry estate of the London Company of Clothworkers and from his position as Agent-General of the Irish Society. In the months following their arrival in the area Jackson frequently shared his house in Coleraine with the Macartneys.[49] Thereafter he began a long series of periodic visits to Loughguile and Dervock and, until his death in 1789, provided Macartney with regular reports on the state of affairs there. During nearly two decades Jackson's role was a vital one. For, between relinquishing the Irish chief secretaryship and securing the appointment in Grenada, Macartney spent most of his time at his town house in London. His next recorded visit to north Antrim followed his return from India in the mid-1780s. For more than a decade, therefore, Macartney remained largely dependent on Jackson for news of the other major, and costly, development on his estate — the wholesale improvement of the house and demesne at Lisanoure.

The only substantial improvement at Lisanoure for which Macartney's grandfather had been responsible was the extensive repair or rebuilding of St. Mary's Church, which was situated on the demesne — near the eastern bank of the lake from which Loughguile ('the bright lake') derived its name.[50] Apparently, when not resident in Dublin or Belfast, he had been content to occupy the small, plain house on the slight promontory to the north of the lake, where Macartney was born. In 1760 the demesne had accounted for about one-third of the 659 statute acres of the townland of Castlequarter where it lay; by the late 1760s, with some of the property having been let during Macartney's absence in Russia, this proportion had fallen to a quarter, much of which was probably also let for summer grazing.[51] Lady Macartney's abiding impression of her first visit was of a 'place without a single tree'.[52] Having been reared in conspicuously comfortable circumstances and in view of the fact that her father was currently spending a fortune on building and other improvements to his various properties in southern England,[53] she was no doubt also dismayed by the poor accommodation at Lisanoure, by the absence of any sort of external embellishment to either the house or the grounds, and by the demesne's wet and boggy situation at the foot of the Antrim hills. Perhaps Macartney himself was somewhat taken aback on his return for, subsequently, he accorded first priority to the improvement of Lisanoure; and, despite other pre-occupations which necessarily involved him in long absences from north Antrim, he pursued this policy with remarkable vigour and flair over many years.

The Lisanoure demesne was mapped in 1772 (together with the rest of the estate), and again in 1788.[54] While it is clear that progress on the house was particularly rapid during Macartney's tenure of the Irish chief secretaryship, the pace of other developments is more difficult to assess. Before long, however, the demesne took up more than half of Castlequarter, and was later further extended. It ceased to be largely pasture ground, kept partially 'in hand' for the convenience of the proprietor, and was gradually transformed into an elegantly landscaped park. At its centre, facing southwards across the lake, stood the house which, to use his own words, Macartney 'almost entirely rebuilt' to altogether larger and more imposing proportions.[55] With two storeys extending round all four sides of a large rectangular courtyard, the building was fronted by five bays between two three-sided bows. Inside the latter were two octagons: on the ground floor these held the dining and withdrawing rooms, each of which was flanked by a further room (the library and a reception room) on either side of the hall. At the rear of the hall, in a projection jutting out at the back into the courtyard, a spacious double staircase led to the second storey, where the main bedrooms and dressing rooms ran across the face of the house. Behind these, two long ranges ran at right angles to the front on either side of the courtyard, the far end of which contained an arched gateway leading to the rear. Besides servants' quarters, kitchens, a laundry, the steward's office and stabling, these ranges housed a dairy, a poultery, a brewhouse and various storerooms; there was also a wine cellar. An early artist's impression (from the south-east) reveals that the building was substantially Georgian Gothic in design and thus similar to Horace Walpole's contemporary edifice at Strawberry Hill in Middlesex, with which Macartney was familiar. A distinctly curious feature was that only on the front of the building were there external windows: on the other three sides the outer walls were blank and battlemented; the inner walls had pointed Gothic windows with dormer gables above.[56]

Macartney lost no time in getting this major project underway. Building commenced in 1770 and the roofing stage was reached in November 1772. Externally, at least, the building was finished before Macartney set out for Grenada. In the light of this schedule it is possible that the semi-castellated design of the house was motivated by other than personal aesthetic considerations: for between the summer of 1770 and the autumn of 1772 large areas of Co. Antrim were rendered ungovernable by the threatening and destructive activities of the Steelboys, members of an agrarian popular movement more melodramatically known as the Hearts of Steel.[57] On balance, however, it seems more likely that Macartney wished to revive memories of Sir Philip Savage's fourteenth-century fortress, whose ruins lay at one corner of the new building; and, indeed, he named the house Lisanoure Castle. Internally, in that it proved incessantly damp and musty, the Castle was uncomfortably akin to its medieval predecessor. In an effort to solve this problem, which in part may have arisen because of the speed with which the house was

Lisanoure Castle and the Lake, 1772, from the south-east (D.1062/2/4).

built, Macartney replaced many of the window frames, experimented with various types of roofing material and, for several days prior to any visit, ordered fires to be lit in all the major rooms, but to no avail.[58] Despite these and later, more substantial alterations, the building was never entirely free from damp.

Macartney's travels provided him with plenty of experience of current fashions in landscape architecture, a matter in which, to judge from his library, he was also well-read.[59] Much influenced by contemporary notions of the 'picturesque', he set out to develop a 'natural' landscape on his demesne, but in fact produced a highly artificial and distinctly man-made work of art, which must have stood in stark contrast to its bleak rural surroundings. The most dramatic feature of the project involved the transformation of the site of Lisanoure Castle into an island by the construction of two canals which ran northwards from the lake on either side of the house, and which then combined to form another lake behind it. In order to achieve this the road from Ballymoney to Ballycastle (which previously had proceeded across Macartney's property to the rear of the house) was diverted round the southern perimeter of the demesne. The island in the original lake was planted and provided with a 'crannog'; the Castle was fronted by a lawn and flanked by extensive shrubberies; the canals were crossed by elegant wooden bridges; a substantial walled kitchen garden was constructed to the north-west of the house; eventually, three-and-a-quarter miles of tree-lined, gravelled paths proceeded to all parts of the demesne, and, at carefully chosen points throughout, large and extremely varied timber plantations were established.[60] There are no details of the cost of all this work, though its nature and scope ensured that it was expensive. However, it is clear that, while the project was well underway by the time Macartney left for Grenada, such radical improvements took many years to complete and mature. Besides subsequent major additions, for the rest of his life Macartney periodically ordered minor modifications: new shrubs or plants, or a fresh site for those already there; swans to beautify the lakes; apparatus for clearing floating debris from the water.[61] His initial enthusiasm for the new Lisanoure remained undimmed during his prolonged absences and he clearly derived deep personal satisfaction from the ordered elegance he established there.

IV

The transformation of Lisanoure would not have occurred without detailed guidance from Macartney as to his requirements. Though the letters which he received are highly informative, the vast majority of those he wrote have not survived: however, if one extant memorandum of 'standing orders' is representative of his planning, there can be little doubt that it was both meticulous and well-informed. Dating from the early 1770s, this listed thirty-six matters to be attended to, including the following:

14. The dam at the end of the canal to be made firm and staunch, and so continued that in case of necessity all the water may be drawn off. A ditch behind the bank to be made as deep as the spring, otherwise it will never be firm . . .

16. The ditches or work fence to be finished completely, so as to separate the plantation entirely from the plough land. The outside ditches to be built from the bottom with stone to prevent falling in.

17. Mortice locks for the front and back door[s] . . . bolts to be made of the proper breadth of the door[s], and the present bolts, which are too broad, to be taken off. Grates for all the rooms . . .

26. The trees in the nursery to be planted out, and the whitethorn hedge to be transplanted in clumps in different places in the Castle Island. The clumps to be varied with tall elms, ash, oaks, firs, cedars, together with laycocks, laburnum and other tall shrubs mixed with them . . .

NB The best way of planting alders is by truncheons 3 feet high, of which 2 feet should be driven into the earth, which ought to be loosened about them; the proper time is February. Scots fir ought to be at least 2 years old and not more than 3 years old when planted out. The Weymouth pine is to be 4 years old. Receipt [sic] for to make a strong and rich and excellent herbage on an English acre: sow 17 pounds of white Dutch clover, 14 bushels of clean hayseeds, 1½ lbs of rib grass, 1½ lbs of trefoil.[62]

There is little information from the period during which the improvement scheme was inaugurated. The record begins after the fabric of the house was completed and alterations to the demesne were in progress. The Gothic design created problems in regard to the roofing of the building and in November 1772 Jackson advised that much of that work be done again.

All the valleys in the roof of your house must be laid with deals and leaded over, and there are many places where it will be necessary to have upright slating; and where the offices and house join there must be a line of sloping slating where it is now flat, through which the water soaks at present.[63]

Successive inclement seasons and difficulty in obtaining adequate supplies of appropriate materials, particularly slates and lead, greatly delayed this work, which was not completed until July 1775. Moreover, severe frost in the winter of 1774 made it impossible to raise the sluice gate in one of the canals and an accumulation of ice and water caused severe breaches in the banks, necessitating extensive repairs. The planting of the demesne also took longer than expected, with some stocks having to be acquired from Antrim, Lisburn and elsewhere in Ulster, and others being available only from England.[64] On the whole matters took much longer to complete than originally anticipated, though otherwise they proceeded largely according to plan; and on Macartney's return from the Caribbean, Jackson, who had recently furnished him with a copious report, 'was happy to find . . . that you approved of what I had done at Lisanoure'.[65]

However, other problems, several of which were undoubtedly exacerbated by Macartney's absence, were more intractable. Blakemore, the bailiff, and McKay, the steward, proved increasingly incompatible. Apparently, by 1772, i.e. once the work at Lisanoure was well advanced, Macartney had decided to dismiss Blakemore as surplus to requirements, and to allow McKay, who then lived in Antrim, to take up residence in the Castle; but Jackson, occasionally overburdened by his various responsibilities, eventually persuaded Macartney against this. Meanwhile, proceeding on the basis of the original understanding, McKay gradually made Blakemore redundant and repeatedly, but unsuccessfully, requested confirmation of the bailiff's dismissal.[66] In March 1775 the situation was further confused for Macartney when Mrs. Jackson raised fundamental doubts about the McKays in a letter to Lady Macartney.

Mr. Jackson . . . was inclined from his regard for Sir George to enquire after . . . [McKay's] . . . character, and this he had opportunity for at my brother's house near Broughshane, where we went from Lisanoure. Several people agreed in giving their opinion that he was a great bragger, and apt to say more for himself than he could perform. He is supposed to be very ignorant about the management of lands, and has hurt his fortune by taking farms that he could not make to account . . . His wife has a very good character, but is thought to be that indolent, slovenly sort of person that I fear would do your house no good.[67]

Writing to Macartney on 2 June, Blackmore lent substance to some of these charges in a lengthy complaint about McKay. For example:

The horses are but in very indifferent order; they are tracked so much that it is impossible for them to be otherwise. Last week three of them were at Antrim for lead. They had thirteen [? sheets] on each carr which broke two of them to the ground before they got a mile from the town. Mr. McKay was pleased to damn the scoundrels of Lisanoure in the public street for sending such carrs, and said it was of a piece with the rest of their proceedings, and that he had a carr that would carry the three loads. But to his great mortification one of the loads crushed his carr to the ground before it had gone half a mile. Still we had one load that came home, and I wish that had stayed behind too, for the horse was in such condition that it was with difficulty he got into the stable.[68]

Later, in his annual accounts, McKay unwittingly corroborated this evidence by charging £2 11s. 6d. for 'four pair of carr wheels' and 'repairs to carrs which carried lead from Antrim', which compared very unfavourably with the £1 12s. 0d. for the 'carriage of lead' from Belfast to Lisanoure.[69] By this time much business had degenerated into a battle of wits between the two adversaries which eroded the respect of workmen and servants alike. Jackson was acutely embarrassed because, while he was convinced that McKay was largely to blame, Blakemore was clearly the more dispensable of the two. Their inability to work harmoniously together continued to hinder business at Lisanoure until 1779 or 1780, when they were dismissed and when Jackson Wray, Richard Jackson's cousin and the overseer of his Coleraine property, was appointed agent of the estate. A substantial gentleman farmer at Bentfield on the north Antrim coast, whence his family had moved from Co. Donegal, Wray became, according to Jackson, 'so attentive, judicious and correct as to merit my highest approbation': he was thoroughly familiar with the day-to-day problems of estate management, but also of sufficient authority and status to be on easy terms with his new employer.[70]

A prominent feature of the situation with which Wray and his predecessors had to deal was the broad regional distinction in the religious affiliation of the population on the two main parts of the estate. Dervock and its associated townlands contained a majority of Presbyterians, whose ancestors, like Macartney's, had migrated from Scotland during the seventeenth century; whereas around Loughguile (and, except for Scotchomerbane, on the properties purchased by Macartney) the population was mainly Catholic and Irish. Members of the Church of Ireland, including Macartney, were in a minority. For someone of his background and status, Macartney's views regarding disadvantaged religious groups were distinctly liberal.[71] Besides being grounded in intellectual conviction, they may have owed something to his proprietorial experience, though it must be stressed that the major problems encountered by Macartney and his staff did not arise from religious animosities.

For example, in January 1772 during the Steelboy disturbances, Lord Blayney 'heard that . . . [Macartney] . . . was drove out [sic] of the country lately';[72] and in March an anonymous but friendly correspondent, a 'country farmer', warned that, together with two other officials who were also proprietors, Macartney was one of the Steelboys' 'principal objects'.[73] Neither rumour is corroborated by further evidence but there seems little doubt that, until the troubles died down later that year, Macartney felt less than secure on his own property. Nevertheless, although the Steelboys were a predominantly Presbyterian movement, their grievances were economic: they were particularly opposed to landowners who raised capital by letting blocks of property to middlemen for large entry fines and increased rents, and who thereby dashed the hopes of undertenants who wished to become direct tenants of the proprietors concerned.[74] As we shall see, Macartney was not in a position to adopt such a policy in the early 1770s and, proprietorially, showed every sign of being adamantly opposed to it. If he suffered at the hands of the Steelboys, it was due to his tenure of the Irish chief secretaryship rather than because of any action in his private capacity.

At Loughguile difficulty arose because the majority of the local population, being Catholics, refused to pay either the great or the vicarial tithe. Nor, according to Jackson, could they be forced to pay, 'as the laws upon many trials have been found insufficient for the purpose'.[75] In 1775 the rector resigned, being 'quite tired of it'.[76] McKay obtained the post for his recently ordained son, but some years later the position was vacant and the church in a ruinous condition.[77] One local Protestant, a Mr. McCollum (who was not a tenant but an owner-occupier), told Macartney that he proposed to sell up and leave the place, being unable to 'live in Rome and strive with the Pope'.[78] No doubt he hoped that Macartney would be prepared to offer a handsome price for his farm, which abutted on the Lisanoure demesne, and whose acquisition would certainly have facilitated current improvements there. Exactly what transpired between the two is uncertain, though Macartney made no further purchases at this stage and McCollum did not sell. Around the turn of the century Macartney, like his grandfather before him, eventually repaired St. Mary's Church; and long before then, in the 1780s, he helped the Catholics of Loughguile to build a 'large handsome Mass house' for their worship.[79]

In so far as it influenced leasing policy the religious affiliation of the tenantry affected the estate in a more serious and fundamental way. At this stage the overwhelming majority of leases in Ulster were long, though some were much longer than others. Most Protestants held leases for three lives or thirty-one years, whichever was the longer, with rising life expectancy ensuring that for them thirty-one years increasingly constituted a minimum term. Indeed, in certain instances Macartney's grandfather had allowed the number of lives to be made up to three once a thirty-one year term had been completed.[80] Most Catholics, on the other hand, held leases for thirty-one years, which was the maximum the law currently allowed to them. Once economic conditions began to improve from around mid-century all these forms of tenure, which were in common use, posed problems for proprietors. Such terms had been established much earlier, often in times of economic difficulty when good tenants (and sometimes on poor land any tenants at all) had been hard to come by. Moreover, like many other estates, Macartney's contained a few leases in perpetuity, including one for £30 a year of the mountain townlands at Corkey, which comprised almost 2,500 statute acres;[81] in the past such leases had been used to encourage settlement on large, undeveloped properties. Macartney's problem was not that he had inherited a peculiar or even unusual leasing structure: rather that much of his land was of very low quality, and hence subject to very low rents; and that for the forseeable future opportunities for rent improvement were likely to be few, and to occur only on the poorest, and therefore most lowly-valued, holdings. For many of the leases on the Loughguile estate had been in mid-term when Macartney's grandfather had purchased it in 1733, so that during their respective incumbencies both he and Charles Macartney had been able to set fresh terms at new rents. Macartney benefited from rent increases on only one or two holdings there in the years immediately following his inheritance in 1759, though several other leases terminated, and were renegotiated, during the next two decades. However, the majority of the (longer) leases at Dervock were of very recent origin at the point of purchase in 1742: indeed, on *at least* twenty of the twenty-five holdings there, rents remained unchanged from then until some time after Macartney's return from Grenada. The combined gross rental of Loughguile and Dervock rose from £694 in 1768 to £1,119 in 1789, but by far the greatest proportion of that increase came *after* 1780 from *some* holdings in Loughguile.[82]

Far from alleviating this situation, the income from the property which Macartney purchased proved to be negligible, and circumstances there were such as largely to defeat the efforts of both Jackson and McKay to cope with them. There was very little good land in the townlands concerned. Carnbuck, for example, which extended over nearly 3,000 statute acres, had a mere 88 acres of arable: there were also 2 acres of bog, 158 of 'green mountain', 429 of 'mixed pasture', and 2,282 acres of 'coarse mountain'.[83] Consequently, much of the land was not in fact tenanted at all, but given over (rather fitfully, according to current market conditions) to temporary grazing. Indeed, the problems associated with these properties were more acute than even this would suggest. Apparently, soon after the purchases were finalized, the bulk of the leases fell in. McKay was ordered not just to negotiate for higher rents but also to rearrange holdings in severalty where they had previously been worked in partnership or in rundale. Many tenants refused to accept this: some left their holdings, others were required to do so, there were substantial arrears of rent, and McKay was eventually reduced to offering seasonal lettings, and to sowing and stocking some holdings on Macartney's own account.[84] Particularly during Macartney's absence, this latter policy could scarcely be justified economically; indeed, when Chief Secretary he had ordered the cows at Lisanoure to be sold.[85] The policy was pursued nonetheless in order to 'keep up the credit of your land'.[86] In regard to rent receipts, the only extant figures relate to the financial year 1774-5, when Carnbuck, Gruig, Glenbuck and Scotchomerbane together brought in a mere £210.[87] The addition of the rents of Anticur would have made little difference to this total, for Mr. Christopher Fleming's £148 a year was rebated as part of the interest on Macartney's bond for the purchase price of that property and Glenbuck.

Not surprisingly, in view of all these difficulties, the transformation of Lisanoure was unaccompanied by significant improvements to other parts of the estate. The modest income from the property was devoted almost exclusively to Macartney's personal needs, to financing activities on the demesne, and to maintaining a barely effective level of estate administration. The system of long leases which prevailed on the inherited property made for a very loose relationship between landlord and tenants whereby the latter were responsible for providing the bulk of working and new fixed capital. Significantly, in this connection, not a shred of evidence indicates that tenants paid lump sums, or fines, at the outset of leases; Macartney received only annual rents which, throughout this period, became increasingly uneconomic as lease terms progressed. He wished to establish a closer relationship with his tenantry, partly because a future increase in his estate income to some extent depended on it, but also because features of the traditional system were, in his view, agriculturally indefensible. Everywhere tenants were actively encouraged, and where possible required, to farm in severalty, and slow but persistent progress was made in this respect both at Dervock and Loughguile. When leases fell in during his absence in Grenada tenants were allowed to continue from year to year until future conditions of tenure could be negotiated, albeit still at some distance, on his return to Britain. McKay was castigated for granting, without permission, two terms of thirty-one years at Loughguile, Macartney preferring terms of twenty-one years or, on better properties, even less.[88] McKay was also expected to look to other than administrative matters and to meet tenants' requests where they were reasonable and likely to prove productive. In March 1775 one of his subordinates reported that 'nobody makes roads over the ditches now in any part about Lisanoure';[89] and three months later a bull was installed on the demesne, local farmers having insisted that one should be bought if they were to stock the area with cattle.[90] Together with the pre-occupation of estate staff with projects on the demesne, the current leasing structure of the estate presented few other opportunities for developing a closer relationship with the tenantry. When they did occur, interventions in tenurial matters tended to be ameliorative — the collection of rent arrears or the examination of holdings left vacant and in disrepair[91] — rather than more positive or constructive. In their own interests of course some tenants were themselves active improvers. At Urbal James Miller and his partners erected a malt kiln; at Moyaver Henry Clark built a new farmhouse on land that was 'well enclosed'; on the Ballyratahan side of Dervock village Mr. Gamble 'has built a new distillery and sunk a tan yard'; and long before the appearance of the new Catholic chapel at Loughguile the tenants of Carncullagh had provided themselves with a 'new meeting house'.[92] However, if static rents, long leases and better economic conditions permitted such developments, population growth encouraged sub-letting which, besides being injurious in itself in so far as it placed working farmers at a further remove from Macartney, also led to other abuses. For example, the Rev. Alexander Clark sub-let several parts of his 245-acre holding in Moyaver, where there was 'plenty of limestone which . . . [the] . . . undertenants burn and sell'.[93] In the past middlemen tenures had been deliberately established on many estates in Ulster as a means of promoting agricultural development, particularly in sparsely populated, peripheral areas. But with new rents rising, even on poor land, alert proprietors attempted to alter this system, though with little success. While Macartney's leases forbade both sub-letting and the exploitation of mineral resources, he ruefully admitted many years later that the former stipulation had been widely ignored.[94] Apart from formally noting instances where covenants were broken, the most he could do was to re-establish links with working farmers when leases fell in; in the meantime he encouraged the more responsible tenants and subjected the remainder to spasmodic, and largely ineffectual, exhortation.

Had Macartney been resident at Lisanoure (or even visited it regularly) during these years, some of these problems would perhaps have been solved, or at least have assumed less serious proportions.

On the other hand, his presence would have done little or nothing to increase the rental of his estate which, net of fixed expenditure, amounted to significantly less than £1,000 a year throughout this period.[95] Such a sum was paltry in comparison with the cost of expanding and embellishing his property, and it was with considerable tact that one correspondent suggested in August 1772 that Macartney could 'hardly have the time to ruin yourself in tripling the value of your estate'.[96] More to the point, Macartney had never felt able to live comfortably on his estate income even prior to his marriage; and from 1768 the prospect of being obliged to do so was still less congenial, though at times no less remote, than before. Nor, when added to his estate income, did his salaries meet his burgeoning requirements. His only alternative was to fall much further into debt.

V

Although the documentary basis for a precise analysis of Macartney's financial affairs during this period does not exist, it is possible to identify his major debts in the summer of 1780. Together these amounted to some £19,700: he owed £7,000 to the executors of Lord Holland; a total of £7,000 to Mr. Fleming (£5,000) and Mrs. Renouard (£2,000), through whom he had financed the expansion of his north Antrim estate; £1,000 to the executors of James Coutts, who had originally lent Macartney £2,000 on the security of the house in Charles Street; and finally, £4,700 to Thomas Coutts, his London banker, on a mortgage executed in July 1780.[97] However, this figure, which greatly exceeded the £12,000 mentioned to Lady Ossory in August 1780,[98] certainly did not represent the sum total of Macartney's debts. In addition there had been a variety of smaller loans on bonds: several of these had been discharged by 1780; others were then converted (via the mortgage from Thomas Coutts) into a single, sizeable loan; and a few, at least, remained unpaid until a later stage.[99] There is no doubt, therefore, that, though Macartney was financially embarrassed on his return from Grenada, he had been in much worse straits before he set out.

The records of Macartney's account with Coutts throw considerable light on earlier developments, though the picture remains incomplete because throughout the 1770s and beyond he also held an account (which has not survived) with Latouche in Dublin. The account with Coutts was balanced at irregular intervals, at Macartney's convenience. As one would expect, a list of these balances (See Table)[100] strongly suggests that until he relinquished the Irish chief secretaryship Macartney kept his main account with Latouche. Indeed, before he arrived in Grenada the account at Coutts was, with a single, modest exception, either precisely in balance or in surplus. There is likewise little doubt that from 1775 Macartney conducted most of his business through his London account; and from mid-1776 until the early months of 1780 that account was persistently, and often heavily, in deficit, due primarily to regular and heavy repayments of short-term loans. The entries in the ledgers are almost always brief, often ambiguous, and refer to numerous individuals who have proved impossible to identify, many of whom were perhaps agents of the creditors concerned. Yet over twenty of the entries for the period 1776-80 refer explicitly to repayments of loans: these amounted to £8,300 in 1776, £3,700 in 1777, £5,000 in 1778, £4,335 in 1779, and £1,571 in 1780.[101] Unfortunately in seeking to estimate the extent of Macartney's indebtedness before these payments began, one cannot simply add these totals to the major debts outstanding in the summer of 1780. Not only does the figure of £19,700 exclude some short-term loans which remained undischarged at that point; also, from 1775 onwards — and no doubt earlier too — some loans were interlinked, one being raised to discharge another, and so on. Once these factors have been taken into consideration, however, it would appear that Macartney's gross

	Account at Coutts' Bank 1768-80		
Date	*Credit*	*Debit*	*Carried Over*
1768	£2,152.10. 0.	£1,452.10. 0.	+£700. 0. 0.
—	5,500. 0. 0.	5,500. 0. 0.	
1769	1,107. 1. 1.	1,107. 1. 1.	
1770	1,280. 0. 0.	1,280. 0. 0.	
1771	1,045. 6. 8.	1,045. 6. 8.	
1772-3	1,041. 7. 0.	500. 0. 0.	+541. 7. 0.
1773	541. 7. 0.	541. 7. 0.	
1774	2,511.10.10.	2,148.15. 2.	+362.15. 8.
—	4,547.12.11.	4,310.16. 1.	+236.16.10.
1774-5	236.16.10.	261.16.10.	—25. 0. 0.
1775	2,647.16. 8.	2,647.16. 8.	
1776	5,225. 0. 0.	5,225. 0. 0.	
—	1,111.13. 8.	1,852. 4. 2.	—740.10. 6.
1777	2,288.11.11.	2,837.10. 6.	—548.18. 7.
—	3,971.14. 0.	4,030.18. 2.	—59. 4. 2.
1778	2,289. 8. 6.	3,203. 4. 8.	—913.16. 2.
—	4,766.19.10.	6,056. 7.11.	—1,289. 8. 1.
1779	3,107. 7. 0.	4,433.10. 7.	—1,326. 3. 7.
1779-80	6,672. 9.10.	7,785. 4. 5.	—1,112.14. 7.
1780	3,700. 0. 0.	3,700. 0. 0.	

liabilities could scarcely have been less than £30,000 in the mid-1770s and may even have approached a total of £35,000.

Whether Macartney was still more heavily indebted earlier in the 1770s must remain uncertain. Together with the £2,000 worth of stocks provided by Lady Jane, the £4,000 borrowed from Lord Holland in November 1768 was quickly devoted to various expenses which arose after Macartney's marriage in that year.[102] Subsequently, most of the cost of the land purchases in north Antrim was borrowed and no doubt other loans were raised in the early 1770s to finance the rebuilding at Lisanoure. Yet Macartney repaid half of the mortgage on the Charles Street house as early as May 1770[103] and during the next two years spent most of his time in Ireland, where at least his day-to-day expenditure was lower than it was apt to be elsewhere. On the whole it seems likely that his indebtedness reached its peak in the period prior to his departure for Grenada, when he was without a salary, living in London and, latterly, obliged to equip both himself and Lady Jane for their forthcoming trip abroad. Indeed, shortly before setting out for the Caribbean Macartney was obliged to sell (for an unknown sum) his sinecure, so laboriously exchanged for his pension, in order to discharge debts still outstanding from his period in Russia.[104]

While in the Caribbean Macartney clearly stuck to his earlier decision to use most of his salary in discharging his debts, but was deprived by the French of the opportunity of continuing to do so for as long as his situation required. The task was in any case a difficult one because of the nature, as well as the scope, of his indebtedness. He was unable to use his inherited estate as security for loans as it had already been settled to other purposes; and his purchased property was encumbered by the loans which had financed its acquisition.[105] Consequently, he had to take up many of his loans on annuity bonds, which frequently carried interest rates of around 16%.[106] Thus, at the root of his anxiety as he left the Caribbean was the realisation that, minus absolutely essential expenditure, his estate income alone was insufficient even to service his debts. The fact that he and Lady Jane had recently lost the bulk of their personal possessions was of relatively minor consequence in the face of this.

The public acclaim and official approbation which greeted Macartney's return to England towards the close of 1779 were accompanied by news of some private good fortune. He must have been gratified by the result, if not the fact, of his father's death earlier that year, whereby he at last inherited the Killinchy and Porter estates. Overnight these added some £700 to his annual income, though the properties were scattered and many of the rents were fixed forever.[107] Nevertheless, he remained heavily indebted in relation to his private income and, once again, was unemployed.

CHAPTER VI

INDIA 1780-1786

I

In the summer of 1780 Macartney began to campaign for the office of President of Fort St. George, the East India Company's possession at Madras in south India. Success in securing this post promised to mark a significant advance in both his public career and his personal fortunes. In the hierarchy of appointments which was then emerging in Britain's world-wide empire, the Madras governorship offered a considerable promotion over that of Grenada; and, if it could be successfully undertaken, might lead to substantial further advancement. However, despite the high hopes and enthusiasm with which Macartney embarked on his successful campaign for the appointment, the post was to offer him little but constant vexation, worry, ill-health and the ultimate frustration of an honourable, if somewhat tactless, man striving to fulfill his obligations in the face of circumstances which he could rarely control. For he could not have gone to India at a time when Britain faced greater danger on a global scale or when the constitutional position of the East India Company's possessions was so ill-constructed.

The complexity of these problems can only really be appreciated in the light of circumstances which long pre-dated Macartney's Indian aspirations. The Presidency over which he hoped to assume responsibility fell into four distinct parts and displayed a bewildering welter of conflicting allegiances. At its core was the long-established settlement of Fort St. George on the Bay of Bengal surrounded by a small territory, known as the *jagir,* which had been ceded to the East India Company. From there the President had to look to the surrounding country of the Carnatic, an extensive Hindu area theoretically ruled from the city of Arcot by its Muslim Nawab, Muhammad Ali Walajah, but which had been under the Company's protection since the time of Robert Clive. To the south lay the little Hindu kingdom of Tanjore, whose Raja claimed descent from late seventeenth-century Maratha raiders. A long-standing enemy of the Nawab, the Raja had seen his kingdom fall to the Carnatic, and hence under the President's responsibility, as the result of controversial wars in 1771 and 1773.[1] Next, extending along the Bay of Bengal to the northwards of the Carnatic, but owing no allegiance to it, were the five Northern Sarkars, extensive administrative districts originally granted to the French by the Nizam of Hyderabad during the south Indian wars. As the result of a Mughal *firman* of 1765 and a treaty with the Nizam the following year, however, they had been transferred to the East India Company in return for annual tribute, and became the charge of Fort St. George. Macartney was to be considerably vexed by the ambivalent status of Tanjore and the Sarkars, but as the Carnatic was to dominate his Indian career some analysis of its peculiarly intractable problems is essential.

The Carnatic's history has to be set within the context of the collapse of central power in the sub-continent following Aurangzib's ill-conceived attempts to impose Mughal authority and the Muslim faith upon south India in the late seventeenth century. The rapid erosion of effective Mughal administration after his death was the essential pre-condition for the advance of British power in Bengal and the Carnatic from the 1740s, though only the latter directly concerned Macartney. In 1692, in an attempt to buttress Mughal power in south India, Aurangzib had appointed Zulf'iqar Ali Khan to the new dignity of Nawab of the Carnatic. Although the Carnatic supposedly acknowledged the authority of the Subahdar of the Deccan, subsequently better known as the Nizam of Hyderabad, by the 1720s both powers had effectively asserted their independence of the Mughals. In 1744, the original Nawab's descendants were overthrown by the Marathas and in an effort to restore the situation the Nizam appointed Anwar-ud-din, a trusted soldier, to the office. It was at this juncture that the quarrels of the rival claimants to the Carnatic became subsumed in the battle for supremacy between the British and the French which brought the War of the Austrian Succession to south India. The contest left the British East India Company as the effective military power in the Carnatic with their protégé, Anwar-ud-din's son, Muhammad Ali Walajah, as the new Nawab. It was with Muhammad Ali Walajah that Macartney had to deal during his Presidency and it is of the utmost relevance to the dispute between the two men that neither the title of Nawab nor his family's claim to it were of ancient provenance.

It was the Nawab's tragedy that in the fighting between 1750 and 1761 which ended in the defeat of the French and his rivals in the Carnatic he incurred debts and obligations which robbed him of any enjoyment of his victory; indeed, his success had only been won by troops paid for by the East India Company. On the cessation of hostilities he presented himself to the Company's representatives at

Madras with the request that he be installed in effective control of the Carnatic, but the latter were far too conscious of their newly-awakened military power to acquiesce without conditions.[2] Remembering that he was the executive of a commercial undertaking which had spent enormous sums during the war in south India, the Company's President, George Pigot, replied that he could only restore the Carnatic to the Nawab on the cession of a tract of land around Fort St. George, the *jagir,* and the payment of the bulk of the 2,593,801 pagodas (£1,037,520) which the campaigns had cost.[3] It was in an attempt to meet the second condition that the Nawab embarked upon the course of action which was ultimately to bedevil Macartney's Presidency and grow into what was arguably the most notorious financial scandal in British imperial history. In seeking to pay the sum, he turned for credit to the native *soucars* and to East India Company servants who were only too anxious to oblige him on the security of his country's revenues. By the end of 1766 he had reduced his debt to the Company to 830,977 pagodas (£332,391) but his debts to his British and Indian *soucars* stood at 2,250,000 pagodas (£900,000).[4]

Although this is not the place to recount at length the sorry history of the Nawab's increasing indebtedness, certain relevant features cannot be ignored. Such was the magnitude of his debts that by the 1770s the dominant power in the Carnatic seemed to be neither the Nawab nor the Company but rather the creditors led by the man who was to become Macartney's *bete noire*, Paul Benfield, an official as unscrupulous as he was skilled in the mechanics of finance. The situation was later outlined with superb polemic, but accurately enough, by Edmund Burke:

> The presidency presses for payment. The Nabob's answer is, I have no money. Good. But there are soucars who will supply you on the mortgage of your territories. Then steps forward some Paul Benfield, and from his grateful compassion to the Nabob, and his filial regard to the Company, he unlocks the treasures of his virtuous industry: and for a consideration of twenty-four or thirty-six per cent. on a mortgage of the territorial revenue, becomes security to the Company for the nabob's arrear.[5]

After the conquest of Tanjore in 1773, the creditors' activities were extended to that country, with Benfield again well to the fore in being assigned its crops. By this time the Nawab had apparently been reduced virtually to a cypher even in his court at Arcot, where influence had passed to his second son, Benfield's friend the Amir al-Umara.[6] In August 1776 the Amir and Benfield startlingly revealed their power by combining with Colonel James Stuart and others to

Map of India, 1781-85.

seize the President, Lord Pigot, who was contemplating the
restoration of Tanjore and its revenues to its Raja.[7] The luckless
Pigot died in their custody the following year. By any standards this
was a scandalous assertion of the power the Nawab's creditors were
prepared to exert in defence of their financial interests; it was also a
precedent which, it became clear, Macartney could ignore only at
his peril. What was at stake may be deduced from the fact that in
1784 the Nawab's debts were officially estimated at the remarkable
sum of 14,844,583 pagodas (£5,937,833).[8] The exact nature of his
debts to particular individuals may never be known as the details of
many transactions were concealed, but in 1785 Burke, admittedly a
sworn enemy of Benfield, conjectured that the 'smallest of the sums'
being mentioned in connection with Benfield's subventions to the
Nawab stood at an accumulated principal and interest of
£592,000.[9] That such a sum might credibly be suggested indicates
the nature of the deep-rooted financial interests and corruption
which Macartney had to fight against at Madras. Concerned at the
scale of the problem, in 1777 the East India Company recalled
Benfield to London to explain his actions, but even this did not ease
the situation. Sir Thomas Rumbold, who replaced Pigot as Governor
in February 1778, far from opposing these financial interests, soon
became identified with them. It quickly became clear that he was
remitting to England sums far in excess of his salary and in January
1781, as Macartney was about to leave for India, the Directors of
the East India Company dismissed Rumbold, together with four of
his council. Order and financial regularity had to be introduced into
the government of the Madras presidency and only the appointment
of a man of proven record in the public service, who, moreover,
stood outside the contending factions there, offered any prospect of
success.

II

Although the records relating to the selection of Macartney are
disappointingly elusive on this point, there is little reason to doubt
that this priority was uppermost in the minds of the powerful men in
British politics who advanced his claim. The prospects might have
deterred a man less sanguine about his personal abilities or less
financially embarrassed, for there is little mystery about Macartney's
interest in the appointment. While it had steeled his character and
enhanced his reputation among the country's ruling élite, his ill-fated
governorship of Grenada had not solved his long-standing financial

difficulties. Though the property which he had inherited on his father's death promised him some relief, by the summer of 1780 his situation was such that only the acquisition of some lucrative official position could restore them. He certainly felt that his service under the crown had left him ill-rewarded and was prepared to use this argument both to explain his interest in seeking the Madras appointment and to justify his claim on official patronage.[10] Madras, with its substantial salary of £15,000 and subsidiary benefits amounting to another £1,000, and the possibility of future advancement to the Governor Generalship in Bengal at £25,000, explain the lure of India to an unemployed, financially embarrassed but still fiercely ambitious man.

It is unlikely that Macartney, with his lack of previous Indian connections, took the initiative; much more probably, those concerned with the affairs of the sub-continent turned to him as someone who had recently shown his mettle in most trying circumstances. The memoirs of Nicholas Wraxall point to governmental influence behind his candidacy and emphasize the high level of patronage which was to ensure its successful conclusion:

> On all great occasions, when the concealed springs of that complicated machine, denominated the East India Company, were necessary to be touched, application was made to Lord Sandwich. Even the intimations sent from the Treasury often remain inefficient, till confirmed by him, and when the First Minister, towards the close of the year 1780, was prevailed on to recommend Lord Macartney for Governor of Madras, as successor to Rumbold, he found that no serious attention was paid to his wishes, before the Admiralty lent its cooperation.[11]

Although the records amply bear out the essential contribution which John Montagu, fourth Earl of Sandwich, First Lord of the Admiralty, made to Macartney's success, they do not reveal who initiated the recommendation to Lord North. Nonetheless, government influence, notably in the shape of Sandwich and John Robinson, North's man of affairs and Secretary to the Treasury, was the decisive element in his candidature.

Wraxall's date notwithstanding, Macartney's active canvassing for the post began in the summer of 1780. On 23 August Horace Walpole informed Lady Ossory that he was writing letters and soliciting votes for him; four days previously Macartney, in an attempt to broaden the basis of his support to include the opposition to North's government, had himself written to Lady Ossory pleading for her assistance in enlisting the patronage of Lord Shelburne.[12] Apparently, 'he had made at least 600 visits to India voters'. 'I have', he continued written as many letters with my own hand and yet I have as much more to do. Perhaps after all to little purpose. If ever man deserved to recover his fortune and independence, surely I do, for no man ever took greater pains for the purpose.

Such pains were necessary in view of the hurdles which had to be surmounted before he could be appointed, as this was no straight-forward governmental matter. The East India Company was still an independent business concern, governed in the first instance by its Court of Proprietors, which well over a thousand investors (each holding £1,000 of stock) were entitled to attend; and then by the Court of Directors, comprising the twenty-four most powerful men in its affairs. Chief among the latter at this time were the chairman, William Devaynes, and his deputy, the veteran Company politician, Laurence Sulivan. The Madras appointment hung on the votes of these two bodies.

Macartney's preliminary soundings were sufficiently encouraging for him to write individually to the directors of the East India Company on 25 August offering himself as a possible candidate for Madras.[13] The next day he prepared another letter to the proprietors intimating his interest and informing them that he would be calling to solicit their votes.[14] His hat was now clearly in the ring. Reliance on patrons like Lady Ossory and Horace Walpole was no longer sufficient; he had to undertake the systematic accumulation of votes in the Courts whose members would decide the success or failure of his venture. It was here that the government's support was crucial. The necessary introduction to the centres of power in the East India Company was provided by Sandwich who visited William Devaynes on his behalf. It was a decisive meeting, for Devaynes responded by advising Macartney to submit his formal application to the Court of Directors. Sandwich was also able to tell his client to contact Devaynes, as 'he seems disposed to give any advice and assistance that he thinks may be useful to you'.[15] Thus encouraged, on 9 October 1780 Macartney addressed a formal letter of application to the Court of Directors, in which he pointed to the motives of the men who were supporting him:

> Nor should I have ventured it [his candidacy], had not several of my friends, men of high character and large property, perfectly versed and deeply interested in Indian concerns, expressed a strong opinion that the situation of things on the Coromandel Coast would probably require at this particular juncture, the appointment of a Governor of Madras out of the usual course, of one totally unconnected with any of the contending interests there, and absolutely free from any local passion or prepossession.[16]

As evidence of his suitability, he adduced his career as a reliable public servant in Russia, Ireland and the Caribbean, a record of service which, he claimed with an obvious eye to the Company's trading function, had rendered him especially sensitive to the needs of commerce. But the appointment of someone new to India had not happened before and Macartney could hardly have expected that his claim to one of the Company's most lucrative positions would go forward uncontested.

His rival was Claud Russell, an East India Company servant of twenty-eight years' service, who had formally applied for the post on 14 January 1780.[17] He naturally appealed to those who considered Macartney an interloper. 'Most of the Indians', Macartney confided in his old friend from Grenada, George Leonard Staunton, 'declare against an interloper, as they term me, and are trying to form a strong opposition to my appointment'.[18] This was the nub of Russell's case: with some justice he regarded the prospect of Macartney's appointment as 'unjust to me, injurious to the Company, and mortifying to the expectations of my fellow servants who have hazarded their lives and exerted their best abilities to promote the interests of the Company'.[19] Russell's candidature was supported by a group of men who were opposed to the dominant Sulivan-Devaynes group in the Company with their links, strongly forged during the previous April, with North's government. The man who emerged as the principal spokesman and canvasser against Macartney, General Richard Smith M.P., was an established critic of these connections. Nor was Macartney's sensible attempt to link the parliamentary opposition with his application successful. On 13 October he wrote to Lady Ossory, observing, on the basis of a letter he had just received, that 'the Lord Shelburne seems shy of exerting his interest', and asserting that 'an Indian appointment such as I solicit is really a great national object, nor a party business at all'.[20] That such a concept was more than just empty electioneering may be seen in the response of one of Macartney's supporters:

> As you know I am no friend in general to the connections of the present administrations. It is conviction alone of the necessity of a *new man's* being appointed to Madras at this juncture, and the very preferable opinion I have of your Lordship that have induced *me* to think as I do on this subject.[21]

Nonetheless, the opposition leaders, Shelburne and Lord Rockingham, remained aloof from his candidacy, and significantly it was the leading Rockinghamite, his old friend Edmund Burke, who opposed him in the Court of Proprietors. But Burke's hostility, which was prompted by more than his attitude to North's government, suggests a further dimension to the Macartney campaign, one in which the established financial interests in Madras tried to influence the future course of events.

The principal architects of the alliance between the Sulivan-Devaynes faction in the Company and the North government were the Scottish cousins, James and John Macpherson, each of whom was deeply involved in the affairs of Benfield and the Nawab.[22] The year 1780 was replete with rumours of the corrupt influence which this group had exerted upon the recent Westminster election in which Benfield and his friend John Macpherson had been returned for the old Cotswold town of Cricklade. Rumours circulated in the press and in the private correspondence of men like Walpole that Benfield had returned up to nine members and that even so high a dignitary as Sandwich, one of Macartney's chief partisans, had been tainted by what was described as the 'Arcot interest'.[23] Whatever degree of truth lay behind these allegations, Macartney's candidacy was clearly associated to some extent with these dubious financial interests; this was the source of Burke's opposition. It is vital to assess the nature of the links which connected Macartney with Benfield and John Macpherson at this time because his subsequent Indian career was to turn on his relations with them.

Macartney's private correspondence shows that he was in close contact with the two men on the eve of his departure for Madras: to the extent, for example, of borrowing £6,000 from Benfield to assist him with the expenses of getting there.[24] It seems a fair construction of their motives, certainly consistent with their conduct once in India, that they believed they could turn Macartney's ignorance of Indian affairs to their advantage. The opposition's estimate of Benfield's political influence may be regarded as excessive but even so it was no less a figure than John Robinson who introduced him to Macartney.[25] Indeed, the evidence suggests that Robinson forced Benfield upon the Macartney camp, though it is unclear at what stage of the candidacy this occurred.[26] What interested such an influential political figure in a man who had already become publicly notorious is equally obscure, though their intimacy at this time is well attested.[27] Nevertheless, Macartney and other members of the government regarded Benfield with suspicion. In trying to reassure Burke of the wisdom of Macartney's appointment, Lord Loughborough predicted that the new Governor could call upon sufficient reserves of character to withstand the influence of Benfield, for whom he evidently had no time:

> He will disappoint me very much if any of the connections you allude
> to should bias him improperly, and I shall be still more disappointed

if such a line of conduct is not marked out to him as will make it impossible for one who means to live the remainder of his life in as good company as he has spent the early part of it, to pursue the measures you dread — notwithstanding the suspicion which the name of Benfield may justly excite.[28]

This also provides significant further indication that the government were placing their trust in Macartney's steadiness and integrity; and they were right to do so as he was too experienced in public affairs not to be wary of a man like Benfield. 'Remember what I said to you of him', he later confided in John Macpherson, 'you will one day remember what I say to you now: *il finira mal'*.[29]

However, Macartney's candidacy, though powerfully backed by Sandwich, Robinson, Loughborough and the rest of the government, by the Sulivan-Devaynes group in the Company, not to mention the shadowy Benfield-Macpherson connection, had still to win the necessary majority in the Court of Proprietors. A committee was formed which from its headquarters at the *George and Vulture* inn set about the formidable task of visiting and circulating Court members. Prominent in it was Thomas Allan, who throughout Macartney's time in India was to serve as his 'confidential correspondent' in London, reporting on events and acting as a lobbyist on his behalf.[30] Macartney and his associates had at their disposal a printed, but incomplete, list of 1,042 electors. Although this was obviously used as the basis of their canvass, its annotations are frustratingly difficult to interpret; while many names are ticked off, they include some, notably General Smith, who were avowed opponents.[31] Much more interesting are the lists which reveal the nature and extent of government patronage at this time. A handwritten list of 259 names appears to indicate a basic vote which the government might have been able to influence on Macartney's behalf. Of these names, 106 bear the simple endorsement 'Government', while others were more specifically assigned to bodies like the Customs or the Post Office. Twenty-two names were associated with Sandwich and five with Robinson, along with another twelve marked 'Treasury'.[32] A truer estimate of the latter's influence may be seen in a letter from his private secretary to Macartney in which he indicated that 'those names to which is attached *Government* are usually applied to directly from the *Treasury'*.[33] But the ways in which the government had to approach Company voters were rather more intricate than this might suggest and other lists show interlocking chains of patronage which had to be used. A group of forty-four names was endorsed 'Ordnance List, if Lord Sandwich and Government approve'.[34] Two of these also appeared on the list of Anthony Todd of the Post Office, where the names were divided between 'In all ten to oblige Mr Todd' and 'In all twelve which Mr Todd can very well ask'.[35] The 'List of Mr Burt's votes for Lord Macartney' accounted for a further eleven voters, only one of whom may have been synonymous with one of the names appearing in the general government list. Burt's names included that of Gompertz, whose allegiance brought with it a further accession of support, as Gompertz himself commanded a list of seven, clearly Jewish, voters, one of whom, Israel Solomons, could offer four votes.[36]

It was from these blocks of votes that the necessary mosaic of support had to be accumulated, but formidable though government influence was it did not obviate the necessity for hard work by Macartney and his supporters, notably, it seems, by Sandwich. One voter in Blackheath, who had already been canvassed by Smith, wrote to assure Macartney that 'Lord S. deliver'd your obliging letter to me yesterday evening and, as his Lordship's carriage is now at the gate', he had 'scarce an instant' to convey his support.[37] Sandwich's efforts persisted until the very day of the meeting of the Court of Proprietors on 23 November. James Tierney of Lincolns Inn Fields then wrote to Sandwich in terms which strikingly emphasize the First Lord's decisive influence. 'I do not know', Tierney assured him, 'that I have ever given a vote in Indian affairs for many years which I did not believe to be consistent with your Lordship's views'. 'I would show', he added, 'how sensible I am of your Lordship's favours. I doubt not many of them are out of your Lordship's memory, but I shall never forget them'.[38] Not surprisingly, some votes were traded for favours. 'You cannot, in the situation you are now placed, expect to be free from troublesome solicitations', Sandwich advised Macartney after his election.[39] Israel Solomons followed up his four votes by negotiating with Macartney for his custom, should he or his friends wish to send diamonds from the east; while Sir Clifton Wintringham's condition was that Macartney solicit Lord Bute's permission for him to pass through Richmond Park with his carriage 'as his villa being in that neighbourhood would thereby be rendered more commodious, as also more capable of contributing to his health and satisfaction'.[40] Through such complex mechanisms were the East India Company proprietors engaged in Macartney's support.

Thus marshalled by Sandwich, Robinson and the *George and Vulture* committee, the East India Company voters saw Macartney safely on his way through the Court of Proprietors on 23 November 1780. General Smith's motion that the Company appoint as

Governor a person who was currently, or had been, in their service was rejected, leaving the way clear for the Court of Directors on 14 December to appoint someone with no previous Indian experience.[41] Had they but known it, they were creating a precedent for the appointment to the major Indian governorships which, with minor exceptions, was to remain to the end of the British period. On the following day Macartney appeared before the Court to be sworn in. In his acceptance speech he made two promises to which he remained remarkably, even stubbornly, faithful. The first was that their instructions 'would ever be his guide and their orders he would steadily obey'. The other related to the integrity of his rule. On his return from India, he assured them, he would appear before them 'with a heart as pure and hands as clean as any servant they have ever employed'.[42] However unctuous this might now appear, it provided an unequivocal assurance to the Directors that, as far as their newly-appointed Governor had it in his power, they need fear no repetition of the financial scandals which had for so long disgraced their presidency. Both promises were hostages to fortune and the implications of holding to them were to prove far more difficult than Macartney imagined in the flush of assuming the new dignity which, he believed, would assure his future prosperity.

III

Stimulated by his irrepressible curiosity about foreign parts, Macartney eagerly anticipated his first encounter with the east which, he claimed, had become a 'sort of passion' with him.[43] During the prolonged period of his candidacy he had acquainted himself with Indian affairs and the directors were clearly anxious that he should now be on his way to attend to the problems of Madras, which had suddenly become more acute as the result of the entry of the Dutch into the war. He spent little more time in London, leaving for Ireland on 15 January 1781 preparatory to sailing from Limerick on the *Swallow* on 21 February.[44] Accompanying him as his secretary was his friend, George Leonard Staunton. It was a judicious choice. Not only was his fellow Irishman a man of intelligence and upright character, but the two men enjoyed a perfect understanding. Staunton proved a tower of strength at Madras; indeed, it is difficult to see how Macartney could have borne the trials which lay ahead without his unfailing support. Lady Macartney did not go with them. It was their intention that she and Mrs. Staunton should join them at some point, but conditions never allowed this.[45] Madras in the 1780s was no place for European women and, if Macartney was thereby deprived of companionship, the changing nature of politics in London meant that his wife was well employed using what talents she possessed in lobbying for him and in generally overseeing his private affairs.

What constitutional authority did Macartney carry with him to Madras? This question must be examined as his time there was rarely free from haggles with the Governor General in Calcutta and with the military operating in south India. The statute which set out his relationship to the Governor General was the celebrated Regulating Act of 1773, the first attempt of the British parliament to intervene in India, but hopelessly imprecise in its provisions. It had established the office of Governor General and Warren Hastings was subsequently appointed as its first incumbent. So much has been written about this seminal figure in Anglo-Indian history that little needs repetition here, except that Hastings encountered grave problems in India, armed only with ill-defined powers over the other two presidencies of Madras and Bombay, and even over his own council at Calcutta. The 1770s had been a period of incessant wrangling with his council. This had largely been resolved by the time of Macartney's arrival; but, as Staunton discovered on visiting Calcutta, Hastings had 'suffered his temper to be somewhat affected by the long opposition he had met in council there'.[46] Hastings's dispute with Macartney was to show that his council remained an uncertain instrument. Macartney had to try to co-operate with a great but embittered man, vulnerable to pressure and unwilling to brook independence in the Madras government. Given Macartney's sense of his own worth, it could scarcely have been other than a fraught relationship, ill-served both by the provisions of the Regulating Act and by the fact that they never met. Article IX of the act gave Bengal the 'power of superintending and controlling' the other two presidencies, 'so far and in as much' as they could not

> make any orders for commencing hostilities, or declaring or making war, against any Indian princes or powers, or for negotiating or concluding any treaty of peace, or other treaty, with any such Indian princes or powers, without the consent and approbation of the said Governor General and Council first had and obtained.

This was the basis of Hastings's right to supremacy, which included the power to suspend a Governor disobeying such instructions. But it was far from comprehensive and it also enshrined two significant exceptions. It expressly allowed a Governor to act, firstly, 'in such cases of imminent necessity as would render it dangerous to postpone such hostilities or treaties until the orders from the Governor General and Council might arrive'; and, secondly, 'in such cases where the said Presidents and Councils respectively shall have received special orders from the said United Company'.[47] Macartney had recourse to both these exceptions in his disputes with Hastings.

His precise position in relation to the military was also open to interpretation. By the terms of the East India Company resolution appointing him, Macartney was designated

> our Governor and Commander in chief of our fort and garrison of Fort St George and town of Madraspatnam, and of all the forces which are now or hereafter shall be employed in the service of the said United Company within the said fort garrison and town.

Furthermore, the Company did

> strictly require, charge and command all commission officers, non-commission officers, soldiers and others belonging to our military forces, and all the people and inhabitants employed or residing in our fort garrison and town, to yield you as Governor and Commander in chief due obedience accordingly.[48]

A military dignity was clearly implied. Whether this extended to an active military role, and whether that extended beyond the confines of Madras and over the royal (as distinct from the Company's) troops, was less evident; but Macartney's predictably positive interpretation carried him into incessant disputes with the armed forces which obstructed his other policies. However, in discharging these powers, Macartney was explicitly required to obey any military and naval instructions issuing from the Committee of Secrecy of Devaynes and Sulivan, which had been considered necessary because of the critical situation facing the Company and the country.[49]

His appointment could not have come at a more difficult time in the world war which had grown out of the American rebellion. Britain was under pressure at various points of the globe from a vengeful combination of European powers, eager to reduce her gains of 1763. In July 1778 news had reached India of the opening of hostilities between Britain and France. This presented little immediate threat, as Pondicherry and the other scattered French possessions were captured by the end of the year, but the long-term prospects were more ominous. As the French had never reconciled themselves to the loss of the strong position Dupleix had created in south India in the 1740s and later lost to Robert Clive, Macartney had every reason to believe that a strong expedition would arrive, and it was to prove fortunate for him that the fleet commanded by an admiral of genius, the Bailli de Suffren, did not sight the Madras coast until February 1782. Macartney's departure had, of course, coincided with news of the Dutch entry into the war. Although Dutch settlements in the Carnatic were ill-guarded, the directors feared that resources from that quarter, especially the port of Negapatam, might be used in conjunction with French and Spanish forces; in addition, Dutch possessions in neighbouring Ceylon presented a considerable strategic threat to Madras should a French fleet arrive. Accordingly, Macartney had left London with precise orders from Devaynes and Sulivan as to how to stifle the Dutch, being instructed to secure every one of their settlements and ships. within his reach. He was specifically charged to conduct operations against their chief settlement and port of Negapatam, to negotiate with the King of Candy for joint operations against the Dutch in Ceylon, and to initiate the total destruction of their fortifications should his garrisons prove insufficient to hold them.[50] Unfortunately, in early January 1781 no one in London yet knew that the situation in south India was infinitely more precarious than these orders implied. When Macartney landed at Madras after his four months' voyage on 22 June 1781, he was faced not only with the ramshackle Dutch forts and the prospect of a French expedition but also with the potential collapse of the entire British position in south India at the hands of a much more dangerous and skilful foe.

What made one of Staunton's correspondents 'apprehensive that Lord Macartney will find no government to take charge of' was news that in July 1780 the Carnatic had been invaded by Haidar Ali, the Muslim ruler of Mysore.[51] Justly regarded by his contemporaries as 'the most formidable enemy with whom we had to contend in the East', Haidar Ali was probably the ablest of those soldiers of fortune who exploited the era of Mughal collapse to set themselves up as independent rulers.[52] Gaining control of Mysore in the 1760s, thereafter he devoted his formidable talents to the expansion of his dynasty; and, as any hope of northward expansion was countered by the military strength of the Marathas and of the Nizam of Hyderabad, his attention turned to the Carnatic. Irritated by certain actions of Sir Thomas Rumbold's government and doubtless inspired by his knowledge of Britain world-wide embarrassments, he entered the Carnatic in July 1780 with a force which his enemies estimated at 150,000 men.[53] His principal striking force was his cavalry, believed to muster 30,000, and he also enjoyed the services of some 200-400 Frenchmen under Colonel Lally.[54] To oppose what was patently a formidable army stood the honest but lacklustre Major-General Sir Hector Munro, with a single British regiment, the 73rd or Lord Macleod's Highlanders, a battalion and a grenadier company of the East India Company's European troops, and some five sepoy battalions, as well as the unpaid and hence unreliable troops of the Nawab. It is unnecessary to accept at face value

Burke's view that 'when the British armies traversed, as they did, the Carnatic for hundreds of miles in all directions, through the line of their march they did not see one man, not one woman, not one four-footed beast of any description, whatever', to appreciate the disastrous effects of this invasion on Macartney's presidency. The opening of the campaign saw the fall of the Nawab's capital at Arcot, the piecemeal erosion of the British garrisons, and the appearance of Mysore cavalry on the very outskirts of Madras. Although by the time of Macartney's arrival Hastings had taken urgent measures to restore the position, the initiative remained firmly with Haidar Ali and his seemingly omnipresent horsemen. When news of these events reached London, the Committee of Secrecy felt obliged to send Macartney instructions, however general. On 31 May 1781 they informed him that he should expect the arrival of 1,000 royal troops, as well as 200 recruits for the Company's forces and another 200 for the 73rd Highlanders. Nevertheless

> You will always remember that our first and grand object is peace with the country powers of India upon safe and honourable terms. Our Governor General and Council must take the lead in all negotiations, and direct, or authorize, the plan of operations for all our settlements; and all their instructions and requisitions must be obeyed.[55]

This last clause clearly referred to the terms of the Regulating Act, but it was the first sentence which was to fix itself upon Macartney's consciousness as a definite statement of policy which actual experience at Madras only served to underline.

Finally, how was Macartney expected to tackle the matter which lay at the root of the presidency's problems, the Nawab's debts and their consequent effects upon its financial stability? Here, too, prior to his departure he was in receipt of advice from Laurence Sulivan who confided in him that 'Madras is become a heavy burden'. Because of the presidency's empty treasury and the increasing expenses of its government, Macartney was to practise economy. Sulivan pointed to the three reasons for these financial problems. The first was spiralling military costs. Here Macartney was instructed to press for the abolition of the 'present unruly rabble' belonging to the Nawab and to concentrate instead upon building up the Company's own troops: if an increase in the military budget proved unavoidable, 'the Carnatic, not the Company, should bear the excess'. All public contracts were to be submitted to 'a minute inspection', something he was to enforce with unforeseen con-sequences. Finally, there was 'the greatest evil' of all, the Nawab's debt, which was, as Sulivan reminded him, 'of such a magnitude as to spread misery throughout the settlement; and while so large a share of almost all the private fortunes is at stake, discord and faction must continue to prevail'. Macartney was given detailed advice on how to consolidate the debts into a single bond, but as this was quickly rendered redundant the important advice that he should make the Nawab assign such revenues as were necessary to pay the annual instalment need only be noted.[56] The thrust of Sulivan's advice was clear. He proposed that the Company take a much firmer hold over the Carnatic's affairs, which policy Macartney endorsed.

These instructions regarding the Dutch, the Mysore war and the Carnatic's finances together formed the foundation on which Macartney built his policies while at Madras: but any hope he entertained of setting his presidency's affairs on a more honest and regular basis was impeded, if not entirely blighted, by the return to India of two men, John Macpherson and Paul Benfield, who had been deeply involved in the Nawab's debts. Macpherson returned to Bengal as a member of Hastings's council, leaving his cousin, James, in London as the Nawab's agent. Macartney seems to have liked Macpherson and looked to him for support in Calcutta, but the Scotsman was not to be trusted. He was a close friend of Benfield who, on the day that Macartney's appointment was approved by the Court of Directors, managed to secure their agreement to his return to Madras, despite the opposition of four directors led by the Rockinghamites, Henry Fletcher and Robert Gregory, who entered a minute of dissent.[57] As Thomas Allan reported to Macartney, it was only achieved with difficulty:

> We were hard run with Benfield and must have been beat, but for my particular and good management. He has followed his success not having a moment to lose. I know but little of him. In truth do not much approve his connexions.[58]

Although Macartney shared these reservations about Benfield, no less a figure than John Robinson had emphasized the benefits of his great experience in Madras. Macartney with all his faults was an honest man and within a few months he was to learn that a crook had followed him to India.

IV

On 21 June 1781, after a seventeen-week passage from the Shannon, the *Swallow* made a rendezvous off Pondicherry with the naval squadron operating in Indian waters under Vice-Admiral Sir Edward Hughes. It is not known whether any intimation of Haidar's invasion had reached Macartney during his voyage; if not, his discussions with the admiral were his first intimation of this disturbing turn of events and of the measures Hastings had taken to relieve the crisis. The Governor General had marched overland a force of 3,800 Indian infantry, with some artillery and a tiny cavalry contingent, under the command of Colonel J. D. Pearse.[59] Pearse's force brought with it so much *impedimenta* that its progress down the Bay of Bengal was ponderous; Pearse failed to rendezvous with the main army until 3 August 1781.[60] More immediate relief for the hard-pressed presidency was provided by the despatch from Bengal of the veteran commander-in-chief, Lieutenant-General Sir Eyre Coote. Coote had first been appointed commander-in-chief in India as far back as 1759 and, two years later, as the result of his victory over the French at Wandewash, had established as good a claim as any man to be considered the preserver of British power in south India. Now a prematurely ageing, peevish fifty-five year-old, plagued by illness, he returned to the scene of his earlier triumph. Despite his ailing physical powers, Coote was still a commander of rare distinction who has been justly ranked alongside his fellow Irishmen, Wellesley, Roberts and Auchinleck, as one of the four ablest officers ever to serve the British cause in India.[61] By 1 July 1781, as yet unaware of Macartney's arrival, Coote had inflicted a signal victory over Haidar at Porto Novo which, even if it was not decisive in ending the war, considerably reduced the immediate pressure on the presidency.[62]

The day after his meeting with Hughes, Macartney landed at Madras. Despite the pressing danger from Haidar, his immediate measures showed a curious indifference to the Mysore problem; at this stage, apparently, he was preoccupied with his promise to the directors faithfully to execute their orders. At a meeting of his council that day, he informed his colleagues of his determination to fulfil his instructions to wage war upon the Dutch, a measure which, he maintained, Haidar's invasion had only made more necessary. Accordingly, orders were issued for the immediate capture of the nearby Dutch fort and factory of Sadras.[63] Not only did this first action in Madras reveal Macartney as a rigid interpreter of instructions drafted in ignorance of the real conditions in India; it also showed he was prepared to take an active hand in waging military operations. Fully occupied by the greatly superior Mysore forces, Coote could scarcely have been expected to relish the prospect of pockets of his command being ordered around by a military ignoramus like Macartney. The Dutch proved to be no formidable foe. Despite the presence of a garrison which was numerically superior to the British force sent to invest it, Sadras fell without protest on 29 June; and three days later, Pulicat, another Dutch factory, followed.[64]

The first sign of divided counsel between the two men came when Coote ordered the lieutenant in charge at Sadras to cease the demolition of its fortifications, which Macartney had ordered, and to put the place in a state of defence.[65] Macartney allowed the officer to suspend demolition, but asked Coote to reconsider the matter in a letter typical of the officious literary style which had such an attraction for him. 'But unless you have particular reasons (which as yet I am a stranger to)', he wrote, 'I am persuaded you would not wish to disappoint the intentions of the Company on this point. They are founded on very good reasons, and should be delayed as little as possible'.[66] Coote complied with Macartney's wishes but this seemingly trivial skirmish did not augur well for future relations between the civil and military powers.

As the autumn of 1781 wore on, Coote and Macartney drifted inexorably apart. Low in spirits because of his failure to carry the war to a decisive conclusion and finding his operations constantly frustrated by lack of money and bullocks for the army, the general found Macartney's constant interference in military matters intolerable. Macartney had no high regard for the military profession. Not only did he order major expeditions against his commander's advice but he posted officers and offered advice to the hard-pressed Coote on how to find provisions for the men. Towards the end of October, the tensions working inside Coote forced him to assert his position as commander and to attempt to put Macartney in his place:

> I am satisfied that if you reverted to the Company's instructions, which are too clearly expressed by them to admit of a double meaning, your Lordship would see that as Governor of Madras you have no military power or authority vested in you out of that government; and even there it is in some degree limited. You will therefore excuse me if I say that you are not warranted either in placing officers in the command of garrisons, or in recalling them. This is so strongly and plainly stated in the instructions, which I allude to, that I shall make no further comment upon it than by saying; that it could be otherwise [sic] no man in his senses would command the army. I am sure I would not.[67]

But this magisterial rebuke did not deter Macartney. For some time his main military aim remained the destruction of the Dutch settlements, especially the stronghold of Negapatam to the south of Madras. With its garrison of 7,000 men and 200 cannon it seemed, on paper at least, to offer a major threat, especially if its troops were to combine with Haidar's forces in Tanjore. There was good reason, as Coote conceded, to suppose that contact had been established between the two powers.[68] Nonetheless, Coote's eyes were fixed on the war with Haidar and he opposed the despatch of an expedition to capture Negapatam.[69] Taking great care not to remove any troops from Coote's command, Macartney organized a combined naval-military operation under Hughes and Munro which captured Negapatam on 12 November. He followed up this major success by using Negapatam as the base for an expedition against the Dutch port of Trincomali in Ceylon, again in precise obedience to his instructions 'that your attempt against the Dutch settlements in Ceylon should be made so soon as possible after the reduction of Negapatam'; and again in the face of Coote's opposition.[70] In early January 1782 Hughes sailed from Negapatam with a force of 500 Indian troops and on the eleventh Trincomali fell.[71] Macartney had secured two major military successes and carefully adhered to his instructions. Later when Suffren's fleet began to operate in the Bay of Bengal, he took justifiable pride in forestalling the disastrous consequences which would have befallen the British position in south India had the Dutch been able to offer their ally the port facilities of Negapatam.[72]

But all this was bought at the price of Coote's undying enmity. Until the time of Coote's departure for Bengal on 20 September 1782, Macartney had constantly to endure what Macpherson, from the safety of Calcutta, could dismiss as 'the caprices and disgusts of a worn-out warrior'.[73] To the great annoyance and inconvenience of the Select Committee in Madras, Coote ignored all appeals to attend its meetings, further alienating the military from the civil power.[74] Coote's sulk, while understandable, was a great pity for Macartney genuinely respected his professional ability and tried to treat him with a tact that was, for him, remarkable. 'I am convinced' he told Macpherson, 'that no man would have borne with him half so much, or half so long'.[75] Proof of Macartney's desire to remove the cause of friction came in the spring of 1782. The Governor General had become alarmed at the depths to which relations between the two men had evidently sunk. Writing to Macartney that he considered his actions over Negapatam totally justified, he confided in him his fear that if Madras were lost Bengal would quickly follow and tact-fully requested that Coote be allowed 'an entire and unparticipated command over all the forces acting under your authority in the Carnatic'. Believing that there was no alternative to Coote, Macartney complied.[76] Even more tangible evidence of his good faith toward Coote was the fact that it was his effort to provide money and bullocks for the army which pushed Macartney into two developments which determined the course of his presidency, the Carnatic assignment and the breach with Benfield. Yet it is undeniable that his failure to establish good relations with Coote was

unfortunate in itself and all too typical of his early months in India.
But the general was notoriously a difficult character as Macartney
told Sulivan in August 1782:

> In God's name how could you send such a man as old C[oote] here.
> He may have military talents for anything I know (I am no judge of
> them) but if he has, they are the only ones which he possesses and I
> own it puzzles me to think how a man can be a good soldier and be good
> for nothing else. I was for a great while imposed upon by his military
> reputation in this country, till I found from persons of his own silly
> trade how little bottom there was to support it.[77]

Events were to show that his troubles at the hands of the 'silly trade'
were very far from being over and that in Coote he had made an
enemy who was to cause him the utmost mischief.

V

Despite the ceaseless pressures of the war, Macartney was soon
involved in the details of the administration of his new responsibility.
Throughout his time at Madras, the files of the Select Committee
and its subordinate committees show the hand of a man who was an
able and confident administrator, even in times of considerable
pressure. The crispness and efficiency with which he conducted day-
to-day affairs, often at times when he was under the most severe
mental and emotional stress, commands considerable respect. From
the beginning he knew that money was at the root of the *malaise*
which affected the Madras presidency. Not only had he been carefully briefed on its financial difficulties, but within days of his arrival
he realized that the Mysore war had compounded the problem as an
empty treasury was preventing effective military operations. Although
the official records of the Madras Select Committee naturally reflect
his daily preoccupation with the war, his private correspondence
reveals that he quickly addressed himself to the task of placing
Madras on a sound financial basis, which in effect meant drawing
money from the debt-ridden Nawab to finance the war which was
crippling his country. Within a fortnight of his arrival Macartney had
applied to the Nawab either to supply him with money or else to
assign to him the exclusive management of the Carnatic's revenues
for the rest of the war; Sulivan had already advised him to adopt this
latter course in connection with the payment of the debt. In refusing
both requests, the Nawab emphasized that he had no money and
informed Macartney that the type of arrangement he proposed would
run counter to the terms of a treaty he had just made with Hastings,
the text of which had yet to arrive from Calcutta.[78] Besides reflecting

Macartney's desire to regularize the presidency's revenue, this early move strongly suggests that from the start of his appointment he was anxious to extend direct British control over the Carnatic's affairs.

This 'imperial' dimension to Macartney's rule also comes across forcibly in his first dispute with the Governor General. Immediately prior to Macartney's arrival in Madras, Hastings had written at length to the presidency strongly advocating that the British surrender their position in the Northern Sarkars. Correctly anticipating the unpopularity of this proposal, Hastings supplied figures showing that in time of war the area was a financial liability. He also castigated their possession on military grounds, maintaining that the Sarkars ate up troops while being generally indefensible because of their topography. As to the overall consolidation of the British position in the sub-continent, he dismissed the argument that the Sarkars aided communication between the Bengal and Madras presidencies; on the contrary, he believed that their possession had weakened British standing by appearing to sustain the general opinion of 'the spirit of encroachment influencing our policy', thus alienating the Nizam of Hyderabad.[79] In his reactions to this proposal Macartney showed not only that he had sufficient steel to stand up to the Governor General in this first encounter with him, but that he had already formed distinct views on the nature of the East India Company's presence in India. He met each one of Hastings's arguments head on, demonstrating statistically the financial benefit accruing from the Sarkars and emphasizing that for some time they had yielded 'the most valuable part of our cargoes for Europe'. He countered the strategic argument by observing that as a coastal area the Sarkars could be defended by the navy, the strongest and most flexible arm of British power. But he was not merely interested in winning debating points. Unlike Hastings, he saw the Sarkars as pointing to the ultimate consolidation of the Company's territory along the Bay of Bengal; he saw no reason 'to cede a valuable, solid, permanent possession, for the hollow friendship, and precarious assistance of an Oriental Prince [i.e. the Nizam], who had already betrayed us'. The imperial cast of his mind could not have been made more plain, a sentiment strongly reinforced by an interesting observation which anticipated the central issue associated with his rule, the assignment of the Carnatic:

> They [i.e. the Sarkars] are our own immediate property. In the Carnatic, it is with reluctance that the present Nabob submits to our influence... No double government, such as subsists in the Carnatic, can be durable, uniform or prosperous.[80]

Confronted with this powerful reply, Hastings quietly dropped his plan to return the Sarkars to the Nizam but its tone must have made him think about the mettle of the man who had assumed the Madras government. It seems likely that his dislike of Macartney dated from this episode.

Certainly, relations between them never seemed to recover from this unfortunate start. Their next major exchange showed that Macartney could be imperious as well as imperial. In his first major despatch to the new Governor, Hastings went to considerable pains to brief him on the terms of the revenue agreement he had concluded with the Nawab's emissaries on 2 April 1781. While reassuring Macartney of his general unwillingness to interfere with his government, he nonetheless made it perfectly plain that this particular agreement had to stand:

> But as it has been made an act of this government, and its faith pledged in the most sacred manner to the performance of it, it can neither be revoked, nor qualified.[81]

Macartney found this intolerable. He was already formulating his own plans for the Carnatic's revenue and was provoked into writing a despatch which in its potential for giving offence far outdid that on the Sarkars. This time he chose not to meet Hastings point for point, implying instead that the agreement could not be effective in providing revenue as the Nawab had conceded nothing he had not given before. He maintained that its practical result was 'to bind our hands from attempting to improve this plan of finances if deficient, or if it should fail, from substituting another in its room'. He could not be so constrained, making it clear not only that the threat of suspension by the Governor General held no terrors for him but that he believed Hastings's interference in the Carnatic to be counter-productive. 'Very soon after my accession to this government', he wrote, 'I had a strong instance of the disadvantage of the interposition of your authority and the imbecility into which it cast this presidency'. He obviously felt it necessary to make it clear from the start that 'there is no alternative between taking away the management from this presidency entirely or leaving to it the means of managing with advantage and effect'.[82] As if to underline his independence of Calcutta, Macartney ignored the presence in Madras of Richard Sulivan, who had been sent by Hastings from Calcutta to superintend the working of his agreement with the Nawab. Within weeks of Macartney's arrival, then, the two men had quarrelled seriously over two major issues, the latter one already involving the constitutional arrangement of the Company's Indian possessions. Once Macartney proceeded with his own policy for the Carnatic's revenue there could be nothing but conflict, given the vague terms of the Regulating Act.

VI

This crucial step was not long in coming. On 6 October 1781, after prolonged negotiations with the Nawab's son, the Amir al-Umara, Macartney was at last able to inform the Select Committee that he had apparently reached an agreement on the future of the Carnatic's revenue.[83] He had done this in the knowledge that a settlement of the country's dire financial plight was close to the heart of his masters in London and that the matter had been rendered even more pressing by the need to provide money for Coote's army. When the presidency's accounts were finalized in the middle of December, the full extent of Macartney's financial task was revealed. He reported to his colleagues that the presidency's treasury held only 200,000 pagodas (£80,000), against which arrears of 386,156 pagodas (£154,462) were owed to Coote's army and an additional 247,800 pagodas (£99,120) to the Bengal contingent of Pearse, a total of 633,956 pagodas (£253,582). To emphasize the gravity of the deficit, Macartney attempted a financial projection through to the following May. Setting the money due to the troops each month against expected revenue from all sources, the total arrears would by then have increased to 694,806 pagodas (£277,922).[84] This, then, was the financial reality which, added to the long-established problem of the Nawab's debts, impelled Macartney to find a means of securing stable revenue.

In attempting this, however, he could not ignore the financial agreement between the Nawab and Hastings, especially as its merits had been so strongly impressed upon him. Hastings's attempt at a solution resulted from a number of pressures which converged upon him early in 1781, as the Mysore war exerted unbearable strain upon the debt-ridden Carnatic. In early January the Nawab had assigned to the Madras government the annual sum of 300,000 pagodas (£120,000) from four of his districts. As its security for this arrangement, the government took into its service two regiments of the Nawab's cavalry and was allowed to station its agents in each of the assigned districts.[85] Interestingly, in view of what was to develop under Macartney's scheme the following year, the assignment soon dissolved in mutual recrimination and led to an appeal from the Nawab to Hastings. The distraught ruler laid bare the extent of his financial extremity. Admitting to a debt owing to his European creditors of 7,000,000 pagodas (£2,800,000), he pointed to the impossible burden placed upon him by Haidar's invasion. As he could foresee no way of resolving this, he proposed that a firm treaty be made which might offer him some relief while safeguarding his dignity as undisputed sovereign of the Carnatic.[86] At the same time Hastings received a petition from the Nawab's principal creditors at Fort St. George in which they, too, pleaded for his intervention, instancing the failure of all the previous attempts to secure for them a due return on their investments.[87] His task, then, was to reach an agreement which, while satisfying the creditors and safeguarding the Nawab's position, might set to right the Carnatic's chaotic finances.

The resulting compact seemed to do this. In a key financial concession the Nawab assigned to the Company the entire revenue of the Carnatic for the duration of the Mysore war, except for one-sixth which was to be returned to him for his own purposes. He was nevertheless determined not to be reduced to the position of a Company pensioner; it is clear that Hastings sympathized with him. The agreement reassured the Nawab that he was still to be 'the Master of his own Country' and its terms showed that this was more than an empty sop. Collection of the assigned revenue was to be entrusted to the Nawab's own Amildars, or revenue officials, who would subsequently transfer the funds to the agents of the Madras government.[88] By leaving the revenue collection firmly with the Nawab's government, Hastings was enshrining the principle of 'double government' which Macartney was to hold in such disdain. It was Macartney's belief that the provisions for implementing the assignment meant that the Nawab had conceded nothing; hence his forceful denunciation of the agreement.

His irritation was doubtless compounded by the knowledge that Hastings's agreement inhibited his freedom of action. The negotiations with the Nawab's son showed him trying to work within its broad terms of reference while displaying considerable perseverance in trying to amend it in order to ensure its effective implementation. The actual financial provisions of the agreement, which he was able to announce to his Select Committee on 6 October, did not depart from Hastings's scheme. In it the Nawab repeated his readiness to assign to the Madras government the Carnatic's entire revenue for the duration of the war, one-sixth of the total being returned to him for the expenses of himself and his family. But Macartney's ideas on implementation were much more concrete than those Hastings had entertained; and his proposals showed that his earlier castigation of the principle of double government had found institutional expression, for the terms envisaged the presidency's direct participation in the everyday management of the Carnatic's affairs. His scheme still envisaged the Amildars transferring the revenue to the Company's agents, but with the latter now assuming a different role. They were to form a new class of official, termed Company's Collectors, and the Nawab was to be asked to give them the power of Tahsildars, the men customarily employed by his government to supervise revenue officials. Thirteen Collectors were to be appointed to superintend each district in the Carnatic and an additional one for the Company's own *jagir* around Madras. As Tahsildars they were to have the power 'to act and superintend in all matters of revenue of whatever kind'. Their own actions were to be scrutinized by a new body, the Committee of Assigned Revenue, with Macartney anticipated exercising wide-ranging powers. It was to consist of six men under the direction of a senior member with a casting vote; because of his 'experience and abilities' Paul Benfield was to hold this office and his subordinates were to include his agent, Hall Plumer, and a future Governor of Madras, Charles Oakley. Benfield's committee was to receive the reports from the Collectors and issue instructions to them, but its proposed functions were to extend much further, intruding far into the authority of the Nawab's government. It was to be 'the particular duty of the committee to attend to the state and progress of the cultivable produce, revenue and collectors, throughout the country'. Members were to tour the various districts, not simply inspecting accounts, but enquiring into such things as the state of village tanks and watercourses and how they might be improved. Such solicitude was, of course, prompted by the hope of improved revenue, but in pursuing this policy Macartney had moved towards a more paternalistic view of the Company's role in India:

> By attending to these points the Company may arrive at much useful knowledge; they may be able gradually to recover the lands and manufactures from their present most deplorable state, greatly to improve the revenues, and finally to establish wealth, credit and prosperity throughout the country.[89]

While Macartney's proposed assignment of the Carnatic's revenues remained congruent with the financial provisions of the agreement Hastings had concluded, the former far outreached the latter in its clear extension of British power. That the revenue was still to be collected by the Amildars certainly preserved the form of the Nawab's authority; but real power was henceforward to lie with the Collectors under the direction of the Committee of Assigned Revenue. The wish to extend British power, discernible from the time of Macartney's arrival, now stood revealed.

Benfield's committee set to work in the succeeding weeks, selecting and appointing Collectors for each district, and recommending to

Macartney that no revenue transaction be permitted unless one of their officials signed jointly with one of the Nawab's Amildars.[90] But it soon became clear that the Nawab and the Amir al-Umara were in no mood to stomach the diminution in their authority contemplated by Macartney and his new committee. The Nawab was far too wary of his position not to recognize the threat posed by granting the power of Tahsildar to the Collectors. In refusing to concede this, the Nawab reminded Macartney that events in the recent past hardly suggested that the direct involvement of the Company's servants in the Carnatic's affairs would result in honest dealing, and hoped that in any agreement 'my rights, privileges, and authority, over my country, subjects, and servants, may be carefully preserved'.[91] Nonetheless, in the course of the negotiations the Amir had announced that rather than yield the power of Tahsildar to the Company's servants, his father was prepared to consider a system of renting the revenue, and Macartney promised to lay this before the Select Committee and the Committee of Assigned Revenue.[92] The latter, realizing that the absence of Tahsildar powers would render the proposed assigned ineffectual, considered the Nawab's willingness to rent the revenue to responsible men a possible alternative.[93] This compromise, the realization of which was in Macartney's words 'extremely uncertain to the last moment', formed the basis of the agreement with the Nawab. In doing this Macartney knew that he could not push the Nawab too far, partly because of local ramifications and partly because of possible adverse reactions amongst other Indian rulers. But he was set on a reduction of the ruler's power 'as a more effectual management of the revenues and a more certain application of them to the promotion of the common cause depended on his Highness ceasing for a time to have any interference in that department of the administration of the Carnatic'.[94]

The fateful agreement for the assignment of the Carnatic's revenue was at last signed on 2 December 1781. Its financial provisions remained faithful to Hastings's agreement of the previous April, while the terms relating to its implementation, which Macartney believed to be the crux of the matter, reflected the maximum concessions he could secure. The compromise enabled the Amildars to become renters and to be appointed by Macartney, subject to the Nawab's approval. Macartney would then settle with them the rent due for a fixed period of three to five years, during which he would have the sole right to dismiss them. Finally, the Nawab yielded up his authority to issue orders relating to the revenue.[95] Macartney and his colleagues clearly felt that they could congratulate themselves on a major revolution in the Carnatic's internal affairs, which they could set alongside the recent capture of Negapatam. Without doubt, the agreement was intended to shift the balance of authority in the Carnatic from the Nawab to the Governor. Following its conclusion, Macartney indicated to the various Company representatives in the district that, while they were to pay due respect to the Nawab's 'dignity and importance in the eyes of his subjects', they were to become actively involved in establishing the new system. 'New Amildars', he informed George Ram at Trinchinopoly, 'will everywhere be appointed (but this is only to yourself) as soon as possible'.[96] In minuting the agreement, the Select Committee revealed their belief that they had changed the nature of the Carnatic:

> at the same time that the difficulties which have been experienced from a divided government in the country will have been removed, sufficient will be left with the Nabob to satisfy the just purposes of power and to preserve his dignity and consequence in the eyes of his subjects.[97]

But events soon demonstrated that Macartney's apparent triumph suffered from three serious defects. The Nawab and his son had not the slightest intention of allowing the forceful new Governor to relegate them to mere puppets in the affairs of their country. Within a few months they demonstrated their ability to act in defence of their interests. Secondly, the terms of the assignment had moved much further in terms of the extension of the Company's role than Hastings had anticipated. Finally, the Committee of Assigned Revenue was under the direction of Benfield, who was soon to emerge as one of Macartney's most dangerous enemies.

VII

As we have seen, John Macpherson and Paul Benfield returned to India soon after Macartney, the former to serve on Hastings's council, the latter to his old haunts in Madras to safeguard his considerable investments. Although Macartney entertained reservations about Benfield, he had borrowed heavily from him and knew that Benfield was highly regarded by Robinson, who had substantially assisted his election. Small wonder, then, that in early November 1781 he felt able to write to Macpherson as follows:

> Your Cricklade colleague seems satisfied; and I shall endeavour to give every reasonable man occasion to be so; his abilities, knowledge, and connections entitle him to my particular attention.[98]

Proof of Macartney's current faith in the man is seen in his appointment of Benfield as senior member of the Committee of Assigned Revenue, the key appointment as far as his hopes for the future of the presidency was concerned. But the delicate business of negotiating the assignment was still under way when Macartney gave a clear signal that his official attitude toward the Benfield 'interest' would not be one of uncritical compliance, and that his government was going to set new standards of honest dealing in the presidency's affairs.

By the late 1770s, securely established as one of the Nawab's principal creditors, Benfield had expanded his activities to become one of the presidency's leading contractors. Under Macartney's predecessor he had been awarded the contract for major public works to the west of Fort St. George, including the construction of an esplanade on the north-west bastion which involved the levelling of an inhabited area known as Hog Hill.[99] On 6 November 1781 Macartney and the Select Committee considered a request from the Committee of Works that the outstanding balance due on the contract be paid to Benfield's agent, Hall Plumer.[100] Plumer's claim was in two parts. The first related to the outstanding sum of 10,703 pagodas (£4,281) owed to Benfield's contract of 55,402 pagodas (£22,160), a sum which the Committee of Works reported the chief engineer as believing to be 'very reasonable'.[101] Plumer also submitted a supplementary account for 1,686 pagodas (£674) for work carried out at the government's request in preparing ground to house the dispossessed inhabitants of Hog Hill.[102] In examining Benfield's account, the Select Committee uncovered startling irregularities and abuses, highly revelatory of the manner in which the presidency had previously been governed. On the first part of Plumer's claim, Macartney discovered that the chief engineer had refrained from submitting any reports on the state of Hog Hill or on how far the terms of the contract had been fulfilled; in regard to the second part there was no record of the work ever having been oficially sanctioned.[103] Not only were these lacunae exposed, but further problems emerged. The luckless Indians who had been removed from Hog Hill petitioned Macartney, accusing Hugh Maxwell, the Superintendent of Company Grounds, of failing to provide them with the agreed compensation for the destruction of their houses, and of not allotting new ground to many, who were in consequence forced to live on the streets.[104] In his defence Maxwell uncovered a widespread system of fraud in the purchase of Company ground, against which, he claimed, he had repeatedly complained without having been given the authority to remedy the situation.[105]

Here, too, Macartney, showed himself to be the faithful servant of his masters in London, having been told by Sulivan to examine carefully all contracts and introduce regular and decent government. Benfield's principal claim was referred back to the Committee of

Macartney and G. L. Staunton in 1784, by L. F. Abbott (National Portrait Gallery, No. 329).

Works until proper reports on the state of the contract had been submitted. In addition, the Select Committee delivered a stern message to the Committee of Works that it was not in future to authorize work without the Governor's sanction. Maxwell was directed to prepare a list of the dispossessed inhabitants of Hog Hill with the financial compensation and ground due to them. He was also permitted to institute a survey, independent of the Committee of Works, to investigate the system of fraud in land purchase of which he had complained.[106] Macartney had shown how he intended the affairs of his government to be conducted. While none of this yet ran counter to Benfield's primary financial interests, it was a significant pointer to the future bitter conflict between the two men.

The clash came to a head in a dispute over the crucial question of the army's bullock supply, which had been festering since the summer campaigns. The despatches of Coote and Pearse constantly returned to it and everyone in the Madras administration agreed that the dearth of bullocks was rendering the fighting against Mysore ineffective. The extent to which military operations relied on these beasts may be illustrated by the fact that Pearse's command of around 4,000 men required 1,165 bullocks; he brought with him from Bengal some 6,000 of them for the main army, a total which Coote, who mustered 8,500 men, found disappointingly small.[107] Macartney was keenly aware of this priority, for he allowed a mere five days to elapse from the completion of the assignment before entering into discussions with Coote on 7 December 1781 as to the best means of putting the bullock supply on a proper basis. He suggested to the general, who concurred, that, as no one had more experience of the country or a more substantial financial base, Benfield should be offered the contract.[108] Benfield had, in fact, been urging such a course for some months and the following day was able to reassure Macartney of his willingness to assume the role of contractor, and to supply the army with 20,000 bullocks, together with two drivers to each beast and the necessary girths and saddles. Any loss in battle or capture by the enemy was to be his liability. In return, he proposed that the Company should pay him at the rate of 4 pagodas a month for each animal.[109] Under such an arrangement, the army's needs would have been satisfied and Benfield stood to profit by the substantial sum of 80,000 pagodas (£32,000) a month. The scheme, of course, was only feasible if the new assignment succeeded in yielding regular income for the presidency, but as chairman of the Committee of Assigned Revenue, Benfield was confident that this would be the case.

Macartney was inclined neither to accept Benfield's first bid nor to allow him free rein. He was under instruction to submit all public contracts to the most careful scrutiny; had been alerted by the terms of the Hog Hill agreement; and certainly knew enough about Benfield's business reputation to ensure that any agreement was as watertight as possible. After much discussion he succeeded in reducing Benfield's proferred 4 pagodas to 3¼.[110] Macartney then proceeded to prepare a detailed contract, agreed by the Select Committee on 26 December, which went far beyond the terms of Benfield's original proposal. Clearly Benfield was appalled by the end it meant to the free and easy methods by which his fortune had hitherto thrived, and he offered detailed objections. In his attempt to make the contract as binding as possible, he maintained, Macartney had taken little account of what was practicable. It was impossible, he complained, to supply all 20,000 trained bullocks within thirty days of the contract being signed, to replace all dead animals within fifteen days, to produce an extra 20,000 within thirty days if so required, or to feed the drivers at all times. He objected to the stipulation that he be paid only in Madras and, in particular, that payment would only be made after his accounts had been passed by the Auditor of Accounts and members of the Select Committee. He was especially perturbed by the way in which the initiative in the contract remained with the government: the power of ending it was vested in the Select Committee, and should he fail to fulfil any part of the contract, he was liable to a penalty of 100,000 pagodas.[111] At a crucial Select Committee meeting, following Benfield's submission of a new draft contract, Macartney refuted to his colleagues' satisfaction every one of his opponent's points. Reminding them that 'during the war with Hyder Ally, that loud and frequent complaints were made against the contractors, whose engagements had not been made so binding upon them, as to secure the army against disappointment in the conveyance of provisions and ammunition', he castigated Benfield's proposals as 'framed in that loose and indefinite manner, which leaves no security to the Company'.[112] As a result, the committee resolved that Benfield had refused their offer. Even so, they made some attempt to maintain good relations with him, offering Benfield the indeterminate position of agent for the supply of bullocks. Increasingly acrimonious negotiations over what this meant spluttered on in the early days of January 1782, until Benfield eventually accused the committee of denying him the means of effective action. By 11 January the committee had had enough. Benfield was sacked and another agent appointed.[113] Macartney lost no time in completing the rupture. He seized the first chance to remove Benfield as head of the Committee of Assigned Revenue, the key appointment in his presidency, replacing him by Charles Oakley, 'a man of open character and of honourable principles', who soon became one of the strongest props of his government.[114]

It is difficult to overestimate the importance of these events for Macartney's subsequent career at Madras. Benfield had taken an active part in his election and lent him a considerable sum to finance his trip to India. No man had wider connections in the presidency and he could reasonably assume that an inexperienced Governor would simply allow him to continue unfettered on the path which had already brought him such great wealth. Yet by the beginning of 1782 he knew not only that Macartney felt no sense of obligation to him but also that he was determined to put the presidency's affairs on a regular and honest basis. Over the next few months Macartney prudently shed his financial obligation, repaying the entire loan of £6,000 by August 1782.[115] This was not, however, the end of the matter. Benfield had a considerable talent for intrigue, as he had shown in the Pigot affair of 1775. His old friend, John Macpherson, was at the side of Warren Hastings whose feelings toward Macartney were already chilly. Thus, Macartney had left himself dangerously exposed at a time when his cares were multiplying alarmingly. Within two months of the breach with Benfield, Suffren's fleet arrived off Madras and Macartney's scheme for the assignment began to collapse.

Knowing that he had made a dangerous and influential enemy, Macartney tried hard to strengthen his position, aware apparently that his recent actions were approved by those in higher authority. His actions had always been guided by the wishes of those who had sent him to India and in January he received a long despatch from Bengal which seemingly showed strong support for his policies. He was congratulated on the fall of Negapatam as its strategic importance was well appreciated; on the vital revenue question he appeared to be given *carte blanche*. The letter did refer to the rights of the Nawab and of the Raja of Tanjore but in such terms and with such significant reservations that it merits close attention, especially in view of attitudes later adopted in Calcutta:

> But these rights cannot exist to their own prejudice and destruction, and such is our confidence in your integrity, your prudence, moderation and public zeal that we shall not hesitate to give our sanction to any measures which you may think the most effectual to realize the resources of every district of the Carnatic that can be wrested from the enemy, or which he has not yet been able to lay waste. Those resources in being applied to relief and support of the Carnatic are

applied to their just purposes. Nor could either the condition of alliances nor [sic] in any degree the spirit of them contradict the principle of such obvious and necessary justice.[116]

This was welcome reassurance to Macartney that his actions were finding favour in Calcutta. Nevertheless, the letter was signed, in Hastings's absence, by Edward Wheler and Macpherson at a time when the latter still considered himself closely intimate with Macartney; and it was written in ignorance of the Benfield affair.

Confident, then, in the soundness of his policies, Macartney prudently began to insure himself against possible counter-attack from his erstwhile colleague. On the day after the decisive Select Committee meeting of 11 January he wrote to John Robinson in London, seeking to explain the breach. 'He is a man', Macartney reported, 'who entertains such ideas as appear to me very dangerous, and the more so, because he seems well disposed to realize them when he can'. He then turned to what was to be a consistent theme in his correspondence throughout the next three years:

Allow me to say one thing, and everybody here who knows me, knows it; that there never was a more laborious man in my station, and I will add never was so disinterested a one. I have now been 7 months here; and it will appear most astonishing to any man in the least acquainted with this country; but it is a fact, and I declare it to you upon my honour, since my arrival here, I have never accepted any present whatsoever worth a dozen pagodas. Standing upon this ground I trust I shall be supported against the attacks which I have reason to expect from interested malignity and disappointed avarice.[117]

Financial integrity was a point of honour to which Macartney frequently returned, particularly as he knew it would be set against the record of his opponents. Towards the end of January he wrote at length to his principal patrons in London, Sulivan, Sandwich, Robinson, Lord Hillsborough and Charles Jenkinson, advising them that 'Mr B. is a man whom I think the Company ought never to employ on any pretext whatsoever'.[118]

Having done his best to present his case in London, he then turned to the key to his immediate situation, Bengal. He failed to appreciate the extent to which Hastings had been alienated by the early disputes between them and by the effect on Macpherson's sympathy of the quarrel with Benfield, though he was apprehensive on both accounts. He waited until 21 January before writing to Macpherson about the Benfield affair, by which time he was about to follow advice the Scotsman had earlier given him that he should send Staunton to Bengal in an attempt to establish an amicable relationship with Hastings.[119] But on 7 February, even before Staunton arrived in Calcutta, Macpherson declared his views on recent events:

The breach with B gives me infinite pain. I have read the papers that all sides recur to in these cases. Your contract was severe, and out of the common line, and the offers upon the part of B to provide bullocks and manage the arrears of the army gain even a validity by the interest he had to save the country.[120]

From this point the intimacy which Macartney had hoped for between Macpherson and himself slowly evaporated. During the next three years Macpherson played an ambivalent but ultimately treacherous role as far as Macartney was concerned. The two men continued to correspond until August 1783, even though their early *rapport* had gone. Macpherson, too, was a dangerous man. His sympathies were avowedly with Benfield and he had the ear of the Governor General, while Macartney was in distant Madras. Moreover, he had his own ambitions on the Governor Generalship and Macartney was a known rival. It is easy to criticise his unprincipled behaviour towards both Macartney and Hastings over the next few years but this son of a Skye minister was an outsider trying to make his way, with even fewer advantages of birth and connection than Macartney enjoyed.

Not surprisingly, Staunton's mission achieved nothing. Arriving at Calcutta on 23 February, he was received amiably enough by Macpherson, and on the following day had the first of a series of unsuccessful meetings with Hastings. Staunton was unimpressed by the Governor General:

He is plain in his manner; nor does his figure or usual conversation announce great abilities or a very strong steady mind. He has, as far as I can judge, some imagination tho' not great quickness, and little solid judgement.[121]

More depressing was the news that Hastings had been totally alienated by the rebuffs from Macartney, the fatal effects of whose letters were now clear. Staunton told his friend that Hastings had resented the charges of 'encroachment, incompetence, folly and ignorance' which had come from Madras and that he 'considered all friendly and confidential intercourse at an end between you.[122] If initially Macartney was at fault for the insensitive manner in which he handled Hastings, the latter could scarcely be excused for the brusque and final way he thrust aside the olive branch offered to him by Staunton. Macartney now entertained no illusions about how his actions would be regarded in Calcutta. His remaining years in Madras were characterized by two long and embittered disputes with the Governor General: the first over the assignment, and the second over the Mysore war.

VIII

Prior to the spring of 1782 Macartney derived little peace of mind from the discharge of his responsibilities in India; thereafter his troubles multiplied alarmingly. Not least among them was the arrival in February of ten French ships of the line and two frigates under Suffren. Sailing from Brest in March 1781, Suffren had already by bold naval action secured the Cape of Good Hope for his Dutch allies. On 8 February 1782 Macartney and his Select Committee were presented with hurried despatches from several parts of the coast, all with the same unpalatable news that a large fleet, almost certainly hostile, was bearing down on Madras.[123] A week later, Suffren anchored off the settlement in sight of Sir Edward Hughes's squadron of nine ships. This was the start of a dogged conflict between the two sailors which lasted until the Frenchman's departure from Indian waters on the conclusion of peace in October 1783. Each side had certain advantages. Hughes benefited from Macartney's foresight in securing Negapatam and, for a time at least, Trincomali, for Suffren's main problem was his lack of a major land base for refitting and victualling; and after the destruction of the British squadron the main French strategic aim was the capture of these two places.[124] But if they lacked facilities, the French enjoyed a clear advantage in leadership, for Suffren demonstrated that he was one of the finest admirals of the eighteenth century. He first engaged Hughes two days after his arrival off Madras, on 17 February, and a series of battles followed over the next few months. In that of 6 July 1782 Suffren finally wrested the initiative from the gallant, but inferior, British admiral. Interestingly, it was to Negapatam that Hughes sailed to refit his squadron, but Suffren seized the advantage to rob the admiral and Macartney of their prize of Trincomali which fell to him on 31 August 1782. Naval warfare continued off the Madras coast for the next year, the relative merits of the two commanders having been aptly summarized as follows:

> Suffren had genius, energy, great tenacity, sound military ideas, and was also an accomplished seaman. Hughes had apparently all the technical acquirements of the latter profession, would probably have commanded a ship equally well with any of his captains, but shows no trace of the qualities needed by a general officer.[125]

Such was the dismal new dimension to Macartney's strategic dilemma. Not only was he still faced with an unwinnable war against Mysore on land; at sea the commerce and very existence of British rule at Madras were under constant peril from a seemingly invincible French squadron. By October 1782 joint pressure from land and sea had produced a desperate famine in the presidency which became the depressing background to his rule. It had also added Hughes to the growing list of the Governor's enemies, for the distraught Macartney quarrelled violently with Hughes's decision to ride out the easterly monsoon at Bombay, leaving the presidency still more dangerously exposed.

IX

With Benfield removed from its head, the Committee of Assigned Revenue under Oakley set to work in January 1782 to operate the terms of the assignment, but within a matter of weeks it became clear that the task was far more difficult than the agreement of 2 December had anticipated. The stubborn way in which the Nawab and his son had conducted the negotiations should have alerted Macartney to the fact that the ruling house was loathe to surrender such authority as it still enjoyed. The Amir al-Umara, fully appreciating that the steady encroachment of British rule pointed to the fact that the throne he intended to occupy would be little more than ornamental, exerted his influence to hamper Oakley's work.[126] Arguably, Benfield might have been more successful, albeit, as Macartney cynically observed, 'for his own purposes', especially as he had for some time been *persona non grata* at the Nawab's court.[127] However, Benfield now turned to the Nawab and Amir as fellow sufferers under the new regime. Macartney had become so disabused of his former colleague that he credited him with the entire collapse of his arrangement with the court. 'Till the friendship between them and B was revived', he lamented, 'all went on very well', although this was rather an over-simplification.[128] Benfield was generally believed to be the guiding spirit behind the torrent of complaints which began to flow from the court to Calcutta and London.

The effectiveness of the new axis soon showed itself. On 6 February 1782 the Committee of Assigned Revenue reported to the Select Committee that the Nawab was not allowing the Amildars unrestricted authority in the collection of revenue, but was using his local police officials, the Faujdars, to control them.[129] The Nawab was requested to desist but a fortnight later, pre-occupied with measures to combat Suffren's fleet, the Select Committee could only

> observe with concern the various impediments and embarrassments thrown by the Nabob's people in the way of the collection and management of the revenue. There seems but too much reason to conclude that they are encouraged and countenanced by some persons of the Durbar [i.e. the Nawab's court], with a view to frustrate the object of the late government.[130]

As far as Macartney's government was concerned, the agreement had already broken down. Before taking the matter further, however, Macartney forcefully reminded the Nawab that the Company had long borne the expenses of the war, and taxed him with the various frustrations suffered by his men since they had tried to implement the agreement, instancing particularly the interference of the Faujdars and the refusal of officials to let him see any accounts for the Carnatic's districts. He also chose this occasion to raise Sulivan's suggestion of requesting the Nawab to disband his undisciplined troops.[131]

Perhaps Macartney did not intend this to provoke a final confrontation with the court, but it did. The reply sent by the Nawab, or more probably by his son in conjunction with Benfield, vented all the resentments which had been festering since Macartney's arrival and, more ominously, threatened to destroy all that he had so far accomplished. As this response formed the basis of all the memorials which later went in the Nawab's name to London and Calcutta, its arguments merit close examination. It tried to refute Macartney's complaints about the Nawab's failure to comply with the agreement, attributing these to the Governor's unfamiliarity with the country and its established procedures. That the accounts had not been produced was Macartney's fault; as he had issued the relevant orders on 6 December, in the middle of the financial year, the Amildars had been at a loss how to respond. Equally, it was argued that Macartney knew little of the state of the Nawab's troops. The letter claimed that the Nawab no longer possessed any, but then proceeded to the contradictory assertion that those under his command were stationed in the districts to enforce the collection of the revenue. On the central matter of the alleged intervention of the Faujdars it was claimed that Macartney had failed to understand their function, which was to protect the peasantry from the rapacity of the Amildars. If they were prevented from doing this, the Amildars would be free to embezzle. All this was carefully presented in such a way as to highlight Macartney's ignorance of local conditions, but what clearly underpinned the despatch was the desire to stop him before he destroyed what remained of the Nawab's authority. Alleging that Macartney had interfered in a judicial matter between an Amildar and a peasant, the letter asserted that 'such an interference never took place before from any Governor of Madras'. Macartney's policies, it was argued, had reduced the Nawab in the eyes of his subjects. The Nawab had heard that Macartney wished to assume the power of the Faujdars and, contrary to the terms of the agreement, prolong the assignment after the end of the Mysore war.

'I think from this', the Nawab concluded, 'that if even all the affairs of my government and people were put under your authority as the business of the revenue has been it will not be sufficient'. In this the Nawab was not far from the mark. Interestingly, in view of Benfield's connection, he complained of Macartney's total neglect of the creditors and made it his 'first request' that justice be done to them. The logical conclusion to this was the demand that the agreement of 2 December be cancelled and the Nawab restored to full authority over his revenue. The letter was an unambiguous challenge to all that Macartney was trying to accomplish.[132]

This was obvious to the Committee, who moved quickly to a confrontation:

> It is now evident to the Committee from the Nabob's whole conduct that they are to expect the most determined opposition to every measure they adopt. The Nabob seems to have entirely thrown off the mask, and the question now is, whether the Company shall passively sink under the embarrassments of their situation, or endeavour to extricate themselves at all events, by such exertions as are still left in their power. In other words whether they shall yield to the artifices used by the Nabob to defeat the purposes of his solemn agreement, or proceed by their own authority to render that agreement effectual.[133]

No more seminal decision was made by Macartney at Madras; he was proposing the final assumption of power over the Carnatic. His challenge to the Nawab was to be couched within the terms of the agreement. The renters of the revenue who had been approved by the committee were to be appointed without delay and the Torana chits, authorizing them to act, were prepared along with a letter to the Nawab. As Macartney was ill, the negotiations were entrusted to his Persian translator, David Haliburton. Macartney's letter to the Nawab was terse. It informed him that under the terms of the agreement the Governor had appointed renters for three of the Carnatic's districts and invited him to sign the necessary Torana chits allowing them to start work. Haliburton's mission moved to a predictable conclusion. The Nawab proved unavailable, the actual negotiation being conducted by the Amir with Benfield in attendance.[134] The court produced a temporising reply, refusing to authorize the appointments on the grounds that the proposed renters were unfit and that the Torana chits had been improperly prepared.[135] The Select Committee now took the fateful step of authorizing Macartney to sign the Torana chits for the three renters, instead of the Nawab, and of resolving 'that all the power of Government be exerted, if necessary, to establish and support their authority'.[136] Thus it was on Macartney's authority, not that of the country's ruler, that the new revenue officials set to work, with, as it turned out, considerable skill and effect.

But these few weeks had witnessed the turning-point of Macartney's presidency. Against the background of the arrival of the French fleet, all pretence of good relations with the Nawab disappeared, the cherished agreement with him collapsed in bitter recrimination, and Macartney openly assumed full responsibility for the Carnatic's revenue: a development of which he entirely approved but also one which he could argue he had gone to considerable pains not to provoke. However controversial his action in signing the chits, Macartney stood revealed as a ruler of steely courage and determination, for a man of lesser metal would not have chosen so perilous a course.

In subsequently defending his action, Macartney stood firmly on the record of his patient negotiations with the Nawab, but he could also point to a considerable degree of encouragement and approval from Bengal and London. The Calcutta government's letter of 26 December apparently sanctioned the type of move he made in the following April. Macartney took care to keep Hastings well informed of how the Nawab was trying to circumvent the assignment and of his proposed counter measures. By their response to this on 5 April 1782, Hastings's government not only confirmed their approval of the agreement of 2 December but mildly reproved Macartney for his moderation in handling the Nawab; and then appeared in the most emphatic manner to sanction his assumption of unfettered power:

To persons whose integrity we did not hold in the highest estimation we should not offer the advice which we now give to you, which is, that you do hold and exercise the entire and undivided administration of the revenues of the Carnatic and of every power connected with it. In a word the whole sovereignty of it shall be necessary to the effectual exercise of such a charge, not admitting the interposition of any authority whatsoever which may possibly impede it, until the necessity which has required the suspension of the constitutional control shall cease and it shall revert of course to its original and regular channel.[137]

Such approval continued throughout most of the summer of 1782, though on 5 August Hastings suggested that some of the complaints levelled against the Nawab appeared to have been exaggerated. In the autumn, however, the Bengal government reversed its previous position, condemning Macartney's actions in no uncertain manner.

This dramatic shift in policy derived from the continuous representations made by the Nawab, his son and Benfield at Calcutta and the effects these had on Hastings and Macartney's other enemies. To earlier complaints the Nawab was able to add details of Macartney's final overthrow of his power. In contrast to Macartney's formal despatches, the Nawab's 'distressing letters' carried 'great weight' with members of Hastings's council.[138] Hastings's repudiation of Macartney's actions, though slow in coming, ultimately became total and unrelenting. There is no reason to suppose that he was part of the network of financial scandal surrounding the Nawab, though in appearing to take that side against Macartney he did his reputation small credit. Yet he held no high opinion of Macartney, whom he dismissed as 'a paltry fellow'; and as Governor General he was right to be dismayed by the 'scene of disorder, perplexity and extravagance' which was being regularly conveyed to him from Madras.[139] A much more substantial fear began to grow in Hastings's mind during the summer of 1782; namely the effect that the *de facto* overthrow of the Nawab's authority was likely to have on the other Indian princes at a time when he was trying to secure allegiances and consolidate peace with the Peshwa of the Marathas.[140] Exacerbated by Macartney's unconcealed contempt for the Indian rulers, this became the main issue of principle between the two men. At all events, Hastings was ready to pay heed to Macartney's detractors, of whom there was no shortage.

Chief amongst them was Benfield, now the principal prop of the Nawab. However, the latter's proposal to send Benfield to Calcutta as his Vakil, or representative, was unanimously vetoed by the Select Committee, so that his influence was only felt at second-hand.[141] Although Benfield's friend, Macpherson, stood close to the Governor General, his role is difficult to establish. He had consistently taken Benfield's part earlier in the year, his cousin James was the Nawab's agent in London, and from the start of their association he had emphasized to Macartney how 'the Nabob as our friend and best ally is to be first attended to'.[142] Despite the fact that he had every reason to decry Macartney's actions, examination of his correspondence for the summer of 1782 shows that he was anxious to remain on good terms with both parties and ultimately did not support the Governor General's more draconian proposals, thus earning him the soubriquet of 'Johnny MacShuffle'. His real attention was directed towards the succession to Hastings and whatever might best assist his prospects of securing it. Sadly for Macartney, his most inveterate enemy was Coote, for whose immediate benefit he had negotiated the assignment and broken with Benfield. Cultivating the general was a clever move on the part of the court, for, despite Macartney's earnest attempt to help him in every respect, their early disputes, especially over Negapatam, still rankled with Coote.[143] The Nawab's principal gesture to his vanity came in May 1782 when he offered to delegate to him the entire government of the Carnatic, a snare which he sensibly avoided.[144] Significantly, it was only on Coote's return to Bengal in October 1782 that opposition to Macartney there began to assume alarming dimensions.

On 19 October Hastings indicated to Macartney that his sympathies were inclining firmly towards the Nawab whose complaints, 'if founded on facts that were not justified by public necessity of which they could scarcely conceive the extremity, were serious to their national character and might prove the cause of very extensive mischief to the present negotiations for peace and alliance with other native powers.[145] Nothing could have been in starker contrast to Hastings's former attitude to Macartney's policies. The dispute between the two governments now moved towards an open breach. In early January 1783 the council in Calcutta met to consider the whole affair of the assignment. The proceedings could not have been more heavily weighted against Macartney, those questioned being Coote, the Nawab's Vakil, Said Asam Khan, John Hollond, the former resident at Hyderabad, and Richard Sulivan, whose presence at Madras had earlier been ignored. Asam Khan recited the Nawab's familiar litany of complaints. Coote submitted a paper 'desiring that the Nabob's grievances be redressed'. Sulivan offered an account of relations between Nawab and Macartney, highly prejudicial to the latter, which he confessed was largely based upon hearsay. Hollond testified that the Nizam of Hyderabad regarded Hastings's agreement with the Nawab of April 1781 'as a decided breach of faith', and that 'this circumstance was urged by his ministers as a warning for regulating his own conduct', an ironic comment on the Governor General's criticisms of Macartney.[146] Hastings himself averred that Macartney had place a false construction on his government's rather embarrassing despatches of 26 December 1781 and 5 April 1782. After this travesty of a hearing, the council decided that Macartney's signing of the Torana chits 'was an usurpation of the sovereign power not justified but by valid authority and evident necessity' and hence all subsequent actions of the Madras government were illegal. Macartney was ordered to free the Nawab from the agreement of 2 December 1781 and to operate instead a modified version of Hastings's earlier assignment.[147]

Macartney could scarcely have anticipated this, but well before Hastings's orders reached him on 28 March, he had received welcome reassurance from London in the form of a despatch from the Court of Directors, dated 12 July 1782, and another from the

Committee of Secrecy of 15 September 1782. The first, while annulling Hastings's agreement of 1 April 1781, expressed approval of Macartney's assignment; the second, drafted in the light of his subsequent complaints about the Nawab, directed him to render it effective.[148] Nothing could have been more welcome to the embattled Macartney. But the first despatch enabled the Nawab to return to the assault. As the Directors' letter of 12 July 1782 had annulled his original agreement with Hastings, he argued, it naturally followed that his subsequent treaty with Macartney was also void. Macartney naturally countered this with London's seemingly unambiguous sanction of his actions. News of this latest joust between the two men reached Calcutta a few days before Coote was due to return to Madras to reassume command of the army from the incompetent hands of his successor, General James Stuart. To avoid a return to earlier friction, Coote had already been endowed with sole control of military affairs; now, his powers were widened considerably. On 20 March 1783 Hastings asked his council to consider whether, as a result of Macartney's latest refusal to surrender the assignment to the Nawab, he was likely to disobey the orders which had been sent to him and thereby lay himself open 'to the penalty prescribed by the act of 1773'. In effect, Hastings was asking for agreement to suspend Macartney if he did not comply with the order to restore the assignment, but his control over his council was far from absolute. John Stables and, interestingly, Macpherson refrained from comment, believing the move to be premature. Of those present, only Coote agreed with Hastings; but as 'the Governor General undertook Mr Wheler's concurrence', the motion was carried.[149]

With this sanction at his disposal, Coote sailed for Madras eight days later. He did not carry an order for Macartney's suspension, though this was widely rumoured. His brief from Hastings was to restore the assignment. As the council had just resolved that Macartney would be liable to the penalty of the 1773 act if he disobeyed, the future course of events seemed clearly marked. Macartney's principal friend at Calcutta, the Irish lawyer, William Dunkin, had tried to keep himself abreast of what was being planned and their correspondence reflects the degree of alarm felt at Coote's impending arrival.[150] On receiving the ominous news from Dunkin, Macartney hid his papers and prepared for the worst.[151] He was only spared humiliation by Suffren who, learning of Coote's departure from Bengal, sent six ships to intercept him. Sighting Coote's ship in the Bay of Bengal, the French pursued her for four days, during which the anxious old general 'repeatedly fainted and remained long insensible from the effect of excessive weakness and fatigue'.[152]

Three days after reaching the safety of Madras he died, on 27 April 1783, and with him passed the severest crisis which had yet faced Macartney in India.

If Coote's death was a reprieve for Macartney, it was an unmitigated calamity for Hastings, for not only did it rob the Governor General of the only man who had sufficient authority to act for him in Madras, but it further weakened his precarious hold over his own council. The consequences were seen in the next few months. Given fresh heart by the removal of the immediate threat, Macartney and his committee on 25 May 1783 sent their formal rejection of the order to restore the assignment, outlining their reasons in a 160-page document. Hastings's impotence soon became apparent. In August he repeated his earlier order that the Madras government restore the assignment but at a meeting on 16 September, while facing yet another crisis with the military, the Select Committee resolved on defiance. When this new gesture of disobedience was received, Hastings summoned his council on 13 October and formally moved that Macartney and his Select Committee be suspended. But Wheler, now his one sure ally, was absent and Macpherson and Stables overruled him.[153] These final events demonstrated, if proof were needed, the utter inadequacy of the 1773 act. Irrespective of the merits of the case, the Governor General could neither enforce his will over a subordinate presidency nor carry his own council. Macartney's defiance had succeeded.

X

If Macartney was lucky in Coote's timely death, his troubles with the military were far from over. Between September and December 1783, while he was still wrestling with Hastings over the assignment and trying to reach peace with Mysore, there occurred a series of events which caused him grave anxiety and considerable vexation on his return home. When ill-health forced Coote to leave the army in the autumn of 1782 and Sir Hector Munro returned to Scotland, the command fell upon Major-General James Stuart, who had perhaps stronger claims as a political intriguer than a field-officer and had lost a leg in the fighting not long before. By common consent the army languished under his command and at the end of the year he let slip a unique chance to deliver a telling blow at the Mysore forces. On 7 December 1782 Haidar died while his son, Tipu Sahib, was absent conducting operations on the west coast. Despite promptings from Macartney to act decisively, Stuart did nothing and, in the jaundiced view of one report, the army 'did not march to take advantage of so favourable an event'.[154] By the time the army ventured forth on 2 January 1783, Tipu had returned and successfully asserted his claim to his father's throne.

Complaints about Stuart's generalship continued into 1783 and by September Macartney and his committee began to fear that he was contemplating the type of coup against them that he had joined against Pigot in 1775.[155] It is not clear whether this was connected with the committee's contemporary defiance of Hastings. If so, it was probably a general apprehension on their part as Hastings thought no more highly of Stuart than anyone else. On 17 September the Select Committee informed Stuart of their desire to dismiss him, but the latter asserted that as a royal officer he would retain the command of the king's troops. Believing that he was now powerless, the committee left him at liberty and appointed as his replacement Major-General Sir John Burgoyne, who had earlier arrived at Madras with his regiment of light dragoons.[156] But Macartney had not reckoned on the jealousy subsisting between royal officers and those in the service of the Company, nor on the grey area which had always bedevilled him in the role of commander of Madras. Burgoyne, too, was in a delicate position. After meeting the dismissed general, he immediately reported to Macartney that as a royal officer he was bound to remain under Stuart's orders until the king commanded otherwise.[157] He also told the Select Committee that Stuart was busy drafting orders which he intended to issue to the troops that evening. Believing this to be the anticipated coup, the committee ordered Staunton to arrest the general. Marching with a force of sepoys to his house, Staunton found Stuart with his aides engaged on what appeared to be the drafting of orders. Staunton went upstairs and confronted Stuart with drawn sword. It was a delicate moment. Neither Staunton's sepoys nor those of Stuart had the remotest idea what was going on other than that the general they were used to obeying was being threatened with a sword. Fortunately for Macartney's friend, Stuart was too preoccupied with the destruction of his papers and arguing the point of law to issue orders to his men. Stuart was arrested and taken to the fort.[158]

If Macartney's handling of affairs had so far been well-judged, his actions now became more open to question. As Burgoyne still refused the command, Macartney now used his powers as commander in chief to appoint a reliable Company officer, Colonel Ross Lang, as Stuart's successor with the rank of lieutenant-general. Perhaps events had left him little option, but Burgoyne and his fellow officers were incensed at such an insulting supercession. In a rather ingenious compromise, Burgoyne put his troops under the command of a regimental officer junior to Lang's colonelcy, and then withdrew from the army. On 20 September he wrote offering this surrender, which in the 'spirit of moderation' Macartney accepted, assuring him that 'there is not the least intention of calling upon you to give any account of your conduct here'.[159]

But the events of these four days had left too much bitterness for any compromise to last. On 31 December 1783 Burgoyne was arrested for 'his contempt, disobedience to and mutinous resistance of the orders and directions of the said Government and of Lieutenant General Lang, Commander in Chief of the forces'.[160] Given the highly dubious nature of Lang's promotion, this was hardly surprising. The subsequent court martial in the summer of 1785 reflected badly on Macartney's treatment of Burgoyne who had, after all, dutifully informed him of Stuart's presumed intentions. Burgoyne was acquitted on all the charges brought against him. In particular, it was found that by quitting the camp on Lang's promotion he had 'prevented many evils that might have arisen and was productive of the most salutary consequences'.[161] By his decisive action in the early stages of this affair, it is probable that Macartney had forestalled a coup against him and Stuart was to find no supporters of any consequence in Britain. But the accelerated promotion of Lang over the head of royal officers, though arguably forced on him, and the later arrest of Burgoyne did Macartney's reputation no good. Most seriously, these moves contributed to the hostility of King George III, who later ordered Burgoyne to be informed that he considered his conduct to have been 'temperate, wise and meritorious, evidently preventitive of much disorder among the troops, and possibly of the most fatal consequences'.[162] Stuart's reward for requesting an investigation into his treatment was dismissal from the Company's services.[163] Macartney and the military could never, it seems, find enough common ground on which to co-exist in harmony. Once again, he had survived, but at the price of royal disfavour.

XI

The fate of the assignment continued to dominate events throughout Macartney's stay in India, but in the second half of his presidency a new issue, peace with Mysore, further clouded his relations with Bengal. His instructions from the Committee of Secrecy had ordered him to work for peace as 'our first and grand object' under the guidance of the Governor General; and he had not been long in India before he concluded that the war was unwinnable.

As early as September 1781, nearly three months after his triumph at Porto Novo, Coote had advised him that the only alternative to a decisive victory was a peace settlement.[164] Yet Coote's victories had yielded no conclusive result and under Stuart the war dragged on to the continuing misery of the Carnatic's inhabitants. The principle of peace was never really in doubt, except by some military commanders who felt that their local successes might be exploited to bring about an overall victory. Hastings believed that he had laid the basis for a settlement in the Treaty of Salbai which he concluded with the Peshwa of the Marathas on 17 May 1782. As an integral part of that treaty, the Peshwa was to put pressure on Haidar to evacuate the territories of the British and their allies. Accordingly, when in September 1782 Macartney, faithful as ever to his instructions, applied to Hastings for permission to negotiate with Haidar, he was refused.[165]

Months passed with no sign of the promised intervention from Poona and in the meantime famine raged in the Carnatic and the army seemed no closer to defeating Mysore. Not only did Stuart fail to profit from Haidar's death but an initially promising offensive into Tipu's territory on the Malabar coast produced another frustrating stalemate. In February 1783 the important port of Mangalore was captured by a small force of Black Watch and sepoys commanded by Colonel Colin Campbell, but in May Campbell was besieged by Tipu's main army with French assistance. Campbell's staunch defence of Mangalore from May 1783 until the following January was an epic of heroism but brought no relief to the Carnatic's starving inhabitants, whose distress was intensified by an embargo on food supplied from Bengal which Hastings had imposed in the spring of 1783. Macartney believed that this was part of the rancorous aftermath of Coote's death, while Hastings justified himself on the grounds of crop failure in his own province.[166] Tipu, too, had his problems, losing valuable support when the French ceased hostilities in July 1783. As a result, an armistice was agreed in August and once more Macartney requested power to negotiate for peace. However, Hastings disagreed, maintaining that the basis of a settlement had been laid through the Treaty of Salbai and the ending of the war with France.[167]

What changed Hastings's mind was the arrival at Madras in October 1783 of two emissaries from Tipu, offering terms which seemed to Macartney to hold out the prospect of peace on the basis of a mutual restitution of territory.[168] This time Hastings, who was well aware of the desire in London for a general end to hostilities, allowed the fact that the initiative had come from Tipu to reverse his previous attitude and sanctioned Macartney's negotiations.[169] Accordingly, on 9 November Staunton and Anthony Sadleir left Madras for Tipu's camp at Mangalore, being joined by John Hudleston a month later. Their task was a long and frustrating one. Sadleir proved a difficult colleague and Tipu kept up sufficient military pressure to show his potential for waging prolonged defensive warfare once the monsoon broke. The prime result of his successful procrastination was the surrender on 26 January 1784 of Campbell's garrison, now reduced through scurvy to less than a third of its original strength. Campbell, a grandson of Lord Bute, died at Bombay less than two months later. The heroism of Campbell's men stood in stark and embarrassing contrast to the incessant squabbling amongst Macartney's negotiators.

Macartney watched Tipu's success and his emissaries' lack of progress with mounting alarm and despair. By February 1784 he had reached one of the blackest periods of his career. Convinced of the ultimate failure of the negotiations, he wrote to Staunton: 'and yet if it fails, I know not *how* it will be *possible* to *carry on the war*'.[170] Two weeks later, as the negotiations still yielded no successful result, he sent this anguished appeal to his friend: 'adieu, I look most anxiously for *favourable* news from you — I think really if this *business fails,* I shall not survive it'.[171] It was, then, with a profound sense of relief that he learned on 24 March that a treaty had at last been concluded with Tipu on the eleventh. On the face of it, the Treaty of Mangalore gave the British the substance of what they needed to rebuild their power in south India. In return for the evacuation of British forces from the occupied areas of Mysore, Tipu promised to return all his European and Indian prisoners, to surrender to the Company its factory at Calicut on the Malabar coast, to withdraw his troops from the Carnatic and to renounce any future claim upon its territory. Given the state of the Carnatic's finances and food supplies, it might have seemed fortunate that the Mysore war had been ended without loss of prestige or territory, but the treaty had two omissions which made it objectionable to the Governor General. It made no reference to the Treaty of Salbai and, more seriously, it was concluded between the 'Company and the Nabob Tippoo Sultaun Bahadaur, and their Friends and Allies, particularly included therein, the Rajahs of Tanjore and Travancore'.[172] It was a challenge which could not be ignored. Not only was the Nawab of the Carnatic's name pointedly omitted but that of the Rajah of Tanjore, whom he regarded as a dependent, specifically appeared. Given the drift of events over the previous two years, the Nawab's outraged reaction at this latest evidence of his supercession and the support he could count on from Hastings were predictable; even so, it was with some confidence that Macartney despatched the treaty to Bengal for Hastings's agreement.

The Nawab's complaints about this latest affront brought a ringing denunciation of the treaty from Hastings's council. True to their now established policy of trying to restore the Nawab's authority, they castigated the treaty as debasing the 'sacred character of the British nation for fidelity to their allies'. Accordingly, while ratifying the treaty, they sent an additional declaration which specifically included the Nawab as a party to it. Macartney was ordered in unequivocal terms to transmit the new version to Tipu for his agreement.[173] The order represented a clear challenge to him either to re-open negotiations with Mysore or face the probable consequences. Yet again his relations with Hastings's government on the issue of the Nawab's powers had reached a crisis point and at a lengthy meeting of the Select Committee on 15 July 1784 he defended his conduct and outlined his proposed response. He argued that the Nawab was implicitly included in the treaty and that, if he was not named, it was because this had not been done in either the 1769 treaty with Haidar or the Treaty of Salbai. He further pointed out that the Nawab of Bengal had not been named in treaties made by Hastings's government and justified the inclusion of the Rajahs of Tanjore and Travancore by maintaining that their territories did not fall strictly within the Carnatic. There was much justification in all of this: but his true feelings surfaced when he asserted that the Nawab was not a true hereditary prince, merely an officer of the Mughals; and that his name could not have been included as a party to the treaty as he had already broken so many agreements. To approach Tipu with an amended version of the treaty would, he believed, merely offer a pretext for re-opening the war. Aware that he was courting suspension, Macartney told his colleagues that he would resign rather than comply with the order, assuring them that he would assume full responsibility.[174]

Macartney allowed his committee two weeks to ponder the serious step they were being asked to take before putting the motion formally before them on 31 July that they request Hastings's government to reconsider its decision. He was supported by Robert Maunsell but by neither Alexander Davidson nor Sadleir, who, though they considered Calcutta's proposal to be ill-advised, still believed that the Governor General's order had to be obeyed. Macartney only carried his motion on his own casting vote. A long despatch was prepared in which he repeated for Hastings's benefit the arguments he had presented to the Select Committee meeting of the fifteenth. If the discussion had so far reflected the committee's uneasiness, this was somewhat relieved when Davidson, Sadleir and Maunsell passed a motion 'that the suspension of Lord Macartney, or his being obliged to quit the chair at this important juncture, would most probably throw the Presidency of Fort St. George into anarchy and confusion', a gesture which showed that the Governor's qualities were at least appreciated amongst those who had worked closely with him.[175]

The reply sent by Macpherson and Wheler to this act of defiance was a masterpiece of invective which masked their inability to coerce Macartney's government. It contained few arguments of detail which Macartney could not effectively counter, but the real issue was not peace with Mysore but the way in which he had extended the Company's power over the Carnatic, confirmed by the exclusion of the Nawab's name from the treaty. 'The real and only question in dispute' was the Nawab's position. Macartney's actions, they contended, had effectively transferred the Carnatic to the Company and its ruler's authority

> had been limited by you to the walls of his garden, under the guns of your fort, and that there was no other spot in all his dominions where his command or power was equal to that of your native servants, or which he could call his own. Yet the Nabob had by no transgression forfeited the friendship or justice of the Company for a course of thirty years.[176]

But as the Bengal government was still reluctant to proceed to the fateful step of Macartney's suspension, his defiance was again successful. Although the despatch contained threatening noises, it was clear that nothing would be done until orders came from London which would reveal where judgement stood on the dispute between Madras and Calcutta. Three things stood out in the dispute. The first was Macartney's overriding, indeed desperate, desire for peace, which arose not just out of his punctilious regard for orders but from a desire to rid the people of the Carnatic of the miseries which had so long afflicted them. Secondly, his subsequent dispute with Bengal emphasized yet again the inadequate power given to the supreme government over the presidencies. But ultimately the real significance of the episode lay in the omission of the Nawab from the Treaty of Mangalore. Macartney seemed resolved to underline the Company's ascendancy in the Carnatic, while Bengal insisted on upholding the Nawab as the country's legitimate ruler. This had come to be the ultimate point at issue between the two governments.

XII

Although their attention was necessarily focussed on events in India, both Macartney and Hastings were uneasily aware that their prolonged duel was taking place against a background of rapidly-changing events at home. The fall of Lord North's government in March 1782 heralded a period of governmental instability with the administrations of Rockingham, Shelburne and the Fox-North coalition following in rapid succession until William Pitt's election victory in the spring of 1784 inaugurated a new phase of more stable government. The coalition of interests which had ensured Macartney's election in 1780 had fallen apart; for a man heavily dependent on patronage this was an unsettling development, though events were to show that Hastings had derived no advantage in the interim. It was, moreover, a time when Indian issues were much in the public eye. The hopeless inconsistencies in the Regulating Act were now painfully obvious to everyone. In 1783 Henry Dundas's bill and the two celebrated India bills of Charles James Fox (which, of course, occasioned the fall of the Fox-North coalition) indicated that the nation's legislators were turning their attention to the imperial issues in south Asia which were assuming ever greater significance following the loss of territory in north America. Here, too, William Pitt proved decisive, for his India Act of 1784 established the broad principles on which the Indian empire was to be governed until the upheaval of 1857-58. Although the Company retained its trading functions and powers of patronage, the decisive voice was henceforth to be that of a new governmental body, the Board of Control, which under the forceful direction of its first president, Henry Dundas, quickly assumed the function of a ministry for the Company's Indian possessions. Although detailed news of these developments was inevitably slow in reaching India, Thomas Allan tried to keep Macartney informed of the drift of events. Macartney was keenly aware that he had to take them into account in justifying his actions and planning for the future.

Well aware of the controversy his actions had provoked, Macartney made the considerable personal sacrifice of sending Staunton to London at the end of July 1784. His friend's mission, as Macartney confided to Fox, was 'personally to represent the true state of affairs of this presidency', and Staunton carried with him letters to a variety of prominent men, notably North, Sandwich, Sulivan, Loughborough, Robinson and Burke.[177] It was with the last that Staunton had his greatest, perhaps historic, success. Burke, who already had strong family reasons connected with Tanjore for hating

Benfield and the Nawab, was preparing the case which culminated in his classic speech on the Nawab of Arcot's debts, delivered on 28 February 1785. His correspondence shows that he was in consultation with Staunton up to the eve of its delivery and again in the summer of 1785, accepting his revisions as he prepared the text of his speech for publication.[178] Burke was able to use this up-to-date information on recent Indian events from Macartney's secretary to powerful effect in one of the late eighteenth century's most vitriolic orations.

Burke's masterpiece of invective must be judged against the background of the decision of the Court of Directors, approved by the Board of Control on 15 October 1784, to annul the assignment of the Carnatic. This decision found against Macartney's actions in every important respect. While commending him for his 'ability, moderation, and command of temper' and for his success in extracting so much revenue from the Carnatic under such difficult circumstances, it castigated him for issuing the Torana chits in his own name without allowing more time for negotiations with the Nawab. Had Macartney not done this, it may be argued, the 'vigorous and effectual' collection of the revenue would not have been accomplished. But sufficient justification of the order to surrender the assignment was their acceptance of Hastings's argument that the Nawab should be restored to control of his country 'and for removing from his mind every idea of secret design on our part to lessen his authority over the internal government of the Carnatic, and the collection and administration of its revenues'.[179] Macartney's policy thus stood condemned in practice and in principle.

Burke, at least, considered that in favouring the Nawab over Macartney those responsible had preferred corruption over honest government. Moreover his words carried more weight because he had been an opponent of Macartney's appointment to Madras. The ministers, he argued:

felt nothing for a land desolated by fire, sword, and famine; their sympathies took another direction; they were touched with pity for bribery, so long tormented with a fruitless itching of its palms; their bowels yearned for usury, that had long missed the harvest of its returning months; they felt for peculation which had been for so many years raking in the dust of an empty treasury; licking their dry, parched, unbloody jaws. These were the objects of their solicitude.[180]

For Burke the true victor had been Benfield, 'a criminal, who long since ought to have fattened the region's kites with his offal'.[181] If Macartney had no other compensation for his time in India, he at least had his actions upheld in one of the most celebrated speeches of the time, though it did little to advance him in the estimation of either Pitt or Dundas.

This, then, was the domestic political background against which Macartney laboured on, increasingly wearily, from the final months of 1784. His concerns showed no sign of diminishing, particularly as the presidency's financial problems had never been entirely solved. In September 1784 he had been forced through lack of funds to cease paying the half Batta, the special allowance to troops in the field which had been the custom for many years. This provoked an angry remonstrance from 256 British officers, many of whom argued that they had suffered beatings and forcible circumcision whilst in captivity in Mysore, and ensured that the deplorable relations which had always subsisted between him and the army continued to the end of his stay.[182] At the same time he was engaged in yet another tedious wrangle with Hastings over the presidency's accounts, though this eased when the Governor General sailed for home in February 1785, leaving Macpherson in an acting capacity.

It had become a thankless task, made no easier by the recurrent ill-health from which Macartney had suffered as early as the spring of 1782. His initial enthusiasm for India had long since waned. Thus, in January 1783, at the height of his dispute with Hastings over the assignment, he had informed Lord Ossory that he had no interest in advancement to the office of Governor General.[183] This was less than candid, as Thomas Allan's correspondence shows that in the summer of 1782 he and Lady Macartney had been actively campaigning for his translation to Bengal in the event of Hastings's removal.[184] But too much had happened for that to remain an attractive proposition and in the spring of 1785 he seems genuinely to have dreaded such a development, confiding in his friend, Thomas Mercer, on the approach of a vessel from home that 'God forbid she should bring anything that could possibly detain me another year in India'.[185]

All that seemed to be keeping him at his post was his belief that he should not relinquish his appointment until a proper successor could be designated and a desire to preserve his financial settlement, but on 28 May the fatal news arrived that his superiors had ordered the restoration of the assignment of the Nawab. The effect of this humiliating repudiation of everything he had worked for in Madras was immediate and irrevocable. It signalled his departure from the presidency, as he ruefully, but defiantly, informed his colleagues:

> I candidly confess it would be utterly impossible for me to carry on the Company's administration under the orders just received for surrendering the Nabob's assignment. These orders are founded in

sentiments directly opposite to the opinions which I have invariably entertained, and communicated to my employers, of the actual situation of their affairs, and I cannot help supposing from them that the Hon'ble Court of Directors have withdrawn their confidence in my administration and by establishing a system, which tends to throw an absolute discredit upon all that I have done, and represented upon this important subject, it would appear, as if they meant, tho' they have not expressed it, that my resignation should immediately follow the receipt of their orders.[186]

But Macartney was a tough fighter and he had no intention of leaving India without first making an attempt to preserve his settlement. For some time he had been curious to see Calcutta before returning home; he now decided to try to persuade Macpherson's government to intervene in favour of his policies.[187] With this aim in mind, he wasted no time before sailing from Madras. Having set in hand measures which he hoped would delay the surrender of the assignment to the Nawab, he embarked on 2 June leaving Alexander Davidson as acting governor. Five days later, as his ship touched the final port of the Northern Sarkars, he sent Davidson his letter of resignation.[188]

Macartney's purpose in going to Calcutta was to use Macpherson's powers as acting Governor General to freeze the situation over the assignment until he could present his case personally in London.[189] Although Macpherson can scarcely have relished the arrival of the man who had been widely regarded as the possible successor to Hastings, he invited Macartney to present his views and initial contacts seemed promising.[190] On 20 June Macartney presented his case to the council, reiterating his familiar contention that the restoration of the Carnatic's revenues to the Nawab would lead to such financial chaos that the Company's position there would be ruined. He formally requested Macpherson to maintain the *status quo* until fresh orders could be received from London.[191] Despite Macartney's early optimism, on 28 June Macpherson's council decided to refuse all his requests. It was naive to have believed that Macpherson might do otherwise, but Macartney was bitterly stung by this rebuff from a man he had once considered a friend. In refusing his support, 'the Governor General and Council see the justice, and feel the policy of leaving to orders so evidently founded on principles of national justice, and directed to the public good, their full scope, and proper effect'.[192] Of course, Macpherson was fully justified in upholding the orders which London had sent, but it is hard not to suspect that he relished this revenge for Macartney's treatment of the Nawab and Benfield.

Macartney lingered in Calcutta for another six weeks, in the course of which he received, to his evident surprise, a despatch from London appointing him Governor General. He had known earlier that there were moves in London to secure this for him but in view of the decision over the assignment he had naturally discounted the possibility.[193] It was true that he was very much the second choice. From October 1783 until his rejection of a formal offer by Pitt in early February 1785, the favoured candidate had been Earl Cornwallis, the defeated commander at Yorktown.[194] But by December 1784 Macartney's friends in Company circles were actively promoting his claims.[195] Cornwallis's refusal gave Macartney's supporters their chance and at the meeting of the Court of Directors on 17 February 1785 they secured his election, though only by lot after a tied vote, 'by the turn of a straw', as one friend described it.[196] Interestingly, the Directors were so apprehensive that the dispute with Hastings over the Treaty of Mangalore might have led to his suspension that their letter of appointment made specific provision for his re-instatement.[197] Had Macartney been desperately ambitious for the office of Governor General, it was now his, but despite this welcome indication of confidence, there were pressing political and personal reasons which impelled him to return to London with certain conditions of acceptance. Having indicated to Macpherson his displeasure over his treatment at Calcutta, he sailed down the Hughli on 13 August 1785, finally ending his active links with the Indian sub-continent.[198]

XIII

Macartney arrived home in December 1785 after the long voyage which he had considered necessary to restore his health and spirits. Still smarting from his humiliation at the hands of Macpherson, he had had ample time to consider the terms on which he would be prepared to assume the Governor Generalship, which he presented to the Chairman and Deputy Chairman of the Company on 13 January 1786. Justifying his return on the grounds of ill-health and the need to determine the extent of his support, given the peculiar way in which he had come by the appointment, he then set out his terms, the fruits of his four years' experience. First among them was the clear subordination of the military to the civil power; there was to be no repetition of his brushes with Coote, Stuart and Burgoyne. He was to be given the power to act independently of the Governor General's council, which was to assume the role of an advisory body, an interesting condition in view of the fact that it had been

Macartney c.1786, following his return from India (G. D. Burtchaell and
T. U. Sadleir, *Alumni Dublinenses,* Dublin, 1924).

Hastings's inability to control his colleagues which had prevented his suspension. On the personal level, he requested Macpherson's recall because of the 'marked and personal opposition on his part to Lord Macartney's public conduct and sentiments'; this was his revenge for what he regarded as betrayal by a friend.[199] A further vital condition was left unspoken at the meeting. The 'Friends of Lord Macartney' had begun to canvass for 'some distinguished mark of Royal favour', their euphemism for the conferring of a British peerage.[200] This elevation was a prime reason for his return home. He believed that his services had earned him such a reward and in the negotiations with Pitt and Dundas his wife had let it be known that this would be the price of his acceptance of the post. It was not, he confided in his father-in-law, a matter of 'personal vanity'; rather the necessary seal of authority as Governor General.[201] Be that as it may, his none-too-subtle canvassing for this substantial promotion in the hierarchy proved fruitless. It all depended on the King and George III, keenly resenting his treatment of Burgoyne, viewed his resignation from Madras as 'not an unfavourable event'.[202] Royal chilliness was evident in an audience Macartney had on the same day as his discussions with the Company officials. In the course of this bleak interview no mention was made of a peerage, the King merely reporting to Pitt:

> Nothing dropped from him that marked any desire of accepting the offer the East India Company have made him, or that enables me to think he is resolved to decline it. As it was certainly no object to me to dive into his future intentions I supposed he had no other views but of having his conduct whilst at Madras examined by his employers, which he had very decidedly stated to me.[203]

This was an unmistakable signal that the desired British peerage was not about to be forthcoming. Any lingering hope Macartney might have entertained of returning to India as a British peer was finally killed when he met Pitt and Dundas on 20 January. Pitt's readiness to accept the conditions Macartney had presented to the Directors was clear. He told Macartney that he would grant the Governor General powers to act independently of his council, that he would allow some time to elapse but would then extend the civil power over the military; and he sensibly pointed out that Macpherson would hardly wish to remain in India as Macartney's subordinate. Macartney was also assured that he would return to India with Pitt's 'decided countenance and support'. If Macartney's sole aim had been the Governor Generalship, it was now his on the terms he had demanded, but the 'distinguished mark of favour' had not been mentioned. Alluding to this omission, Macartney at once caught

Lady Jane Macartney in 1786, by Abbott (Coll. Mr. L. Mackie).

Pitt's hostile expression but went on to press his claim, being forced to plead that he had 'been 22 years in public business of that kind and hoped it was not unreasonable to aspire to the King's favour, as a reward for past service and an encouragement to future'.[204] It was not to be. After a long silence Dundas mercifully ended everyone's embarrassment by observing that 'Lord Macartney seems to shew not only no inclination to the Government of Bengal, but a reluctance to accept of it'.[205] Macartney's aspirations to the British peerage had been checked and his Indian career had ended. Cornwallis went in his stead with the powers Macartney had demanded and was to preside over a distinguished administration.

XIV

Failure to secure the coveted British peerage seemed merely to underline the lack of success which had characterised Macartney's time in India. By any standards it had proved a trying experience which had brought him little but constant ill-health, worry, disappointment and the frustration of cherished plans. He had seemingly shown scant talent for human relations, having provoked the bitter enmity of Hastings, Coote, Stuart, Burgoyne, Benfield, Macpherson and the Nawab, not to mention the fatal alienation of his sovereign. As a result of his quarrels he had fought two unsuccessful duels, one with Sadleir in India in 1784, and a second with Stuart in Hyde Park in June 1786 in which he suffered a severe wound. Little had happened at Madras to lighten or enrich the cares of administration. The pressures of war and famine had meant that social life in the presidency had been of a rudimentary nature, though Macartney seems to have entered with amused tolerance into the male-dominated dinners and dances, attended both by Europeans and by Indians. His voluminous correspondence shows little of the intellectual curiosity about local life which so distinguished Hastings, and which Macartney himself displayed in other circumstances. He did not cease to be concerned with Indian affairs on his return home. Between 1786 and his departure for China his patronage for Indian appointments was constantly sought; and later, on his return from the Cape, he was offered (but did not accept) the increasingly powerful office of President of the Board of Control, a belated recognition of his worth at Madras. In general it seems that he recollected the place with small affection. When in 1789 he was visited at Lisanoure Castle by a young Co. Antrim man who hoped to enlist his patronage for an Indian career, Macartney diverted the youth to Canada with the remark 'that we heard a great deal of those who came from India with fortunes, but not a word of the hundreds who fell victims to the climate, and the excesses into which young men were liable to be led in such a voluptuous country'.[206]

Yet Macartney's time in Madras is replete with insights into the way in which the British empire in India was emerging out of the revolutionary changes of mid-century. Moreover, in personal terms it was by no means a disaster for him. If he quarrelled with most of the prominent men in India at that time, his immediate circle — Staunton, Oakley, Hudleston and Davidson at Madras, Dunkin and Mercer at Calcutta, and Allan in London — devotedly stuck by him at times when it must have seemed more profitable to give their allegiance elsewhere. Even Sadleir, a notoriously cantankerous man, was generally the faithful executor of his wishes. His honesty and upright character retained for him the regard of influential men of different parties in London, as his elevation to the Governor Generalship bore witness. He started badly by alienating Hastings and Coote, though in each case the arguments were not one-sided. But once his troubles multipled from the start of 1782 he showed toughness and resolution in times of the utmost stress, even if Coote's fortuitous death spared him the ultimate choice between bowing to Hastings and dismissal. The most satisfactory outcome of his time in India was that during his four years he managed to save the sum of £32,718, without recourse to the financial peculation which had disgraced the Company's name in south India.[207] This successful financial aspect to his Indian career enabled him to discharge many of his debts and establish an investment portfolio, as well as to continue with improvements to his north Antrim estate. This new financial security helped compensate for the adverse effect India had had on his health. As early as April 1782, despite the crisis in their relationship, he had been too unwell to negotiate personally with the Nawab; and another serious bout of ill-health had afflicted him during his Calcutta visit. Nor was his health improved by the wound which he sustained in the duel with Stuart on his return. His absence from public life for a period after 1786 was probably necessary for him to rebuild his health and certainly enabled him to put his new-found financial means to constructive use.

But it is in the public sphere that Macartney's Indian career must ultimately be judged. It was a period of experiment in Britain's relationship with the Indian sub-continent as the way in which he and his patrons had to campaign for the governorship demonstrated. Although Lord North's government and leading men in the Company were anxious to send him to Madras, they could only do so through the cumbersome exercise of patronage. The ways in which they went about this illuminates the problems created by the East India Company's transformation from a trading body into an instrument of national policy. Once Macartney arrived in India his policies and the reactions they provoked further exposed the inconsistencies in Britain's Indian position. In regard to specific acts of policy, by general consent his insistence on the seizure of the Dutch settlements was timely in view of Suffren's arrival and the Treaty of Mangalore allowed the hard-pressed presidency a respite until war with Mysore resumed in 1790. He went to the Presidency of Fort St. George at a time of acute military and naval danger and left it intact. A great deal of the credit for this must go to others, but it must be remembered that Macartney bore the ultimate responsibility for the survival of his government.

On the central matter of the assignment of the Carnatic and his consequent dispute with Hastings opinions must differ. Macartney and Hastings were honourable public servants, each trying to resolve problems as they found them, and it was an abiding pity that neither man could acknowledge this quality in the other. Macartney's initial handling of Hastings was tactless, but that hardly merited the Governor General's unrelenting opposition. The two men expressed profoundly different views on Britain's position in India. Hastings based his opposition to Macartney's policies on the need to sustain the authority of the Indian rulers, though this seems odd in view of his own policies in north India. It was an honest principle: but, in implementing it, Hastings seemed to reverse the previous encouragement given by his government to Macartney, and to adopt the arguments of parties deeply tainted by corruption and self-interest. In taking their side against an honest man Hastings diminished his own stature.

In contrast, Macartney's policies came to be based on the unashamed assertion of the Company's power to the detriment of what remained of indigenous authority. He successfully averted the return of the Northern Sarkars to Hyderabad; above all, by signing the Torana chits and omitting the Nawab from the Treaty of Mangalore he attempted to establish undisputed British power in the Carnatic. The morality of such a course must be debated within the context of the nature of European imperialism, but Macartney was a man of his time and he believed he was following the only logical course. He attempted to replace the Nawab's authority, which was tainted by corruption and had for years been little but a shadow, by the rule of the Company. In this respect he saw more clearly than Hastings, for the future of India followed this direction. He must claim credit for the uncompromising honesty of his government. By fearlessly challenging the corruption of Benfield and his associates, he cut a bench-mark by which the standards of government might be judged. Despite all temptations to the contrary, he remained remarkably faithful to his pledges to remain true to his employers' wishes and to return to them with 'hands as clean as any servant they have ever employed'. It was a considerable achievement.

CHAPTER VII

CHINA 1792-94

I

The embassy which Lord Macartney undertook to the Court of Ch'ien-lung, Emperor of China, in 1793 marks the beginning of a cultural confrontation between Chinese and European attitudes and values which culminated, in its crudest form, in the period after 1840. Macartney consciously confronted the Chinese Empire, then apparently at the zenith of its power and prosperity, with the increasing power and achievement of the British Empire. The affairs of the embassy were conducted on both sides in a spirit of cultural superiority, with Macartney and the gentlemen of his suite trying to impress the Chinese with their good manners, good discipline and technical achievements, and the Chinese officials seeking to outface the Englishmen with the spectacle of Chinese culture, prosperity and good order, without admitting the claims of the 'barbarians' to any distinction whatever, except that of unruliness. This aspect of the embassy will become more apparent as we follow the course of events through quotations from the official Chinese documents as well as from Macartney's own account.

British trade with China was not firmly established until the beginning of the eighteenth century, when the East India Company started to trade regularly at Canton. At first the system was somewhat flexible, but the local Chinese officials continually tightened their control over the foreign merchants and imposed heavier fees and duties on them. During the decade 1750-60 the system was formalized and the Chinese officials laid down detailed regulations which were confirmed by an imperial edict of 1760.[1] As a result foreign merchants trading at Canton did so in face of considerable restrictions and vexations. Trade had to be conducted through a small group of licenced Chinese merchants known to westerners as Hong merchants. These merchants were formed into a monopoly, known as the Co-hong, under the control of the local officials who were able, thereby, to tighten their control more effectively over the foreigners. From about 1770 onwards the pattern of British trade at Canton gradually became more complex because of the arrival of private merchants in the Country trade.[2] In 1784 William Pitt introduced the Commutation Act by which duties on tea imported into England were drastically reduced. This lowered the price of tea considerably, made smuggling unprofitable, and increased revenue through greater legal sales. But if the price of tea in England was to remain reasonable it was necessary that conditions of trade at Canton should remain stable, and that no further increases should be made in the amount of fees, duties and 'presents' exacted there. Thus in 1791 Pitt himself, as head of the Ministry, had good reason for considering an embassy. Furthermore it was about this time that the industrialists in England began to look round for wider markets for their growing volume of manufactures. By this time the East India Company, tired of the constant difficulties confronting its trade at Canton, began to consider that perhaps the only way in which conditions might be improved was through an ambassador who could represent their case direct to the Emperor at Peking. In 1791 Henry Dundas, a close friend of Pitt, and the administration's authority on Eastern affairs, was made Home Secretary, and since he was anxious to enlarge the trade of England and India with China it was decided to send an embassy.

This was not, in fact, the first attempt to send an embassy to China. In 1787 Lieutenant-Colonel the Hon. Charles Cathcart had been appointed Ambassador to China, but he had died on the outward voyage and the embassy was not carried out.[3] Dundas now turned to Lord Macartney who, with his previous diplomatic and administrative experience abroad, was highly qualified to undertake this difficult and delicate task. Dundas first approached Macartney in the autumn of 1791, and discussions continued into December. Macartney's first reaction was a qualified one. Writing to Staunton (who, since returning from India, had become Sir George Staunton Bart.), he explained that he did not wish to undertake the embassy unless there was a fair prospect of making 'an honorable and prosperous voyage. I am myself pleased with the idea, and should therefore be sorry to find myself disappointed'.[4] Dundas and Macartney had a meeting on 22 December 1791 when the final decision to send an embassy appears to have been taken.[5] Macartney accepted the appointment on the following terms. He asked that the choice of all members of the embassy be left in his hands, and this was settled as he wished.[6] He asked that his salary should be nearly equal to his previous earnings at Madras, and proposed a figure of £16,000 a year. After some negotiation he accepted a salary of £10,000 a year as Ambassador with an allowance of £5,000 a year.[7] Macartney also wanted promotion in the peerage, and requested an Irish earldom. This request was met when he was granted the immediate title of Viscount with the promise of an earldom later. He was created Viscount Macartney of Dervock in the County of Antrim on 28 June 1792; and Earl Macartney on 1 March 1794, shortly after his return to England.[8]

For over a hundred years ideas about China had been filtering into England, but this knowledge had mostly been obtained at second-hand through the accounts of the Jesuits, who were apt to be over-enthusiastic, or from the superficial reports of previous European embassies. Here, then, was the opportunity of the century, a splendid chance to penetrate the subtleties of the Chinese character, to find out at first-hand their method of government and the way their minds worked. In fact the Macartney embassy proved to be an early attempt at penetrating the bamboo curtain of Chinese exclusiveness. It was something of a European reconnaissance, carried out by experienced men, since in his suite Macartney took scientists ('natural philosophers'), draughtsmen, army officers and others, most of whom made copious observations and sketches of what they saw. Preparations for sending the embassy, which began late in 1791, were made with this in mind. Several things had to be done simultaneously. Macartney's first care was to obtain a capable deputy who would serve as his principal secretary and also hold credentials as Minister Plenipotentiary in case Macartney himself died, or was unable to carry out the embassy for any reason. Luckily he was able to persuade his old friend and colleague, Sir George Leonard Staunton, to undertake this post, and Staunton, because of his experience and personal loyalty to Macartney, played a considerable part in the efficient running of the embassy. Staunton's first task was to search for a suitable interpreter in Europe. Eventually he found two young converts at the Chinese College at Naples who had completed their training for the priesthood and were now waiting for a ship to take them to Macao from whence they could hope to enter China. They did not speak English but were capable of interpreting between Chinese and Italian or Latin. In exchange for a passage to China the two priests, Jacobus Li and Paolo Cho, agreed to accompany the embassy as interpreters. Meanwhile Macartney was busy appointing the members of his suite which in the end consisted of ninety-four persons, including two under-secretaries, two interpreters, a comptroller, a surgeon, a physician and 'natural philosopher' (Dr. Hugh Gillan M.A. Aberdeen, M.D. Edinburgh), a mechanic or 'experimental scientist' (Dr. James Dinwiddie M.A. Edinburgh), a painter, a 'draughtsman' (William Alexander), a metallurgist, a watchmaker, a mathematical instrument maker, a gardener-botanist, a page (Master George Thomas Staunton), his tutor, a valet and five German musicians. There was also a military escort under a Lieutenant-Colonel and two Lieutenants consisting of ten dragoons, twenty artillerymen and twenty infantry.[9]

Another important task to be carried out was the selection and packing of the presents intended for the Emperor and the more important officials with whom the embassy might have contact. In Chinese theory all foreign envoys were regarded as tribute envoys, who should arrive at the capital bringing local produce to show their 'dutiful submission'. However, it was well known to the English supercargoes at Canton that Ch'ien-lung and his great officials were amused by valuable and ingenious articles such as clockwork automata which told the time, played tunes and performed various gyrations. Quite apart from sending presents to conform with the tastes of the Chinese Court and to impress the Chinese with the wealth and advanced technical skill of English craftsmen, it was also decided to send a selection of samples of English manufactures which could be displayed to Chinese officials and merchants and given away as presents whenever opportunity offered. With this in view prominent manufacturers were invited to submit specimens for inclusion among the embassy's baggage. Eventually specimens of manufactures were received from Thomas Gill of Birmingham (sword blades), Josiah Wedgwood (Staffordshire pottery) and from Matthew Boulton of Birmingham (various items of hardware).[10] Also some outstanding recent inventions were taken by Dr. Dinwiddie for public display, including a diving bell by Smeaton, an air balloon, an air pump and apparatus with which to demonstrate experiments in electricity, mechanics and so on.[11] The official presents to the Emperor included, among others, a planetarium by P. M. Hahn, an orrery by William Fraser, ornate clocks by Vulliamy and Son, two eighteen-light lustres and a great lens (or burning glass) by William Parker and Son, Staffordshire vases and figures by Josiah Wedgwood (including a copy of the Portland vase), and a telescope made by Sir William Herschel.[12] Thus the embassy was to be both a reconnaissance sent to bring back information on China, as well as a trade mission to popularize British inventions and manufactures abroad. To transport the embassy in a fitting manner Macartney was promised a large warship, H.M.S. *Lion*, sixty-four guns, to carry himself and part of his suite, and also the *Hindostan*, East Indiaman, one of the newest and largest of the East India Company's fleet, to carry the presents and the remainder of his staff.

The instructions which Macartney received, both from the government and from the East India Company, show clearly the reasons for sending an embassy and the attitude in Britain towards commerce at the end of the eighteenth century. In general the East India Company wanted to preserve its monopoly of British trade to China with the minimum of disturbance, and was prepared to put up with a good deal of extortion and annoyance at the hands of the Chinese officials in Canton. If possible Macartney was to obtain permission for the Company to trade to one or more ports north of Canton, to obtain information about Chinese manufactures and trade, and to find out what new articles might profitably be exported from China to England. The attitude of the Company was one of caution and patience, tinged with scepticism. The government, on the other hand, was being nudged forward by the thrusting English manufacturers, the Boultons, Garbetts and Wedgwoods, who wanted to find and expand markets abroad for their growing range of products. It was also being pushed by private merchants, who wanted government support in recovering debts owed them by bankrupt Hong merchants and, in general, a stronger reaction to what they considered the extortions and irregularities of the Chinese officials at Canton. The instructions which Dundas gave Macartney before he sailed can be summarized as follows: to create as favourable an impression on the Chinese as possible, both by the good conduct of his suite and also by demonstrating England's scientific knowledge and technical achievements. He was also to obtain all the information he could about China's relations with Russia and other countries. More specifically he was to attempt:

To negotiate a treaty of commerce and friendship and to establish a resident Minister at the Court of Ch'ien-lung.

To extend British trade in China by the opening of new ports, especially in northern China where British woollens might be sold.

To obtain from China the cession of a piece of land or an island nearer to the tea and silk producing area than Canton, where British merchants might reside the whole year, and where British jurisdiction could be exercised.

To abolish the existing abuses in the Canton system and to obtain assurances that they would not be revived.

To create new markets in China, especially in Peking, for British products hitherto unknown, such as hardware and the like, samples of which were taken by the Ambassador as presents.

To open Japan and Cochin China to British trade by means of treaties.[13]

Before relating the events of the embassy itself it will be helpful to have some knowledge of the Chinese milieu in which it took place in order to visualize the embassy in its historical setting and to avoid, as far as possible, anachronisms. For instance, the Chinese at that time had no conception of Europe and merely wrote 'western ocean' and 'western ocean barbarians' in their documents. The ideas of even the highest officials concerning the geography of the 'western ocean' were extremely vague. From the European point of view it was 'the embassy of Lord Macartney to the Court of the Emperor of China', but from the Chinese point of view it was 'the English envoy bringing tribute to the Emperor of China'. From the Chinese point of view China was the centre of the world, and outside her frontiers dwelt only various barbarian peoples of inferior culture.[14] When European merchants started coming to China their behaviour and customs did not impress the Chinese scholar-officials as in any way cultured. The small number of Catholic missionaries who went to Peking, learned to speak Chinese, wore Chinese clothes and ate Chinese food, quoted the Confucian classics and entered the Emperor's service where they received appointments in the hierarchy of officials, merely served to reinforce the Chinese belief that barbarians would naturally wish 'to come to be transformed' by higher Chinese culture. According to Confucian theory the 'virtue' of the Emperor, as Son of Heaven and universal ruler, would inevitably attract the barbarians to his Court where, briefly, they could see for themselves China's superior culture. The barbarians would naturally be eager 'to come to be transformed' by Chinese culture while the Emperor, as universal sovereign, would be compassionate towards them in his 'tender cherishing of men from afar' and would 'treat them all with equal benevolence'.[15] Thus the tributary system evolved whereby the barbarian envoy came to Court to show 'the humble submission' of his own ruler and to acknowledge Chinese cultural superiority. A detailed Court ritual was laid down in the dynastic statutes for the reception of tribute envoys in audience by the Emperor. The envoy, and his assistants taking part in the audience, must perform the full kotow and then deliver their presents, which traditionally should consist of 'native produce', and which would compare unfavourably in value and elegance with the Emperor's presents, consisting of rolls of silk, sets of porcelain and other artistic Chinese products. In essence the tributary system was *symbolic*. It was a *ritual* whereby barbarous peoples outside the borders of China could be given a place in the Chinese world system, and take their place under the Son of Heaven. The practical purpose of the system was strictly to control the relations of barbarian countries with China *on China's own terms*.[16]

Before his arrival in China Macartney prepared himself as thoroughly as possible for the task ahead by drawing on the experience of the East India Company trading at Canton, by talking to people with knowledge of China, and by reading 'all the books that had been written upon that country in all the languages I could understand'.[17] In spite of his efforts Macartney was only able to gain a vague impression of the Chinese system of government. Certainly he started his embassy under the impression that European diplomatic methods modified slightly to suit oriental ideas of pomp might succeed, and that it might be possible for him to reside continuously at Peking while negotiating a treaty of trade and friendship.

Final preparations for the embassy were made during the late summer of 1792 and on 2 August Macartney, Staunton and Captain Erasmus Gower, commanding H.M.S. *Lion*, were received in audience by George III. The Ambassador and his suite sailed on 26 September, touching at Madeira, Teneriffe, the Cape Verde islands and at Rio de Janeiro where they stayed on shore two weeks. The voyage proceeded, by way of Tristan da Cunha, through the Straits of Sunda to Batavia, where they stayed about six weeks and were well entertained by the Dutch authorities. From Batavia they sailed to the Bay of Tourane in Annam.[18] Macartney kept two journals during the embassy. The first covered the outward voyage as far as Tourane Bay and the second covered the period until his arrival in Macao at the conclusion of the embassy on 15 January 1794.[19] It is clear from more than one passage in these journals that Macartney wrote daily notes of events and impressions. Thus in his journal entry for 16 August 1793 he wrote: 'but before I proceed further I must set down a few particulars which have struck me, lest in the multiplicity of things before me they should slip from my memory. Indeed observations ought always to be written upon the spot; if made afterwards upon the ground of recollection they are apt to vary their hue considerably'.[20] Again, in a footnote to an entry for 15 December he wrote: 'but at the same time I must add that I wrote the above description immediately on my returning to my yacht, merely for the purpose of aiding my recollection and certainly without any intention of imposing upon myself or upon others'.[21]

II

On 20 June 1793 H.M.S. *Lion* and the *Hindostan* East Indiaman anchored several miles off Macao and Sir George Staunton went ashore for intelligence. He reported that the embassy seemed likely to enjoy a good reception in Peking, but that the Portuguese at Macao appeared hostile towards it.[22] On 7 July Staunton went ashore at Ting-hai on the main island of Chusan to obtain pilots to take the ships to Tientsin.[23] Finally on 25 July the ships anchored off

(Above) Macartney on the *Lion* during the Chinese Embassy: a good likeness according to Barrow, and one which put on record Macartney's 'habit of putting his gloves in the corner of his cocked hat' (B.L. Add. MS.33931, f.2).

(Left) Macartney, n.d. but c.1792, by J. Hall after T. Hickey (B.L. Add. MS.33931, f.3).

the bar in the Gulf of Chihli which was as close as they could proceed to the mouth of the Peiho, on which river Tientsin is situated. Two Chinese officials then came aboard the *Lion*, being charged by the Emperor to escort the Ambassador and in general to oversee the arrangements for the embassy. In his journal Macartney called them Van and Chou. However, Van is not a Chinese name, and Macartney was referring to an official named Wang Wen-hsiung, while by Chou Macartney was probably referring to Ch'iao Jen-chieh.[24] For convenience they will be referred to here as Wang and Chou. Wang, at this time, was commander of the Tungchow brigade, having recently distinguished himself in action against 'bandits', while Ch'iao was Taotai (Circuit Intendant) of Tientsin.

On 5 August Macartney and his suite disembarked into Chinese junks which were to take them up river to Tientsin and then to Tungchow, twelve miles from Peking. Macartney now began to react to the Chinese people and scenes around him and to record his impressions for writing up in his journal. Where present-day travellers to China would take coloured photographs Macartney noted down his immediate impressions, while his 'draughtsman', William Alexander, made innumerable rough sketches from which to work up his colour-wash drawings later.[25] 'The river here appeared to be as broad as the Thames at Gravesend. Great numbers of houses on each side, built of mud and thatched . . . and inhabited by such swarms of people as far exceeded my most extravagant ideas even of Chinese population . . . The children are very numerous and almost stark naked. The men in general well-looking, well-limbed, robust and muscular'.[26] The following day Macartney went ashore to a temple where he met Liang K'en-t'ang, Governor General of the province of Chihli, who had come to greet him. In his journal Macartney gives a description of a highly cultured, great official of the Chinese empire receiving a highly cultivated, great minister of the British empire, and shows how a representative of Chinese civilization and a representative of the European Enlightenment played the diplomatic game together. 'The Viceroy received us at the gate with distinguished politeness and an air of cordiality'. After recounting the compliments they paid each other Macartney concluded: 'it is impossible to describe the ease, politeness and dignity of the Viceroy during the whole conference [and] the attention with which he listened to our requests . . . He is a very fine old man of seventy-eight years of age, of low stature, with small sparkling eyes, a benign aspect, and a long silver beard'.[27] Only one thing disturbed Macartney's peace of mind. The Viceroy had

224

offered to supply the English ships with twelve months' provisions immediately. 'I hope this does not forbode his wishes for our speedy departure'.

The two following days were spent in preparing for the departure upriver of the junks. 'In this we were assisted by the different mandarins appointed to attend us, with regularity, alertness and dispatch that appeared perfectly wonderful. Indeed, the machinery and authority of the Chinese government are so organized, and so powerful, as almost immediately to surmount every difficulty, and to produce every effect that human strength can accomplish'.[28] With a little imagination one can picture the pageant of colour and movement of the embassy's progress as described in Macartney's journal. There were thirty-seven junks 'each having a flag flying at her masthead to distinguish her rank and ascertain her station in the procession'. There were many other boats to carry the hundred or more mandarins allotted to the embassy. 'At noon the gongs or copper drums began to beat with a most deafening noise, and gave the signal for all being ready for departure. In less than an hour our whole fleet was under sail, and we proceeded up the river with a good breeze and flowing tide at the rate of about four miles per hour'.[29] On 11 August Macartney arrived at Tientsin where he was met by an official, senior in rank to Wang and Chou, whom he called Chin, and whom he described as the Emperor's legate, especially deputed to conduct him to the Emperor who was now at his summer hunting-palace at Jehol, north of the Great Wall. This official was Cheng-jui, a Manchu, who at that time was Salt Commissioner of Chang-lu (an area south of Tientsin), an important and lucrative post.[30] Macartney explained in his journal that Cheng-jui had been deputed, together with Wang and Chou, to accompany the embassy to Jehol, 'the viceroy's age and infirmities disabling him from any fatiguing service'. However, in a military despatch of 31 August, from the Emperor's favourite minister, Ho-shen, to Cheng-jui and others, a different reason was given. It was explained that the Governor General's rank was an exalted one, and that if he were to accompany the tribute envoy on the journey it might enhance the envoy's arrogant bearing.[31] There were a number of instances during the course of the embassy when Macartney was thinking one thing while the Chinese officials were thinking something very different, such being the nature of the diplomatic blind man's buff when two very different cultures briefly met.

Amid 'the clangour of various instruments of warlike music' Macartney went ashore with his whole entourage to a conference with the viceroy and the legate. Two questions caused difficulties.

Macartney wanted to leave the larger and more delicate presents at Peking (the planetarium, the globes, the great lens, the lustres, the clocks and certain other articles) and to take to Jehol only the presents which were not likely to be damaged by a long overland journey.[32] Cheng-jui, out of anxiety not to depart from precedent, objected, and urged that all the presents be sent to Jehol. Macartney finally won his point but antagonised Cheng-jui. The other question concerned the performance of the kotow ceremony at the imperial audience, which was still not settled. In a Court Letter of 5 August instructions for dealing with the barbarian envoy were issued:

Although the tribute envoy himself declared that he is an Assistant Minister of State[33] of his country and is a person in the close confidence of the King, nevertheless, whenever barbarian envoys enter our country to present tribute, the etiquette for the meeting of vassal officials with ministers of the Celestial Empire is governed by a definite code... When the envoy waits on Cheng-jui he naturally ought to be very reverential. In dealing with barbarians it is all the more important to weigh up the situation and to hit the mean, being neither too servile nor too overbearing. Since that country has sent an envoy sailing across the sea from afar, on no account should he harbour any slight which might deflect him from turning towards civilization. Show him kindness and it will be all right. But if he is treated with too much ceremony then, the barbarian nature being greedy to gain advantage, the more liberally we treat them the more haughty they will become, and instead we will cause the barbarians to lose sight of the ceremonial system and dignity of the Celestial Empire and they may slight us.[34]

A Court Letter of 14 August from Ho-shen discussed the difficulty of performing the kotow in the 'western ocean' style of dress, and Cheng-jui was instructed to tell the envoy in the course of conversation that 'as regards the various vassal states, when they come to the Celestial Empire to bring tribute and have an audience, not only do all their envoys perform the ceremony of the three kneelings and the nine knockings of the head, but even the princes who come in person to Court also perform this same ceremony'; and then to suggest that when Macartney was given audience by the emperor he should temporarily loosen the bindings round his legs.[35] The whole document illustrates the Chinese attitude towards barbarian envoys and the importance attached to the proper performance of the kotow, especially at the imperial audience. The battle of the kotow was now joined. Macartney's instructions stated: 'you will procure an audience as early as possible after your arrival, conforming to all ceremonials of that court which may not commit the honour of your Sovereign or lessen your own dignity, so as to endanger the success of your negotiation'. This left it to his own discretion, but it is clear from his journal that he was determined to avoid the kotow unless he obtained something in return.[36]

The kotow ceremony was not the only matter with which the Ambassador had to contend. As they proceeded upriver towards Tungchow Macartney noted: 'we are much troubled with mosquitoes, or gnats, and other insects . . . and we are stunned day and night by the noise of a sort of cicada which lodges in the sedgy banks and is very obstreperous'.[37] Added to this, the members of the embassy had to endure the noise of the copper drums which the Chinese in the boats were continually beating. Sleep must have been difficult especially since the weather was hot, the temperature reaching around 88 degrees Fahrenheit, and the first victim of dysentery died. Macartney, meanwhile, had begun to have some doubts about the outcome of the embassy: 'for all along, ever since our departure from Tientsin, I have entertained a suspicion, from a variety of hints and circumstances, that the customs and policy of the Chinese would not allow us a very long residence among them'.[38] He now began to realize that in China things were not necessarily what they appeared to be, and that the reality beneath appearances was more difficult to fathom. 'The most refined politeness and sly good breeding appeared in the behaviour of all those mandarins with whom we had any connection; but although we found an immediate acquiescence in words with everything we seemed to propose, yet, in fact, some ingenious pretence or plausible objection was usually invented to disappoint us'.[39] Furthermore he realized that he and his staff were being 'very narrowly watched, and all our customs, habits and proceedings, even of the most trivial nature, observed with an inquisitiveness and jealousy which surpassed all that we had read of in the history of China'. Macartney always tried to put the best face on things, and therefore shut his eyes to the flags on the junks carrying the embassy which bore Chinese characters meaning 'The English Ambassador bringing tribute to the Emperor of China'.[40] From the Chinese point of view these 'western ocean barbarians' needed watching. It was known that their country had conquered a part of India, and Wang and Chou startled Macartney during the course of conversation by claiming that some British troops from Bengal had recently given assistance to insurgents in Tibet. Subsequently, Macartney was very circumspect in what he said on this subject.[41]

In spite of these preoccupations Macartney was alert to anything of interest concerning the Chinese people and their way of life; for instance, at Tungchow the removal of the heavy crates of presents from thirty-seven boats in less than a day. He attributed this to the fact that 'everything is at the instant command of the state', and then explained how the Chinese could lift almost any weight by the use of strong bamboo poles, multiplying the use of these poles and using more bearers 'till they can master and carry it with ease'.[42] Later he commented from experience on the very hard labour of the trackers who hauled the boats over the shallows or against the wind. 'I doubt whether the labour of a negro in our West Indies be near so constant, harassing, toilsome, or consuming as that of the Chinese boatmen'.[43]

III

Macartney and his entourage set out for Peking, some riding horses, some in palanquins, and others in Chinese carts; the road was dusty and the day hot. Soldiers, brandishing whips, walked in front of them in order to clear a passage through the jostling crowds. It took the procession two and a half hours to get through Peking and a further two hours on the road to Yuan-ming Yuan, the famous Summer Palace eight miles north-west of the city.[44] While there Macartney met some of the European missionaries in the service of the Emperor. Macartney's interpreter, Jacobus Li, explained that Wang and Chou would be much out-of-pocket since the Emperor's allowance did not fully cover the expenses of the embassy. There was no question of Macartney paying for the provisions, accommodation and services he required for his suite since, while in China, he was a 'guest' of the Emperor, so he agreed to give them a present of five hundred dollars each. However, the next day his interpreter came to say that Wang and Chou 'could not possibly think of accepting any presents of money'. Macartney noted in his journal: 'the Chinese character seems at present inexplicable'.[45] This phrase can be contrasted with the Chinese phrase, used repeatedly in documents dealing with 'western ocean barbarians', both at this time and later: 'the barbarian nature is unfathomable'. This difficulty of understanding each other's natures was at the heart of the cultural confrontation now taking place. Two completely different ways of thinking and acting, two different psychologies, now met head-on and the epithets 'inexplicable' and 'unfathomable' were the symbols of the attitude of the Chinese and the English ministers towards each other.

The problem of the kotow ceremony was raised again and Macartney was urged to practise it. He managed to have a written statement translated into Chinese to the effect that he was willing to conform to the etiquette of the Chinese Court, provided that a Chinese official of equal rank should perform the same ceremony before the King of England's portrait! While Macartney was taking this stand on the kotow question, letters were passing back and forth between the Court at Jehol and the legate in Peking on the same subject. For Cheng-jui to report to the throne that the barbarian envoy steadfastly refused to practise the ceremony would have been to admit that his own powers of persuasion had failed, and so to have lost face and rank. Instead he reported: 'the English envoy and others are deeply ashamed at being unversed in the etiquette of the Celestial Empire, and have daily been practising it, and are now gradually learning to kneel and kotow'.[46] Presumably he was hoping that before they reached Jehol Macartney would acquiesce. The members of the Grand Council were thus given false information, though they may have felt some slight suspicion, for in a Court Letter of 18 August from the Grand Council to Cheng-jui they stated: 'but after he has arrived the tribute envoy must first practise the etiquette. If he still does not conform fully to the etiquette you must instruct him point by point. Only when he is versed in the salutation of the kotow may he be ushered into an imperial audience'.[47] The Chinese conductors of Lord Amherst found themselves in an identical position in 1816 when they consistently reported that he was practising the kotow right up to the time due for the audience when, in fact, Amherst had consistently refused to do so. The question of the kotow brooded, like a summer storm, over Macartney's embassy as it moved towards Jehol.

While in Peking Macartney held open house to the senior officials who came to look at the presents and specimens of different manufactures which the ambassador had brought for distribution in the hope of starting a demand for these things in China. Portraits by Sir Joshua Reynolds of King George III and Queen Charlotte in their royal robes also attracted considered notice, and the embassy band, consisting of five German musicians, gave a concert every evening. Among the audience was 'the chief mandarin of the Emperor's orchestra, who attended constantly and listened to the performance with all the airs of a virtuoso'.[48]

On 2 September Macartney and the majority of his suite set out for Jehol. 'At six o'clock a.m. we began our journey. Young Staunton and myself travelled in a neat English post-chaise which I had provided, and which was drawn by four little Tartar horses not eleven hands high, being, I believe, the first piece of Long-acre manufactory that ever rattled upon the road to Jehol'.[49] Sir George Staunton, who had a touch of gout, rode in a palanquin, while the others rode on horses or in Chinese carriages. Macartney's account of the journey to Jehol, which took nearly seven days, is a mixture of precise notations of such things as agriculture, bridges, fortifications, the Great Wall and so on, interspersed with more lyrical descriptions of the countryside and the feeling of exhilaration at spanking along in a carriage-and-four, out of the dust of Peking into the cooler air of 'Tartary', with the prospect of distant hills and eventually of the Great Wall itself. On 5 September the pass of Ku-pei-K'ou and the Great Wall came into sight. Naturally they determined to visit this famous wonder. Had not Macartney's friend, Dr. Johnson, said that the children of any man who had visited the Great Wall of China would have a lustre reflected on them from his spirit and curiosity.[50] In his journal Macartney gave a somewhat technical description of the wall with various measurements, very much in keeping with the 'scientific' attitude of the natural philosophers of that period in Europe. At the same time Lieutenant Parish, of the Royal Artillery, was making his sketches and notes in order to produce a plan, with sections and measurements and observations. Macartney recorded the reactions of the accompanying Chinese officials to this burst of sight-seeing and note-taking. They appeared uneasy and impatient at the length of time spent on the wall, and 'were astonished at our curiosity, and almost began to suspect us, I believe, of dangerous designs'.[51] On 8 September the ambassador with his cavalcade, all neatly marshalled, made his public entry into Jehol, watched by the Emperor Ch'ien-lung.[52] Summarizing his impressions of the journey Macartney noted the imperial lodges along the route, the Chinese taste in landscape gardening, and the fact that a separate road, parallel to the common one, was maintained for the Emperor's sole use, 'no other person being permitted to travel upon it, a circumstance of Imperial appropriation which I don't recollect even in Muscovy or Austria'.[53]

IV

Soon after reaching Jehol Sir George Staunton delivered Macartney's written statement on the kotow ceremony to the chief minister, Ho-shen. As a result the legate, together with Wang and Chou, came to urge Macartney to give up the suggestion of a reciprocal ceremony in front of a portrait of George III; but Macartney maintained that it was necessary to distinguish between the homage of tributary princes and the ceremony used for a great and independent sovereign. At this point Macartney was still fairly hopeful that he might be able to remain long enough at Court to negotiate with Ho-shen. However, what he did not know was that already, on 3 August, before he had even landed on Chinese soil, an edict dismissing him was drafted and submitted to the Emperor, and was held in readiness to hand to the envoy on his departure from Peking.[54] Thus, even before the audience and before Macartney had a chance to discuss the business of his embassy, the machinery for dismissing him from Court had already been put into operation. On 10 September Cheng-jui, Wang and Chou had another session with Macartney on the ceremony to be followed at the audience. Macartney argued that it was not natural to expect an Ambassador to pay greater homage to a foreign prince than to his own sovereign, unless a return were made which would warrant him doing more. When they asked him what audience-ceremony was followed at the English Court, Macartney explained it to them and even demonstrated it. Later Cheng-jui and Chou came to say that it had finally been decided to adopt the English ceremony, but that since it was not the custom in China to kiss the Emperor's hand, they had proposed that Macartney should kneel on both knees instead. Macartney insisted that he would kneel on one knee only on those occasions when it was usual for the Chinese to prostrate themselves. Cheng-jui and Chou insisted that kissing the Emperor's hand must be omitted. Macartney agreed, and wrote in his journal: 'thus ended this curious negotiation, which has given me a tolerable insight into the character of this Court, and that political address upon which they so much value themselves'.[55] However, on the same day a Court Letter from Ho-shen, in the name of the Emperor, to the princes and ministers remaining at the capital, put the matter in a different light: 'at present instructions have been given for him to practise the ceremony but he still pretends to be ill and procrastinates. We are extremely displeased at his unwarranted haughtiness, and have given instructions to cut down their supplies . . . Also it is not necessary to prepare entertainments and opera at the capital'. The letter concluded: 'if, when the barbarians come for an audience with the Emperor, they are sincere and reverential, we always grant them our favour, so as to display our "cherishing by kindness". If they tend to be in the least haughty then they are not destined to receive our favour. Also we should immediately cut down the ceremony of their reception in order to demonstrate our system. This is the way to restrain foreign dependencies'.[56]

On 11 September Macartney had his first interview with Ho-shen and recorded his own impressions of the 'chief minister' which are a useful addition to the Chinese sources for his biography, which tend to be over hostile. 'He is a handsome, fair man about forty to forty-five years old, quick and fluent'. Macartney began by paying an elaborate compliment to the Emperor in the course of which he managed to say, *à propos* of the Emperor's good health, that it 'would give sincere pleasure to the greatest sovereign in the West to hear such good news from me of the greatest sovereign of the East'. Ho-shen then made compliments in return and said that 'on account of the very great distance from which the embassy had been sent, and of the value of the presents, some of the Chinese customs (which had hitherto been invariably observed) would now be relaxed, and that I might perform the ceremony after the manner of my own country, and deliver the King's letter into the Emperor's own hand'. According to Macartney, when he rose to leave Ho-shen 'took me by the hand, and said he should be happy to cultivate my acquaintance, and hoped to have frequent opportunities of seeing me familiarly at Yuan-ming Yuan'.⁵⁷ It would be interesting to know exactly what Ho-shen said in Chinese and how Jacobus Li translated it into Italian. Macartney, perhaps, received too optimistic an idea of what Ho-shen actually intended. Thus the first meeting between the two courtier-ministers ended with honours fairly even.

On Saturday 14 September 1793 Macartney had his official audience with the Emperor Ch'ien-lung in a large circular tent. This was the great moment of the whole embassy and Macartney devoted a detailed description to it in his journal.⁵⁸ From this account it appears that, as Chi'ien-lung passed, the envoy and members of his suite present at the ceremony 'paid him our compliments by kneeling on one knee, while all the Chinese made their usual prostrations'. Macartney described how he handed the King's letter, in a large gold box enriched with diamonds, to the Emperor, and received various presents in return, and the lavish banquet which followed. He characterized Ch'ien-lung thus: 'his manner is dignified, but affable and condescending, and his reception of us has been very gracious and satisfactory. He is a very fine old gentleman, still healthy and vigorous, not having the appearance of a man of more than sixty'.⁵⁹ He also mentioned that three ambassadors from Pegu in Burma and six ambassadors from the Kalmuck tribe of the Mongols were also present at the audience. The last paragraph of Macartney's description began: 'thus, then, have I seen "King Solomon in all his glory" '. In contrast the official Chinese record of the audience was almost the opposite of Macartney's lively account. It was extremely terse and matter-of-fact, placing no particular importance on the reception by the Emperor of a barbarian tribute envoy from a 'western ocean' country, together with envoys from Burma and the Kalmuck tribe. It read: 'on the day *keng-wu* [14 September] the Emperor took his seat in a great tent in the Garden of Ten-Thousand-Trees. The chief English envoy, Macartney, and the assistant envoy,

Staunton, had an audience, and were feasted, along with the princes, dukes and ministers in attendance and the Mongol princes with their sons and grandsons, dukes, imperial sons-in-law and nobles, as well as the Burmese tribute envoy and others. They were given presents according to rank. The Emperor composed a poem recording the fact that the King of the red-haired English had sent his envoy, Macartney, and others, who had arrived bearing a state message and tribute'.[60]

On the following day Macartney, Staunton and others were conducted round the eastern part of the imperial gardens at Jehol by Ho-shen and other senior ministers, including Fu-k'ang-an, who had recently returned from commanding a Chinese army in Tibet against a Gurkha invasion from Nepal.[61] 'During the whole day the first minister . . . paid us very great attention, and displayed all the good breeding and politeness of an experienced courtier, though I am afraid I can already perceive that his heart is not with us'. In contrast Macartney found the attitude of Fu-k'ang-an 'formal and repulsive'. Knowing that he was a powerful official, in good standing with Ho-shen, and therefore with the Emperor, Macartney attempted to flatter him. 'I told him that I had often heard of his reputation as a warrior, and therefore I hoped that the exercise of my guard and their military evolutions, with the latest European improvements, might afford him some pleasure and entertainment'. Fu-k'ang-an declined the proposal coldly, 'saying that nothing of that kind could be a novelty to him'. Macartney speculated on the reasons for his hostility and came to the conclusion that while Governor General at Canton 'he may have remarked . . . and felt, with regret and indignation, that superiority which, wherever Englishmen go, they cannot conceal from the most indifferent observer'.[62] Although Macartney requested Ho-shen for a short conference during the next day or two, the minister excused himself but repeated that he hoped to have frequent opportunities of seeing Macartney at the Summer Palace on their return to Peking.[63]

A kind of diplomatic duel now developed between Macartney and Ho-shen: the one pressing every opportunity to start negotiations concerning the business on which he had been sent by the king; the other, on behalf of his emperor, parrying every attempt to discuss business and simply keeping to the precedents for the entertainment and speedy dismissal of tribute envoys. From the Chinese point of view the English barbarians had now, for the first time, dutifully presented tribute to the Emperor, they had 'turned towards civilization' and had 'come to be transformed' by Chinese culture. There was nothing further to detain them in China. In fact

Macartney now began to realize that the procedure of the Court of China was very different from that of any European Court, and that he must be prepared to act accordingly. There was a slight note of disappointment in his journal for 16 September when he wrote: 'thus I see that the same strange jealousy prevails towards us which the Chinese government has always shown to other foreigners, although we have taken such pains to disarm it, and to conciliate their friendship and confidence'.

On the same day Ho-shen sent a request that Macartney's physician, Dr. Gillan, should visit him and give an opinion on his ailments. In his report on the state of medicine and surgery in China, which Gillan wrote for Macartney to include in the observations attached to his journal, he gave an account of Ho-shen's ailments. Apparently Ho-shen had suffered for some years from recurrent rheumatism with violent pains in his joints; also for about eight years he had suffered from a hernia in the lower abdomen which gave him considerable pain. 'When the interpreter translated to him my explanation of the nature of his complaints, and the method of cure, he seemed quite lost in astonishment. He conversed again with his physicians and at last desired the interpreter to tell me that my ideas and all that I had said were so extraordinary that it appeared to them as if it had come from an inhabitant of another planet'.[64] This was another aspect of the cultural confrontation.

The Emperor Ch'ien-lung's eighty-third birthday was celebrated on 17 September and Macartney described the ceremony vividly in his journal. The envoy, with a few of his suite, set out for the Court at 3 a.m., and there waited for two hours before the ceremony began. The Emperor did not appear in person but remained behind a screen. Here is Macartney's description of the event:

Slow, solemn music, muffled drums, and deep-toned bells were heard at a distance. On a sudden the sound ceased and all was still; again it was renewed, and then intermitted with short pauses, during which several persons passed backwards and forwards, in the proscenium or foreground of the tent, as if engaged in preparing some *grand coup de théâtre.* At length the great band both vocal and instrumental struck up with all their powers of harmony, and instantly the whole Court fell flat upon their faces before this invisible Nebuchadnezzar. 'He, in his cloudy tabernacle shrined [sic], sojourned the while'. The music was a sort of birthday ode or state anthem, the burden of which was 'Bow down your heads, all ye dwellers upon earth, bow down your heads before the great Ch'ien-lung, the great Ch'ien-lung'. And then all the dwellers upon China earth there present, except ourselves, bowed down their heads, and prostrated themselves upon the ground at every renewal of the chorus. Indeed, in no religion either ancient or modern,

234

has the Divinity ever been addressed, I believe, with stronger exterior marks of worship and adoration than were this morning paid to the phantom of his Chinese Majesty.[65]

After the ceremony the same great officials who had shown Macartney and others round the eastern part of the park now took them to see the western part which was wilder. Macartney's description is well worth reading for its own sake, but it is also important as the source for a passage in Wordsworth's *The Prelude.*[66] Even while enjoying the romantic beauty of the scenery Macartney was trying to pursue the business of his mission with Ho-shen, but to no avail. 'I could not help admiring the address with which the minister parried all my attempts to speak to him on business this day, and how artfully he evaded every opportunity that offered for any particular conversation with me'.

On 18 September Macartney and some of his suite saw the day-long entertainments to celebrate the Emperor's birthday. In his journal he gives a long description of the Chinese opera, the 'grand pantomime', dancing, tumbling, wrestling, acrobatics, and finally a magnificent display of fireworks.[67] At the end of the performance Wang and Chou explained that the ceremonies and entertainments at Jehol for the visiting envoys were now ended and they proposed that Macartney and his entourage should set out for Peking.

V

The Ambassador and his suite left Jehol on 21 September and arrived in Peking five and a half days later. Another member of the guard died of dysentery on the way. Wang and Chou continued to be friendly, 'but the legate still preserves the same vinegar aspect without relaxation'. Cheng-jui informed Macartney that it was customary for envoys as well as for the great officials of the Court to greet the Emperor on his return to Peking at a point beyond the Summer Palace. Macartney was in very considerable pain from rheumatism and decided to sleep the night at Yuan-ming Yuan. By 4 a.m. the next morning he was *en route* for the appointed place. The Emperor was carried past 'in a kind of sedan chair' and Macartney and his party paid their compliment to him.[68] He then returned to Peking 'extremely tired and very much out of order'. It seems that Macartney's health was beginning to feel the physical strain of the embassy, and his anxiety over the outcome of his mission may have contributed to his disorder. At this point Wang and Chou brought a message from Ho-shen requesting Macartney to meet the minister in the Imperial city, and adding that the Emperor's letter to the King would probably be handed to him then. They advised him to ask permission to depart without delay.[69] Thus, finally, on 2 October Macartney had to admit to himself what he had begun to fear several weeks earlier, namely that he would not be allowed to remain in Peking to negotiate with Ho-shen.

On 3 October Macartney entered the famous 'Forbidden City' for his first and only time, to go to one of the pavilions where the Emperor normally came to receive the congratulations of the Court on New Year's Day. Cheng-jui came early to escort him. 'Being ill in bed when he came, and scarcely able to rise, I don't remember ever having received an unpleasanter message in my life'. Macartney was conducted to the foot of the steps leading to the T'ai-ho Tien ('Palace of Supreme Harmony') where he saw 'a fine yellow silk arm-chair, representing the majesty of China and containing the Emperor's letter to the King. After making our usual reverences, we proceeded to the hall, the chair and letter being carried up in great state before us'. Here Ho-shen explained the meaning of all this ceremony, and then pointed to some tables on which were bundles wrapped in yellow silk, which, he said, were the remainder of the Emperor's presents to the King and some presents for the envoy and all those who had come with him from England. When Macartney wanted to give some 'magnificent presents' to Ho-shen and the other Grand Secretaries, they firmly refused them. 'I was now almost fainting with fatigue and therefore requested the minister's leave to retire, but first reminded him of the points I had mentioned to him yesterday'.[70] Ho-shen replied that Macartney might send him a note of these requests. 'It is now beyond a doubt, although nothing was said upon the subject, that the Court wishes us to be gone, and if we don't take the hints already given, they may possibly be imparted to us in a broader and coarser manner, which would be equally unpleasant to the dignity of the embassy and the success of its objects'.[71] Macartney immediately sent a note to Ho-shen consisting of six main points abridged from his instructions.[72]

In his journal for 4 October Macartney discussed the reasons, as he understood them, for the difficulties which faced his embassy and the reasons why it had failed to achieve its main objects. He came to the conclusion that it was wisest both for the public service and his own character to depart with a good grace, and without delay.[73] As he realized, the decision did not really lie with him. In fact from 9 September onwards the Chinese documents concerned with the embassy contain plenty of instructions about his departure from Peking and the subsequent journey by inland waterways to Canton, and for the security measures to be taken *en route.* For example on 23 September a Court Letter was despatched to the Governor General designate of the two Kwangs[74] and the Governor of Kwantung, which, among other points, contained the following suggestions:

> Perhaps they intend to spy; this definitely cannot be allowed... Now, after the tribute envoy arrived he made many entreaties and repeatedly pestered us. It seems that these barbarians after all are ignorant... But perhaps they may conspire to stir up trouble in Macao, and we must be prepared to guard against it. After Ch'ang-lin has arrived in Canton he must act circumspectly and must at all times be on the alert. Although the tribute envoy has seen the Celestial Empire's strict and stern system with his own eyes, and that the barbarians on all sides are overawed into submission, nothing must be left to chance... If they make unwarrantable requests you ought to speak sternly and justly, rejecting them categorically. You must not be too tolerant or this will encourage them to pester you endlessly.[75]

This is a revealing letter because of its almost brutal frankness, and it is just as well that Macartney did not know of its contents. All the Chinese documents preserved for the period 22-30 September reiterate the need to get Macartney out of Peking at the beginning of October, and not to allow him to leave anyone behind at the capital.

The final act in the drama took place on 7 October. Macartney and his suite set out at noon *en route* for Canton, and on the way through the city stopped where Ho-shen and several great officials (all in their ceremonial robes) were ready to receive the envoy at his leave-taking. Ho-shen pointed to a table covered with yellow silk on which were two large rolls; one of them, he told Macartney, contained the Emperor's answer to his six requests; the other a full list of presents from the Emperor. As they parted Macartney noted that 'the minister had a smile of affected affability on his countenance during the greater part of the time, but I thought Fu-ch'ang-an and his brother looked confoundedly sour at us.'[76] The two main protagonists, Ho-shen and Macartney, having played out their roles, now went their differing ways. Ho-shen hung himself with a silken cord in 1799, having been impeached on sixteen different counts, and found guilty of massive corruption. He received gracious permission to commit suicide from Ch'ien-lung's successor, Chia-ch'ing.[77]

VI

After leaving Peking Macartney continued to keep a detailed journal, and many of his entries for the period from 7 October until his arrival in Canton on 19 December are of considerable interest, especially since he travelled part of the way on the Grand Canal, which he described, and also because he passed by such famous cities as Soochow and Hangchow and also crossed the Mei-ling pass. This part of his journal gives a superb account of a journey through China at the end of the eighteenth century, and includes a particularly romantic portrayal of the rock-hewn temple of Pusa in northern Kwangtung.[78] At times Macartney's description of scenery is remarkably vivid. For example:

> the mist grew every moment darker and heavier, and so magnified the objects around us that no wonder our senses and imaginations were equally deceived and disturbed, and that the temples, turrets, and pagodas appeared to us through the fog, as we sailed along, like so many phantoms of giants and monsters flitting away from us, and vanishing in the gloom.[79]

Macartney and his suite reached Hangchow on 9 November where he met the Governor General designate of Kwangtung and Kwangsi, Ch'ang-lin, who was to escort him on the remainder of the journey. Naturally Macartney used this opportunity to discuss the trade at Canton, and Ch'ang-lin asked him to set down in writing the English merchants' grievances. However, he warned Macartney that he would have to face opposition in Canton from those with vested interests in maintaining the source of these grievances, and that his predecessor as Governor General, Fu-k'ang-an, would not be pleased to see him adopt measures which were opposite to his own while in office there.[80] On 4 December they talked about the value of the foreign trade at Canton and Macartney noted: 'he suspects great peculation among the public officers at Canton and that the Emperor is much defrauded in his revenue there'. The conversation then turned to 'natural philosophy' and various technical inventions. 'But when I told him of many things in England, and which I had brought people to instruct the Chinese in, if it had been allowed, such as the reanimating [of] drowned persons by a mechanical operation, restoring sight to the blind by the extraction or depression of the glaucoma, and repairing or amputating limbs by manual dexterity, both he and his companions seemed as if awakened out of a dream and could not conceal their regret for the Court's coldness and indifference to our discoveries'.[81] The journal then contains an interesting passage on Ho-shen's reactions to Macartney's offer to send someone up in an air-balloon to demonstrate it, and on the policy of the Chinese Court 'in endeavouring to keep out of sight whatever can manifest our pre-eminence'. This is followed by a purple passage about the human mind being of a 'soaring nature' and struggling against every difficulty to reach the highest goals, a kind of hymn of faith to the spirit of progress. He ends this entry with a reference to troubles inside China itself. 'Scarcely a year now passes without an insurrection in some of the provinces'. On 18 December Macartney and his party arrived at the garden-houses belonging to the Chinese Hong merchants at Canton, where they found the three East India Company Commissioners. After fifteen months absence from England it was good to receive the most recent news, and letters from home.

VII

In the course of a long entry in his journal dated 2-7 January 1794 Macartney reviewed the problems faced by the East India Company in its trade with China and offered some suggestions for improving the situation. In lengthy observations and closely reasoned arguments Macartney went on to reflect on relations between England (and by extension other countries of Europe) and China as he saw them at the end of his embassy while staying in Canton. In his remarks one can discern the quintessence of the growing confrontation as seen from the English point of view. They also contain some remarkably prophetic passages viewed in the light of subsequent Chinese history — both as regards domestic affairs and as regards relations with the 'western ocean barbarians'.[82] He argued that Britain had the power to damage China effectively 'for a few frigates could in a few weeks destroy all their coast navigation and intercourse from the island of Hainan to the gulf of Pei-chihli', while the forts guarding the mouth of the river leading to Canton 'might be demolished by half a dozen broadsides', and the river made impassable without Britain's permission. But he advised against the use of force because of the severe repercussions it would have on England's trade at Canton. On the grounds of reason and humanity, also, it would be wrong to think of offensive measures whilst there was any hope of succeeding by peaceful ones. The only argument in favour of hostile actions would be the firm conviction that a policy of forbearance had failed. This point was not reached until fifty years later when England sent a force from India to threaten Canton and Nanking during the Opium War. Macartney then defined the real position of China in the modern world, showing that already, in 1793, he had discerned the growing weakness and unrest in China, despite superficial appearances of solidarity.

The empire of China is an old, crazy, first-rate man-of-war, which a fortunate succession of able and vigilant officers has contrived to keep afloat for these one hundred and fifty years past, and to overawe their neighbours merely by her bulk and appearance, but whenever an insufficient man happens to have the command upon deck, adieu to the discipline and safety of the ship. She may perhaps not sink outright; she may drift some time as a wreck, and will then be dashed to pieces on the shore; but she can never be rebuilt on the old bottom.[83]

These words are so apt and so vividly expressed that they deserve to find a place in every modern history of China. They can serve as an epitaph on the Ch'ing dynasty, for although it survived a further one hundred and eighteen years, modern historical research is corroborating in detail Macartney's claim that already by the end of Ch'ien-lung's reign the dynasty was very sick.

On 9 January 1794 Macartney took leave of the Governor General and the East India Company Commissioners, said farewell to Wang and Chou, and with his suite sailed down the Pearl River to Macao. At this point Macartney closed his daily journal. The final paragraph was addressed directly to the reader.

Should any accident throw this journal under the eyes of a stranger unacquainted with me and the country I am now quitting, he might possibly imagine that I had too much indulged myself in local description and political conjecture. But nothing could be more fallacious than to judge of China by any European standard. My sole view has been to represent things precisely as they impressed me. I had long accustomed myself to take minutes of whatever appeared of a curious or interesting nature, and such scenes as I have lately visited were not likely to obliterate my habits or to relax my diligence. I regularly took notes and memorandums [sic] of the business I was engaged in and the objects I saw, partly to serve for my own use and recollection, and partly to amuse the hours of a tedious and painful employment. But I will not flatter myself that they can be of much advantage or entertainment to others.[84]

Macartney need have had no doubts of the interest which his journal has aroused in readers from the time when quotations from it first appeared in 1797 until now when the full text is available in print. The sentence 'but nothing could be more fallacious than to judge of China by any European standard' is still true today. Thinking about China in European (or Western) terms and categories was a basic part of the cultural confrontation as it existed then and as it has remained until the present.

VIII

The object of the embassy was to establish regular diplomatic relations with China in an effort to improve, permanently, the conditions under which English subjects traded at Canton. It was hoped that this might be achieved by a treaty of commerce and friendship. The two edicts from Ch'ien-lung to George III, which Macartney brought back with him, show the wide gap between English wishful thinking and Chinese state policy. A brief analysis of both will make this clear.

The Emperor's answer to the King's state message is of outstanding significance in the study of Sino-Western relations because it shows the Chinese position in the cultural confrontation of 1793 with stark clarity. The English version of this edict, translated from the Latin version made from the Chinese original by two of the European missionaries in the Emperor's service, is less condescending in tone than the official Chinese text. It is difficult to convey the cumulative effect of the original by giving short quotations and it needs to be read in full in order to appreciate the flavour of the rebuff which the Emperor of China gave to the King of England's letter.[85] Firstly, it is worth noting that none of the objects of the embassy, as set out in the King's letter to the Emperor, was attained. The request to have an English envoy resident at the capital was rejected on the grounds that it did not conform to the Celestial Empire's system, and that, in any case, it would not be practicable. Only those who have entered the imperial service (such as European missionaries) may reside in Peking, and even they are confined to certain buildings, must wear Chinese costume and are not allowed to return home. Matters which arise concerning foreign trade at Canton and Macao are fully taken care of by the Chinese officials there. The Emperor does not value rare and precious things; in fact so great is the virtue and power of the dynasty that envoys from the various states have come to pay homage to the Emperor, with the result that all manner of precious things have been collected at the capital as the English envoy and those with him have seen for themselves.[86] The edict claimed that the Emperor had 'never valued ingenious articles', though this hardly coincides with Ch'ien-lung's known admiration for these things. However, when the edict went on to state 'nor do we have the slightest need for your country's manufactures' it was nearer the truth. With the exception of pepper and tin,[87] which were fairly extensively imported through Canton at that time, China needed no other articles from outside her boundaries. Thus, there was no need for England to have an envoy resident at the capital. At the end of the edict King George III is exhorted to strengthen his loyalty and to swear perpetual obedience 'so as to ensure that your country may share the blessings of peace'. This is the only document dealing with the Macartney embassy which is known to historians generally; it has been quoted fairly often, usually in the translation by E. Backhouse and J. O. P. Bland.[88] This version has held the field for seventy years but perhaps the time has come when this edict should be studied in a more literal translation which attempts to bring out the full flavour of the original Chinese. Nor is it sufficient to translate it from the Latin version translated by the European missionaries since, as Fr. Poirot made clear in a letter to Macartney, they were accustomed to modify certain obnoxious expressions here and there while making translations of this nature.[89] Many of the Chinese characters used in this edict have a condescending tone and echo classical Chinese phrases which strongly imply a superior addressing an inferior in the hierarchy of 'all under heaven'. These nuances of superiority may have been extremely reassuring to the Emperor and his officials but were lost on the 'western ocean barbarians' in their English translation.

Apart from this famous document Macartney received a reply to the six requests which he submitted, in the name of the King, to Ho-shen on 3 October. This was in the form of an edict from the Emperor to the King, and it was ceremonially delivered to Macartney as he left Peking on 7 October. This edict is not composed in such elegant language as the previous one, but it does give detailed reasons for refusing each of the points which Macartney had set down from his written instructions. In general the same reasons are given as in the main edict, namely that there is no precedent in the Chinese system, or that it would be of no practical value, or simply that it is 'inconvenient', in other words impossible. I have paraphrased some of the more important points, but in doing so much of the impact of the original has been lost.[90] The envoy has petitioned the great officials to memorialize concerning his country's trade, but the requests he has made, if carried out, would alter all the established regulations; therefore they cannot be granted. China has an abundance of every kind of product and has never had to rely on goods from distant barbarians; therefore it does not need to exchange what it has for what it does not have. But because tea, porcelain and silk are necessities for 'western ocean' countries, therefore the Emperor has treated the English with kindness and 'foreign hongs' have been established at Canton so that they can obtain their daily necessities and 'share in our superabundant riches'. But now the envoy has gone beyond the established regulations and has requested things which are contrary to 'the Celestial Empire's way of treating men from afar generously' and caring for all barbarian peoples. 'Moreover, the Celestial Empire, in ruling over the myriad countries, regards them all with equal benevolence'. England is only one among several countries trading at Canton. The Emperor realizes that England lies in a remote part of the world and has never been acquainted with the Celestial Empire's system, so therefore he instructed his great officials to enlighten the envoy in detail. The edict then proceeds to reject the requests one by one. The edict ends with clear instructions to George III. 'You, O King, ought, looking upwards, to carry out our wishes, and for ever obey our edict, so that we may both enjoy the blessings of peace . . . Do not say that you have not been forewarned'.

With these two forthright edicts in mind it is hardly necessary to enquire whether Macartney made any major mistake or minor errors of judgment in his handling of the embassy, or whether any other envoy, acting somewhat differently, might have succeeded. Ignorance of the true nature of the Chinese tributary system led Dundas into persuading the government to send an embassy, and Macartney into accepting the post in the belief that he had a reasonable prospect of succeeding. *From the very beginning the embassy never stood the slightest chance of success.* There was never any common ground of understanding between England and China; the two countries possessed two different cultures with totally different outlooks. No treaty of commerce, nor of alliance, and no exchange of ministers could be effected while the Chinese tributary system, and the ethos it stood for, remained dominant.

CHAPTER VIII

VERONA 1795-96

I

Macartney had little enjoyment of leisure after his safe return from China before he was attracted into a very different mission abroad.[1] The man who had waited upon a Celestial Emperor in the (late) high noon of the Ch'ing Dynasty was now invited to confront the Most Christian King at the nadir of French Royal fortunes:[2] not at Versailles, nor even at the Tuileries, but 'at Orto del' Gazzola, a Veronese gentleman's villa... about half a mile without the gates of the city... neither large, handsome nor convenient'.[3] The Earl went there to represent the tutelary providence of Great Britain to a prince whose wretched fortunes, neglect by the rest of the world, and penniless condition alike marked him, at least for the near future, as at best a 'satellite' ally; and Macartney's new mission, characterised as 'private' (or, as we say, unofficial), bore upon its face the evidences of its problematical, uncertain destiny.

At first Macartney viewed Lord Grenville's proposal of Verona with 'some little disappointment... I had only a week's notice of my mission; two days later I should have been half way on my road for Ireland, having packed up and made all my arrangements'. Perhaps he also had misgivings of the outcome; if so, the event proved them justified. But the Foreign Secretary contrived to overcome his reluctance: 'the matter was proposed to me', Macartney later explained, 'in such a manner as to make it eligible for me to undertake it'.[4] In this rather vague indication, he was almost certainly conveying a renewed hope of achieving at last, by means of this new mission, a British barony; for he had now been shown some prospect that — if, with his aid, the cause of Restoration in France soon ripened — the mission would become 'public', in circumstances bringing him greater celebrity and influence than even he had yet envisaged. But he may also have been adverting, no less, conceivably even more, to his own immediate need of further public employment; half-way through his mission at Verona, he was to characterize his post there as not 'lucrative', but still, perhaps when Grenville originally framed the offer of it, in the more glittering

Macartney, n.d. but mid-1790s, by Henry Hudson after M. Brown (Robbins, p.238).

perspectives to which it might lead, Macartney found it, even in itself, too attractive to decline.[5] However all this may have been, once the Earl had accepted, he then set off with his accustomed resolution and good spirits, bearing instructions dated 10 July 1795. Impeded no more by gout than by a large suite (accompanied by Thomas Coutts, the son of his London banker, and by his servant, Russell),[6] he was delayed only by 'the usual distresses of a traveller'; adverse winds at Yarmouth, 'bad roads, bad weather, bad horses'. By 20 July he was at Hamburg: very early on the morning of 6 August he drove into Verona; within a few hours he was 'so well recovered as to be able to dine with His Most Christian Majesty', and only regretting that he had not learned sooner of the twice-weekly post out of Verona that morning, else he would have written to his principal 'immediately on getting out of his chaise'.[7]

II

Macartney's appointment at Verona was a development of the 'metaphysical war' (as Lord Lansdowne called it: ideological war, as we say) which Great Britain was then carrying on against the first Republic. The immediate origin of the mission was the death, 8 June 1795, of the hapless young prisoner, Louis XVII. This transferred the succession to his elder uncle, Louis-Stanislas-Xavier, Comte de Provence, recently claiming (in exile) the Regency. From his obscure headquarters in the territory of Venice, the new Pretender published his assumption of the style, Louis XVIII.[8] To only one Great Power, his paper accession was highly important; and hence the prompt despatch to his side of one of its own most experienced servants.

More than once since war had begun between the Republic and England, Pitt and Grenville had laid it down that George III was bound to seek the overthrow of the *régime* which was so called. Disclaiming any general right of 'interference . . . in an independent country', they 'by no means disputed the right of France to reform its laws'. But they viewed 'all the republican parties in France' as being identified with 'a system destructive of all public order . . ., which attacks the fundamental principles by which mankind is united in . . . civil society', and they had invoked French support for 'some legitimate and stable government . . . the standard of an hereditary monarchy'.[9] It was in pursuance of this policy that Grenville now posted Macartney at Verona; and even when, a few months later, Pitt announced Great Britain's willingness to discuss terms with the enemy *régime* (at last formally 'constituted' under the aegis of the

Directory),[10] it still remained the case that England's rulers preferred, and worked for, a very different system in France.[11]

This did not mean that they were committed, either to the 'constitutional monarchy' of the earlier revolutionary times, 1789-92, or to the hopes of French 'pure' royalists for what appeared in London to be simply the restoration of 'an absolute and arbitrary monarchy' and of all the other features of the vanished old order. Lord Grenville declared that the first revolutionary constitution, 'of 1791', had 'contained in itself the seeds of its own ruin', and had 'led to all that had since happened'.[12] He likewise declared that in London 'no belief was entertained that permanent tranquillity could now be established' upon pre-revolutionary bases; 'your Lordship should express', he emphasized to Macartney at Verona, 'how different this idea is from the sentiments of this government'.[13] Instead of either, the British ministers looked to what was called (by Grenville's most specially trusted envoy, William Wickham) 'a coalition of parties' in France: of French people who would accept the traditional Crown as the foundation and mainspring of their state;[14] but meantime the lawful ruler and his 'pure' Royalist adherents must on their side acknowledge that the world had changed, not wholly for the worse, since 1787: the ancient monarchy would gather the 'coalition' round the throne only in proportion as it convinced its people that it took the change seriously to heart. In particular, it must undertake that there should be no 'reign of terror in reverse', rather, an almost universal Act of Indemnity and Oblivion; 'the most unjust confiscations' which had shaken 'the foundations of all property in Europe' ought certainly to be reversed, but the landowning peasants who had profited by the abolition of the manorial system must nevertheless be convinced 'that their interests would be in some degree consulted'; above all, and most generally, the Crown must make clear that 'at a period of more tranquillity and order', it would not 'preclude' 'the concurrence of [the] people, convoked in some constitutional form', to 'correct former abuses . . . to establish and secure the happiness and prosperity of France'.[15]

Down to the death of Louis XVII, the British government had not achieved much in these directions. The 'pure' royalist emigration was, by its own publicists, committed to programmes of extreme and inhumane reaction. The French 'interior', though by no means wholly enthusiastic for any version of the republican *régime*, dreaded and shunned this polar-opposite alternative. While the lawful claimant was both a minor and a prisoner, his uncle, the self-proclaimed Regent, seemed to identify himself, hardly if at all less than his own brother, the Comte d'Artois, and their soldierly cousin, the Prince de

Condé, with the adepts of simple reaction. England never acknowledged his regency, if only for fear of doing more harm than good in the struggle to sway French opinion. Still, from July 1794 onwards — when the very conservative leaders of the 'Portland' Whigs joined Pitt's administration — British relations with the exiled princes underwent a change for the better. England alone, among the allies, offered the princes much prospect; England alone might free them from their pressing debts. Grenville became convinced that — whatever their extremist adherents might announce — the princes would meet British requirements at least in respect of a liberal amnesty. And early in 1795 the British ministers seemed to warm decisively to a great drive for restoration, provoked by forcible methods, on terms which by no means neglected the aspirations of the princes. Viewing the final political settlement of restoration with a large opportunism, they took up with the Comte de Puisaye's plan of an *émigré* and British descent on the western coast, reviving the Vendéan and *chouan* war, and driving at last towards Paris. Though Puisaye envisaged some kind of 'constitutional' final settlement, the English cheerfully committed this plan to the ultimate direction of Artois. They also subscribed to the invasion of eastern France by Condé's *émigré* army; to an Anglo-*émigré* incursion from the Mediterranean; to ambitious plans of royalist insurrection, in the Jura and in the far south. The princes now professed the most deferential respect for the government in London.[16]

Large opportunism appeared justified by the event when Louis XVIII succeeded his nephew. Before the new plans of forcible action in France were ventured, there now arrived the seemingly golden moment to negotiate, not with a self-styled regent, but with a new lawful claimant of full age, incontestably of many talents and good qualities, and sobered already, it might be thought, by the prospect of ultimate responsibilities. Before England ventured things so great for his cause, there glittered the chance to present to him — for his first manifesto — advice calculated to rally the widest measure of 'interior' support; to eclipse the wilder stars of reaction, no less than the spurious sunrise of the Republic; to direct his conduct towards the throne, no less than to the purposes with which he was to ascend it; to enforce upon him, before he could begin to gainsay them, the claims to 'indemnification', not only of Great Britain but even of Austria. Lord Grenville lost no time. He addressed an elaborate note (22 June 1795) to the new claimant's agent at London, the Duc d'Harcourt. But he resolved also to despatch a special (as yet private) representative of the Court of St. James's to the Court of Verona, who should commend to the new King in person the providence, and the requirements, of London.[17]

Macartney doubtless appeared to his principals to be well-nigh the ideal choice for this mission. His knowledge of French domestic affairs was not unlimited.[18] But neither was it negligible; and he had already achieved reputation at the French Court, in other days, as a doughty enemy. His elder years (he was eighteen years older than the new King), his world-wide experience now involving even China, his distinguished manners, his firmness and good humour, even what Sir Nathaniel Wraxall characterized as his want of 'ductility and powers of conciliation': all these points might well plead in his favour. His striking presence and his wide-ranging familiarity with polite letters must perforce render him agreeable to a prince such as Louis XVIII, adept of friendships and of urbane culture. And however much the Earl, for a moment, regretted the invitation of Lord Grenville, he from his side might well conclude that it was indeed 'eligible'. His 'private' mission, if all went well, would become 'public' in the swelling triumph of restoration, bringing him diplomatic fame to eclipse even that of Lord Malmesbury.

But all did not go well. Even Macartney could not induce Louis XVIII to dance to Great Britain's tune; while a providence more august than that of London persistently disallowed all the British ministers' hopes of better fortune for the French royal cause. Like another French leader in exile at a later date, Louis played a hand weak beyond hopelessness with mastery of the most frustrating kind. The Earl at last retired baffled. The penniless fugitive King persevered with his hopeless cards for twenty years and went home to die secure on the throne of his ancestors.

III

Yet Macartney's despatches and letters of this period are full of instruction and of interest, whether for students of his personality and career, or for those concerned with the no less fascinating subject of Louis XVIII. Let us begin with the Earl's impressions of his royal host:

> Nothing could be more gracious, or proper than the manner of his receiving me, or his expressions . . . of the distinguished marks of friendship shown him by His Majesty [King George], among which he considered my early mission to be not one of the least. Since that time I have had several private audiences of him, one of which lasted near three hours. . . He seemed always desirous of discoursing with me on his affairs, and pressed my attendance upon him almost to my own inconvenience.[19]

And six weeks later Macartney reported 'the most flattering attention ... consideration and regard' which Louis and all his court extended to the spokesman of London;[20] while six weeks later again he explained that he enjoyed at Verona more than ambassadorial privilege, being made privy to Harcourt's despatches from London, and even, occasionally, being called to join the exiled Cabinet.[21] All this was, in the circumstances obtaining, natural enough; and the Earl did not neglect the specially favourable chance which it gave him to study the personal qualities of the French King:

> He appears [reported Macartney to Grenville] to have a good understanding, a respectable share of literature, and to be particularly well versed, not only in the history of France but in that of other nations, as far as connected with it. He talks Italian tolerably well, understands the English language, and speaks his own with great correctness, copiousness and volubility. His manners and address are affable and pleasing, and his deportment to those about him gracious and even familiar, without departing from his dignity, which is still apparent thro' his eclipse. What is his real character, it is impossible for me as yet to judge, but he is said to be discreet, well natured and friendly, and ... his courtiers and attendants ... serve him with respect, zeal and affection.[22]

As time moved on, the envoy felt able to judge that Louis was as realistic as he was intelligent: 'adversity . . . had improved, not exasperated him'; 'misfortune and reflection' had 'softened the prepossessions' of a princely education, so that he was able to talk, whether about the *ancien régime* or about the 'French subversion', 'justly and with great moderation... if he were restored to power, his own disposition would not lead him to abuse it'.[23] Even the King's careful attendance upon his religious duties, the Earl at last concluded, afforded no grounds for fear that he might be, in that aspect of things, over-zealous: 'he is by no means a bigot... he is not even, at bottom, devout, but... an idea of his piety is encouraged and held out... for those of his subjects, who have any religion left, to rally under'.[24] Similarly Macartney read, accurately and reassuringly, the secrets of Louis's personal relations. The Queen, residing at Turin with her father, was 'never mentioned by anybody' (though Louis wrote to her every week); but the King 'never showed any turn towards practical gallantry', and the personal relations which seriously counted in his life were the friendships which bound him to the Comte d'Avaray and to the 'inferior servants' who were the companions of his escape from the revolution in 1791.[25] And although the envoy did not fail to grasp — what was of great moment for the government in London — the subtle ambiguity between Louis 'in common intercourse facile and compliant', and Louis 'in certain points . . . entirely governed by himself', still his mature judgment of the new French King was, on the whole, strikingly favourable. Not every observer of Louis XVIII concluded as did Macartney in January, 1796:

> Louis XVIII has I believe as good an understanding, perhaps as much information, and certainly more virtue, than any of the five kings in the executive directory of Paris . . . I own my favourable sentiments of him; I have seen him almost every day for these five months past, stripped of all those trappings which dazzle common minds . . . if I am imposed upon, he is the most consummate hypocrite that ever was born in purple.[26]

And, on his side, Louis was certainly not 'imposing upon' the Earl *as a person*. He addressed Macartney (in English, at these points), when the Earl's mission lay in the past, as 'my dear Lord', even as 'my dearest Lord'; and to the Comte de St.-Priest at that time, after bitter comments on the British policies which Macartney had transmitted to him, he still concluded: 'Je said distinguer l'homme privé de l'homme public. Je rends avec plaisir hommage à ses vertus'.[27]

Macartney meantime retailed impressions no less vivid concerning the *grandeur et misère* which characterized the exiled Court. It was the latter which first impressed him, and with good cause:

> Everything about the King indicates . . . great distress. His table which is so serious a matter to a Frenchman is scantily and inelegantly served, his servants are few and shabbily dressed, and even in his own private apartments there seems a want of proper furniture . . . There is however a pretty garden . . . the prospect of which alone is a considerable resource to a prince who . . . for several months has never stirred beyond the enclosure. Indeed from the great corpulence and unwieldiness of his figure he is little able to take . . . exercise.[28]

Louis was trying to support his pretensions by the slender munificence of two or three more or less friendly Courts. His Spanish cousin, Carlos IV, had been paying him, 'not very punctually . . . about £1,500 sterling a month': until the abrupt (and disastrous) peace with the conquering Republic, concluded within two months of Louis's accession by Godoy (at whose new title, Prince of the Peace, Louis despite his anger 'could not refrain from smiling'.) His cousin of Naples remitted 'some money', but only occasionally. The Kaiser had guaranteed payment of interest towards debts left by the princes at Coblenz (though these did not include 800,000 *livres* owed to other creditors in Germany), and inadequately took care of the small *émigré* force known as the army of Condé.[29] Louis's best resource, even before his accession, was in London. The Treasury had found him £6,000 as early as November 1792; and it furnished similar sums on three occasions before he succeeded to the royal title — by which time it was also providing £140,000 for the equipment of Condé's army to lead the van in the grand Austrian invasion of eastern France.[30] Yet the Court of Verona still lived on the brink: Louis was trying, not only to keep up some shadow of royal state, but also to provide 'a little pittance' for 'his many dependants (persons of the highest quality)', and to support 'the expence of spies, messengers, agents, etc., both in and out of France' — so that 'his Treasury often remained without a sequin . . . M. de Hautefort, whom he sent . . . to England in the end of July last, was delayed several days for want of £50 to pay the expence of his journey'.[31]

It is, therefore, easy to believe that when the sun of British favour seemed indeed to shine out with the arrival of Lord Macartney, the exiles confidently expected much greater things from the cornucopia of London. They expected to learn of Mr. Pitt's arrangements to meet the debts still outstanding in Germany, and to enjoy the first of a series of much larger subsidies. They were disappointed. The Earl denied all knowledge of a British agreement to wipe out the 800,000 *livres;* but he professed himself empowered to advance up to £8,000 for the King's immediate wants. Louis's principal adviser, the Maréchal-Marquis de Castries, did not conceal his discomfiture; Louis himself thanked King George in rather minimal terms.[32] But Louis by no means abated his efforts to live and act like a King. To the dismay of the Marshal himself, he ordered the reconstitution — not, indeed, at Verona, but under Condé in Germany — of the *Gardes du Corps;*[33] and the Court itself took on, despite its persisting impoverishment, an ever more imposing air:

> Ever since the death of Louis XVII [reported the Earl, towards the end of his mission there] the King's residence here has been assuming more and more the air of a Court, not indeed by any fastuous exterior, . . . but by the numerous correspondences, the arrival and despatch of couriers, . . . the ministerial attendance of different persons who formerly held high office under the monarchy . . . We have at present four Cordons bleus, a Cordon rouge, and two Grand Croix of Mont Carmel and St. Lazare, besides Croix de St. Louis almost beyond arithmetic.[34]

Macartney was meantime gathering impressions no less instructive about the new claimant's advisers. He did his best to establish friendly and confidential relations, not only (as directed by Grenville) with the Marshal (credited with 'ability and steadiness of principle'), but also with two other 'principal persons of business', the Baron de Flachslanden and Mgr. de Conzié, Bishop of Arras.[35] The envoy had some success. He came to appreciate the Marshal as a man of honour and understanding, though broken by age and by the misfortunes of his cause; but he does not seem to have enjoyed the confidence of the others well enough to fathom the real causes of the Marshal's early retirement (in September). Flachslanden he found to be vigorous despite his age, and a quick, resourceful, frank-mannered soldier; Arras a thoroughgoing politician, and a man of more questionable candour.[36] Macartney unavoidably became concerned over the succession to the Marshal, and — to illustrate already a large topic which must later claim fuller attention — emerged somewhat nettled. He learned only belatedly, and not 'from authority', that the Duc de la Vauguyon had been summoned from Spain, and then that 'by the farewell advice of the Marshal', the Comte de St.-Priest had been sent for from Stockholm. He doubted if either was 'eligible': 'they have both been long exercised in the politics of the former French government, and in the habit of counter-acting ours'; had he learned in time, he would have 'represented against' the former (at least) of these two nominations.[37] Fortunately for himself, Macartney did not remain long enough with the exiled Court to discover how right he was to fidget over La Vauguyon;[38] while St.-Priest finally joined his sovereign only much later still.[39]

Besides a few brief references to other notable members of the Court (to Jaucourt, Guiche, Duras and, not least, d'Avaray), the Earl made instructive comments upon the exiled circle as a whole: 'men of fair character, well-bred and correct in their behaviour' — too well-bred to speak of their opponents at Paris as *sans-culottes* — but unable to conjure up any but 'crude ideas' as to how the restored monarchy should be more 'limited' than that of the *ancien régime* (the Bishop of Arras, who had perhaps at least given the matter thought, dreamed aloud of limiting, not the Crown but the spirit of 'the late convulsions', by confining the great portfolios to Princes of the Blood). The social ideals of the exiles were, added the envoy, all of a piece: it was 'not a little entertaining', remarked that complacent devotee of old England, 'to hear them discourse upon the former happiness of *all* ranks of people in France, never conceiving how the lower rank could think of aspiring to a higher'.[40]

At all events, the courtiers in their impoverished state at least introduced Macartney to a happy, if short, social life at Verona wider than that of their own company. Through some of them he met the Marchese (Alessandro) Carlotti ('distinguished by his attention and civilities to the French emigration here'), who became the Earl's very much devoted admirer, and who (as will appear) took the centre of the stage in the final scene of this strange piece; through the Court too, it seems, the Earl met a number of Veronese ladies, about whom one is sorry not to have gathered more: among them, Mme

Verza, who — so soon after Macartney's return home — was hoping to make the (platonic) conquest of General Bonaparte, Commander-in-Chief the Army of Italy.[41]

IV

Now for the more serious business: the 'failure of a mission'.[42] The Earl's immediate charge had been to dictate the new King's accession manifesto. He arrived post haste, but too late: the 'Declaration of Verona' had appeared three weeks earlier; and it had not been such as Lord Grenville desired. Louis had expatiated upon the time-honoured constitution of old France; he had earnestly repudiated the calumnious claim that it bore the character of despotism; he had pointed to its independent courts of law and to the political functions of the *Parlements;* he had admitted its disfigurement by many (unspecified) abuses, but had undertaken to correct these at the restoration; finally, he had offered amnesty to all those involved in the subversion, except indeed to the regicides.

The British envoy saw at a glance that his ministers would regard all this as a very inadequate encouragement to the 'coalition of parties' in France; and his misgivings were fully justified, in due course, by Grenville's despatches to him. Was Louis identifying himself, asked the Foreign Secretary, with the 'feudal' phase of the monarchy, or with something resembling the polity of Louis XIV, or with any particular transition which had occurred between these? Would not most contemporaries suppose that the new King was really driving, under his amiable vagueness, at 'an absolute and unqualified re-establishment of the . . . monarchy, such as it existed in its last stage'? If so, Macartney must 'express how different this idea is from the sentiments of this government'. Grenville noted no less clearly that Louis had not thought it desirable to promise some 'constitutional' consultation of his people for the settlement of the great uncertainty about the character of the monarchy (nor yet, he might have added, for the definition of 'abuses'); and even to the regicides, he insisted, hope of pardon should be left, if they would now render 'great services'.[43]

Macartney cried at some length over the spilt milk of the royal declaration, both in his first conversations with the new King and in his reports home. In the months which followed, he recurred again and again to this theme. But he laboured in vain against the subtle defences of his royal host and adversary. Louis from the beginning perplexed the envoy by speaking of the declaration 'with such a degree of fondness as almost induced me to suppose him the real parent of the offspring' (so the envoy, for all his own urbane culture, was perplexing his own perplexity by such scepticism of the expressive talents of Louis); and thence the Earl found it, 'from this circumstance and from its being past recall . . . a matter of great delicacy and embarrassment to make any comments upon it'. He persevered ('I thought it my duty . . .'), pointing out parts of the text 'less eligible' than they might have been, and showing up Lord Grenville's 'sketch of a manifesto . . . a good deal different'. Louis's defences were impermeably elastic. His declaration matched entirely the suggestions already received from London *via* the Duc de Harcourt, did it not? Oh, there was now a 'sketch of a manifesto' from London? Let me read it ('with great attention'). What a pity it didn't arrive three weeks earlier; Louis might then have 'concerted' with the Earl 'some alterations'. Still, the King knew his own nation, and knew what he was doing (perhaps he anticipated the very words of his cousin, and unlawful successor, Louis-Philippe: 'Allons . . . je connais les Français, je sais comment les prendre'.) For the French were quite unlike the English — as he illustrated 'in a very lively manner, with a good deal of wit and pleasantry'; *for them,* 'the ancient constitution of France' (embodying 'the wisdom of ages, the perfection of reason') was the only possible form of government, alone 'capable of controlling their impetuosity'. As for 'the feudal rights', Louis readily agreed that they should not 'all remain upon the ancient footing'; though he emphasized that 'the losers', whose lands had been granted to the peasants on these 'feudal' terms, must be 'reimbursed' by their tenants. And as for the regicides, even they might indeed be pardoned — though only under condition of banishment.[44]

The new King's offer of amnesty (with or without the regicides) was perhaps the most sensitive topic of his declaration. Could his word be trusted? And, even if so, what would life amount to for a 'pardoned' revolutionary? The French 'interior' — much to the concern of Macartney's colleague Wickham — was unreassured. One of the King's first acts was not calculated to settle the doubt. The *émigré* Prince de Poix, in exile (nominally) *Capitaine des Gardes du Roi,* was abruptly discharged. His only conceivable offence was to have favoured, in June 1789, the union of the three Orders in the Estates-General. His subsequent devotion to Louis XVI seemed not to count. The Prince hardly required a pardon; but his fate hardly suggested well for those who needed one. Wickham prompted Macartney to raise the matter at Verona. The Earl then found himself confronting, not the 'elastic' defences but the steel of self-assured pride:

He had so little resentment [said Louis XVIII in reply] that he should
not be unwilling to employ [the Prince] in various situations . . . but in
a confidential place, as Captain of his Guard, he could not in justice to
himself consent to it . . . His heart revolted at any kind of duplicity,
and he hoped that the frankness of his conduct . . . would recommend
him to every honest man.[45]

The British envoy, labouring on, found the King always equally
'just and moderate' on the subject of the great upheaval in France,
and attentive enough in listening to 'those sentiments of conciliation
which are so necessary to his interests'. But what came of all this
talk? In November, Macartney reported hopefully: 'the King of
France has been gradually relaxing in some points, and is now
nearly brought to the disposition that was to be wished'; Louis had
by that date even conceded (if only by implication) that he would be
willing to convene once more the Estates-General; when the collision
was coming on between the 'moderate' sectional movement at Paris
and the Convention (destined to end in Bonaparte's 'whiff of grape-
shot', 13 Vendémiaire — 5 October 1795) the Earl was able to claim
that (no doubt partly by his own efforts) 'much pains' were taken to
'inspire the Paris malcontents with proper ideas of Louis XVIII' —
just as, a little later, the British were able to secure, in the royal
instructions issued to the Comte de Précy, who was to raise the
Lyonnais against the Republic, the inclusion of conciliatory inter-
pretations of certain features of the declaration. Yet what was Louis
conceding? He was not *promising,* even the Earl, still less his own
subjects, to re-assemble the Estates-General; he was 'thinking aloud'
in a private conversation: even so, he made it clear that he had in
mind the Estates-General 'in their ancient form' (of 1614); he was
still totally unprepared to come to terms with 1789. For the rest, the
King was (verbally) authorizing assurances that his offer of amnesty
was serious, and that he meant to wield power in a mildly reforming
spirit. This was not enough to meet Lord Grenville's requirements
for a 'coalition of parties' in France; nor, we must notice, were these
further gestures published to the world in the only manner likely to
command much attention — by an authoritative addition to the
declaration.[46] Macartney meantime found all his efforts towards
greater concessions inhibited by the ghost of 'the ancient constitution':
always invoked by the King and his advisers, always pursued by the
valiant envoy, always as impalpable as it was inviolate. The 'notions'
he was given of it, he advised Grenville in mid-October, were:

so vague and confused . . . that it is impossible to give your Lordship
any precise answer to your questions about the meaning intended . . . by
. . . the manifesto . . . Two days ago the King himself told me it was

intrinsically as little despotic as our own, that its proper and regular form was to be dated from the time of Philip Le Bel, and that the imperfections it was charged with . . . were mere abuses . . . He added that France . . . requiring an army of 150,000 or 200,000 men to defend its extensive frontier, it was absolutely necessary that the sovereign should be invested with a strong and . . . extensive authority . . . and that such authority was founded in the ancient laws of the kingdom. This is the utmost and least unintelligible matter that I have been able to collect.

And, by that same date, the Earl had already contradicted the more optimistic estimate which he was momentarily to reach in November:

The wish, and perhaps the expectation [of the King and his Ministers] is to re-enter France and restore the monarchy without any conditions at all, fully determined at the same time upon a correction of all . . . abuses . . . And they think that such a measure would emane [sic] with more dignity, simplicity and expedition from the sovereign himself than from any assembly . . . composed from their lively and impetuous nation.[47]

This was apt confirmation of the dismal verdict which Grenville had already reached upon the Earl's seemingly hopeful mission: 'it is impossible not to see . . . that while the King and those who surround him profess an entire disposition to be guided by the counsels of this country, they are in fact pertinaceously attached to their own ideas and systems'.[48]

How well did Macartney manage this, the most important of all his commitments at Verona? Without disparagement of the silkily formidable opponent who was also his host, it is hard to believe that the Earl did himself credit. We have good evidence that he went to Verona determined to act *suaviter in modo, fortiter in re;*[49] and what less should the envoy of the protecting Power have attempted? But there is no trace here of *fortiter in re;* Macartney seems to have been reduced to the part of the Greek tragic chorus, and to groping vaguely for some view of the French 'constitution' which he could not clearly discern. Was he simply dazzled by the charm and majesty of the exiled King? Or too ill-briefed in French constitutional history to play the cross-examiner? Or too ill-provided with British funds to produce (what might have been, though it seems doubtful) the Ace of Spades?

Louis had the means of counter-attack in this game of argument; and he had embarked upon it even before the Earl arrived. Lord Grenville had advised the Duc de Harcourt that England would accord formal recognition of the new King when some part of France rose in arms for him. Harcourt had promptly stood Grenville's proposal on its head: formal recognition by England was precisely what was needed to bring out the King's subjects in their true colours of royalism.[50] The Duke had correctly reported his sovereign's mind on the matter, and Macartney found the King ready with all his address to enlarge upon Harcourt's plea:

> He flattered himself that the formal recognition of his title would soon be added to his other obligations [to the King of Great Britain], which recognition he was by no means solicitous about from any motive of vain ambition (a passion he must be acquitted of by all who knew him) but from a firm persuasion that it would most efficaciously contribute to the success of his cause; that the Empress of Russia was as ready to acknowledge him as a King, as she had formerly not hesitated to recognize him as a Regent, and that if Great Britain were to join her, ... the other Powers would follow the example without delay ... Till England acknowledged him, neither the Prince of Condé's army would be properly arranged, nor Marshal Clerfayt's be quickened into the activity which it was capable of.[51]

Grenville was unimpressed, whether by Harcourt's or by Louis's version of this case. But Macartney, once more, displayed fidgets rather than assured mastery. Late in August, he announced to his principal with some emphasis the arrival at Verona of 'an officer from St. Petersburg, with a letter from the Empress of Russia to the King of France, treating him and acknowledging him as such', and declaring that 'her ministers at London and Vienna were instructed to press both these Courts to a speedy recognition of him'. In November the Earl implicitly acknowledged his relief that Catherine had not yet actually 'taken the steps in consequence' of her letter.[52]

V

Lord Grenville had also instructed his envoy to advise the French King where (pending the insurrection of some important French area in his cause) he ought to reside. Until royalist movements inside France called Louis to go thither and preside in person over the first phase of restoration, urged the Foreign Secretary, he should certainly not linger in Verona, on the territory of a minor Power which had now consented to full diplomatic relations with the French Republic; this was neither dignified nor secure. He should reside, temporarily, in the dominions either of the Kaiser or of the King of Spain: if (added Grenville realistically) one or other of these would consent; failing them, he should have recourse to Rome. This relatively minor question drew Macartney into yet another clash of wills with Louis, and into his own worst defeat of the whole episode. That the defeat involved the British envoy in no disamenities with his charming and masterly interlocutor only makes it the more striking.

He had no wish, said the King to the Earl, to remain at Verona; but what he wanted was to follow his own brother, then (it was hoped) setting off via Spithead to join the royalist revival in western France. There, more than anywhere, the new King might find 'a grave, or a crown'. Why, for the moment, shouldn't he go half-way towards his brother, by taking station near the army of Condé? The Earl cautiously rejoined that such a station must be Austria's, rather than England's, decision; he knew how little love was lost between Habsburgs and Bourbons, and had more sense than to drag his own country into either side of that issue; it was to Rome that he was commissioned to direct the King. Louis, in his most appealing manner, brushed the rejoinder aside: Rome was even further from where he most wanted to be than Verona; to reach western France from Rome involved a 'tedious and unpleasant' sea journey, and 'he had never been to sea himself'. When the envoy persisted about Rome, the French King resorted from the appealing to the grand. It might have been Louis XIV who countered: 'My Lord, you have certainly fulfilled your instructions, and I have expressed my feelings to you upon them'.

What then? Significantly, the Earl resorted to Louis's ministers. With them he took up 'a more elevated tone'; 'if the King was not advised to choose Rome,... instead of England directing his conduct, he directed hers'. Alas for *fortiter in re!* The ministers took up the role of the Greek chorus. Louis was 'entirely governed by himself'. It was the Earl who weakened: the Court should remove to the neighbourhood of Condé.[53]

But even the new Louis XIV could not overrule the providence more august than that of London. Before Macartney could arrive at Verona, the Anglo-*émigré* invasion at Quiberon had been smashed by General Hoche. Artois might still be disembarked in the west to join Charette and other local royalist partisans there; but, until their cause prospered again mainly by their own efforts (ruled Grenville early in September), England must not endanger there the life of the King himself. There would be no point yet, therefore, in his moving nearer Cuxhaven; and his pausing half-way, near to Condé, might well simply worsen his relations with Austria.[54] Yet neither the more august providence, nor (when he learned of it) the latest providence of Lord Grenville, halted Macartney's decline into 'direction' by the Prince whom he had proposed to 'direct'. The envoy acceded to the (vain) effort of Louis to obtain refuge with the Margrave of Baden, then to Louis's still more hopeless request of the Kaiser's permission to move to the Imperial city of Rothenburg, on the Neckar; the Earl even tried to involve in this second proposal his own colleague at

Vienna, Sir Morton Eden. All was in vain.[55] Macartney won no laurels, even when he fought for 'the other side'; while Louis, defeated too, became still more despondent. As October set in, the King was 'a good deal . . . discomposed', 'lamenting' to the Earl 'his unfortunate situation . . . through the Court of London's solicitude for his personal safety, and thro' the Court of Vienna's inhospitality'; he must 'seize the earliest opportunity of getting into France . . . his involuntary inaction was liable to misconstruction, for, his brother being now active in the Vendée, it was difficult to explain . . . the reason why he himself was not there also'.[56]

About this last point, Louis worried needlessly. Artois, under British protection, reached the île d'Yeu, off the Vendéan coast, at the end of September; but, rightly or wrongly, did not venture the mainland. By mid-November he was on his way back to Spithead, and thence to Holyrood, to evade his creditors.[57] But Louis became no more resigned to 'his unfortunate situation'. He still longed to be in France: if not in the Vendée, with his brother and the English, then in eastern France, with his cousin Condé; arm in arm, if not with the Austrians, then with their principal republican opponent, General Pichegru, Commander-in-Chief of the Army of the Rhine and Moselle, whose long-expected treason against the Republic now seemed imminent as he — purposefully? — mishandled his offensive eastward and seemed to encourage, in retort, the counter-invasion of eastern France by Condé and by the hitherto sullen Imperialists.[58] At the end of November, both the King and the Earl were rising from the trough to the crest: Austrian counter-strokes against Pichegru appeared, at last, to open the way for Condé, while Précy seemed set fair to raise the Lyonnais (and far beyond) for the King and against the unpopular Directorial government. Wickham (at Berne) and Trevor (at Turin) now united with various royalist leaders in France to urge upon Macartney a fresh attempt at Vienna to obtain authorization for Louis XVIII's 'temporary refuge' near the Franco-German border: 'in the neighbourhood of the Brisgau'.

The Earl wrote, without reluctance, once more to Eden, and also to Baron Thugut. He even rose to the hope that he himself might now become the agent of the seemingly impossible: *rapprochement* between Franz II and Louis XVIII (whose 'good nature' was 'not inferior to his sensibility').[59] He did his successful best, at the French King's Council table, to put down a complaint raised by Condé against a draft proclamation which he had been instructed to publish, on entering France, by the new Imperial Commander-in-Chief West, Field-Marshal Count Wurmser. The Earl urged (and won Louis's agreement) that 'the great point for the King was once to get a footing in France . . . the Prince of Condé was to take the shortest way, without stumbling at any . . . delicacies'.[60]

But, again, labour in vain. By mid-December it seemed very doubtful that the Imperialists would cross the Rhine in winter conditions; the great Royalist rising in the French Comté likewise receded; Pichegru lent no help; the allies had already incurred shattering defeat by Schérer (Commander-in-Chief of the French Army of Italy) in the Riviera; and on 21 December the Austrian 'winter armistice' with the Republicans on the Rhine front brought an end to the Earl's autumnal optimism. In vain did the French King, in January 1796, urge the British envoy to advise once again that the royal brothers should now be disembarked in western France;[61] Grenville's ears were deaf, and Macartney made no further efforts to open them.

VI

It was the question of (territorial) 'indemnities' for the allies, Austria and England, which called out Macartney's greatest interest, and his most strenuous attitudes, at Verona. *Fortiter in re* here came into its own; suavity seems hardly to have kept pace. The Earl plainly advised the exiled Court that the borders of France had been spread too far, even before the conquering career of the Republic, for the safety of others and even for the true interest of France herself; at the restoration, not only must the Belgian Netherlands be confirmed to the House of Austria, but they must be enlarged on their western frontier at the expense of the Bourbon realm. The King must abandon, not only the conquests of the Republic, but also some of those made by Louis XIV.[62] And when it came to 'compensations' for Great Britain, the envoy both spoke, and wrote home, in the style of a stout-hearted aggrandizing British imperialist (which he was).[63] In both areas of discussion he ran into serious difficulty, from which he found no happy deliverance. So far as concerned Austria, the exiled Court had an abundance of grievances against Vienna, accumulating ever since the abortive Austro-Prussian offensive against revolutionary France in summer 1792. Not least among these grievances was the evident Austrian appetite for territories which had been French long before the revolution. 'Nothing could have so fatal an effect', intimated Louis to the Earl, 'as . . . the slightest suspicion of an engagement to any material cession of towns or territory, as it would equally revolt all Frenchmen . . . whether royalist or republican'. And the King went on to denounce, very much in the terms afterwards employed by Talleyrand at the Congress of Vienna, all such projects of dismemberment and annexation of other Powers' territory as seemed to flourish, he thought, especially in the circle of the Kaiser. The Earl persisted against this 'French buckram of an intangible boundary' on the Belgian side with a lusty appetite for 'Lisle and Valenciennes, or at least one of them';[64] he laboured on, no less, for the genuine reconciliation of the Bourbon with the Habsburg Court — all to no better success.

In pressing the claims of England, to concessions not on the borders of France but in the maritime areas, the envoy could at first savour the promise of better fortune. The exiled Court could not very well decline to contemplate some 'compensation' — in more distant parts — to the only Power which seemed prepared to assist its hopes. But there are clear signs in his correspondence that Macartney approached this part of his duties with at least as much impatience to diminish the future inheritance of the French Crown as he displayed with respect to the interests of Austria;[65] and that, for all his charm of manner, his want of insight and delicacy in this negotiation spoiled whatever slender chance of real success might have been his. He never obtained anything closer to a formal promise of indemnities for England than for the Kaiser.

Had the Earl's mission prospered better in its immediate business, no doubt he would have taken less heavily his instructions 'to correspond, on all subjects that might require it', with other British representatives on the Continent who were concerned with different aspects of the war against the Republic. As things really were, he and his colleagues were groping in vain for the missing keystone of the arch, and he found his correspondence with them little more than a heavy burden. His remaining time was consumed by *émigrés* at Verona, who pestered him for relief which he had not the means to supply. He could not even attend to his own favourite private project, the publication of his account of China.[66]

We have, therefore, no reason to be surprised that, before the end of 1795, Macartney was disenchanted with his situation. In December, he advised Sir George Staunton that it was 'neither pleasant nor lucrative, and considering the places I have already filled elsewhere, not very eminent'. Eminence had indeed now passed him by; 'the King of France' ruled over a villa in north Italy, but not even over the west of France. And, as early as mid-November, the envoy had asked Lord Grenville's permission to take leave, about the turn of the year, 'to make a little tour'. It hardly required the permanent presence of a British representative 'to reconcile the mind of Louis XVIII' (as Grenville put it about that same time) 'to the hard lot which necessity had thrown upon him'; and in due course the Foreign Secretary rejoined to the Earl's request that he saw no objection to the little tour — while Dundas was meantime thinking of Macartney as the proper person to send as Governor of the latest British conquest abroad, the (Dutch) Cape of Good Hope.[67]

But the end was not to be just yet. Macartney's plan of leave was fleetingly disturbed by the hope of an Imperialist winter invasion of France and of a great royalist insurrection in eastern France. The hope faded, however, as rapidly as it had arisen. All that then detained him was the Foreign Secretary's reply to his request. Grenville had replied that he saw no objection; but his reply seems to have been long in arriving. It was only towards the middle of February 1796 that the Earl set off. On 26 February, Grenville conveyed to the itinerant envoy the King's 'approbation' ('amply deserved') of 'the zeal and intelligence manifested throughout Lord Macartney's conduct and correspondence'; and advised him that no new instructions seemed to be necessary. This appears to have been all but a notice of impending recall.[68]

VII

The Earl spent almost two months in what he seems to have viewed as a belated *grand* tour. He had already made two shorter excursions and had gazed upon Padua and Venice, Bologna and Florence; he had been struck by the 'museums' of these latter cities, compared with which he thought 'Great Russell Street . . . quite a paltry collection', and he had heard the great Fontana lecture on anatomy. He now went much further, to Naples, and he called both at Rome and at Florence on his return journey. He seems to have been an assiduous visitor of 'tout ce qu'il y a de plus beau, d'ancien et de moderne'; and he made the happiest impression upon people whom he met: the Neapolitan royal couple, the French King's aunt, Madame Victoire, and the French royalist agent at Rome. He was at Rome to admire the firmness and dignity of Pius VI in rebuffing, like a Roman of nobler times, the first menacing demands ('impudent and ridiculous requisitions') of the French Republic.[69]

These demands were some of the first rumblings of the storm over Italy which was soon to sweep Macartney's mission, and all that it had seemed to portend, into the limbo of forgotten things. Still earlier rumbles had sounded just before the Earl had left Verona. The French Directory had complained to Venice that it sheltered on its soil the French Pretender and other *émigrés*, conspiring against the Republic with which Venice professed full diplomatic relations. Venice had decided to ignore the complaint; the Earl had been well pleased.[70] But the sands were running out. The Directors had authorized, for Spring 1796, a great double offensive against Austria: in Germany and in Italy. On 2 March Bonaparte was appointed General-in-Chief, Italy. The Pope, like the Venetians a little before, heard the anticipating voice from Paris. He, too, thought to ignore it. On the very point of Macartney's return to Verona, the voice spoke to Venice again. This time, the Most Serene Republic crumbled; on 13 April the exiled Court received Macartney's private friend, Carlotti, who explained, as from the Council of Ten, that Louis and his adherents must quit Venetian territory 'within as few days as possible'.[71]

In the final scenes at Verona, the Earl was indeed once more on stage; but with no effective lines to speak. He offered his last advice to Louis, who was now determined both to vent his grandest displeasure upon the Venetian Republic, and also — at last, and regardless of all gainsayings — to make his way to Condé's camp in south-western Germany. Macartney washed his hands of what he considered the 'unreasonable rhodomontado' of the King's rebukes to Venice; but he intervened energetically to dissuade Louis from south Germany, until he had 'an eligible abode' there, and also the approval of 'his best friends'. Would not the King best take temporary refuge, meantime, in Parma, or at Bologna? Alas once more for *fortiter in re:* Louis — no doubt very charmingly — swept the Earl's advice aside: he distrusted the Duke of Parma, had 'an inveterate aversion to reside in the Paral dominions', and doubted the ability of the allies to defend north Italy.[72]

Louis reasoned better than his elder adviser. A month later Bonaparte was in Milan; and presently the rulers with whom Louis was advised to seek refuge were themselves signing armistices, or capitulations, with the victorious republican Commander-in-Chief. And a request for British approval of his joining Condé would simply have been referred to Imperial approval first: which would, as ever, have been unforthcoming. Louis calculated that, in his new circumstances, even the Court of Vienna could hardly refuse him asylum within the Reich — provided it were given no chance to raise fresh objections before he arrived there. The event justified the King, and not the Earl.

It only remained for Macartney to concede his final defeat in the spirit of a gentleman. This, to be sure, he did. He handed over to the exiles the remaining £2,000 which he had been empowered to dispense; and, noted Wickham, Louis 'spoke in the highest terms . . .

of the manner in which his Lordship had conducted himself at Verona, particularly upon this last unpleasant occasion'.[73] It was on 21 April that Louis set out upon his northward adventure; next day Macartney addressed his last despatch home, proposing to 'set out upon his own journey . . . next week'. And his destination was London.[74] Without (apparently) any official recall, he now regarded his mission as terminated. But he also knew, and he knew that Grenville knew, that the mission had lost all clear purpose, and that he himself had been 'nominated' for the governorship of the Cape. The Earl returned safely to London, no longer feeling very well and reluctant to venture the Cape. But there awaited him what made this still further commission 'eligible' after all: a barony in the peerage of Great Britain.[75]

CHAPTER IX

THE CAPE OF GOOD HOPE 1796-98

I

Macartney was appointed Governor of the Cape of Good Hope in December 1796 at the instance of Henry Dundas, Secretary of State for War and the Colonies. It was a post to which Dundas attached great importance. His long involvement in Indian affairs had made him conscious of the strategic significance of the Dutch settlement at the Cape as a key to the protection of British interests in India. He was said to have been 'an enthusiast (as far as a hackneyed politician can be) about the Cape'.[1] As the aggressive intentions of revolutionary France became increasingly evident his concern for the safety of the British position in India mounted. The memory of the French occupation of the Cape in 1781 moved him to propose, in 1791, that the Dutch East India Company should place all its settlements under British protection;[2] and when the French overran the United Provinces in 1794 he pressed for an immediate occupation of the Cape to prevent the French from taking possession of it.[3] This course of action was adopted. Early in the following year a combined naval and military force was despatched to the Cape and, after some resistance, the Dutch authorities capitulated in September 1795. Pending the appointment of a governor, the officer in command of the troops, Major-General James Henry Craig, assumed control of the settlement.

Dundas was convinced that the Cape should never be given up. His immediate task, however, was to provide for its government during the war, and for this he required an experienced and prestigious governor who would rule firmly and inspire respect among an alien population. He had to be a man, too, of sufficient weight to keep the peace between the military and naval commanders at the Cape. As early as March 1796, only six months after the capitulation, Dundas was worried about the bad relations between the commanders of the two services. By this time he had fixed upon Macartney as the ablest man available for the Cape post, but as Macartney had not yet returned from his mission to Verona he was not anticipating a decision from him for some time.[4] Macartney commended himself to

Dundas for the role of governor at the Cape mainly because of his Indian service; it had been at Dundas's insistence that Macartney was offered the governor-generalship of India in succession to Warren Hastings in 1785. Besides, Macartney shared his views on the importance of the Cape to British security and he was well qualified, by his overseas experience, to report fully and accurately on a territory about which very little was known in Britain.[5]

Macartney accepted the appointment with great reluctance. At his age, and with his health already causing him concern, he was not inclined to go abroad again. He went to Court the day after his return from Italy with a view to excusing himself, but the King and Dundas put pressure on him and he was offered highly attractive terms. His salary as Governor and Commander-in-Chief was to be a princely £10,000 a year, with an annual allowance of £2,000 table money, payable in sterling. On his retirement he was to receive an annual pension of £2,000. Macartney also succeeded in extracting from the government permission to relinquish his post and return to England without waiting for his replacement should the state of his health necessitate his resignation.[6]

Once he had committed himself, Macartney was anxious to reach the Cape as quickly as possible. He wrote to Dundas from Plymouth, where the warship *Trusty* on which he was to travel had put in for repairs, of his disappointment and mortification at the delay.[7] Eventually, after a voyage of seventy-one days, he reached the Cape on 4 May 1797. He had with him, as his private secretaries, two young men who had been with him in China, Acheson Maxwell and John Barrow; and also the newly appointed Secretary of the colony, Andrew Barnard, and his wife, Lady Anne. Barnard, the son of the Bishop of Limerick, was a conscientious but undistinguished man, considerably younger than his well-connected wife who, at one time, had come near to marrying Dundas. It was in response to her solicitations that the appointment at the Cape was found for her husband. Since Macartney's wife did not accompany him, Lady Anne became the first lady at the Cape.

II

The settlement in which Macartney and his retinue had arrived dated back to the mid-seventeenth century when the Dutch East India Company established a refreshment station at Cape Town to service its ships on their way to and from the Dutch possessions in the Far East. At first only Company servants were admitted but eventually free colonists (Dutch, Germans and French Huguenots) penetrated the interior and established themselves as wine and grain farmers in the western parts adjacent to Cape Town, and as pastoralists in the more remote areas. By the third quarter of the eighteenth century the cattle farmers, or *boers,* had come into conflict on the eastern border of the colony, in the region of the Great Fish River, with black, Bantu-speaking pastoralists who were moving southwards. At an early stage of the Dutch settlement slaves were imported, mainly from east Africa and the Company's eastern possessions, to provide the labour which the sparse indigenous population was unable or unwilling to supply. This indigenous population was composed of hunters and herders, once called Bushmen and Hottentots and now named San and Khoikhoi. By the time the British arrived, the San had been driven into the more in-accessible parts of the colony and the Khoikhoi were in process of blending into the coloured population which had emerged as the result of miscegenation among whites, slaves, Khoikhoi and San. This was the source from which the free labour force of the colony was drawn. Problems arising from this complex admixture of peoples exercised Macartney, as they had done his Dutch predecessors; he had, in addition, to cushion the impact of the British occupation.

Macartney's instructions, like the terms of the capitulation, were specifically designed to the latter end, for it was the aim of British ministers to reconcile the Cape Dutch to the new regime. The laws, customs and institutions of the colony were left largely intact, and such changes as were made were thought likely to benefit the inhabitants. Besides, the conquest did not involve an influx of strangers; the British presence was confined to the garrison and a few officials at Cape Town. Nor had the Company been particularly popular; indeed, the *boers* in the frontier district of Graaff-Reinet were in revolt against it when the British arrived. Nevertheless, the requirement to take an oath of allegiance to the British monarch encountered resistance and the arrogance of some of the newcomers aroused resentment. A good many people, too, were so sure that the Cape would pass to the Netherlands or France when peace returned that they did not want to associate too closely with the British.

It was clear from the beginning that Macartney regarded his sojourn at the Cape as likely to be of short duration. He was also averse to spending public money on government property in a colony where the future of British rule was uncertain. With these considerations in mind he elected to live in the government house in the Gardens at Cape Town, without having any renovations effected, although it was in a sorry state of disrepair. It was cramped and dirty and had a nearly perpendicular staircase up which, as Lady Anne Barnard said, he hopped, gout and all, like a parrot to his perch.[8] He furnished only what rooms were necessary for his own use, with the result that he was unable to offer accommodation to visitors. 'I have it not in my power to offer you a bed', he told Rear-Admiral Sir Hugh Christian, the naval commander at the Cape, 'but in every other point I beg you to consider my house as your own'.[9] When Lord Mornington stayed at the Cape on his way to take up the governor-generalship of India, Macartney had him installed in a lodging house, until Mornington took refuge with the Barnards to escape the attack of bugs.[10] Hospitality, apart from accommodation, Macartney did provide. For that he had equipped himself in advance: a list he prepared in London of what he should take out with him to the Cape included wines and spirits, tableware, glass and candlesticks, a cook and *maître d'hotel*, and a kitchen range.[11] The more commodious government house in the Castle at Cape Town, which would normally have been occupied by the Governor or the Lieutenant-Governor, he allotted to the Barnards — his second-in-command, General Dundas, a nephew of the Secretary of State, was unmarried at this time and consequently not in need of the superior accommodation. Here, in the Castle, with Macartney's warm approval and support, Lady Anne Barnard set about cultivating the Dutch ladies as a means of winning the allegiance of the leading burgher families. Macartney himself participated in social functions. Lady Anne Barnard records, for example, an occasion on which he danced a Scottish reel, adding: 'I fear the little twinge in the toe next day whispered to his Excellency that he had been rash'.[12]

In his social activites and in his relations with his officials Macartney appears to have been unusually affable. A reputation for being cold and formal, obstinate and self-opinionated, had preceded him to the Cape so that the graciousness and consideration with which he treated his subordinates came as an agreeable surprise.[13] Admittedly, much of the evidence comes from Lady Anne Barnard who enjoyed Macartney's confidence and patronage, but Lord Mornington was surprised to find how Macartney had mellowed at the Cape, and even Lady Anne implied that a change had come over him when she commented: 'wines of strong body and high flavour are sometimes ameliorated by time, and become more gracious to the taste than when new'.[14]

III

Such behaviour was consistent with what Macartney conceived to be his foremost duty at the Cape, to maintain stability and security in the colony. This involved, on the one hand, the exercise of a benevolent paternalism and, on the other, a stern suppression of anything which appeared to challenge his authority or endanger the peace. In the benevolent aspect of his rule he was doing no more than fulfilling his instructions and complying with repeated exhortations to attach the colonists 'to His Majesty's mild and paternal government'. To this end, oppressive monopolies were abolished and greater freedom of trade was allowed; arrears of land rent incurred before the beginning of the British occupation were cancelled; officials were given fixed salaries instead of the fees and perquisites by which they had been paid under the Dutch East India Company; liberty of conscience and the free exercise of public worship were guaranteed; and the administration of justice was improved by the abolition of torture, the reorganisation of the High Court and the creation of appeal procedures.[15] The assiduity with which Macartney inquired into the problem of the depreciated paper money at the Cape, and his concern for the alleviation of shortages, reflected his desire to promote the welfare of the colonists.[16]

Macartney's main task, however, was to enforce the authority of the new government at the Cape and to avoid conflict or friction which might endanger the stability of the colony. Very soon after his arrival he laid down a timetable for the taking of the oath of allegiance. When a number of Cape Town residents allowed the deadline to pass, he followed up his first proclamation with another threatening defaulters with transportation to Batavia or some other Dutch settlement in the east. Meantime troops were billeted on selected offenders. Shortly afterwards he was able to report that even notorious Jacobins had taken the oath, firmness having convinced them that they were not likely to be returned to their former masters.[17] A situation more difficult to resolve existed in the frontier district of Graaff-Reinet where the local magistrate or *landdrost,* Frans Reinhard Bresler, installed by General Craig to restore order, had been expelled by the local *boers.* Macartney reinstated him, with instructions to assure the frontiersmen of the government's good intentions but to warn them of the consequences of disobedience. So that he would not be entirely dependent on a Dutch official he sent his secretary, John Barrow, with Bresler to Graaff-Reinet 'to discover how far the same objects may appear alike to British and Dutch eyes', furnishing Barrow with separate instructions.[18] The resistance in Graaff-Reinet collapsed, however, after the capture of a Dutch ship carrying arms and ammunition intended for the rebels' use, and for the remainder of Macartney's governorship Graaff-Reinet acquiesced in British rule.[19] He also found it necessary to send Andrew Barnard to

Swellendam where about a dozen men were evading the oath. When he arrived all but four had sworn allegiance. Barnard had the recalcitrants rounded up and sent to Cape Town for transportation on the next available ship. Though they conformed at the last moment and were freed, they were kept under military surveillance for a time.[20] One Swellendam man who evaded Barnard was arrested months later and sent to England without trial.[21]

Any manifestation of Jacobin sympathies, however trifling, evoked a sharp reaction. When a Cape resident, Hendrick Oostwald Eksteen, addressed his friends as 'citizen' on invitations to his daughter's wedding, Macartney ordered a party of dragoons to be billeted in his house. They arrived during the wedding celebrations. Eksteen was required 'to retract and redress in the most public manner this wanton and petulant conduct, or to repair to that country where, in the midst of confusion and medley, his meditations would be better relished'. Eksteen pleaded innocent of any intention to give offence, and apologised, but the troops were not withdrawn until he had produced a bond for 500 rixdollars as security for his future good behaviour.[22] Others more discreet than Eksteen, but suspected of being republicans, were appointed to unpaid petty offices; and, if they refused to perform the duties and take the stringent oath required, troops were billeted on them.[23] Towards the municipal body in Cape Town, the burgher senate, Macartney adopted an autocratic attitude. Its duty, he said, was to take care of the common interests of the corporation of burghers and, in case of necessity — for the prevention of disorders, to make representations to the government 'in decent terms'; but it had no right to consider private requests or individual complaints, or to meddle in matters which were the concern of government. When its members pressed him to relieve the labour shortage by importing slaves, he replied that he would be better pleased if, instead of petitioning for things which could not be granted, they turned their attention to the repair of the streets; and they incurred a stiff reprimand for having made difficulties about the use of the town house for the celebration of the King's birthday. In future, they were not consulted and were ordered to hand over the keys of the building to a military officer.[24] Macartney allowed no encroachment on his own position. When his second-in-command, General Dundas, began the draft of a proclamation with the words, 'His Excellency, the Commander-in-Chief', Macartney struck out the word 'Excellency', with the remark that there was only one 'Excellency' in the colony.[25] He was equally jealous of the authority of his subordinates. In a proclamation soon after his arrival he affirmed the primacy of the *landdrosts* in their districts and directed

271

that they should be respected and obeyed.[26] When it came to his notice that a member of the Stellenbosch Board of Heemraden, the local administrative and judicial body, had spoken disrespectfully of the *landdrost* he recommended the offender to behave in future in conformity with his orders.[27]

Macartney realised that recalcitrant *boers* and burghers were not the only potential troublemakers; the tranquillity of the colony could equally well be disrupted by discontent among the rank and file of the occupying forces or by friction within the ruling élite. A mutiny which broke out in October 1797 on a number of naval vessels stationed at the Cape was inspired more by the example of the mutineers at Spithead and the Nore than by any peculiarly local grievances. The restoration of order was essentially a problem for the naval officers but they had Macartney's full support; he was prepared to use shore batteries to bombard the ships if necessary and he moved most of the troops out of Cape Town to prevent dis-affection spreading to the army. Wine houses frequented by the sailors were closed and the proprietor of the principal one, and his wife, were sent off on an East Indiaman.[28] Macartney's prescription for contentment among the private soldiers stationed at the Cape was to pay them in English money, which they were able to exchange for rixdollars at an advantage of from 20% to 30%. To have paid them in rixdollars with full allowance for the rate of exchange would have been less satisfactory, for 'I know the nature of these gentry so well that I could have little hope of their long remaining satisfied, for from their not well comprehending the fluctuation of exchange, and from their suspicious nature, they would be apt to complain of being cheated'. In his first letter from the Cape, and at intervals thereafter, Macartney stressed the need for regular remittances of money from England. On one occasion he was obliged to borrow £2,500 from the governor of St. Helena to pay the troops.[29]

Over the small circle which composed Cape society Macartney kept a tight rein. Gambling was discouraged. No card-playing was allowed in his house, he disapproved of horse racing, refused to subscribe to the Turf Club, and when he learnt of bets being organised at the races he sent a message to the people involved 'to desire it might be the first and last time he heard of such a thing in the colony'.[30] On the other hand, he encouraged Lady Anne Barnard's efforts to provide some social life for the junior officers by inviting them to balls in the Castle; and he enjoyed the salacious stories which circulated about the liaisons between the officers of the garrison and the Dutch ladies in Cape Town. An outcome of this social activity, which was in accord with Macartney's policy, was noted by an observer: 'we shall very shortly see a race of English men grafted on a Dutch stock which in a great measure will conciliate the affections of the people in general'.[31]

IV

The two European communities were not the only source of potential threats to the stability of the colony. Macartney had to turn his attention as well to problems arising from the existence of other peoples within and beyond the boundaries of the colony. The British had inherited a slave economy at the Cape and Macartney was well aware of how sensitive an issue slavery was becoming in England. He was put under considerable pressure by the burgher senate to authorise the import of slaves to relieve the labour shortage in Cape Town, but his response was cautious. A few slaves from ships captured by the navy were brought in and sold, and he granted one licence for the importation of a cargo of slaves. When the ship arrived it was found that it had not been able to acquire half the authorised number of slaves and disappointment in Cape Town was intense. All this information was conveyed in private letters to Henry Dundas. Macartney studiously avoided the subject of slaves in his public despatches, for he was anxious to ensure that 'if all my public letters were to undergo the ordeal either of Parliament or the India House no prejudice would arise to those whom they were addressed to'.[32] Towards the Bushmen or San, whose depredations on the livestock of the *boers* evoked harsh reprisals, he advocated lenient treatment. He tried to induce them to live in peace by giving them presents of cattle, but he also authorised their expulsion to the Kalahari if they proved to be intractable.[33] With the Xhosa tribes from beyond the frontier he also endeavoured to establish good relations, or, as he put it, to avoid rousing the hornets' nest. Those who had broken into the colony he tried to persuade to withdraw. The Great Fish River was fixed as the boundary and movement in either direction was forbidden. Even trade between blacks and whites was discouraged.[34]

To guard the security of the Cape Colony was Macartney's primary duty but he was instructed as well to report on the nature and resources of the territory and to give his opinion on its value as a permanent British possession. Macartney would have liked to have seen the interior with his own eyes. At one time he hoped to make an eight- or ten-day tour if the state of his health and the volume of business permitted. But the tour never took place and Macartney had to rely on information collected by others. His secretary, John Barrow, was one of these. Barrow was sent to Graaff-Reinet with *Landdrost* Bresler, not merely to keep an eye on him, but also to report on the nature of the frontier district and on the peoples living in and beyond it. How necessary such an expedition was appears from Macartney's comments at the time:

> We are shamefully ignorant of the geography of the country; we have no map that embraces one-tenth part of the colony; I neither know, nor can I learn, where this Graaff-Reinet lies — whether it is 500 or 1,000 miles from Cape Town. I am further informed that the Kaffirs with their cattle are in possession of the finest grazing country in the colony, and that these people and the *boers* are perpetually fighting and mutually carrying off each other's cattle.

Barrow prepared the best map of the colony yet to appear and his experiences and observations provided material for a book which he subsequently published.[35] Macartney accumulated information about the population, the natural resources, the extent of government property and the economic activities of the colonists. The conclusion he reached was that the colony's products did not rival or interfere with British interests, but, equally, were unlikely to contribute much to British wealth for some time to come. It was for strategic reasons that he advocated the retention of the Cape when peace came. In his opinion restoration of the Cape and Ceylon to the United Provinces would be tantamount to handing the colonies over to France, but if Britain retained them 'the Indian world will long be our own'. Though his plan of inducing the East India Company to take over the Cape after the war encountered opposition from India House, and though he admitted that, if a choice had to be made, Ceylon should be retained rather than the Cape, he never departed from his conviction of the Cape's strategic importance. As he told Dundas after his return to England, 'I should indeed be a poor geographer and a poorer statesman were I to advise our parting with it, but in the last extremities — putting off the question [of] any commercial advantage that might be derived from it — I would wish it at present to be considered solely as a great military station, and the master key of India'.[36]

V

As Macartney's governorship progressed, it became clear that the ill-health he had feared at the time of his appointment was laying hold upon him. Though he argued against accepting office on health grounds, he seems to have hoped that the salubrious Cape climate

Macartney, c.1802, by Gaettano Bartolozzi after Henry Edridge (B.M. PS.131928).

would do him good. For the first three months he was reasonably well, but by September 1797 he was complaining of fatigue. Next month he confided in Andrew Barnard that he was very ill. He apologised to Barnard for asking him to write some despatches, which he had meant to do himself, but the combination of ailments affecting him was making the business of his office almost too much for him. At this time his illness was not public knowledge and he was still fulfilling his social engagements. Some weeks later he spelled out in detail to Dundas what illnesses he believed he was suffering from. Gout was ravaging his head and stomach; he had piles, if not a fistula; he feared he had a stone in his kidneys; and, what depressed him more than all the rest, he was experiencing an increasing weakness in his eyes. By the new year he was confined to bed by gout and unable to write. Such bouts of illness recurred at intervals and he felt they were sapping his energy. He had become convinced that the climate at the Cape, however healthy, was unsuited to people suffering from arthritic conditions. He struggled on for some months more, with spells of being incapacitated by gout, and then on 21 November 1798 he sailed for home, having handed over power to the Lieutenant-Governor, General Francis Dundas, and surrendered to him the full salary of £10,000, though it was customary for a retiring governor to retain half the salary till his successor was appointed.[37]

Two days before he left the colony Macartney drew up and signed in the presence of the Secretary, Andrew Barnard, and the Fiscal, W. S. van Ryneveldt, a declaration similar to the one he had issued on leaving India. In it he solemnly declared that he had never received any gift or emolument other than the salary and services made available to him as Governor, and that he had never engaged in any commercial or trading venture for his own advantage. Although, as he admitted, the temptations and the opportunities for corruption were much less at the Cape than in other British possessions, he felt impelled to make the declaration 'from a sense of that propriety and consistency which I wish to preserve through the whole course of my political life, now drawing near to its conclusion'.[38] This was his last official act.

Macartney was Governor at the Cape of Good Hope for just over eighteen months, during a wartime occupation and when the future of the colony was far from certain. He was in office neither at the beginning nor at the end of what proved to be the first of two British wartime occupations. His freedom of action was restricted by the terms of the capitulation, by his instructions, and by the necessity of avoiding too deep an involvement in colonial problems. He was often stiff and insensitive in his response to what he regarded as manifestations of disaffection. Some of his arrangements, like his measures to pacify the frontier *boers* and to avoid conflict on the border, broke down almost as soon as he had gone; and the harmony which he had nurtured among members of the governing circle in Cape Town quickly evaporated. Nevertheless, Pitt and Dundas were satisfied that he had discharged what was required of him. He continued to advise on Cape affairs; and when the Addington ministry was being formed, he was offered the presidency of the Board of Control, with a seat in the Cabinet. Macartney declined to accept this or any other public office; as he had said at the time, his public life ended when he left the Cape of Good Hope.

CHAPTER X

LATER YEARS 1780-1806

I

Macartney's youthful ambitions, fierce though they were, could scarcely have encompassed the possibility of membership of the British Cabinet. It was profoundly ironical, therefore, that his public career should have ended with his refusal to accept such a position. While undoubtedly gratified to receive the offer, Macartney had no hesitation in turning it down. In December 1797, almost a year before leaving the Cape, he had informed Thomas Coutts of his determination to quit public life 'for ever' on his return to England.[1] Nor was deteriorating health the sole reason for his carefully considered and irrevocable decision. Many years previously — on his appointment to Grenada, if not before — Macartney had set his sights firmly on two objectives: personal financial security and a British peerage. Both had been achieved by the time he left the Cape; in addition, he had earned an enviable reputation as an honest and efficient public servant and, primarily as a result of his mission to China, had also become one of the most celebrated public figures of his day. It was a measure of his high standing with the government that his appointment at the Cape had been so amply rewarded, and that he had been granted prior permission to return to England immediately should *he* deem it advisable to do so.

The prestige which Macartney derived from his later appointments promoted a perceptible alteration in his behaviour. According to Barrow, for example, he became almost eccentrically conservative in matters of dress, whereas earlier he had been alive to every change of taste in this respect.[2] More significantly, the arrogance for which at one time he had been positively renowned was gradually succeeded by a mildly benevolent paternalism. Soon after his return from India Lady Portarlington found him 'much more agreeable, as he has left off the sneering way he had'.[3] Memories of his own youthful extravagance were no doubt responsible for Macartney's growing aversion to gambling: on the other hand from the mid-1780s he frequently lent money to those of his hard-pressed acquaintances who asked for it, and adopted a casually indulgent attitude if they

278

failed to repay him.[4] He retained the utmost respect of those younger officials, like Barrow, who served under him; but as his old touchiness and acerbity gave way to a more even-tempered urbanity, he also won their affection.

While much of this change may safely be attributed to Macartney's satisfaction with the course of his public career, he was also mellowed by a more relaxed and enjoyable private life after returning from India in 1785. In that year his relationship with Lady Jane reached a critical juncture for, at a time when the couple had already been apart from each other for more than four years, there arose the possibility that Macartney would remain in, or return to, India as Governor General of Bengal. For months Lady Jane was torn between duty to her husband, which urged her to accompany him, and the demands of her mother that she remain at home. In the event Macartney was as glad to decline the appointment as Lady Jane was to avoid the decision, and the two enjoyed long periods of domestic contentment together between and after his later appointments.[5]

It is perhaps appropriate at this point to counter the suggestion, by Robbins, that Macartney's marriage to Lady Jane was not a happy one.[6] Mrs. Robbins, it seems, was strongly influenced by the couple's apparent willingness to remain apart during all but one (Grenada) of the overseas postings which followed their marriage. In reality they had very little choice in the matter. Throughout his career Macartney was obliged to take employment where he could get it; and after Grenada it was always more likely that he would be offered opportunities abroad. Likewise, various considerations kept Lady Jane at home. She was perhaps unnerved by the incidents which marked their departure from the Caribbean. She had a delicate constitution and would not readily have withstood the rigours of India, China or the Cape. She also had a fiercely possessive mother, who bitterly resented Lady Jane's absences in Ireland, and who, after Grenada, would not hear of her daughter going further afield. Moreover, although both he and Staunton had planned that their wives would eventually join them in India, Macartney almost certainly valued Lady Jane's continued presence in London as an insurance against his own inability to deal with unforeseen emergencies, either there or in Ireland. Above all, perhaps, Lady Jane's severe deafness made public duties exceedingly difficult, if not impossible, for her. Thus, the separations which punctuated the marriage were accepted reluctantly; and in spite, and to an extent perhaps because, of them the couple continued to hold each other in great esteem. Macartney corresponded with Lady Jane in the most affectionate terms; during his absences he gave her far-reaching control over his affairs, as well as ready access to the means at his command; and he left her a very wealthy woman at his death.[7]

From 1786 onwards Macartney had much more time at his disposal than previously and used it to considerable effect. Having been deprived of intellectual diversion for more than a decade, he was delighted to be elected a member of the Literary Club in May 1786. This was an informal but highly prestigious group, whose nine founder members had included Samuel Johnson, Edmund Burke and Sir Joshua Reynolds. By the time Macartney was admitted it had a membership of around thirty, the majority of whom were leading public figures. For the rest of his life Macartney attended meetings whenever he could, and served as President of the Club in the period immediately before his departure for China (when he was also elected a Fellow of the Royal Society).[8] In 1786-7 he acquired a further town house in London and a country property in Surrey and, especially after returning from China, was more welcome than ever in polite society. However, from 1786 both he and Lady Jane also spent long periods at Lisanoure. By then economic conditions on the north Antrim estate and in Ulster generally were much more favourable than they had been in the early 1770s. An increase in his low level of income per acre remained a major priority and, not least in this respect, Macartney continued to encounter difficulties which were neither easily nor speedily solved. Nevertheless, reverting to his proprietorial role with commitment and zest, he devoted much careful attention to the development of his property and, by the time ill-health finally overcame him, had completed a number of significant improvements.

All this was a far cry from the anxious, debt-ridden years between his embarkation for Russia and his return from Grenada, when he had possessed neither the time nor the money to pursue other than short-term or exclusively private concerns. Nor, thereafter, was the path to financial ease and personal contentment an easy one. However, a substantial improvement in Macartney's fortunes may be confidently dated from his arrival in India in 1781.

II

At around £16,000 a year Macartney's salary as President of Fort St. George amounted to almost three times the income he had received as Governor of Grenada. Yet, whereas the bulk of his earnings in the Caribbean had been paid into his London bank account in sterling, his Indian salary was paid in local currency (pagodas) at Madras. He was, therefore, obliged to exchange his savings, and also to arrange for their secure transfer via bills of exchange to London. In the long-run neither of these requirements posed insuperable problems, but the risk and uncertainty involved in transferring credit over such a long distance caused both Macartney and Coutts considerable anxiety. In January 1784, for example, Macartney still awaited 'intelligence from you of the receipt of several bills transmitted . . . between the month of March 1782 and . . . [now]'; and other correspondence indicates that Coutts experienced similar delays at his end.[9] In addition to this factor (and the continued existence of the account with Latouche in Dublin), various other considerations render analysis of the account with Coutts (See Table)[10] exceedingly difficult. Thus, some of the money which Macartney borrowed in London prior to his departure, notably the £6,000 from Paul Benfield, was repaid at Madras, though the precise amount involved is uncertain.[11] Moreover, as he reported to Coutts, Macartney frequently borrowed in advance of his Indian salary in order to seize favourable opportunities of making remittances: subsequently, he repaid some of the loans in London, and some at Madras, so that precise, overall analysis is again impossible.[12] Furthermore, soon after arriving in India Macartney struck up a friendship with Thomas Mercer, a wealthy merchant-captain. On being offered the chance, Mercer agreed to purchase the bulk of the north Antrim property which Macartney had acquired between 1769 and 1771 as soon as they both returned home. In the meantime he lent Macartney sums totalling £10,000 at 4%, some (but perhaps not all) of which were included among the remittances to Coutts.[13] Finally, on at least one occasion Macartney transferred money to a creditor whose account was not with Coutts but with another banker, Drummond:[14] there may well have been other such

Account at Coutts' Bank 1780-86			
Date	*Credit*	*Debit*	*Carried Over*
1780-1	£1,124. 2. 4.	£568. 2.11.	+£555.19. 5.
1781	3,645. 5. 8.	3,350.12. 2.	+294.13. 6.
1781-2	2,085. 0. 6.	1,141.15. 6.	+943. 5. 0.
1782-3	6,868. 3. 4.	6,797.14.10.	+70. 8. 6.
1783	10,910. 2. 8.	9,259.19.10.	+1,650. 2.10.
1783-4	12,309.14. 1.	11,667.13. 9.	+642. 0. 4.
1784	1,762. 4.11.	1,118. 0. 1.	+644. 4.10.
1784-5	13,110. 9. 3.	12,045. 2. 0.	+1,065. 7. 3.
1785	1,381.13. 9.	320.11. 7.	+1,061. 2. 2.
1785-6	31,077. 6. 8.	26,654.11. 8.	+4,422.15. 0.

remittances. Nevertheless, together with contemporary correspondence and memoranda, the account at Coutts leaves no doubt as
to the private outcome of Macartney's period in India: by saving hard
for four and a half years he utterly transformed his financial position.

Anticipating that his position at Madras would periodically be
subject to grave uncertainty, Macartney lost no time in attempting to
recoup his fortunes. In February 1781, several months before he left
London, he laid out £1,600 of borrowed money on the first of a series
of investments in government securities. Because of the American
war the government had expanded the national debt with the result
that the price of securities was low; the interest on them exceeded
that due on most of Macartney's debts, and such investment allowed
him ready access to his capital should be require it.[15] His first priority,
however, was the discharge of the most pressing and expensive of his
debts. Within thirteen months of his arrival in India he had repaid
Benfield (£6,000), cleared £5,000 of the £7,000 owing to the
executors of Lord Holland, and in addition had remitted no less than
£18,444 to Coutts. Only £9,000 of these huge sums represented
savings: but, on accruing in London many months later, that was more
than sufficient to repay the remainder (£1,000) of the sum owing to
the executors of James Coutts, the whole of the mortgage from
Thomas Coutts (£4,700), and various short-term debts and tradesmen's bills (£2,892).[16] As yet Macartney had no intention of repaying
the loans raised to finance the expansion of his north Antrim estate.
Instead, as remittances proceeded, he instructed his wife and Coutts
to dispose of 'surplus money . . . to advantage, always taking care it
be in such a manner that I may command it at a moment's warning,
as I know not how soon I may draw . . . for it'.[17] Accordingly, in
addition to more routine income and expenditure, from 1783 the
account with Coutts recorded a growing number of purchases, sales
and profits of investments, particularly in navy and victualling bills.[18]
By the end of that year all Macartney's short-term debts had been
discharged, the investment programme was well underway, and his
London bank account was in persistent, and often substantial,
surplus. In January 1784 he was able to inform Edmund Burke that
so far he had managed to accumulate £20,288 'solely from the
savings of the Company's allowances'.[19] Thereafter Macartney
continued to make significant progress, benefiting both from the low
cost of living in India and from the fact that, in the absence of his
wife, household and associated expenditure could be kept to an
absolute minimum; and during the course of 1784 he ceased
borrowing from East India merchants in advance of his salary.
However, the impact of these developments on the account with

Coutts only reached a climax in the months surrounding Macartney's return to England in December 1785. Between September 1785 and June 1786 over £31,000 passed through the account as final remittances arrived and were cleared, securities were profitably sold, and many of the debts incurred in India were repaid in London. His total savings from his income as President amounted to no less than £32,718.[20]

Among the letters of congratulation which Macartney received soon after his arrival in London was one from an old friend, Dean Marley, in Dublin, who was delighted 'to hear [of] the high reputation you have acquired'. 'Though you have not . . . [returned with] . . . a princely fortune', he went on, 'you have brought home what you certainly value more, your integrity unscathed'.[21] In fact Macartney succeeded on both counts for, in the light of his previous circumstances, his legitimate profits were 'princely' indeed. Moreover, they constituted merely the first instalment of the reward for his services at Madras. The East India Company was so impressed by his 'upright and disinterested conduct' on its behalf that, together with plate valued at £1,600, it granted Macartney a life annuity of £1,500, the first payment of which was made in August 1786.[22] Further payments between then and his death in 1806 more or less equalled the fruits of Macartney's recent retrenchment. During the next few months he continued to recover from what, without doubt, was his most taxing public assignment. No-one any longer doubted his abilities: but, apart from himself, Lady Jane and Thomas Coutts were probably alone in appreciating the importance of the Madras presidency to Macartney's private affairs.

III

The freedom to plan for the future which Macartney now enjoyed was an invaluable aid to his recuperation and before long his new-found prosperity was clearly reflected in his everyday life. There was no return to the gross extravagance of earlier years; indeed, soon after arriving in England he arranged to repay the £7,000 (£5,000 to the Flemings and £2,000 to Mrs. Renouard) still outstanding from the land transactions of the early 1770s.[23] Nevertheless, confident that fresh employment would be offered to him in due course, he embarked on further ambitious schemes at Lisanoure and also acquired two additional residences in the south of England.

Although as yet he made no attempt to sell it, Macartney decided that the rather poky town house in Charles Street, Piccadilly, was no longer adequate; and in 1786, 'partly for its convenience, and partly for grandeur', he purchased a much larger and more imposing establishment in Curzon Street, Mayfair, for £3,500.[24] In the following July he also bought a small country house in a part of the Surrey countryside much favoured by professional and business men who wished to get away from the city whilst remaining within easy reach of it. Situated on the edge of Abingdon Common, Parkhurst was acquired for the modest sum of £1,400: apart from the house, there was a garden (which Macartney greatly improved), an orchard, a farm, outhouses, and forty acres of arable and pasture. Macartney was soon reported to be living 'in a more comfortable style than I have ever known', and as being 'fonder of home than he used to be'; and during the course of the next decade he added a further four parcels of land to the property at a total cost of £610.[25]

As far as Macartney was concerned, however, 'home' meant Lisanoure, and between returning from India and setting out for China he visited north Antrim regularly and spent several protracted periods there. By 1786 Lisanoure Castle had not been occupied, other than by an elderly housekeeper, for well over a decade. Throughout that period the ravages of damp and associated rot had gone largely unchecked, and Macartney decided that they could only be repaired by substantial alterations. The original Gothic front of the house was dismantled and replaced in a plain Classical style.[26] The entire roof of the house and connecting offices was also removed to make way for 'a much more simple [sic] and better . . . [one] . . . than the last'.[27] Once these major tasks had been accomplished, much of the interior was provided with stud walls to keep out further damp, and then extensively re-decorated; and the exterior was freshly rendered and sealed. The courtyard was paved, the paths and lawns at the front of the house were refurbished, and a great variety of shrubs and plants was purchased for the gardens.[28] In the midst of these activities Macartney embarked on further elaborate embellishments to the rest of the demesne. He took over some land to the north-east (which had previously been let for temporary grazing) and, by excavating and flooding 'an ugly bog', created a third lake, which he then separated from the permanently tenanted land beyond by constructing a wall and sunk fence. He built a porter's lodge on the east side of the demesne, and put down a driveway from there to the Castle. On the west side he built a hamlet of six cottages for the demesne workforce, naming it 'Macartney'. And to the south he established further sizeable timber plantations. The canals were cleared, deepened, and at certain points provided with new banks; a stream was diverted into the new lake to maintain its level; and a

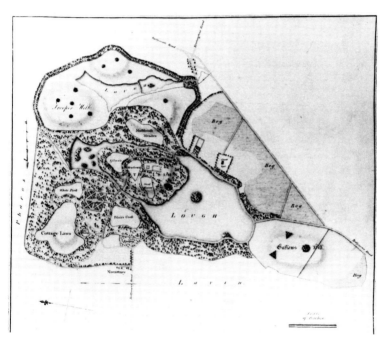

Map of the Lisanoure Demesne, 1788 (D.1062/2/4).

285

'stout boat' was acquired so that the surroundings could be admired from the water.[29]

As these extensive alterations neared completion in 1788, Macartney re-arranged and catalogued his furniture, pictures and library, laid in 'as good claret, port and sherry as I have ever drunk', and had the demesne surveyed and mapped.[30] And then, while maintaining that no-one should expect 'finery, decoration or elegance ... where the owner's fortune is so moderate', he freely encouraged his friends to visit Lisanoure. Apart from Macartney's instructions not to tip the servants and despite his provision of a model timetable for visitors, they were 'to mind no forms, but to do exactly and without constraint just as if [sic] they were at their own homes'. The nearby Giant's Causeway was 'by no means answerable to the descriptions that are given of it': but in Macartney's eyes and, he hoped, in those of his guests too, Lisanoure was now among the 'many other things ... in that neighbourhood which are ... as worthy of observation'.[31]

During the course of these developments Macartney increased the number of permanent staff in his employ. For the first time since Blakemore's dismissal several years earlier, he appointed a bailiff, James Dunn, whose wife, Mary, soon replaced the ageing housekeeper, Mrs. Swindell. Under Dunn, another new employee, Felix Laverty, had particular responsibility for the tree nursery and timber stands, and subsequently Macartney also appointed a full-time gardener. This expansion in the demesne staff was further necessitated by Jackson Wray's occasional ill-health and by the division of his energies between his own establishment at Bentfield, the Jackson estate near Coleraine in Co. Londonderry, and Macartney's property in north Antrim. Particularly after Richard Jackson's sudden death in 1789, Macartney judged it essential for Wray to devote the bulk of his time to circumstances beyond the demesne.[32]

However, even if Wray had worked full-time for Macartney, he could have offered little assistance in regard to the far-flung properties outside north Antrim. In the first place the chief rents from the Killinchy estate in Co. Down, which amounted to some £505 a year, were fixed forever. Secondly, apart from a single townland, Boherna, in King's Co. and some thirty acres in Co. Kilkenny, the remnants of the Porter estate in the south of Ireland consisted of scattered houses and tenements in the cities of Kilkenny and Dublin. The entire property was set on long determinable leases and brought in some £222 a year in rents. Finally, there were the buildings and parcels of land in and around Carrickfergus in south-east Antrim and the property at Auchinleck in Scotland, from which Macartney derived a total of £67 a year in the late 1780s.[33] Because little or nothing could be done to improve such scattered holdings, Macartney soon determined to sell all but Auchinleck and to invest the proceeds in the purchase of further property near his main estate. However, having advertised the fact and received preliminary enquiries regarding the Killinchy estate, his solicitor was advised of certain practical difficulties which had to be overcome if prospective purchasers were to be persuaded to offer the full market value. In regard to the Porter and Killinchy estates it would not only have been necessary (and expensive) to procure an enabling act of Parliament but, in view of the fact that her jointure was partly to be derived from those properties, Lady Jane would have been obliged to swear, either before a panel of judges or before a committee of the House of Lords, 'that her consent [to the sales] was not obtained by coercion'.[34] Eventually, and reluctantly, Macartney decided to retain the properties.

He suffered a further setback in regard to the proposed transaction with Thomas Mercer. In India Mercer had lent Macartney £10,000 on the understanding that, following their return to Europe, he would purchase property of that value from him. The property in question consisted of five of the townlands which Macartney had acquired after returning from Russia, and whose management had caused his staff such difficulty throughout the 1770s. Having visited both Lisanoure and the townlands concerned, Mercer bought Glenbuck, Anticur and Scotchomerbane in 1789 for a total of £6,500: but, following legal advice, declined to purchase either Carnbuck or Gruig.[35] The price which Macartney had paid for Scotchomerbane is unknown. However, in view of the fact that he had paid no less than £5,656 for Glenbuck and Anticur, it seems likely that he failed to break even on the limited transaction with Mercer; and he still owed £3,500 of the original loan.[36]

Although circumstances there remained difficult for him, Macartney's activities on his inherited estate in north Antrim met with greater success. His long-term aim was to develop a closer tenurial relationship with those who farmed his land and, soon after his arrival in 1786, he resolved a potentially sensitive issue at Loughguile in a manner which benefited all concerned. Since the time when the O'Haras owned the property local Catholics had worshipped in a small Mass house on the Lisanoure demesne. Wishing to include adjacent land in his new developments, Macartney persuaded the parish priest, Father McNally, to accept an alternative site nearby. He granted a 999-year lease of the property, and not only subscribed to the cost of the new building but persuaded many of his friends and associates (including Thomas Mercer, Richard Jackson, and Jackson Wray) to do likewise. Macartney reserved a right for himself or his successors to terminate the lease and re-possess the ground, but only on condition that the congregation was paid a sum of £210 from the estate.[37] Due to the refusal of the local populace to pay tithes, the incumbency of the Church of Ireland's St. Mary's was temporarily vacant; and in his last letter to Macartney, in October 1789, Richard Jackson contrasted the dilapidated state of that building, which was also on the demesne, with the 'large handsome Mass house now roofing near Lisanoure'. He went on:

> [It] will be soon fit to receive a great congregation. Many of the Church [of Ireland] people of the parish go now to that worship— the remainder to Kilraughts and Clogh [Presbyterian] Meeting houses. And all the children are baptised by the priest for there is no other minister to do it. I am sorry to send you this state of your church but you are not single: it is the state of almost all the vicarages in the diocese of Connor.[38]

Far from being perturbed by this state of affairs, Macartney allowed more than a decade to elapse before ordering the repair of St. Mary's. His prime concerns were more fundamental and involved, in the first instance, his own thorough familiarisation with local economic conditions.

A leading feature of Macartney's discharge of public responsibilities was the thoroughness with which he prepared for an assignment. Henceforward, he adopted a similar approach to estate affairs. For the first time in his career he became seriously engaged in agriculture, establishing a modest home farm at Lisanoure where he raised crops of potatoes, oats and hay and kept a small dairy herd. This not only reduced his own purchases of food for the household, workforce and stables but raised at least some cash through the sale of surpluses in nearby markets. Macartney was not satisfied merely to vet his employees' accounts but kept his own records of stock, costs and profits.[39] Moreover, he collated a whole range of information concerning farming activities in the surrounding area. Besides noting the locations and dates of all the markets and fairs held in north-east Ulster, he collected details of local postal, carriage and shipping services; and, by periodically listing the prices of a wide range of commodities, identified significant seasonal variations in local income and expenditure. He went on to refine this by calculating the distances involved in transporting produce from one area to another, as well as the cost of producing important crops such as oats, and of feeding cattle and horses.[40] In addition he began to collect local historical manuscripts and data, and at one point, albeit unsuccessfully, persuaded several of his contacts to scour the Dublin bookshops for a dictionary of the Irish language.[41] Most remarkably, in 1790 he procured surveys of 'the inhabitants, livestock, rents, occupations, earnings, religion, etc. etc.' for each of the townlands on his north Antrim estate, though unfortunately these were among several documents which he subsequently lent to friends and which, apparently, were never returned.[42] Eventually, one result of all this activity was a decision to exercise his right to develop a market at Dervock to serve the large and increasingly populous area to the north and east of the village. Another, more immediate consequence was his adoption of a characteristically distinctive policy in regard to the tenures on his estate.

By the mid-1780s, particularly in the eastern half of Ulster, both prices and new rents were rising steadily, and were to rise very rapidly indeed during the agricultural prosperity of the war years from 1793. Where they were free to do so, proprietors responded by shortening lease terms in order to obtain more frequent opportunities of improving rents: henceforward, leases for three lives were granted only in very special circumstances, if at all. However, possession of a lives' lease was one of the major qualifications for the franchise and many landowners were reluctant to sacrifice their political influence by disenfranchising their tenants. This consideration acquired added significance from 1793 when Catholic as well as Protestant lease-holders became eligible for the vote. Accordingly, the most common policy was to grant leases for one life or twenty-one years, whichever was the longer. This meant that many tenants continued to reap substantial profits, often by sub-letting, as rents again lagged behind prices. Only around the turn of the century, when prices proceeded upwards at an unprecedented rate, was there a general move over to tenancies at will. Under this system tenants were not granted leases, but held their property from year to year at rents which could be moved upwards or downwards according to changing agricultural circumstances; and under stipulations, for example against sub-letting, which could be firmly enforced. [43]

Although still largely hamstrung by the policies of his predecessors, Macartney anticipated this last development by more than a decade. In 1789 some fifteen of the twenty-five holdings around Dervock continued under old leases; and, quite apart from the few perpetuities, a similar position obtained on seven of the thirty-three holdings around Loughguile. A total of fourteen leases had fallen in during Macartney's absence in the early 1780s, all of which had been re-set for terms ranging from fourteen to twenty-one years. Thereafter, however, Macartney introduced a new policy of tenancies at will, and by 1789 fourteen properties were held in this way, five at Dervock and nine at Loughguile. He could, of course, have used such tenures to attract the highest bidders or to increase rents repeatedly. In fact rentals for 1789 and 1796 indicate that, where the size of holdings remained unchanged, sitting tenants enjoyed security of tenure, at rents which were set by Jackson Wray and then allowed to stand for several years. On the other hand it was certainly Macartney's purpose to establish a direct relationship with working farmers. Old-established holdings were often large and had frequently been subdivided and sub-let; and, as head tenants' leases fell in, Macartney struck bargains with their sub-tenants, with the result that the average size of holdings was reduced and the rental increased. Nevertheless, by its very nature the new policy could be implemented only gradually and sporadically as existing leases fell in. In 1789 the gross rental of Loughguile and Dervock amounted to some £1,119 which, from a total of some 8,300 statute acres, represented an average rent of only 2s. 10d. an acre. By then new rents on the province's better land often exceeded 10s. 0d. an acre; and Jackson Wray's current valuation of Macartney's property suggested that, had it all been out of lease, it would have fetched an average rent of almost 5s. 0d. an acre.[44]

In the period before he set out for China Macartney's gross rental income amounted to some £2,024 a year — £1,119 from Loughguile and Dervock, £112 from Carnbuck and Gruig, and £793 from elsewhere. When both the India House annuity and the profits of continuing investments in the funds were added to this, he could count on an annual income of between £3,600 and £3,750. Although this was substantially more than he had ever previously commanded

Account at Coutts' Bank 1786-92			
Date	*Credit*	*Debit*	*Carried Over*
1786	£5,642. 7. 7.	£4,405. 0. 0.	+£1,237. 7. 7.
—	7,320.14. 1.	8,120.12. 4.	−799.18. 3.
1786-8	8,816.19. 9.	7,126. 5.10.	+1,690.13.11.
1787-8	8,422.16. 7.	5,390.17.11.	+3,031.18. 8.
1788	7,446. 5. 5.	7,073. 1. 0.	+373. 4. 5.
—	1,333. 3. 8.	1,591. 9. 6.	−258. 5.10.
1788-9	5,786.14. 1.	3,245.14. 1.	+462.16. 4.
1789	2,468. 8. 6.	2,498.19. 2.	−30.10. 8.
1790	3,419.16. 9.	3,353.19. 8.	+65.17. 1.
—	3,032.10. 9.	700.18. 9.	+2,331.12. 0.
1790-1	3,119. 2. 0.	2,537.13. 1.	+581. 8.11.
1791	581. 8.11.	56. 6. 0.	+525. 2.11.
—	1,732. 1. 1.	1,508. 1. 6.	+223.19. 7.
1792	3,131. 1.10.	3,695.18. 1.	−564.16. 3.
—	3,947. 7. 3.	3,197. 7. 3.	+750. 0. 0.

when unemployed, it still demanded more restraint than he was prepared to exhibit. From 1786, for the first time for several years, the
account with Coutts (See Table)[45] began occasionally to run into
deficit; and while surpluses were both more frequent and more substantial, they were largely the result of further borrowing. Although
there is no precise indication of the total cost of his contemporary
purchases and improvements, Macartney borrowed £5,000 from Sir
John Menzies in order to buy and repair the house in Curzon Street;
and the bulk of a further £8,000 worth of miscellaneous debts
appears to have been devoted to the acquisition of Parkhurst, and to
improvements there and at Lisanoure. Moreover, Macartney had
yet to discharge the residue of the debts incurred in previous years:
£3,500 was due to Thomas Mercer; £2,000 of the debt to the
executors of Lord Holland remained outstanding; and at some point
in the future Macartney was bound to repay the £1,500 which
Jackson Wray had lodged with him as security for honest dealing as
his estate agent.[46] By the early 1790s, therefore, Macartney owed a
total of £20,000.

Long before then Richard Jackson, for one, was anxious lest his
friend's 'numberless schemes and fanciful ideas' should provoke a
fresh financial crisis;[47] and, while Macartney himself was confident
that he would eventually be re-called to public service, he was forced
to put a brave face on his disappointment in 1788 when the prospect
of further (but unspecified) employment finally came to nought.[48] By
July 1790 Lady Bute's customary annoyance at being separated
from her daughter (who had recently gone with her husband to
Lisanoure) was coupled with the conviction that Macartney should
have remained nearer the centre of affairs in London if he wished to
get another job.

> Though Lord Macartney may be pleased with his improvements, yet
> I cannot but hope that he will reflect that when people put themselves
> out of society they are soon forgotten, whatever may be their merit; and
> if . . . they retire from it, nothing remains but an old age and infirmity,
> and regret for having done so. As well for his own sake as for yours
> [i.e. Lady Jane's] and mine, I hope he will only pass the summer
> among his trees and shrubs.[49]

In fact Macartney remained at Lisanoure for the rest of that year and
subsequently only the joint exhortation of Lady Jane and Thomas
Coutts persuaded him to return to London. Once the log-jam of old
leases began to crumble, he became progressively more engrossed in
his affairs in north Antrim, though on the eve of his departure for
Curzon Street in January 1791 he also confessed to the fear that he
had been finally 'laid aside'.[50] In 1792 his appointments to the Privy

Council and as Ambassador to China proved otherwise;[51] the latter post also brought about a further substantial improvement in his financial position.

IV

In view of the recent increase in his private income, the level of Macartney's indebtedness was much less serious than it had been a decade or so earlier. Two of his creditors (each of whom was owed £1,000) informed him that they would prefer not to call in their capital as yet, while the £1,500 owed to Jackson Wray was due only on the termination of his employment. Nevertheless, before embarking on the *Lion* in September 1792 Macartney instructed Lady Jane to use his ambassadorial salary, which was paid directly into his bank account in London, to clear the remainder of his debts.[52] His earnings from the trip to China amounted to £22,500: debts of £16,500 were discharged and, shortly after his return in 1794, the residue of £6,000 was devoted to further investments in the funds which, since the outbreak of war in the previous year, had again become an attractive proposition.[53] By the autumn of 1794, exactly three decades after his departure for Russia, Macartney was finally free of all but the most trifling incumbrances. For the rest of his life he remained untroubled by financial difficulties.

However, he had long grown accustomed to a lavish style of life and several more years elapsed before, by his own standards, he became a wealthy man. As indicated above, no official record remains of the terms upon which Macartney embarked on his next appointment, to Verona, in 1795.[54] Nor does the account with Coutts (See Table)[55] throw much further light on the matter. Throughout 1793 and 1794 the account was dominated by the activities associated with the embassy to China. Then, after briefly assuming more modest proportions, it again recorded substantial income and expenditure during the latter part of 1795 and the whole of 1796. However, a large proportion of this money accrued to Louis XVIII rather than to Macartney. The whole of the £10,000 made available by the British government to the exiled King was credited to Macartney's account in three instalments between October 1795 and May 1796, and disbursed to Louis XVIII's representatives almost immediately thereafter.[56] None of the income to the account during Macartney's period in Italy appears to have constituted a salary: individual amounts were small and, apart from the subsidy to the French exiles, the only four-figure sum involved (£3,000 in May 1796) was a loan.[57] The considerable turnover in the account later that year included the receipt of £5,000 from the Pay Office, but this was almost certainly an advance payment of the salary attached to Macartney's future appointment at the Cape.[58] Of course, money may have exchanged hands in a variety of other ways, for example via the account with Latouche in Dublin. On the other hand, in view of the fact that his aspirations in this direction were long-established and well-known, it is quite conceivable that a British peerage was the sole reward for his services at Verona.

On returning from Italy Macartney was no doubt vexed to discover just how slowly old leases in north Antrim continued to fall in. The most unequivocal of his instructions in 1792 had been in this regard: 'on no account' was Lady Jane 'to make any bargain or agreement for longer than one year'.[59] To Macartney's dismay there was little alteration in the situation during the next few years. In 1795 he purchased for £300 the tiny townland of Ballynagabog, which abutted on Carnbuck and Gruig and was subsequently let for £15 a year.[60] In the following year his gross rental income stood at £2,250, the bulk of the increase of £226 since 1789 having come from the Loughguile properties. Not a single old lease had 'dropped' in the Dervock area, where three of the townlands (Urbal, Aghancrossy and Ballyratahan) continued to be held at the rents which had been listed in Macartney's marriage settlement in 1768.[61] This contrast was fully reflected in his

	Account at Coutts' Bank 1792-1800		
Date	*Credit*	*Debit*	*Carried Over*
1792-3	£3,104. 0. 0.	£2,596. 6. 1.	+£507.13.11.
1793	9,467.13.11.	9,241. 2. 4.	+226.11. 7.
1794	9,076.11. 7.	8,715. 0. 6.	+361.11. 1.
—	9,831.11. 1.	9,029.11. 2.	+801.19.11.
1795	2,361.19.11.	2,373.17. 4.	−11.17. 5.
—	10,758.15. 0.	10,677. 6. 4.	+181. 8. 8.
1796	6,898. 3. 9.	5,833.19. 5.	+1,064. 4. 4.
—	13,261.12. 3.	6,764.18. 0.	+6,496.14. 3.
1796-7	7,048. 2.11.	6,104.11. 3.	+943.11. 8.
1797	1,818.17. 2.	928. 6. 0.	+890.11. 2.
—	1,951.15.11.	1,475. 0. 3.	+476.15. 8.
1797-8	12,511.15. 8.	12,026. 6. 9.	+485. 8.11.
1798	7,767. 0. 2.	7,526.11. 5.	+240. 8. 9.
—	4,853.11.11.	2,404. 4. 7.	+2,449. 7. 4.
—	5,171.17. 4.	4,699. 4.10.	+472.12. 6.
1798-9	13,540. 3. 4.	13,999.11. 4.	−459. 8. 0.
1799	24,541. 7. 8.	24,511. 8. 3.	+29.19. 5.
1800	5,781.19. 1.	4,891. 9.11.	+890. 9. 2.
—	6,447. 6.10.	5,677.14. 3.	+769.12. 7.

programme of improvements. At least one tenant at Loughguile was provided with a new house at the estate's expence and, opposite the Mass house, the demesne workforce built what appears to have been a parochial house for Fr. McNally, together with 'a new wall, new road and bridge from . . . [there] . . . to near the porter's gate'. Moreover, one of the mills on the Loughguile estate, at Culbane, was 'thoroughly repaired and a new road made to it'.[62] Macartney was very keen to promote such improvements, but clearly saw no reason why he should do so on properties which still failed to yield reasonable rents.

However, despite his growing frustration with the situation in and around Dervock, Macartney's major concern was with the modest level of his total private income which, at around or somewhat above £4,000 a year, was considerably less than that normally enjoyed by a British peer. Although for several years he was unable to initiate the transactions, by this stage he had decided to sell both Parkhurst and the town house in Charles Street, Piccadilly. Too much of his capital was tied up in too many establishments and for the future he proposed to live either in Curzon Street or at Lisanoure. Yet, as long as future prospects in north Antrim remained uncertain, even this plan threatened to leave him uncomfortably short of resources. It was primarily for this reason that, in spite of increasing ill-health, he agreed to go to the Cape.

The terms of Macartney's final appointment assured his future prosperity. In addition to earning £12,000 a year while at the Cape, he was granted for life an annual pension of £2,000.[63] His salary was paid directly into his London bank account and, because by now there were very few debts to service or repay, Thomas Coutts was instructed to mount a major programme of investment. In earlier years the recovery in Macartney's finances had been partly the result of Coutts' shrewd dealing in the funds, especially in wartime when the government's demands for finance made the terms upon which securities were available highly attractive. By the time Macartney returned from Verona public borrowing had developed on a massive scale, and for several months prior to his departure for the Cape there were major fluctuations in his bank account as profits on exchequer bills were maximised. Thereafter Coutts invested particularly heavily in imperial annuities; and because, as was customary, the bulk of Macartney's salary was paid in arrears, his banker's activities continued throughout 1799 and, indeed, beyond.[64] In July 1799 Macartney sold Parkhurst for £4,660, making a handsome profit on earlier transactions there; and a year later he obtained £1,711 for the house in Charles Street.[65] The whole of this capital was also invested in the funds. By 1800 Macartney was deriving some £400 a year from profits on exchequer bills and no less than £2,000 a year from imperial annuities.[66] At the going rate of around ten years' purchase this latter sum represented a capital outlay in previous years of £20,000, almost the whole of the income from his appointment at the Cape. The India House and Cape pensions brought in a further £3,500 a year which, until recently, had been as much as his total private income had ever amounted to.

However, nothing would have given Macartney greater satisfaction than news of the termination, at some point between 1796 and 1801, of many (though not all) of the old leases in north Antrim. As a result rents from Loughguile rose from £706 to £866 a year, and those from Dervock more than doubled, from £451 to £960 a year. The difference in the value of the two properties was more graphically reflected in their average rents per statute acre, which stood at 2s. 11d. at Loughguile and 9s. 1½d. at Dervock; at 4s. 7d. the gross average of the two properties combined still remained somewhat less than the figure suggested in Jackson Wray's valuation of 1789. Nevertheless, far from being 'laid aside' on his return from the Cape, Macartney could afford to turn down the offer of further employment. In 1801 his gross rental income reached a total of £2,789, a substantial proportion of which was derived from tenancies at will.[67] With a private income approaching £9,000 a year he went into retirement without a shred of anxiety or regret, not only wealthy but free at last to develop the bulk of his main estate as he wished.

V

After selling Parkhurst Macartney decided after all that, in addition to Curzon Street, he needed a further property outside but nearer the capital, so he rented Corney House at Chiswick from Lady Caroline Damer for £300 a year.[68] He continued to be much in demand in London, both socially and as a source of comment and advice on public affairs, and from 1801 until his death in 1806 he served on the Board of Trustees of the British Museum.[69] However, until his ill-health marooned them in London, he and Lady Jane spent most of their time in north Antrim. While acknowledging that Lisanoure was in a 'remote part of the world', Lady Jane assured her friends that journeys to and from the north of Ireland were 'swift' and 'pleasant', and that her home there was 'really very pretty'.[70] As far as Macartney himself was concerned, its 'only drawback' was 'the distance that separates us from our friends . . . [and] . . . great as that privation is, I am afraid we must submit to it . . . as I do not think I can get free from my present engagements here'. In fact he had no wish to do so. He was 'seldom less than five or six hours in the day on my feet abroad in the open air, and often as many on horseback, and my spirits keep pace with my exercise'.[71]

Soon after returning to north Antrim Macartney seized two unexpected and welcome opportunities of extending the demesne at Lisanoure. For many years he had been tenant under Lord Mountjoy of a small property in the townland of Lavin, which lay immediately to the south of Castlequarter. When the whole of Mountjoy's property in that area came onto the market in 1800, Macartney quickly declared an interest in acquiring part of it only to be foiled by Hugh Montgomery of Benvarden, who decided to purchase the entire estate. Two years later, however, Montgomery agreed to sell the townland of Lavin to Macartney for £4,659.[72] In the meantime, for a sum of £1,000, Macartney was able to purchase property to the east of the demesne from the McCollum family: this abutted on St. Mary's churchyard and had been alienated many years previously under a fee farm grant from the O'Haras.[73] The subsequent extension of the demesne to include part of Lavin and the whole of McCollum's land allowed Macartney to increase the acreage of both the home farm and the timber plantations. It also encouraged him to restore St. Mary's: besides putting the fabric and grounds into good order, he provided the church with a steeple; and following extensive repairs, McCollum's house was made available to the rector. Nor was there any lack of activity on other parts of the demesne. The Castle was made a good deal more comfortable by the installation of water-closets. Fish-ponds and a pheasantry were established in the grounds. The home farm was provided with a large barn and extra stabling. New cottages were added to the hamlet of 'Macartney'. And over a period of several years the plantations were enclosed and the roads and ditches in the vicinity of Lisanoure were steadily improved. While it is again impossible to calculate the cost of these developments, one account, which dealt with 'buildings and jobs of work' in the two-year period to July 1804, amounted to £1,668.[74]

Although Macartney could well afford such outgoings, careful monitoring of costs soon convinced him that 'the prices of almost every article is [sic] full as high here as in London, and three times what they were ten years ago, so it is now as expensive living here as there'.[75] Accordingly, he went to considerable pains to ensure that his expenditure on the demesne was at least partially offset or reduced by produce or income from it. By this stage, for example, some of the timber at Lisanoure was either mature or needed thinning: between

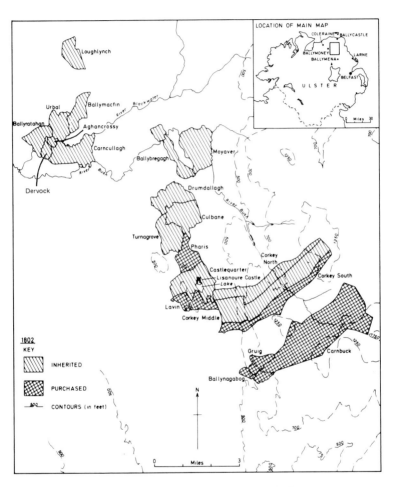

Map of the North Antrim Estate, 1802.

March 1802 and January 1804 Felix Laverty and his men felled 21,470 trees whose value was estimated at £897. Some of the wood was used for various purposes on the demesne and the rest was sold.[76] Large amounts of gravel were dug from pits opened up behind the Castle; a lime-kiln was built on the demesne and supplied from the quarries at Corkey; and in order to reduce the quantity of coal hauled from the collieries at Ballycastle, the demesne workforce spent part of each year cutting and stacking turf. Moreover, the further development of the home farm and the kitchen garden led to the profitable sale of produce when Macartney was absent from Lisanoure, and to self-sufficiency in many commodities when he was resident there. Cattle and sheep were fattened for slaughter, the dairy herd provided milk, and in one year Mary Dunn churned more than six firkins of butter. In a good season enough hay and oats were produced to feed the cows and horses over the following winter and at one point yields were increased by spreading silt from the canals over the fields. Each year several acres were given over to growing potatoes, most of which were used to feed the labourers, while the kitchen garden produced a large variety of additional vegetables and fruit. Many of the walled enclosures which surrounded the timber plantations were built from stone collected from the arable and, wherever possible, similar thrift was employed elsewhere on the estate: for example, most of the stone used in the enclosure of the Fair Hill at Dervock came from buildings in the village which had recently been demolished.[77] Macartney was never loath to spend money on improving his estate, but as he grew older he became increasingly intolerant of inefficiency and waste.

Beyond the demesne one of the most significant developments of these later years was Macartney's purchase of the townland of Pharis for £2,800 in July 1802. This property lay immediately to the north of Castlequarter and was relinquished by the Stirling family of Walworth in Co. Londonderry, who were heavily indebted and borrowed, at the time of the sale, an additional £1,640 from Macartney.[78] Together with Lavin, the acquisition of Pharis admirably consolidated Macartney's holdings in north Antrim. Henceforward he could ride from Corkey South to Drumdallagh without ever leaving his estate, and he also owned further property only slightly to the north and to the south of that route. In addition to his appreciation of the difficulties which local farmers encountered in marketing their produce, these purchases encouraged Macartney to concentrate on improving the roads which passed through his land, especially his section of the important route from Ballymena to Ballycastle. While prepared to devote a good deal of his own resources

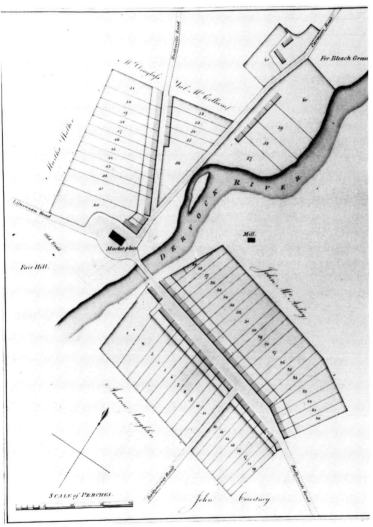

The Building-Plan for Dervock, 1801 (D.1062/2/4).

to this end, he also obtained additional funds from the county grand jury. In this, as in much else, he was ably assisted by Neal McPeake of Ballymena, his solicitor, and by the Revd. George Macartney of Antrim, his cousin. Both men regularly attended meetings of the grand jury at Carrickfergus and, although they were occasionally unsuccessful, a steady stream of proposals attracted public subsidies.[79]

Some years previously McPeake had taken over from Mr. Hutchinson of Ballymoney, who was judged to be both lackadaisical and unreasonable in his charges;[80] and from around 1800 the Revd. Macartney began to assume a role in estate affairs which was similar to that discharged by Richard Jackson until 1789.[81] Before long these changes proved extremely beneficial, for Jackson Wray died in 1802[82] and his son, who replaced him as agent, never lived up to Macartney's expectations.[83] There were a number of reasons for this. Firstly, like his father, Jackson Wray Jnr. divided his energies between Macartney's agency and various other concerns. Secondly, management inevitably became more complex and time-consuming under a system of tenancies at will: in addition to many other tasks, rents had to be regularly reviewed and, as middlemen were by-passed, the number of tenants on the rent roll was substantially increased. Thirdly and above all, with little previous experience to guide him Wray inherited major responsibility for the implementation of Macartney's ambitious plan for the development of a market town at Dervock.

The most important leases to 'drop' on the north Antrim estate during this period were those which had been held by Peter Gamble and his heirs since 1739. In return for a total rent of £45 a year, Skeffington (from whom Macartney's grandfather bought the Dervock estate) had granted Gamble two holdings, one on each side of the River Dervock, for a period of three lives. The first, of over 100 statute acres, comprised virtually the whole of the townland of Dervock; the second, of similar extent, was situated in the adjoining townland of Ballyratahan.[84] Subsequently, in addition to farming, Gamble became involved in a number of other business activities. He built a distillery and a tan yard on the Ballyratahan side of the river and, by sub-letting numerous tenements, some as houses and others as retail outlets, he encouraged the development of the village on the Dervock side.[85] Under his tenancy Dervock became well-known throughout the north of Ulster for the quality of its fairs, which were held on a hill just outside the village on five fixed dates in January, February, June, August and October. Although a variety of livestock was bought and sold at these functions, Dervock Fair was renowned for its trade in horses and by the later eighteenth century the June fair was also the setting for Dervock Races.[86] Soon after inheriting the property Macartney was strongly advised to establish a regular market in the village to complement the fairs, and he obtained the right to do so in 1770.[87] However, because the interests of the head tenant clearly conflicted with his own, and following Gamble's refusal to surrender his leases,[88] Macartney made no attempt to proceed under his patent until the leases fell in at some point between 1796 and 1799. His first move, as elsewhere, was to establish a direct relationship with the occupying tenants. By 1801 the land in Dervock townland which had been formerly let to Gamble for £32 a year was bringing in £168 a year from fifty tenants at will; while the townland of Ballyratahan, previously let in three holdings for £41 a year, was held by thirty-six tenants at will for a total of £232 a year.[89] Macartney then embarked on the wholesale improvement of the village. If Dervock was not to be completely over-shadowed by the long-established market at nearby Ballymoney, it had first of all to be completely refurbished.

Macartney's detailed plans for Dervock were laid during the course of 1801 and towards the end of that year he began to receive tenders for parts of the work.[90] He decided to alter the road system in order to accommodate a Market Hall in the centre of the village. There were to be sixty-one other establishments, thirty-nine on the Dervock side of the river and the rest on the Ballyratahan side. Eleven of the existing structures were retained, thirty-five establishments were completely rebuilt, and a further fifteen were erected on new sites nearby.[91] Each of the new buildings, including five near the bleach green which were allocated to weavers, had a roof of 'Scotch slate'.[92] However, together with the other developments noted above, the death of Jackson Wray Senr. in July 1802 greatly delayed the implementation of the scheme. Demolition did not begin until 1803 and, although the Market Hall was finished 'according to contract' by 1 May 1805,[93] the other buildings were not completed until the autumn of that year. Macartney paid for the Market Hall, provided new pavements and guttering throughout the village and, with some help from public funds, carried out the roadworks. Much of the rest of the construction work was also at his expence, though some of the more substantial tenants agreed to rebuild their homes and, in return, were granted lengthy 'building leases' for one life and a concurrent term of sixty-one years. In the short run the lives of the inhabitants were thoroughly disrupted. Nevertheless, they not only gave the venture their full co-operation but vied with one another to achieve the best results. In October 1805, as the work neared completion,

Jackson Wray Jnr. reported that Macartney 'could get tenants . . . for as many more houses as you already have set'.[94]

Increasingly incapacitated by illness, Macartney had been anxious for some time to proceed to the next stage of the project, the inauguration of the market. However, Wray preferred to wait until nearer Christmas, no doubt hoping to launch the market on a wave of seasonal trade, and also aware that in winter weather many dealers from north and east of the village would prefer to come to Dervock instead of travelling a further eight miles to and from Ballymoney.[95] His judgment was entirely borne out by events. Following an 'elegant Ball and Supper' in the Market Hall, attended by 'forty very genteel people [who] did not part till seven' the next morning, the first market was held on the second Friday in December 1805. 'It blew a hurricane, with heavy showers of snow and hail', and sales included between 300 and 400 webs of linen cloth, £100 worth of yarn, and 'a considerable quantity of flax', as well as provisions and some livestock.[96] The second market, held a fortnight later, was even more successful, with sales of 550 linen webs, 'home-made flannel and drugget', 'near 300 spangles of yarn', flax, pigs, potatoes and meal. In addition there were:

> many stalls covered with gingerbread, cakes etc. [and] a great deal of money was laid out by the country people in the woollen and grocery shops and whiskey houses, which has raised the expectations and spirits of the inhabitants . . . Dervock will soon find its level with other markets, and become a flourishing town, in spite of all the exertions of the Ballymoney people to the contrary.[97]

When the latter retaliated by announcing in the Belfast press that in future they would hold weekly, instead of fortnightly, markets — on Thursdays, Wray introduced weekly markets at Dervock; and within a month businessmen at Coleraine expressed concern at the level of competition from both quarters.[98] The most serious threat to Dervock came not from local competition but from the province's linen drapers, who were loath to see their existing schedules disrupted by a proliferation of markets. However, following hectic canvassing by Wray, Revd. Macartney and several neighbouring proprietors, as well as by Macartney himself, the leading drapers complimented Dervock by placing it on a par with Ballymoney, whose trade had undoubtedly been damaged. Although both continued to have weekly markets, the drapers undertook to 'attend one great market in the month in each town . . . [which] . . . should be held as nearly as possible within a fortnight of each other'.[99] Thereafter, for as long as wartime prices persisted, Dervock's prosperity was assured, and during the last months of his life Macartney sought to promote further development by establishing a post office in the town and arranging for the provision of a local police force.[100]

Unfortunately, there are no details of the rents charged at Dervock in the wake of these events, though *circa* 1804-5 the whole of the northern part of the estate yielded £1,503 a year or, on average, 14s. 4d. an acre — a substantial increase over the 9s. 1½d. an acre derived from the same property in 1801. This contributed to but was by no means wholly responsible for a further dramatic increase in the gross rental of Macartney's Irish property, which rose from £2,739 a year in 1801 to £4,224 a year *circa* 1804-5. Because this last figure is drawn from a summary rather than from a detailed rental, it is impossible either to identify the precise reasons for the increase, or to calculate average rents per acre on the expanded estate around Loughguile. However, such a rapid upward movement of rents suggests that ultimately Macartney derived a very satisfactory return from most of his property. A combination of factors was responsible for this. In the first place, old leases continued to terminate, and not merely on the inherited estate in north Antrim: rents from Carrickfergus doubled from £28 to £59 a year, and those from Carnbuck, Gruig and Ballynagabog rose from £127 to £215 a year. On the other hand the Porter estate still yielded little more than in 1779; at least one old lease of property near Dervock, set two years after Macartney's birth, appears to have outlived him; and, even if added to the purchase of Lavin and Pharis, the dropping of lives cannot explain the rise in the rents of Loughguile from £866 in 1801 to £1,675 in 1804-5.[101] An additional factor was Macartney's ability under a system of tenancies at will to increase rents to match the upward movement of prices. This undoubtedly occurred, although as before Macartney's behaviour in this regard was far from extreme: even at Dervock, average rents remained well below those currently charged elsewhere in east Ulster.[102] Also, from 1801 onwards, when many proprietors were finally discarding life leases, Macartney began to introduce them selectively, granting certain tenants leases for one life and a concurrent term not exceeding thirty-one years.[103] The tenants concerned were probably substantial farmers who had paid economic rents for several years and who, in Macartney's judgment, could be relied upon to adhere to the covenants contained in their leases. Following the introduction of this alternative tenure, tenants at will were provided with an incentive to improve their own performance as farmers. A final factor supported this change of policy. During these later years the overwhelming majority of tenants were directly linked to a proprietor who was himself prepared to plough back the greater proportion of the rents which accrued from his north Antrim estate. At Dervock the estate was substantially improved and at Loughguile it was also expanded and consolidated. By any standard the record was impressive, if only because by this stage Macartney had no personal need of additional income from his property.

None of Macartney's other income, however, was channelled into property and there was no return to the precipitate estate expansion of earlier years. Land prices in Ulster also rose to unprecedented heights and, at around or slightly above twenty years' purchase, property was a poor investment in purely financial terms, especially for someone who was elderly and without a direct male heir. Macartney's ventures into the property market were, therefore, strategic and few: offers of additional property were not taken up and shortly before his death he sold his scattered and outlying holdings in and around Carrickfergus to Sir William Kirk for £1,000.[104] In the meantime Macartney's general expenditure declined as his lifestyle became quieter and more retired; and the account with Coutts (See Table)[105] almost invariably recorded surpluses, which latterly were very substantial. On the financial front his last major decision was to consolidate most of his investments into one type of security. During

	Account at Coutts' Bank 1801-1806		
Date	*Credit*	*Debit*	*Carried Over*
1801	£3,464. 9. 1.	£3,282. 7.10.	+£182. 1. 3.
—	1,507. 1. 3.	2,025.12.10.	−518.11. 7.
—	4,646.10. 2.	3,233.19. 5.	+1,409.10. 9.
1802	3,459.10. 9.	1,085.11. 8.	+2,373.19. 1.
—	12,061. 1.11.	5,403. 0. 2.	+6,658. 1. 9.
—	9,869. 1. 9.	4,574.11. 1.	+5,294.10. 8.
—	5,738.10. 8.	4,201. 3. 0.	+1,537. 7. 8.
1803	5,090.10. 6.	4,344. 4. 6.	+746. 6. 0.
—	7,118.11. 7.	6,272.13. 8.	+846.17.11.
—	2,550.17.11.	1,632. 3. 7.	+918.14. 4.
—	1,493.14. 4.	970. 2. 5.	+523.11.11.
1803-4	2,418.10. 1.	1,967. 5. 1.	+451. 5. 0.
1804	2,038.12. 0.	1,383.18. 2.	+654.13.10.
—	3,591. 7. 0.	1,100. 1. 5.	+2,491. 5. 7.
—	3,360. 9.10.	1,417.12. 0.	+1,750. 8. 5.
1804-5	4,891.14. 5.	1,771. 8. 2.	+3,120. 6. 3.
1805	3,744. 5. 5.	2,033. 9. 8.	+1,710.15. 9.
—	4,009.14. 1.	1,221. 1.10.	+2,788.12. 3.
—	3,693. 3. 2.	1,817.15.11.	+1,875. 7. 3.
1804-6	4,394. 0. 7.	1,808.15. 5.	+2,585. 5. 2.
1806	2,585. 5. 2.	121.14. 9.	+2,463.10. 5.

1802 he sold many exchequer bills, together with a few short annuities, and used the proceeds to acquire further blocks of imperial annuities. By October 1803 his total income from this latter source amounted to some £3,000 a year. If he had laid out his capital at 'legal interest', it would, according to his own calculations, have returned an income of 'only £1,750' a year,[106] and further investment in the expansion of his estate would have been similarly unremunerative. To the very last, therefore, Macartney continued to derive the greater proportion of his income from sources other than property.

VI

For almost three years after returning from the Cape Macartney enjoyed reasonably good health and was able to walk and ride (albeit on a suitably docile horse) in moderate comfort.[107] In October 1802, however, 'repeated indisposition' delayed his return from Lisanoure to London, and a year later he was confined to bed for some time following one of his rare attendances in the House of Lords.[108] He was last resident in north Antrim during the summer of 1804 when the rebuilding work at Dervock was at its height.[109] By then his mobility was increasingly restricted. Early in 1805, perhaps because he judged that his employer would never see Lisanoure again, the Revd. Macartney moved house from Antrim to within ten miles of Loughguile so as to be 'more frequently able to see how things go on there and at Dervock'.[110] Macartney planned to return to Ireland in the summer of that year but illness prevented him from doing so. By November 1805 he felt much better and proposed 'going over as early as possible in the [following] summer', but this was not to be.[111] Towards the end of February 1806 he was finally confined to bed and obliged to conduct his correspondence through an amanuensis.[112] He died at Curzon Street on 31 March, aged sixty-eight, and was buried, very quietly, at Chiswick on 9 April. According to a report in the *Belfast News Letter:*

A hearse and four, two mourning coaches, and one private coach, viz. that of the Marquess of Hertford, constituted the whole funeral procession. The privacy observed upon the occasion was so great that not even his Lordship's old friend and companion in India, Sir William Duncan [sic — Dunkin], was allowed an opportunity to pay a tribute of respect to the memory of the deceased. By this course his Lordship's numerous and dear friends may feel disappointment, but it was the only mode, short of a public funeral, to avoid jealousy.[113]

While Macartney had continued to pay the closest attention to his affairs until a fortnight or so before his death, he had long been reconciled to his lack of a son or daughter to or through whom to transmit the fruits of his success. At his death his various titles became extinct. And having himself inherited the bulk of his main estate from a childless uncle, he was obliged to look to the offspring of his sister, Elizabeth Belaquier, for a successor at Lisanoure. Although he disposed of his considerable fortune by a will of 30 April 1801 (to which he added a codicil of 3 July 1804),[114] Macartney would appear to have formulated the major element in his dispositions many years previously. He took an early interest in the welfare of Mrs. Belaquier's daughter, Elizabeth, and saw her regularly following her marriage to the Revd. Travers Hume in 1787.[115] By his will Macartney vested all his real estate in trustees for the use of Elizabeth Hume for life. Thereafter, provided they assumed the surname and arms of Macartney by due course of law, the property was to pass to Elizabeth's eldest son, George (born in 1793); and, after his death, to his male heirs in succession. Having been widowed in 1805, Elizabeth Hume lived on until 1825. By that time George had long assumed effective control of the estate. By royal licence he took the surname and arms of Macartney as soon as he came of age in 1814, and subsequently presided at Lisanoure for over half a century until his death in 1869.[116]

The other major element in Macartney's will was his lavish provision for Lady Jane. Besides a legacy of £2,000, she was left the unexpired term in the lease of Corney House, the use for life of the house in Curzon Street, and all the personal estate within them. More remarkably, she was granted the proceeds of all Macartney's investments in securities which, at the time of his death, exceeded £3,000 a year: following Lady Jane's death, any residue was to be divided equally between Elizabeth Hume's surviving children. And finally, in lieu of the modest jointure of £400 a year which was all she was allowed under her marriage settlement, Lady Jane received a life annuity of no less than £2,400, which was to be derived from the Irish estate.

In so far as he was able Macartney attempted to perpetuate the policies which he had adopted in regard to his estate. Leases were to be for a maximum term of one life and a concurrent period of thirty-one years; the life was to be that of the lessee; and tenants were to be required to pay a full economic rent but no entry fine. The trustees were instructed to sell the remnants of the Porter estate for the best available price and to invest the proceeds in land which was 'as near as may be' to the main estate in north Antrim. While these stipulations left George Hume Macartney considerable room for manoeuvre, he assumed his responsibilities against a background of mounting agricultural distress in Ireland. Following the end of the Napoleonic wars agricultural prices fell precipitately. The majority of farmers experienced difficulty in paying their rents and the profitability of domestic textile production was increasingly threatened by the onset of fierce competition from factory-based industry at home and abroad. Above all, however, the income which accrued to the new regime at Lisanoure was severely depleted by the longevity of Lady Jane, who outlived Elizabeth Hume and died at the advanced age of eighty-five in 1828.[117] Only then was George Hume Macartney able to share the residue of his great-uncle's financial investments with his surviving brothers and sisters; and only then did he come into all the income from his estate. Like Macartney before him, his fortune was based on an indirect inheritance; and he too had to wait for many years before he could enjoy it to the full. Macartney had transformed his own and his family's circumstances: but in one respect at least he allowed the wheel of fortune to turn a complete circle.

CHAPTER XI

CONCLUSION

Towards the end of his life Macartney was inclined to put a favourable gloss on his earlier experiences. After his death his biographers did likewise, fostering the belief that his progress had been steady and cumulative, and had flowed naturally from the brilliant start which he made to his career in 1764. The evidence considered in this study points to a quite different conclusion. Macartney's success was neither easily come by nor uninterrupted. The problems which he encountered in public life were numerous and significant; they were not readily solved; and for many decades they were exacerbated by his private lack of substance.

Although he achieved a great deal during the earlier part of his mission to Russia, Macartney's indiscretions at St. Petersburg were long remembered both there and in London, and seriously jeopardised his future prospects. Subsequently, he had little choice but to accept relegation to the Irish chief secretaryship, and may have been obliged to settle for even less had it not been for the intervention of his father-in-law, the Earl of Bute. His next appointment, to one of several governorships in the Caribbean, took him still further from the centre of public affairs without raising any expectation of a speedy or propitious return. It was only at Madras in the 1780s that Macartney finally enhanced his early reputation, and during much of his gruelling service there such a successful outcome appeared unlikely. Moreover, his later appointments were a distinct anti-climax in comparison with what had gone before. It was not Macartney's fault that the embassy to China never stood the slightest chance of success. At Verona, on the other hand, he was thoroughly outwitted by Louis XVIII, while his duties at the Cape of Good Hope constituted little more than a lucrative interlude prior to his retirement. This declension was scarcely evident to his contemporaries, however, and with great satisfaction but not much further effort Macartney ultimately reached a pinnacle of official and public esteem.

Any assessment of the factors which contributed to Macartney's success must pay tribute to his great good fortune. Had he inherited little or no property, he would probably never have come to public attention. Without stumbling on the hapless Stephen Fox and thereby becoming intimate with Lord Holland, he could not from the start have aspired to, still less have obtained, major public office. After sullying his record in Russia and grimly enduring the Irish chief secretaryship, he was fortunate indeed to emerge from the loss of Grenada to public acclaim *and* in time to compete for the presidency of Fort St. George. His duties at Madras frequently brought him to the very brink of personal disaster: his treatment of Sir John Burgoyne alienated the King and neither Pitt nor Dundas was unduly disappointed when he refused the governor-generalship of Bengal. Yet, overall, Macartney's performance in India met with almost universal applause. Moreover, his next and most prestigious post — the Chinese embassy — arose only because a previous appointee, the Hon. Charles Cathcart, had died before reaching China. Above all, having inherited a sizeable but not very valuable estate and fallen into serious financial difficulties during the earlier part of his career, Macartney had the good fortune to obtain sufficient consecutive employment thereafter to enable him both to recoup his finances and, latterly, to amass considerable wealth.

Nonetheless, besides being lucky, Macartney was an extremely able man. Although much younger than the majority of his colleagues, he was clearly among the brightest students of his year at Trinity College, Dublin. Subsequently, his education continued on a less formal basis, producing wide-ranging interests and a general intellectual curiosity which were lifelong, and which undoubtedly played some part in his acceptance of a long series of far-flung posts overseas. There is no telling how much Macartney owed to his contacts with Dennis, Burke and their acquaintances in the years which followed his undergraduate career: but, to judge from the itinerary which he planned for his first European tour, he lost no opportunity as a young man of widening his physical and mental horizons. By the time he had reached his mid-twenties he was not only knowledgeable and articulate, but also self-confident and of a distinctly independent cast of mind. It was no doubt these latter qualities which attracted Lord Holland, for it took more than charm, youthful precocity and friendship with Stephen Fox to win the confidence and support of that hardened politician. Moreover, Holland's judgment was quickly vindicated: arguably — his record in India apart — the negotiation of the commercial treaty with the Russians was Macartney's single, most durable achievement in public life. Even when dealing with more routine matters, which was his lot for most of his period as Governor of Grenada, the quality of his despatches earned the admiration of his ultimate superior, George III.

However, once it became impossible for Macartney to return to St. Petersburg as Ambassador, his future prospects were clouded by uncertainty. In the absence of wealth and strong connections, personal ability and growing experience were insufficient for his cause, and had to be bolstered by the utmost tenacity and a willingness to calculate his every move. Marriage to Lady Jane Stuart, which helped him to obtain the Irish chief secretaryship, also initially encouraged him to hold out for something better. Before long, however, he not only accepted what was available to him, albeit with a bad grace, but continued in the post for longer than he would have wished. It was during this period in Dublin that Macartney finally dismissed any thought of a political career. Henceforward, he looked solely to administration or diplomacy for the bulk of his wherewithal and, until his financial position was beyond threat, never refused an offer of employment. He was utterly disgusted by his treatment in the Irish Parliament and later maintained, more generally, that the cut and thrust of party politics offended his love of 'consistency' and 'uniformity'.[1] In reality, however, Macartney's reasoning at this earlier stage was a good deal more prosaic. Marriage had connected him to the Earl of Bute, who was among the most unpopular public figures in Britain. It had also promoted his innate tendency to extravagance, with the result that the debts which he had brought back from Russia multiplied rapidly. Within a few years he was unable to afford either a seat in Parliament or long-term unemployment. Because he could not look to his property for much additional income, Macartney hoped to earn a succession of substantial salaries; and he judged that his chances of achieving this would best be served if he remained as loyal as possible to the government of the day, whatever its complexion, whilst at the same time avoiding undue alienation from its critics. He believed this to be the safest course open to him and stuck to it for the rest of his life. Such a strategy did not come naturally to him. A frank and open approach to public affairs had to give way to greater circumspection in word and deed. He was obliged to distance himself somewhat from the younger generation at Holland House. His relations with Edmund Burke and others became strained. And at times, especially during the fierce contest for the presidency of Fort St. George, he feared that he had lost favour with both government and opposition.

A variety of other matters worried Macartney before and during his decisive appointment at Madras. Until the outcome of the contest was known he could not be confident of overcoming his financial difficulties. Moreover, many years previously he had adopted *mens conscia recti* as his personal motto [2] and had reason to confirm his choice following the outbreak of controversy over Lord Holland's profits from office. In addition Edmund Burke stood ready to pounce on the slightest evidence of maladministration in the sub-continent; and, with his intimate knowledge of Macartney's background and connections, would no doubt have done so to deadly effect. Thus, Macartney's utter rectitude at Madras was, despite his private needs, entirely in his own best interests: indeed, his brief required him to rid the presidency of Fort St. George of the peculation with which its former incumbents had long been associated. However, no-one anticipated the extent of his difficulties with Hastings on the one hand, and with the military on the other, both of which put him under severe duress. Macartney needed a successful and, therefore, extended period at Madras in order to accumulate enough savings to discharge his debts; and irrespective of whether or not he completed this task, he could ill afford to return to Britain with a record which denied him further opportunities in public life. Eventually, after stubbornly adhering to his instructions and displaying considerable nerve, he emerged nearly solvent, physically exhausted, and otherwise largely unscathed. Publicly, his reward was a reputation which was never again in serious doubt; privately, besides repairing his fortunes, he regained a degree of equanimity which he had not enjoyed for twenty years.

During the earlier part of his career Macartney often complained that ability and preferment rarely went hand in hand in public life. His own later experience demonstrated that the allocation of the rewards of office was no less irrational. For another important element in his long-term strategy was the relentless pursuit of title, not merely for its own sake, but also as a means of strengthening his position in any future bargaining over office and salary. Several of his initial requests for an improvement of title were refused: but he stubbornly returned to the matter whenever an opportunity arose; and progressed from a knighthood and the Polish White Eagle, via a knighthood of the Bath, to a barony, viscountcy, and earldom of Ireland, until finally he became a baron of Great Britain. In the interim, with the probable exception of Verona (which earned him his last honour), the level of his salaries was roughly commensurate with his rank. The highly favourable outcome of his endeavours was evident at the Cape where, having acceded to the British peerage, he obtained (if we include his pre-arranged pension) his most lavish financial reward in return for his least taxing assignment. So successful was he in securing honours as well as income that only towards the very end of his life did his private means begin to match his public status; and had it not been for the fruits of office, they would never have done so.

For very many years this disparity caused Macartney acute concern. He entered public life with property which was scattered, remote and poor; and, although he was keen to improve it, many years elapsed before he had sufficient time, money, and other resources to devote to the task. Fortunately, his career co-incided with a period of steady, and then rapid, economic growth in Ireland, particularly in the north-east of the country, which ultimately did much to enhance the value of his estate. Nevertheless, for most of his life his property produced insufficient income for him to fall back on when unemployed and, in several other respects, could not be regarded as an adequate private base from which to pursue an ambitious public career. In general Macartney's attempts to remedy this situation mirrored his behaviour in other spheres. His earliest efforts were ill-considered; thereafter a more cautious approach eventually produced positive results; and he finally achieved considerable success.

During the 1760s Macartney learned a good deal about estate affairs in southern England, where circumstances were radically different from those which pertained in north Antrim. A decade passed before he was able to devote much, if any, attention to his own property: but, following his marriage to Lady Jane Stuart and his appointment as Chief Secretary for Ireland, he set out to make his mark among the Ulster landed gentry. Even before he returned to Lisanoure with Lady Jane he embarked on a series of land transactions which weakened his financial position without proportionately improving his property; and much of his initial work on the Castle had later to be substantially altered. At this stage, however, the difficulties which arose from his hasty endeavours were less significant than other, more fundamental problems which were largely beyond his control. In particular, the tenurial system which he and many of his fellow Ulster proprietors had inherited was not susceptible to wholesale reform; it allowed rents to lag far behind prices; and, particularly in a period of rapid population growth, it encouraged sub-letting and subdivision. In such circumstances it was exceedingly difficult to foster a sense of common purpose between landlord and tenant: financially, at least, the interests of the two parties sharply diverged. In contrast to what was common practice in Britain, estate stewards and bailiffs in Ulster were rarely drawn from the local farming community. Indeed, reliable and experienced employees (not to mention solicitors, surveyors and other consultants) were few and far between, with the result that the more capable of them often served several employers, as well as managing their own concerns.

Thus, even where they were free to do so, conscientious proprietors experienced considerable difficulty in translating policy into effective action. If, like Macartney, they were unavoidably absent from their property for long periods, their capacity was still further reduced. At regular intervals he transmitted copious instructions to his staff, but was quite incapable of monitoring either the nature or the extent of their implementation. During the earlier part of his career his subordinates proved inadequate, and for some two decades after the event his efforts in regard to his first inheritance met with little success.

As with the rest of Macartney's affairs, matters slowly but steadily improved following his return from Grenada in 1779. The death of his father in that year brought him a further inheritance which significantly increased his income; and in Jackson Wray Senr. he gained an estate agent whose services were as valuable to him in a private capacity as George Staunton's were in a more public one. Moreover, on his return from India a few years later Macartney was wiser, more experienced, and no longer unduly pre-occupied with his public career. At last he became thoroughly conversant with circumstances at Loughguile and Dervock and, because his subsequent absences from Lisanoure were much less prolonged than hitherto, he was able to tackle the problems which confronted him there with persistent energy and enthusiasm. Old leases terminated slowly and irregularly but, as they did so, Macartney got rid of middlemen and, by introducing tenancies at will, established a close and continuing relationship with those who lived and worked on his land. This policy met with no resistance primarily because his other activities complemented the general improvement in economic conditions: in addition Macartney ploughed back an increasing proportion of his profits, and eventually rewarded his more successful tenants by granting them a medium-term stake in his property. He developed one of the most impressive small demesnes in Ulster, consolidated his other holdings, improved many local services, and finally created a market town at Dervock. In so far as it boosted others' income as well as his own, and enhanced the quality of life in the locality, this last achievement symbolised Macartney's entire approach to the management of his estate during his later, more leisured years.

Little of this would have been possible had Macartney's own tenure at Lisanoure not been long enough to allow him to bring his private concerns more into line with his public success: indeed, only during the last months of his life was he able to view all aspects of his affairs with equal satisfaction. No doubt he regretted his inability to bequeath his fortune to a son or daughter. On the other hand, without the indirect inheritance from his childless uncle, Macartney's life would have followed a very different course, while his own lack of children left the bulk of his income at his personal disposal. Yet, although Macartney's inheritance provided him with an indispensable modicum of respectability, he acquired most of his wealth from salaries and pensions; and, following early mistakes, he determined not to dissipate his fortune in nurturing his Irish estate. After returning from the Caribbean he became aware of the more lucrative and assured returns to be derived from investment in the funds; for someone who had once been chronically short of cash, such investment had the added attraction of rendering capital much more readily accessible. Thus, while Macartney's proprietorial behaviour was strongly influenced by what he saw in Britain, in the case of his financial strategy the importance of that experience was paramount.

The final key to an understanding of Macartney's career is provided by a fundamental element in his attitude towards it. If there was a single strand which ran throughout, it was his fear that a hard-won reputation would be undermined by the discovery of his modest background among the middling Irish gentry. Macartney never doubted his own abilities and rarely lost confidence in his future prospects: yet there was a brittle core to his arrogance and, in a society whose upper reaches were replete with gossip and intrigue, he endeavoured to conceal not only his lack of means but also his antecedents. George Benn, the shrewd and fair-minded historian of Belfast, went so far as to surmise that Macartney was somewhat ashamed of his ancestors;[3] if so, Macartney's attitude towards their endeavours was in stark contrast to his careful preservation of manuscripts and memorabilia relating to his own career. Perhaps this explains why, once his career was underway, Macartney saw little or nothing of his father; why he was so ready, despite repeated injuries, to throw down the gauntlet, or take it up, in defence of his honour; why he craved enhancement of title; and why, even at the height of his success, he took such care over the facilities which he had to offer at Lisanoure and elsewhere. Macartney provides a graphic illustration of how someone could rise from obscurity to wealth and status in eighteenth-century public life: but he preferred his admirers to focus on his achievements rather than on the foundations on which they were erected, or the manner in which they came about.

REFERENCES

The following abbreviations have been used throughout:

B.L.   British Library
D.N.B.   *Dictionary of National Biography*
Ec. Hist. Rev. *Economic History Review*
H.M.C.   Historical Manuscripts Commission
I.M.C.   Irish Manuscripts Commission
N.L.I.   National Library of Ireland, Dublin
P.R.O.   Public Record Office, London
Proc. R.I.A.   *Proceedings* of the Royal Irish Academy
P.R.O.I.   Public Record Office of Ireland, Dublin
P.R.O.N.I.   Public Record Office of Northern Ireland, Belfast

PREFACE
1. Sir J. Barrow, *Some Account of the Public Life and a Selection from the Unpublished Writings of the Earl of Macartney,* 2 vols. (London, 1807).
2. H. H. Robbins, *Our First Ambassador to China* (London, 1908).

CHAPTER ONE   EARLY YEARS 1737-64
In preparing my contributions to this volume I have received assistance from many quarters. Staff at the New University of Ulster Library, the British Library, the Trinity College, Dublin, Manuscripts Room, the Registry of Deeds, Dublin, and the Public Record Office of Northern Ireland have been unfailingly helpful. At Coutts Bank in the Strand the authorities made special arrangements for me to consult Macartney's accounts; the archivist, Miss V. Stokes, and her assistants went out of their way to assist me; and the British Academy made a generous grant in support of this aspect of my work. In Ulster I have been able to draw freely on the knowledge and resources of several local historians: Mr. H. A. Boyd, Mr. D. MacLaughlin, and the Rev. Dr. and Mrs. T. H. Mullin. Mrs. F. Bach very kindly translated a number of letters in Italian among the Macartney papers in the P.R.O.N.I. and Mrs. S. Speers provided me with information relating to Macartney's holdings in Carrickfergus, and in regard to the O'Hara family. Several friends and colleagues, Dr. T. G. Fraser, Mr. S. J. S. Ickringill, Mr. G. Kirkham and Dr. A. P. W. Malcomson, read my text in whole or in part, and made valuable suggestions for its improvement. In this connection my greatest debt is to Dr. S. J. Connolly, who scrutinized my work in draft and saved me from numerous errors and infelicities. Mrs. R. Rainey typed my manuscript with exemplary patience and skill; and, as always, my wife, Fiona, encouraged and sustained me throughout.
1. J. Lodge, *Peerage of Ireland,* rev. M. Archdall (Dublin, 1789), VII, 89.
2. 'Brown George' Macartney (a member of a collateral branch of the family) of Blacket in Scotland also settled in Ulster at about this time.

315

Ibid. p. 88; G. Benn, *A History of the Town of Belfast* (2nd ed. London, 1877), I, 259, n. 1.

3. A portrait of Bartholomew Macartney (father of 'Black George'), completed in 1625, was among the collection of paintings at Lisanoure in 1791. Macartney's catalogue of the collection described his great-great-grandfather as 'Laird of Auchinleck in Kircudbright Stewartry'. P.R.O.N.I. D. 557, Macartney's Memorandum Book, [from] 1790, f. 46.

4. For the early history of the Donegall estate in Ulster, see P. Roebuck, 'The Making of an Ulster Great Estate : the Chichesters, Barons of Belfast and Viscounts of Carrickfergus, 1599-1648', *Proc. R.I.A.* LXXIX, sect. C, no. 1 (1979); and 'Landlord Indebtedness in Ulster in the 17th and 18th Centuries' in J. M. Goldstrom & L. A. Clarkson, eds. *Irish Population, Economy and Society : Essays in Honour of the Late K. H. Connell* (Oxford, 1981).

5. Lodge, *Peerage,* VII, 89; Benn, *Belfast,* I, 213, 254-58, 455; Government of N. Ireland, Public Record Office, *Report of the Deputy-Keeper of the Records for 1960-65* [Cmd. 521] (Belfast, 1966), pp. 121-22.

6. P.R.O.N.I. D. 1184, Will of 'Black George' Macartney, 22 April 1691.

7. Benn, *Belfast,* I, 259, n. 1.

8. P. Roebuck, *Yorkshire Baronets, 1640-1760 : Families, Estates and Fortunes* (Oxford, 1980), pp. 25-26.

9. Lodge, *Peerage,* VII, 90-91.

10. Ibid. p. 92.

11. *Ormonde Mss.* new ser. VIII (H.M.C. 1920), 312-13. I am indebted to Dr. D. W. Hayton for this reference and for further elucidation of George Macartney's political career.

12. Benn, *Belfast,* I, 257-59; Lodge, *Peerage,* VII, 92.

13. Lodge, loc. cit. Originally a not very successful member of the English Bar, Porter had been appointed Lord Chancellor of Ireland by James II. The property which passed to his children was specifically excluded from the Act of Resumption of 1700. J. G. Simms, *Jacobite Ireland 1685-91* (London, 1969), p. 25 and *The Williamite Confiscation in Ireland 1690-1703* (London, 1964), p. 115. I am indebted to Dr. S. J. Connolly for these references.

14. Lodge, loc. cit. For further details of the Porter and Dobbin inheritances, see below, pp. 11-12, 14, and P.R.O.N.I. T. 2408/7, Abstract of Title of Lord Macartney, c. 1804; D. 572/21/101, Estate Rental, 1801, with Macartney's marginal notes on the descent of his property.

15. M. Drake, 'The Irish Demographic Crisis of 1740-41' in T. W. Moody, ed. *Historical Studies VI* (London, 1968).

16. P.R.O.N.I. T.2408/7; D.572/21/101; D.1062/2/1/8, Abstract of Title of George Macartney to the Freehold Estate of the Route, c. 1734; Registry of Deeds, Dublin, Book 73, p. 452, No. 51924; Book 106, p. 564, no. 75621.

17. Lodge, loc. cit.

18. P.R.O.N.I. D.1062/2/7, Memoranda by Macartney's grandfather, 18 July 1745.

19. Ibid.; G. D. Burtchaell & T. U. Sadleir, eds. *Alumni Dublinenses* (London, 1924), pp. xxii, 525.

20. P.R.O.N.I. D.1062/2/7.
21. J. W. Stubbs, *The History of the University of Dublin from Its Found-ation to the End of the 18th Century* (London, 1889), p. 204.
22. P.R.O.N.I. D.1062/2/7; R. B. McDowell & D. A. Webb, 'Courses and Teaching in Trinity College, Dublin, during the First Two Hundred Years', *Hermathena,* LXIX (May, 1947), pp. 21-23.
23. Trinity College, Dublin (hereafter T.C.D.), Mun. V, 23/3, Entrance Book 1725-58, f. 192.
24. Ibid.
25. T.C.D. Mun. V, 27/2 Examination Returns, Entries under 'Term ending 16 December 1750', 'Christmas Examinations 1750', 'Hilary Term 1751', and 'Easter Examinations 1751'. For the general back-ground, see R. B. McDowell & D. A. Webb, op. cit. and *Trinity College, Dublin 1592-1952 : An Academic History* (Cambridge, 1982).
26. T.C.D. Mun. V, 52/39a, 41, 43, Bursar's Books, Dec. 1747 - Jan. 1755. I am indebted to Mr. G. Kirkham for assistance with these records.
27. T.C.D. Mun. V, 10/2, Degrees Conferred Feb. 1743 - Feb. 1834.
28. Ibid.
29. Professor R. B. McDowell confirms this judgment.
30. Sir J. Barrow, op. cit. I, 2.
31. G. D. Burtchaell & T. U. Sadleir, eds. op. cit. p. 224.
32. Sir J. Barrow, op. cit. I, 2-3.
33. H. H. Robbins, op. cit. p. 7.
34. P. Melvin, 'Colonel Maurice Griffin Dennis, 1805-63', *The Irish Sword,* XIII (Summer, 1977), p. 45.
35. Ibid. p. 46; B.L. Add. Mss. 51389 (P.R.O.N.I. Mic. 227/1), Dennis to Macartney, 12 Nov. 1766, 29 Sept. 1767; N.L.I. Ballitore Mss. Mic. P. 1089, Letter A/43, Dennis to R. Shackleton, 15 Aug. 1767, attaching a poem which Dennis sent to Macartney to mark the latter's return from Russia. I am indebted to Mr. G. Kirkham for this last reference.
36. Registry of Deeds, Book 192, p. 127, no. 126786; P.R.O.N.I. T. 2408/19, Will of Charles Macartney, 10 July 1758.
37. H. H. Robbins, op. cit. p. 8; see above, p. 4.
38. P.R.O.N.I. T. 2408/18, Will of George Macartney, 7 Aug. 1756.
39. Registry of Deeds, Book 192, p. 127, no. 126786.
40. Sir J. Barrow, op. cit. I, 3.
41. Ibid.; H. H. Robbins, op. cit. p. 8.
42. Lodge, *Peerage,* VII, 92.
43. P.R.O.N.I. T. 2408/19, Will of Charles Macartney, 10 July 1758.
44. P. Roebuck, *Yorkshire Baronets,* pp.283-87.
45. Lodge, loc. cit.
46. See above, pp. 6-7.
47. Macartney's grandfather appointed the Rt. Hon. Arthur Hill and Charles, Macartney's uncle, as executors of his will and guardians of Macartney. P.R.O.N.I. T. 2408/18.
48. G. E. C[ockayne], *The Complete Peerage,* ed. V. Gibbs & others (London, 1910-40), VIII, 323; P.R.O.N.I. D. 572/2/53, G. Portis to Macartney, 9 Oct. 1771.
49. A careful search of all the appropriate archives has yielded neither a

will nor any reference to a will. Moreover, the 'Index to the Dublin Grant Books' lists a George Macartney of Dublin, a gentleman, as having been found intestate in 1779. *Twenty-Sixth Report of the Deputy-Keeper of the Public Records in Ireland, Appendix* (Dublin, 1894), p. 546. I am indebted to Dr. S. J. Connolly for assistance in this matter.

50. P.R.O.N.I. D. 557, f. 46.
51. Registry of Deeds, Book 192, p. 127, no. 126786, endorsement; Book 196, p. 580, no. 131197 and endorsement.
52. P.R.O.N.I. D. 562/1518, Revd. Tisdall to Lord Chief Baron Foster, 2 Oct. 1766.
53. P.R.O.N.I. D. 572/16/2, Boscovich to Macartney, 23 June 1760.
54. P.R.O.N.I. D. 572/16/3, List of persons in Italy to whom letters of introduction could be sent, n.d.; D. 572/16/4-15, Letters of introduction from Boscovich and others to various individuals, June 1760 - Feb. 1761.
55. Earl of Ilchester, *Henry Fox, First Lord Holland : His Family and Relations* (London, 1920), II, 169-70.
56. K. Garlick & A. MacIntyre, eds. *The Diary of Joseph Farington* (London, 1978), II, 103.
57. Earl of Ilchester, loc. cit.; P.R.O.N.I. D. 572/16/15, A. Hoffman, Geneva, to Revd. G. Maria della Torre, Naples, 30 Nov. 1760.
58. Earl of Ilchester, op. cit. II, 170.
59. Ibid. pp. 169-70; Lodge, *Peerage,* VII, 90-91; see above, p. 4.
60. Quoted in B. Fitzgerald, ed. *The Correspondence of Emily, Duchess of Leinster* (I.M.C. 1949), I, 106; see also *D.N.B.* VII, 535.
61. Earl of Ilchester, op. cit. II, 262.
62. B. Fitzgerald, ed. op. cit, I, 322, 328, 343, 350, 352.
63. Earl of Ilchester, op. cit. II, 169-70.
64. T. Besterman, ed. *Studies in Voltaire and the 18th Century :* XLIV, Sir G. de Beer & A-M. Rousseau, eds. *Voltaire's British Visitors* (Geneva, 1967), pp. 56-59; Besterman, ed. *The Complete Works of Voltaire: Correspondence and Related Documents,* XXVI (Banbury, 1973), pp. 198-200; H. H. Robbins, op. cit. p. 9. I am indebted to Dr. G. Gargett for the first two references.
65. B.L. Add. Mss. 51388 (P.R.O.N.I. Mic. 227/1), Macartney to H. Fox, 16 Nov. 1762.
66. Earl of Ilchester, op. cit. II, 262-63.
67. B. Fitzgerald, ed. op. cit. I, 364, 366, 372, 376, 386.
68. B.L. Add. Mss. 51388, Macartney to H. Fox, 16 Nov. 1762; see also same to same, 8 Dec. 1762, 14 Oct. 1763; and Add. Mss. 51389, H. Fox to Macartney, 5 Nov. 1762, 19 April 1763, 28 Sept. 1763.
69. B.L. Add. Mss. 51388, Macartney to H. Fox, Lord Holland, 14 Oct. 1763.
70. See below, pp. 132, 150. Lord Ilchester listed Macartney among Holland's creditors at 4% (op. cit. II, 357); yet Holland told Macartney that 'what you owe me I shall be in no sort of haste for, will never take any interest for, and [will] take care [that] those that come after me shall have the same way of thinking'. B.L. Add. Mss. 51389, Holland to Macartney,

13 Jan. 1768.

71. P.R.O.N.I. T. 2408/22, Deed of Settlement on the marriage of Macartney and Lady Jane Stuart, 1 Feb. 1768. In 1768 the Loughguile estate brought in £354 a year, compared with £329 in 1759 (P.R.O.N.I. D. 1375/5/2/2, Loughguile Rent Roll, 1 May 1759). There are no details of the rents of the Dervock estate before 1768.

72. B.L. Add. Mss. 51389, S. Fox to Macartney, 24 Oct. 1765; Add. Mss. 51388, Macartney to Lord Holland, 3/14 May 1765.

73. B.L. Add. Mss. 51389, Lord Holland to Macartney, 22 May 1764.

74. B.L. Add. Mss. 51388, Macartney to Lord Holland, 26 Oct. 1764.

75. B.L. Add. Mss. 51388, Same to same, 31 Oct. 1764.

76. B.L. Add. Mss. 51389, Lord Holland to Macartney, 22 May 1764.

77. Earl of Ilchester, ed. *The Journal of Elizabeth, Lady Holland (1791-1811)* (London, 1908), I, 228-29.

78. See, for example, B.L. Add. Mss. 51388, Macartney to Lord Holland, 12 Dec. 1764; Macartney to Lady Holland, 31 July 1765; Add. Mss. 51389, C. J. Fox to Macartney, 13 Feb. 1765; S. Fox to Macartney, 3 Jan. 1767.

79. B.L. Add. Mss. 51389, Lord Holland to Macartney, 23 Nov. 1764.

CHAPTER TWO   RUSSIA 1764-67

1. This chapter is a shortened version of the author's *Macartney in Russia,* which appeared as a Special Supplement (No. 7) to *The English Historical Review* (1974). The excerpts are here reprinted with the kind permission of the editors of that journal. All references have been omitted, and the reader is referred to the full-length version.

CHAPTER THREE   IRELAND 1769-72

1. W. L. Clements Library, Ann Arbor, Michigan, Townshend Letter Book, V, Townshend to Bute, 2 Jan. 1770. All further references to Townshend Letter Books are to those in this library.

2. Ibid. VII, Grafton to Townshend, 11 Dec. 1768.

3. Derby Borough Library (hereafter D.B.L.), Catton Collection (Ireland), Wilmot Papers, Sir R. Wilmot to T. Waite, 21 Nov. 1768.

4. [Sir G. Macartney], *An Account of Ireland in 1773, by a Late Chief Secretary of that Kingdom* (privately printed, 1773), pp. 69-70.

5. B. Fitzgerald, ed. *The Correspondence of Emily, Duchess of Leinster* (I.M.C. 1949), I, 332.

6. *Donoughmore Mss* (H.M.C. 1891), p. 236.

7. W. J. Smith, ed. *The Grenville Papers* (London, 1853), IV, 301.

8. [Macartney], *Account of Ireland,* pp. 70-71.

9. This account is based on T. Bartlett, 'The Townshend Viceroyalty 1767-72' in Bartlett & D. W. Hayton, eds. *Penal Era and Golden Age: Essays in Irish History 1690-1800* (Belfast, 1979), pp. 88-113, and Bartlett, 'Viscount Townshend and the Irish Revenue Board 1767-73', *Proc.* R.I.A. LXXIX, Section C, no. 6 (1979), 153-75.

10. H. H. Robbins, *Our First Ambassador to China* (London, 1908), pp. 66-67; T. Bartlett, ed. *Macartney in Ireland 1768-72 : A Calendar of the Chief Secretaryship Papers of Sir George Macartney* (P.R.O.N.I. 1979), p. xi.

11. R. Hoffman, ed. *Edmund Burke, New York Agent* (Philadelphia, 1956), p. 456.
12. T. Bartlett, ed. *Macartney Calendar,* p. 3, Townshend to Macartney, 2 Jan. 1769.
13. P.R.O.I. M. 733/22, S. Fraser to Townshend, 16 June 1769.
14. W. Anson, ed. *The Autobiography and Political Correspondence of Augustus Henry, Third Duke of Grafton* (London, 1898), p. xxiv.
15. Townshend Letter Book, V, Townshend to Lord F. Campbell, 30 Oct. 1769.
16. Bartlett, ed. *Macartney Calendar,* pp. 32-33, Townshend to Macartney, 28 June 1769.
17. Quoted in H. H. Robbins, op. cit. p. 58.
18. Townshend Letter Book, V, Townshend to Bute, 30 July 1769.
19. As early as 1766 Macartney had expressed interest in the embassy to Spain, 'an employment which few people seem to care for, which I should like and for which on several counts I think myself not absolutely unqualified'. B.L. Add. Mss. 51388, Macartney to Lord Holland, 19/30 June 1766. See also below, pp. 78, 80, and Bartlett, ed. *Macartney Calendar,* p. 43.
20. Bartlett, ed. *Macartney Calendar,* pp. 41-42.
21. Ibid. pp. 42-43.
22. Townshend Letter Book, II, Townshend to Grafton, 23 Dec. 1769.
23. See *Freeman's Journal* (Dublin), 15 Aug. and 4 Nov. 1769.
24. D.B.L. Wilmot Papers, Waite to Wilmot, 12 March 1769.
25. For the political and constitutional significance of this, see T. Bartlett, 'The Irish House of Commons' Rejection of the Privy Council Money Bill in 1769', *Studia Hibernica,* no. 19 (1979).
26. [Sir G. Macartney & R. Jackson], *A Comparative State of the Two Rejected Money Bills in 1692 and 1769, by a Barrister* (Dublin, 1770), pp. 72-73, 75.
27. R. Hoffman, ed. op. cit. pp. 459-60.
28. Townshend Letter Book, VII, Weymouth to Townshend, 22 Feb. 1770; Bartlett, ed. *Macartney Calendar,* p. 54.
29. J. Redington, ed. *Calendar of Home Office Papers 1766-69* (London, 1879), p. 552, Macartney to Weymouth, 28 Dec. 1769.
30. D.B.L. Wilmot Papers, Macartney to Wilmot, 22 Jan. 1770.
31. Quoted in H. H. Robbins, op. cit. pp. 76-77.
32. But note Grattan's withering remarks: 'Macartney, if possible, is more disliked than Lord Townshend. An eternal sneer, a nauseating affection and a listless energy make him (they say) disgusting in general and give him the name of the Macaroni Prime Minister'. H. Grattan, ed. *Memoirs of. . . Henry Grattan* (Dublin, 1839), I, 162.
33. D.B.L. Wilmot Papers, Waite to Wilmot, 7 June 1769, endorsed 'most private and to be burnt'.
34. Bartlett, ed. *Macartney Calendar,* pp. 129-30, Allan to Macartney, 17 Dec. 1770.
35. Ibid. p. 130.
36. Ibid. p. 202.
37. This was the second time that Macartney had been informed that he

was not 'in the first rank'. See P.R.O. S.P. 91/77/201-2, H. S. Conway to Macartney, 1 Aug. 1766. I am indebted to Professor M. Roberts for this reference.

38. Quoted in H. H. Robbins, op. cit. p. 77.
39. Lord Townshend's salary was around £16,000 a year, and yet during his five years in Ireland he spent over £25,000 of his own money and returned to England almost a bankrupt. Macartney's expenses, though not as considerable as this, were also very heavy.
40. Townshend Letter Book, II, Townshend to Rochford, 31 Jan. 1771.
41. Bartlett, ed. *Macartney Calendar,* p. 60, Townshend to North, May 1771.
42. Townshend Letter Book, VI, Townshend to Mrs. Grenville, 17 June 1771. Henry Flood was a leading opponent of Townshend's administration.
43. Ibid. Townshend to Lord Ferrers, 26 March 1771.
44. Ibid. Townshend to Mrs. Grenville, 17 July 1771.
45. J. Fortescue, ed. *The Correspondence of George III* (London, 1927), I, 512-13, 'Thoughts on Lord Townshend's Proposals' [Sept. 1771]; Townshend Letter Book, VII, North to Townshend, 30 Sept. 1771.
46. Bartlett, ed. *Macartney Calendar,* p. 139. Rochford had succeeded Weymouth as Secretary of State for the Southern Department.
47. D.B.L. Wilmot Papers, Macartney to Wilmot, 30 Aug. 1771.
48. For Macartney's speeches in this session, see Bartlett, ed. *Macartney Calendar,* pp. 343-58.
49. D.B.L. Wilmot Papers, Macartney to Wilmot, 1 Jan. 1771 [i.e. 1772].
50. Ibid. 10 Oct. 1771.
51. Bartlett, ed. *Macartney Calendar,* pp. 61-62.
52. Ibid. p. 43.
53. *Freeman's Journal,* 23 July 1772.
54. Bartlett, ed. *Macartney Calendar,* p. 47, Townshend to Macartney, 31 Aug. 1772.
55. D.B.L. Wilmot Papers, Macartney to Wilmot, 11 June 1772. For the later history of Macartney's pension, see below, pp. 89-90.
56. *Donoughmore Mss* (H.M.C. 1891), Macartney to John Hely-Hutchinson, 21 Jan. 1773.
57. P.R.O.N.I. D. 1606/1/77, Macartney to Sir A. Acheson, 23 July 1773.
58. Bartlett, ed. *Macartney Calendar,* pp. 337, 340.
59. Ibid. p. 341. The 'test' referred to was the Sacramental Text imposed in 1704 on all office-holders. Presbyterians especially resented this text, which was abolished in 1780.
60. N.L.I. MS. 11, 967, 'A Sketch of the Revenue of Ireland in 1773' (by Sir G. Macartney). Macartney's letter to Lord North is dated 28 May 1773, and is pasted onto the inside cover of this manuscript.
61. Macartney received help from Robert Waller, a Commissioner of the Irish Revenue Board, in amassing his material. He may also have gained some assistance from G. E. Howard, *History of the Exchequer and Revenue of Ireland* (Dublin, 1776). Although Howard's book was not published until 1776, the manuscript of it was available for inspection at the Custom House, Dublin early in 1772 *(Freeman's*

Journal, 25 April 1772). Evidence of Macartney's interest in Howard's work is provided by the fact that, when the book came to be published, Macartney put his name down for six copies, equalling the order placed by the Lord Lieutenant and being many more than anyone else ordered.

62. [Macartney], Account of Ireland, p. 55.
63. Bartlett, ed. *Macartney Calendar,* p. 325. Further documents relating to this mission are printed in ibid. pp. 315-32.

CHAPTER FOUR   GRENADA 1775-79

1. R. Hoffman, ed. *Edmund Burke, New York Agent* (Philadelphia, 1956), p. 458.
2. *Donoughmore Mss* (H.M.C. 1891), p. 274.
3. For brief biographies, see the entries in *D. N. B.* and Sir L. Namier & J. Brooke, *The House of Commons 1754-90* (London, 1964). For Bute's belief that he could govern the country through His Majesty's favour, see *Various Collections,* VI (H.M.C. 1909), p. xxvi.
4. R. Hoffman, ed. op. cit. p. 456, 4 Nov. 1769.
5. B.L. Add. Mss. 51388, Macartney to Lord Holland, 19/30 June 1766.
6. *Fortescue Mss,* III (H.M.C. 1899), p. 113; see also E. M. Johnston, *Great Britain and Ireland 1760-1800* (Edinburgh, 1963), pp. 10, 43.
7. Sir L. Namier & J. Brooke, op. cit. I, 500-01. Macartney did have a small estate in Scotland — see below pp. 137-38.
8. Ibid. III, 79.
9. H. H. Robbins, *Our First Ambassador to China* (London, 1908), pp. 95-6. This work quotes from private correspondence, some of which I have been unable to trace.
10. P.R.O. C.O. 101/1, ff. 5-8 give the state of Grenada in 1763; C.O. 101/22, ff. 70 et seq., Macartney's report on the defences of the Grenadines, which also gives details of their produce and topography.
11. P.R.O. C.O. 101/1, ff. 5-8.
12. P.R.O. C.O. 101/21, f. 22, Macartney to Germain, 12 Oct. 1777.
13. P.R.O.N.I. T. 2480/3, Macartney to Lady Ossory, 2 Sept. 1777.
14. P.R.O.N.I. T. 2480/2, same to same, 25 Sept. 1776.
15. P.R.O. C.O. 101/20, Macartney to Germain, 15 March 1777.
16. P.R.O. C.O. 152/52, f. 101, Payne to Dartmouth, 5 Sept. 1772.
17. P.R.O.N.I. T. 2480/2, Macartney to Lady Ossory, 25 Sept. 1776.
18. P.R.O. C.O. 152/84, Lavington (Payne) to Hobart, 17 Dec. 1802.
19. See F. W. Pitman, *The Development of the British West Indies 1700-63* (New Haven, 1917), pp. 386-90; P.R.O.N.I. D. 2225/3/5.
20. P.R.O.N.I. T. 2480/2, Macartney to Lady Ossory, 25 Sept. 1776.
21. H. H. Robbins, op. cit. p. 102; P.R.O. C.O. 101/20, Macartney to Germain, 20 July 1777.
22. See L. J. Ragatz, *The Fall of the Planter Class in the British Caribbean* (American Historical Association, 1928), pp. 21-2; R. Pares, *A West India Fortune* (London, 1950), pp. 76, 102, 141-52 and *passim;* E. Long, *History of Jamaica* (London, 1774), I, 455-63; Ragatz, 'Absentee Landlordism in the British Caribbean 1750-1833', *Agricultural History,* V (1931), 7-24; R. B. Sheridan, 'The Rise of a Colonial Gentry : A Case Study of Antigua, 1730-75', *Ec. Hist. Rev.* 2nd ser. XIII (1960-1).

23. For example, see P.R.O. C.O. 101/20, Lt. Gov. Campbell of Tobago to Macartney, 27 May 1777; C.O. 101/23, f. 76, Macartney to Germain, 28 Jan. 1779; Sir G. T. Staunton, *Memoir of the Life and Family of the Late Sir George Leonard Staunton* (London, 1823), pp. 21-2.
24. R. Hoffman, ed. op. cit. p. 458; P.R.O.N.I. T. 2480/2, Macartney to Lady Ossory, 25 Sept. 1776.
25. P.R.O.N.I. T. 2480/2, Macartney to Lady Ossory, 25 Sept. 1776.
26. P.R.O. C.O. 101/16, Leybourne to Hillsborough, 6 and 30 Jan. 1772; C.O. 101/19, 7 Nov. 1775.
27. P.R.O.N.I. T. 2480/2, Macartney to Lady Ossory, 25 Sept. 1776.
28. P.R.O. C.O. 101/1, ff. 5-8 contains a summary of French colonial government as it operated in Grenada at the time of the conquest.
29. P.R.O. C.O. 101/21, f. 63, Macartney to Germain, 22 Oct. 1777.
30. P.R.O. C.O. 101/23, f. 95, same to same, 10 Jan. 1779.
31. P.R.O. C.O. 101/23, f. 1, Germain to Macartney, 3 Feb. 1779.
32. P.R.O. C.O. 101/20, Macartney to Germain, 12 Feb. 1777; P.R.O.N.I. T. 2480/3, Macartney to Lady Ossory, 2 Sept. 1777. See also W. L. Clements Library, Ann Arbor, Michigan, A.M. 21, List of Offices in North America and the West Indian Colonies, c. 1775, Grenada, and H. H. Robbins, op. cit. p. 101. Colonial money was discounted against sterling.
33. P.R.O.N.I. T. 2480/2, Macartney to Lady Ossory, 25 Sept. 1776.
34. P.R.O. C.O. 101/11, ff. 1-12.
35. P.R.O. C.O. 101/10, 'Ordinance for regulating the elections for the General Assembly of Grenada, the Grenadians, Dominica, St. Vincent and Tobago', 10 Feb. 1766. Colour was a sensitive and complicated issue: the fifth generation of successive white unions from a mixed union was white, while the fourth generation of successive black unions was black — see B.L. Add. Mss. 12438, f. 2.
36. P.R.O. C.O. 101/21, ff. 22-3, Macartney to Germain, 12 Oct. 1777.
37. P.R.O. C.O. 101/12, ff. 53-6, Melvill to Hillsborough, 27 July 1767.
38. P.R.O. C.O. 101/11, f. 132, Melvill to the Lords Commissioners of Trade and Plantations, 28 May 1766.
39. P.R.O. C.O. 101/12, f. 53, Melvill to Hillsborough, 27 July 1767.
40. P.R.O. C.O. 101/5, Leybourne to Hillsborough, 22 Nov. 1771; C.O. 101/16, Protest of suspended members of the Grenada Council to the Earl of Hillsborough, 5 Dec. 1771.
41. P.R.O. C.O. 101/16, Leybourne to Hillsborough, 5 May 1772 and 25 July 1772.
42. Ibid. 25 April 1772.
43. P.R.O. C.O. 101/19, Lt. Gov. Young to the Earl of Dartmouth, 10 Jan. 1776, and Macartney to Germain, enclosing address of 2 April 1776.
44. P.R.O. C.O. 101/20, Macartney to Germain, 12 Feb. 1777.
45. P.R.O. C.O. 101/20, same to same, 8 June 1777.
46. Ibid.
47. P.R.O. C.O. 152/56, f. 183, Burt to Germain, 17 Sept. 1777.
48. P.R.O. C.O. 101/12, f. 25, Melvill to Shelburne, 16 Nov. 1769.

49. P.R.O. C.O. 101/20, Macartney to Germain, 27 Feb. 1777; also C.O. 101/23, f. 76, same to same, 28 Jan. 1779.
50. H. H. Robbins, op. cit. p. 104.
51. P.R.O. C.O. 137/33, f. 228, Lyttleton to Lords Commissioners of Trade and Plantations, 20 Aug. 1765.
52. P.R.O.N.I. T. 2480/2, Macartney to Lady Ossory, 25 Sept. 1776.
53. P.R.O. C.O. 152/49, ff. 41, 59, Gov. Woodley to Hillsborough, 9 June 1769, and the Post Masters' reply.
54. P.R.O. C.O. 101/22, f. 137, Macartney to Germain, 8 Oct. 1778. These were the hurricane months.
55. P.R.O. C.O. 101/20, Macartney to Germain, 8 Oct. and 14 Dec. 1776. Despatches were numbered so that the recipient knew if any were delayed or missing.
56. See G. Metcalf, *Royal Government and Political Conflict in Jamaica, 1729-83* (London, 1965), p. 17. Another useful study of constitutional matters is D. J. Murray, *The West Indies and the Development of Colonial Government* (London, 1965), Chapts. 1 and 2.
57. P.R.O. C.O. 101/20, Macartney to Germain, 1 March 1777.
58. P.R.O. C.O. 101/20, same to same, 30 June 1776.
59. P.R.O. C.O. 101/20, same to same, 2 April 1777.
60. P.R.O. C.O. 101/20, same to same, 30 June 1776.
61. P.R.O. C.O. 101/21, f. 179, same to same, 10 April 1778.
62. See above, p. 98.
63. H. H. Robbins, op. cit. pp. 96-7.
64. P.R.O. C.O. 101/20, Macartney to Germain, 30 June 1776.
65. P.R.O. C.O. 101/22, f. 155, same to same, 25 Oct. 1778.
66. P.R.O. C.O. 101/23, ff. 30-1, same to same, 1 Dec. 1778. There are a number of letters referring to the financial administration of individual cases in the Macartney Papers, W. L. Clements Library, Ann Arbor, Michigan.
67. P.R.O. C.O. 101/22, ff. 155-58, same to same, 25 Oct. 1778.
68. See L. M. Penson, 'The London West India Interest in the Eighteenth Century', *English Historical Review,* XXXVI (1921), reprinted in R. Mitchison, ed. *Essays in Eighteenth-Century History* (London, 1966), pp. 1-20; Pension, *The Colonial Agents of the British West Indies* (London, 1924).
69. L. J. Ragatz, *Statistics for the Study of British Caribbean Economic History 1763-1833* (London, 1928), pp. 10-11, esp. Table VI. Grenada's refusal to pay the 4½% duty was upheld in Campbell v Hall, 1774.
70. See F. W. Pitman, op. cit. pp. 70-1, 98.
71. Ibid. p. 334 et seq. See also Ragatz, *Statistics,* p. 9.
72. See R. Pares, *Yankees and Creoles* (London, 1956), p. 1 et seq. for details of this trade.
73. For details of West Indian society, slavery and the economy, see E. Goveia, *Slave Society in the British Leeward Islands at the end of the 18th Century* (Yale, 1965), and B. W. Higman, *Slave Population and Economy in Jamaica, 1807-34* (Cambridge, 1976). Both are later than the period of this study but they are interesting and important.

74. P.R.O. C.O. 101/9, General Scott to Lord Egremont, 19 Jan. 1763.
75. E. Long, op. cit. I, 455-63. B. Edwards, *History of the British Colonies in the West Indies* (London, 1807), II, 287-300 estimated that capital investment of £30,000 was necessary for 'a fair prospect' of success. See also S. G. Checkland, 'Finance for the West Indies 1780-1815', *Ec. Hist. Rev.* 2nd ser. X (1957-8), 461-69.
76. Anon., *Some Observations . . .* (London, 1764). For a study in estate management, see R. Pares, *West India Fortune*, esp. pp. 40-1 on planting partnerships, and pp. 15-16 on sugar cultivation.
77. P.R.O. C.O. 101/20, Macartney to Germain, 30 June 1776.
78. P.R.O. C.O. 101/19, Young to Dartmouth, 1 Feb. 1776.
79. P.R.O. C.O. 101/20, Macartney to Germain, 20 June 1776.
80. P.R.O. C.O. 101/20, Macartney to Germain, 30 June 1776.
81. R. Pares, 'The London Sugar Market, 1740-69', *Ec. Hist. Rev.* 2nd ser. IX (1956), 254-70. See also L. J. Ragatz, *Falls of the Planter Class*, pp. 100-01, and Ragatz, *Statistics*, p. 8.
82. P.R.O. C.O. 101/17, Leybourne to Dartmouth, 26 June 1774.
83. L. J. Ragatz, *Fall of the Planter Class*, p. 135. For the customs figures, see P.R.O. C.O. 3/63.80, printed in Ragatz, *Statistics*, p. 14. Eighteenth-century customs figures are unreliable, and the nature of the West Indian trade made those relating to the Caribbean notoriously so: the difference over the ten years 1763-72 averages at 29.78; in 1778 it was 30.95; and in 1777 5.27!
84. P.R.O.N.I. T. 2480/2, Macartney to Lady Ossory, 25 Sept. 1776.
85. P.R.O. C.O. 101/18, f. 1; C.O. 101/20, Macartney to Germain, 1 Aug. 1776.
86. P.R.O. C.O. 101/20, Germain to Macartney, 22 April 1777. See also C.O. 71/7, f. 15, Gov. Shirley of Dominica to de Bouillé. British law discouraged debtors from taking refuge in British islands.
87. P.R.O. C.O. 101/20, Macartney to Germain, 27 May 1777.
88. P.R.O. C.O. 101/23, ff. 6-14, various letters to Baker explaining his predicament, 13 Feb. 1779; requesting leave of absence, 19 Feb. 1779; Macartney's recommendation, 26 May 1779.
89. P.R.O. C.O. 101/19, Macartney to Germain, 3 Sept. 1776; C.O. 101/21, ff. 65-6, same to same, 22 Oct. 1777; C.O. 101/22, f. 54, 22 July 1778.
90. P.R.O. C.O. 101/20, same to same, 8 June 1777.
91. P.R.O. C.O. 101/22, f. 110, same to same, 2 Sept. 1778. See also C.O. 152/59, Burt to Germain, 2 Nov. 1778, regarding a cartel for the exchange of prisoners.
92. P.R.O. C.O. 101/20, Macartney to Germain, 9 April 1777.
93. P.R.O. C.O. 101/21, f. 63, same to same, 22 Oct. 1777; C.O. 101/20, same to same, 6 March 1777.
94. P.R.O. C.O. 101/20, same to same, 11 July 1777.
95. P.R.O. C.O. 101/21, f. 65, same to same, 22 Oct. 1777; C.O. 152/59, f. 9, Burt to Germain, 2 Nov. 1779. See also W. L. Clements Library, Ann Arbor, Michigan, Macartney Mss. Admiral Byron to Macartney, 11 March 1779.
96. P.R.O. C.O. 101/22, f. 145, Macartney to Germain, 18 Oct. 1778.

97. P.R.O. C.O. 101/21, f. 68, same to same, 24 Oct. 1777.
98. P.R.O. C.O. 101/22, f. 145, same to same, 18 Oct. 1778.
99. P.R.O. C.O. 101/20, same to same, 11 July 1777.
100. Ibid.
101. For the complexities of British trade in the West Indies, legitimate and illegitimate, see R. Pares, *War and Trade in the West Indies 1739-63* (Oxford, 1936), and F. Armytage, *The Freeport System in the British West Indies 1766-1822* (London, 1954).
102. P.R.O. C.O. 101/23, f. 148, Macartney to Germain, 10 April 1779.
103. P.R.O. C.O. 101/23, f. 96, same to same, 10 Jan. 1779. See also C.O. 152/59, f. 117, Burt to Germain, 3 May 1779, and C.O. 152/57, ff. 90-103 for an acrimonious exchange of letters in 1777 between Gov. de Graaf of St. Eustasius and Gov. Burt of Antigua, regarding de Graaf's assistance to the Americans. See also J. F. Jameson, 'St. Eustasius and the American Revolution', *American Historical Review,* VIII (1902-3), esp. pp. 686-87.
104. P.R.O. C.O. 101/21, f. 64, Macartney to Germain, 22 Oct. 1777. Much West Indian trade was carried on in barter, particularly with rum.
105. L. J. Ragatz, *Fall of the Planter Class,* p. 161.
106. P.R.O. C.O. 152/57, f. 151, Burt to [Germain], 1 Dec. 1777. For a list of goods supplied to the West Indies from America in 1771, see R. Pares, *Yankees and Creoles,* p. 25.
107. P.R.O. C.O. 101/20, Macartney to Germain, 25 Nov. 1776. See also W. L. Clements Library, Ann Arbor, Michigan, Macartney Mss. Admiral Barrington to Macartney, 7 Jan. 1779.
108. P.R.O. C.O. 101/23, ff. 42, 58, Burt to Germain, 31 Dec. 1778 and 10 Jan. 1779.
109. Ibid. f. 42, same to same, 31 Dec. 1778.
110. P.R.O. C.O. 101/20, Macartney to Germain, 20 July 1777 and corrected list in C.O. 100/21, f. 39; C.O. 101/22, ff. 41, 100.
111. P.R.O. C.O. 101/23, f. 159, Macartney to Germain, 23 May 1779.
112. P.R.O. C.O. 101/23, f. 181, same to same, 6 June 1779. The convoy started in Barbados and collected produce from the Windward and Leeward Islands before returning to England.
113. P.R.O. C.O. 101/23, f. 183, Germain to Macartney, 5 Aug. 1779.
114. P.R.O. C.O. 101/23, f. 194, Macartney to Germain, 4 Sept. 1779, from La Rochelle.
115. P.R.O. C.O. 101/23, f. 258, printed in Sir J. Barrow, *Some Account of the Public Life and a Selection from the Unpublished Writings of the Earl of Macartney* (London, 1807), I, 65-6.
116. Sir J. Barrow, op. cit. I, 62-3, 66; H. H. Robbins, op. cit. p. 110.
117. P.R.O. C.O. 101/23, f. 258, Germain to Lieut. Gov. Graham, 4 Nov. 1779.
118. *Various Collections,* VI (H.M.C. 1909), p. 141, J. Pownall to W. Knox, 11 Nov. 1777.
119. It has been possible to collect the material for this chapter through the generosity of the Research Fund of the University of Sheffield, to whom I should like to offer my sincerest thanks.

CHAPTER FIVE   **MIDDLE YEARS 1764-80**

1. See above, p. 20.
2. Quoted in H. H. Robbins, *Our First Ambassador to China* (London, 1908), p. 101.
3. See above, p. 87.
4. P.R.O.N.I. T. 2480/5, Macartney to Lady Ossory, 19 Aug. 1780.
5. B.L. Add. Mss. 51388 (P.R.O.N.I. Mic. 227/1), Macartney to Lord Holland, 26 Oct. 1764.
6. B.L. Add. Mss. 51388, same to same, 12 Dec. 1764.
7. B.L. Add. Mss. 51389 (P.R.O.N.I. Mic. 227/1), S. Fox to Macartney, with postscript by Lady Holland, 1 April 1766.
8. B.L. Add. Mss. 51389, C. J. Fox to Macartney, 13 Feb. 1765.
9. B.L. Add. Mss. 51388, Macartney to Lord Holland, 3/14 May 1765. For example, soon after returning from Russia Macartney lost a hundred guineas at the card table in the course of a single evening. *The Letters and Journals of Lady Mary Coke* (privately printed 1889-96, fac. ed. London, 1970), II, 195.
10. B.L. Add. Mss. 51389, Lord Holland to Macartney, 20 June 1765.
11. Ibid. same to same, 14 Aug. 1766.
12. Ibid. same to same, 13 Oct. 1766.
13. Ibid. same to same, 30 June 1766.
14. B.L. Add. Mss. 51388, Macartney to Lord Holland, 19/30 June 1766.
15. Sir J. Barrow, *Some Account of the Public Life and a Selection from the Unpublished Writings of the Earl of Macartney* (London, 1807), I, 48, n. 1.
16. B.L. Add. Mss. 51388, Macartney to Lord Holland, 19/30 June 1766.
17. *Letters and Journals of Lady Mary Coke*, II, 169; J. Davies, *Cardiff and the Marquesses of Bute* (Cardiff, 1981), pp. 5-6.
18. *Letters and Journals of Lady Mary Coke*, II, 372.
19. Ibid. II, 169; W. S. Lewis, ed. *Horace Walpole's Correspondence* (London, 1937-), VII, 181, Walpole to Lady Ossory, 14 Oct. 1779.
20. B.L. Add. Mss. 51388, Macartney to Lord Holland, 19/30 June 1766.
21. *Walpole's Correspondence*, XXI, 472, Walpole to Sir H. Mann, 27 Jan. 1761; Coutts Bank Archives, London, Ledger 48, f. 453A; Ledger 50, f. 400A.
22. P.R.O.N.I. T. 2408/22, Marriage Settlement, Macartney and Lady J. Stuart, 1 Feb. 1768.
23. *Letters and Journals of Lady Mary Coke*, II, 178, 187 (quote); B.L. Add. Mss. 51388, Macartney to Lord Holland, 12 Jan. 1768; Add. Mss. 51389, Lady Holland to Macartney, 5 Jan. 1768; Lord Holland to Macartney, 13 Jan. and 3 Feb. 1768. See above, pp. 57-58.
24. B.L. Add. Mss. 51389, Lord Holland to Macartney, 13 Jan. 1768.
25. B.L. Add. Mss. 51388, Macartney to Lord Holland, 19/30 June 1766; *Letters and Journals of Lady Mary Coke*, III, 115, 134, 139. See above, pp. 70-72.
26. See above, p. 8-9. Macartney's M.A. degree certificate is at P.R.O.N.I. D. 2731/1.
27. P.R.O.N.I. D. 1375/5/2/2.
28. B.L. Add. Mss. 51388, Macartney to Lord Holland, 12 Dec. 1764,

postscript.

29. Huntingdon Library, Los Angeles, HM 686, Macartney's Commonplace Book 1767-77, ff. 92-95; P.R.O.N.I. D. 572/21/96.

30. P.R.O.N.I. D. 572/4/33, R. Jackson to Macartney, 13 July 1770. See also D. 572/18/43, Lady Macartney to Lady Staunton, 10 July 1801 in which Lady Jane declared that she had first seen Lisanoure 'one and thirty years ago'.

31. P.R.O.N.I. D. 573/2/25, 26, Mrs. A. Macartney to Macartney, 26 Dec. 1769, 3 Jan. 1770. See above, p. 73.

32. See above, pp. 11-12, 14. The statute acreage has been calculated from the Irish or 'plantation' acreage recorded in the survey and valuation of 1767 (P.R.O.N.I. D. 572/21/96).

33. The rental has been calculated from the detailed figures listed in Macartney's marriage settlement of 1 Feb. 1768 (P.R.O.N.I. T. 2408/22). See also P. Roebuck, 'Rent Movement, Proprietorial Incomes and Agricultural Development, 1730-1830' and D. McCourt, 'The Decline of Rundale, 1750-1850' in Roebuck, ed. *Plantation to Partition: Essays in Ulster History in Honour of J. L. McCracken* (Belfast, 1981).

34. The earliest reference to the Latouche account is Coutts Bank, Ledger 57, f. 437B, 20 Aug. 1771.

35. P.R.O.N.I. D. 572/5/1-7, R. Waller to Macartney, 26 March, 5 and 15 April, 6 and 26 May, 23 June, 9 August 1770. See above, p. 77.

36. P.R.O.N.I. D. 1062/2/1/44, Deed of Covenants, Macartney and Portis, Dec. 1786, reciting developments from 9 Oct. 1767.

37. P.R.O.N.I. D. 572/21/101, Estate Rental, 1801, with Macartney's marginal annotations, f. 16; D. 572/3/22, J. Allen to Macartney, 10 Dec. 1770; W. A. Maguire, 'Lord Donegall and the Hearts of Steel', *Irish Historical Studies,* XXI, no. 84 (September 1981). For Lord Donegall's subsequent lease to Allen, see Registry of Deeds, Dublin, Book 314, p. 377, no. 218465.

38. P.R.O.N.I. D. 1062/2/1/32, 33, Declaration of Trust, Stewart and Portis, reciting background to and details of the transaction, and letter, Portis to Macartney, 22 April 1769; Registry of Deeds, Book 270, pp. 595-6, nos. 175685-6.

39. P.R.O.N.I. D. 572/21/101, f. 16; Registry of Deeds, Book 277, p. 487, no. 178947.

40. P.R.O.N.I. D. 572/21/101, f. 6.

41. Registry of Deeds, Book 380, p. 385, no. 256654.

42. P.R.O.N.I. T. 2480/26, Bill of Costs, May 1771; Registry of Deeds, Book 287, p. 202, no. 186497. For details of the arrangement with Fleming, and maps and surveys of the newly-expanded estate, see P.R.O.N.I. D. 1062/2/4, Volume of Estate Maps, [mainly] 1772.

43. Coutts Bank, Ledger 53, f. 336B, which records the repayment of £1,000 of this mortgage on 23 May 1770.

44. P.R.O.N.I. D. 1062/2/1/43, Redemption of Mortgage, reciting mortgage of 12/13 Aug. 1771; Registry of Deeds, Book 287, p. 593, no. 188314.

45. P.R.O.N.I. D. 572/2/21, Mrs. C. Macartney to Macartney, 26 March 1770; D. 1062/2/4, Map and Survey, 1772; J. Lodge, *Peerage of Ireland,* rev. M. Archdall (Dublin, 1789), VII, 90-91.
46. P.R.O.N.I. D. 1062/2/1/34, Letters Patent, 6 Nov. 1770.
47. P.R.O.N.I. D. 572/21/96, Survey and Valuation, 1767; D. 2225/7/17, Sloane to Macartney, 10 Feb. 1768.
48. P.R.O.N.I. D. 1062/2/4, Volume of Estate Maps, [mainly] 1772.
49. T. H. Mullin, *Coleraine in By-Gone Centuries* (Belfast, 1976), pp. 144, 155-6, 176; P.R.O.N.I. D. 572/33-35, 37, 38, 44, Jackson to Macartney, 13 July, 14 Sept. and 20 Nov. 1770, 15 Jan. and 27 June 1771, 6 Oct. 1772. See also *Londonderry Journal,* 8 Aug. 1772 (kindly drawn to my attention by Mr. G. Kirkham).
50. S. Lewis, *A Topographical Dictionary of Ireland* (London, 1837), II, 315.
51. P.R.O.N.I. D. 1375/5/2/2, Loughguile Rental, 1759; D. 572/21/96, Survey and Valuation, 1767.
52. P.R.O.N.I. D. 572/18/43, Lady Macartney to Lady Staunton, 10 July 1801.
53. J. Davies, op. cit. p. 6; *D.N.B.* XIX, 97-98.
54. Both maps are in P.R.O.N.I. D. 1062/2/4.
55. P.R.O.N.I. D. 2225/7/54, Note on the History of the Estate by Macartney, c. 1793.
56. M. Bence-Jones, *Burke's Guide to Country Houses,* I, *Ireland* (London, 1978), p. 188; P.R.O.N.I. D. 577, ff. 50-59, An Inventory of Furniture at Lisanoure, Jan. 1791, which lists the rooms and outhouses.
57. W. A. Maguire, op. cit. See below, pp. 145-46.
58. P.R.O.N.I. D. 2225/7/22, Memorandum (by Macartney) of work to be done at Lisanoure, n.d. (but early 1770s); D. 572/4/42, R. Jackson to Macartney, 24 Nov. 1772; D. 572/18/22, Mrs. A. Jackson to Lady Macartney, 21 March 1775.
59. There are three catalogues of Macartney's books: P.R.O.N.I. T.D. 4779, Curzon St. n.d.; Mic. 395, 1786; D. 577, ff. 64-78, Lisanoure, Jan. 1791.
60. Compare the maps of the demesne of 1772 and 1788 in P.R.O.N.I. D. 1062/2/4. See also Macartney's notes on various aspects of his developments on the demesne in D. 557, ff. 2-3, 32.
61. For discussion of the later development of the demesne, see below pp. 284, 286, 296, 298.
62. P.R.O.N.I. D. 2225/7/22, Memorandum, n.d. (but early 1770s).
63. P.R.O.N.I. D. 572/4/42, Jackson to Macartney, 24 Nov. 1772.
64. P.R.O.N.I. D. 572/18/5-7, 13, 14, J. Mackay to Macartney, 26 Nov., 12 and 31 Dec. 1774, 10 and 24 April 1775; D. 572/18/11, A. Kindell to Macartney, 20 March 1775; D. 572/18/22, Mrs. A. Jackson to Macartney, 21 March 1775.
65. P.R.O.N.I. D. 572/18/24, R. Jackson to Macartney, 1 May 1781.
66. P.R.O.N.I. D. 572/4/42, same to same, 24 Nov. 1772; D. 572/18/3, 5, 6, 8, J. Mackay to Macartney, 1 Oct., 26 Nov., 12 Dec. 1774, 4 Feb. 1775.
67. P.R.O.N.I. D. 572/18/12, 21 March 1775.

68. P.R.O.N.I. D. 572/18/15.
69. P.R.O.N.I. D. 572/18/18, J. Mackay's Account with Macartney, Aug. 1774 - July 1775.
70. P.R.O.N.I. D. 572/9/5, R. Jackson to Macartney, 4 March 1786; C. V. Trench, *The Wrays of Donegal, Londonderry, Antrim* (Oxford, 1945), pp. 277-90.
71. See above, pp. 85-87.
72. P.R.O.N.I. D. 572/3/152, Lord Blayney to Macartney, 26 Jan. 1772.
73. P.R.O.N.I. D. 572/7/22, Anon. to Macartney, 13 March 1772.
74. W. A. Maguire, loc. cit.
75. P.R.O.N.I. D. 572/9/33, R. Jackson to Macartney, 19 Oct. 1789.
76. P.R.O.N.I. D. 572/18/16, J. Mackay to Macartney, 24 June 1775.
77. P.R.O.N.I. D. 572/18/17, same to same, 29 July 1775; D. 572/9/33, R. Jackson to Macartney, 19 Oct. 1789.
78. P.R.O.N.I. D. 572/18/2, J. Mackay to Macartney, 15 Aug. 1774.
79. P.R.O.N.I. D. 572/9/33, R. Jackson to Macartney, 19 Oct. 1789. See below, pp. 287-88.
80. Registry of Deeds, Book 159, p. 281, no. 106973; P.R.O.N.I. D. 2225/7/47, J. N. Magawley to J. Wray, 23 June 1790.
81. P.R.O.N.I. D. 426/5, Estate Rental, 1789, ff. 1, 6.
82. P.R.O.N.I. D. 1375/5/2/2, Loughguile Rental, 1759; T. 2408/32, Macartney's Marriage Settlement, 1768; D. 426/5, Estate Rental, 1789.
83. Details of the quality of the land at Carnbuck and throughout the estate arc given in P.R.O.N.I. D. 1062/2/4, Volume of Estate Maps and Surveys, [mainly] 1772.
84. P.R.O.N.I. D. 572/18/2, 3, 5, 6, 8, 13, 14, 17, J. Mackay to Macartney, 15 Aug. 1774 - 29 July 1775. Details of rent arrears and of receipts from direct farming are in D. 572/18/18, J. Mackay's Accounts, Aug. 1774 - July 1775.
85. P.R.O.N.I. D. 2225/7/22, Memorandum, n.d. (but early 1770s), Item 2.
86. P.R.O.N.I. D. 572/18/13, Mackay to Macartney, 10 April 1775.
87. P.R.O.N.I. D. 572/18/18, Mackay's Accounts, Aug. 1774 - July 1775.
88. See Macartney's marginal annotations in P.R.O.N.I. D. 2225/7/47, Summary Rental, 1790.
89. P.R.O.N.I. D. 572/18/11, A. Kindell to Macartney, 20 March 1775.
90. P.R.O.N.I. D. 572/18/18, Mackay's Accounts, outgoing for 5 June 1775.
91. See for example P.R.O.N.I. D. 572/18/8, 14, Mackay to Macartney, 4 Feb. and 24 April 1775.
92. See 'Observations' in P.R.O.N.I. D. 572/21/96, Estate Survey and Valuation, 1767.
93. Ibid.
94. See Macartney's marginal annotation to P.R.O.N.I. D. 572/21/101, Estate Rental, 1801, f. 6.
95. As Reference 82 above.
96. P.R.O.N.I. D. 572/2/95, Col. E. Smith to Macartney, 15 Aug. 1772.
97. For the debts to Fleming, Renouard, and the executors of James Coutts, see above, pp. 136-37, and below, pp. 282-83; and for the debt to the

executors of Lord Holland, see B.L. Add. Mss. 22462, f. 6, Macartney to J. Powell, 28 March 1782; and for the mortgage to Thomas Coutts, see Coutts Bank, Ledger 75, f. 441A and Add. Mss. 22462, ff. 1-2, Macartney to Lady Macartney, 27 March 1782.

98. See above, p. 128.
99. See for example Coutts Bank, Ledger 79, ff. 477B, 779B.
100. Coutts Bank, Ledgers, 48, 50, 53, 57, 59, 61, 63, 65, 67, 69, 71, 73, 75.
101. Coutts Bank, Ledgers 65, 67, 69, 71, 73, 75.
102. Coutts Bank, Ledger 50, f. 399B.
103. Coutts Bank, Ledger 53, f. 336B, 23 May 1770.
104. Sir J. Barrow, op. cit. I, 64-65.
105. See above, pp. 132, 136-37.
106. For examples, see Coutts Bank, Ledger 67, f. 456B; Ledger 69, f. 436B; Ledger 71, f. 430B.
107. P.R.O.N.I. D. 426/5, Estate Rental, 1789. For further details of the inheritance, see above, pp. 11-12, 14, and below, pp. 286-87.

CHAPTER SIX   INDIA 1780-86

In the course of preparing this work I have acquired many debts, the most important of which can only be inadequately expressed. It could never have been completed without the encouragement at every stage of the Editor, who first suggested to me the possibilities offered by an investigation of Macartney's Indian career. In addition to the substantial assistance provided by the Public Record Office of Northern Ireland, I must thank the staffs of the British Library, the India Office Library and Records, the Bodleian Library and the New University of Ulster Library, as well as the Norfolk Record Office and the Charles Patterson Van-Pelt Library, University of Pennsylvania, for their assistance with microfilms. The Macartney Papers in the British Library have been cited according to the British Library catalogue, although the Public Record Office of Northern Ireland holds much of this material on microfilm and this was used extensively. Sources which might otherwise have escaped my attention were suggested to me by Dr. A. P. W. Malcomson, Mr. A. T. Harrison, Mr. S. J. S. Ickringill and my wife, Mrs. G. F. Fraser. I gladly acknowledge the assistance of the Research Committee of the New University of Ulster which enabled me to work in Oxford.

1. P.R.O.N.I. T. 3428, 'Concerning the indeterminate rights of the Nabob of Arcot and the Raja of Tanjore with respect to each other'. These are photocopies and microfilms of Walsingham Papers held at the Norfolk Record Office and consulted by permission of the County Archivist. The affairs of the Carnatic feature prominently in this collection as Walsingham was a member of the Board of Control instituted in 1784.
2. P.R.O.N.I. T. 3428, 'Extract of the representations of the Court of Directors to the Board of Commissioners for Indian affairs . . . relative to the private debts of the Nabob of Arcot', 2 Nov. 1784.
3. Ibid.
4. Ibid.

5. 'Speech on the Nabob of Arcot's Debts', *The Works of the Rt. Hon. Edmund Burke,* IV (London, 1803), 283. For a recent edition, see P. J. Marshall, ed. *The Writings and Speeches of Edmund Burke* (Oxford, 1981).
6. P.R.O.N.I. Mic. 407/3, 'Translation of a letter to the Court of Directors by Orndut ud Omrat', 19 Sept. 1782. The writer was the Nawab's eldest son. This collection is a microfilm copy of the originals held by the Charles Patterson Van-Pelt Library, University of Pennsylvania, and consulted by their permission.
7. Ibid.
8. P.R.O.N.I. T. 3428, 'Principal of the several debts due from the Nabob of Arcot to the Company and to individuals in their service or under their protection'.
9. Burke, 'Speech . . . ', p. 307.
10. P.R.O.N.I. T. 2480/5, Macartney to Lady Ossory, 19 Aug. 1780.
11. N. Wraxall, *Historical Memoirs of My Own Time* (London, 1904), pp. 321-22.
12. W. S. Lewis, ed. *Horace Walpole's Correspondence* (London, 1937-), XXXIII, 219, Walpole to Lady Ossory, 23 Aug. 1780; P.R.O.N.I. T. 2480/5, Macartney to Lady Ossory, 19 Aug. 1780.
13. P.R.O.N.I. D. 572/19/13, Macartney to E.I.C. Directors, 25 Aug. 1780.
14. P.R.O.N.I. D. 572/19/14.
15. P.R.O.N.I. D. 572/20/10, Sandwich to Macartney, n.d.
16. P.R.O.N.I. D. 572/19/43.
17. P.R.O.N.I. D. 572/20/14, Russell to Court of Directors, 23 Sept. 1780.
18. Sir G. T. Staunton, *Memoir of the Life and Family of the Late Sir George Leonard Staunton* (London, 1823), p. 254, Macartney to Staunton, 18 Sept. 1780.
19. As 17 above.
20. P.R.O.N.I. T. 2480/6, Macartney to Lady Ossory, 13 Oct. 1780.
21. P.R.O.N.I. D. 572/19/49, J. Hume to Macartney, 3 Nov. 1780.
22. L. S. Sutherland, *The East India Company in Eighteenth-Century Politics* (Oxford, 1952), pp. 346-52.
23. *Walpole's Correspondence,* XXIX, 244, Walpole to Lady Ossory, 26 Nov. 1780.
24. B.L. Add. Mss. 22462, f. 18, Macartney to T. Coutts, 8 Aug. 1782.
25. P.R.O.N.I. D. 572/19/70, Robinson to Macartney, 1 Feb. 1781; Mic. 407/2, same to same, n.d. 1781; C. C. Davies, ed. *The Private Correspondence of Lord Macartney, Governor of Madras (1781-85),* Royal Historical Society, Camden Third Series, LXXVII (London, 1950), p. 177, Macartney to Robinson, 12 Jan. 1782.
26. P.R.O.N.I. D. 572/19/84, T. Allan to Macartney, 9 June 1782.
27. As 25 above.
28. J. A. Woods, ed. *The Correspondence of Edmund Burke,* IV (Cambridge, 1963), pp. 323-25, Loughborough to Burke, 20 Dec. 1780.
29. *Private Correspondence of Lord Macartney,* p. 10, Macartney to

Macpherson, 3 Jan. 1782.
30. P.R.O.N.I. D. 572/19/73, T. Allan to Macartney, 6 Feb. 1781.
31. P.R.O.N.I. D. 2225/4/60, 'A list of the voters in the city of London, etc. Westminster and suburbs', 1780.
32. P.R.O.N.I. D. 572/20/6 (10), Untitled list of electors.
33. P.R.O.N.I. D. 572/19/38, W. Brummell to Macartney, 30 Sept. 1780.
34. P.R.O.N.I. D. 572/20/6 (9), Ordnance list.
35. P.R.O.N.I. D. 572/20/6 (4).
36. P.R.O.N.I. D. 572/20/6 (2), Burt's list; D. 572/29/6 (5), Gompertz's list.
37. P.R.O.N.I. D. 572/20/1, Anon. to Macartney, n.d.
38. P.R.O.N.I. D. 572/20/8, J. Tierney to Sandwich, 23 Nov. 1780.
39. P.R.O.N.I. D. 572/19/60, Sandwich to Macartney, 24 Dec. 1780.
40. P.R.O.N.I. D. 572/19/62, I. Solomons to Macartney; D. 572/19/53, Sir C. Wintringham to Macartney.
41. India Office Records (hereafter I.O.R.), B/96. 450, East India Company Court Book, 14 Dec. 1780.
42. I.O.R. B/96. 455, E. India Company Court Book, 15 Dec. 1780. Dame Lucy Sutherland believed that 'he owed his adoption as candidate in the first instance to a group of company politicians', and emphasised the role of Robinson and the Treasury in ensuring Macartney's election. While the evidence is not conclusive, it seems to point to governmental initiative behind Macartney's candidature, especially as Sandwich had to approach Devaynes to allow the application to go ahead. While Robinson's contribution was clearly important in the election, the surviving evidence reveals an astonishing degree of personal commitment and activity by Sandwich, confirming the assessment of his importance in Company elections in Wraxall's memoirs. See L.S. Sutherland, 'Lord Macartney's Appointment as Governor of Madras, 1780 : the Treasury in East India Company Elections', *English Historical Review*, XC (1975), 523-35.
43. P.R.O.N.I. T. 2480/6, Macartney to Lady Ossory, 13 Oct. 1780.
44. Sir G. T. Staunton, op. cit. p. 258, T. Staunton to G. L. Staunton, 3 March 1781.
45. Ibid. pp. 267-68, G. L. Staunton to Mrs. Staunton, 6 Nov. 1782.
46. *Private Correspondence of Lord Macartney*, pp. 265-66, G. L. Staunton to Macartney, 24 Feb. 1782.
47. North's Regulating Act, 1773, P. J. Marshall, *Problems of Empire : Britain and India 1757-1813* (London, 1968), pp. 111-16.
48. P.R.O.N.I. Mic. 407/2, Macartney's patent from the E. India Co.
49. P.R.O.N.I. Mic. 407/1, Instruction to Macartney and the Select Committee.
50. I.O.R. L/P & S/5/537, Devaynes and Sulivan to Macartney and Hastings, 8 Jan. 1781.
51. Sir G. T. Staunton, op. cit. pp. 259-60, Rev. P. B. Brodie to G. L. Staunton, 3 June 1781.
52. N. Wraxall, op. cit. p. 572.
53. This was Coote's estimate; there was, of course, no way of accurately knowing Haidar's strength.

54. B.L. Add. Mss. 22415/140, G. Proctor to Madras, 13 May 1781.
55. I.O.R. L/P & S/5/537, Sulivan and W. James to Macartney 31 May 1781.
56. P.R.O.N.I. Mic. 407/2, Sulivan to Macartney, 8 Jan. 1781.
57. I.O.R. B/96. 449 & 464-5, Court Book, 14 and 18 Dec. 1780.
58. P.R.O.N.I. D. 572/19/73, T. Allan to Macartney, 6 Feb. 1781.
59. B.L. Add. Mss. 22415/9, Pearse to Madras, 10 June 1781.
60. B.L. Add. Mss. 22415/503, Coote to Macartney, 3 Aug. 1781.
61. See P. Mason, *A Matter of Honour* (London, 1974), pp. 150-54.
62. B.L. Add. Mss. 22415/116, Coote to C. Smith, 2 July 1781.
63. B.L. Add. Mss. 22415/4, Select Committee minute, 22 June 1781.
64. B.L. Add. Mss. 22415/31, Capt. Mackay to Macartney, 29 June 1781; 22415/66, Major Elphinstone to Macartney, 2 July 1781.
65. B.L. Add. Mss. 22415/325, Coote to Lt. Baillie, 19 July 1781.
66. B.L. Add. Mss. 22415/342, Macartney to Coote, 20 July 1781.
67. *Private Correspondence of Lord Macartney,* pp. 167-68, Coote to Macartney, 10 Oct. 1781.
68. Ibid. p. 166, same to same, 10 Oct. 1781; B.L. Add. Mss. 22417/1662, Munro to Macartney, 18 Nov. 1781.
69. *Private Correspondence of Lord Macartney,* p. 126, Macartney to Hastings, 22 May 1782.
70. I.O.R. L/P & S/5/537, Committee of Secrecy to Macartney, 8 Jan. 1781.
71. *Private Correspondence of Lord Macartney,* p. 126, Macartney to Hastings, 22 May 1782.
72. Ibid. p. 39, Macartney to Macpherson, 22 April 1782.
73. Ibid. pp. 88-89, Macpherson to Macartney, 5 July 1782.
74. B.L. Add. Mss. 22418/332, Select Committee minute, 6 Feb. 1782.
75. As 72 above.
76. B.L. Add. Mss. 22416/954, Hastings to Macartney, 11 March 1782 and Select Committee minute, 6 April 1782.
77. *Private Correspondence of Lord Macartney,* pp. 199-202, Macartney to L. Sulivan, 29 Aug. 1781.
78. Ibid. p. 109, Macartney to Hastings, 11 July 1781.
79. P.R.O.N.I. D. 2225/4/55, Hastings to C. Smith, 2 July 1781.
80. *Private Correspondence of Lord Macartney,* pp. 110-14, Macartney to Hastings, 10 Aug. 1781.
81. Ibid. pp. 139-43, Hastings to Macartney, 23 July 1781.
82. Ibid. pp. 116-20, Macartney to Hastings, 26 Sept. 1781.
83. B.L. Add. Mss. 22416/1211, Select Committee minute, 6 Oct. 1781.
84. B.L. Add. Mss. 22417/1756, Select Committee minute, 18 Dec. 1781.
85. P.R.O.N.I. T. 3428, 'A statement of the several assignments of revenue etc. from the Nabob of Arcot to the E. India Co. and of the proceedings had in respect thereof'.
86. B.L. Add. Mss. 22415/673, 'The requests of the Nabob to the Governor General', n.d.
87. B.L. Add. Mss. 22415/690, Nawab's creditors to Hastings, 15 Feb. 1781.
88. B.L. Add. Mss. 22415/690, 'Replies from the Gov.-General to the

requests of the Nabob', 2 April 1781.
89. B.L. Add. Mss. 22416/1211, Select Committee minute, 6 Oct. 1781.
90. B.L. Add. Mss. 22417/1494, Select Committee minute, 6 Nov. 1781.
91. B.L. Add. Mss. 22417/1670, 'Translation of a letter from the Nabob to Lord Macartney', n.d.
92. B.L. Add. Mss. 22417/1669, Select Committee minute, 27 Nov. 1781.
93. B.L. Add. Mss. 22417/1676, Benfield to Macartney, 15 Nov. 1781.
94. B.L. Add. Mss. 22417/1708, Select Committee minute, 4 Dec. 1781.
95. B.L. Add. Mss. 22417/1710, Agreement with the Nawab, 2 Dec. 1781.
96. Bodleian Library, Ms. Eng. Hist. c. 98, Macartney to Ram, Trinchinopoly, 3 Dec. 1781; Macartney to Proctor, Tinnevelly, 5 Dec. 1781.
97. B.L. Add. Mss. 22417/1712, Select Committee minute, 4 Dec. 1781.
98. *Private Correspondence of Lord Macartney,* p. 2, Macartney to Macpherson, 3 Nov. 1781.
99. B.L. Add Mss. 22417/1489, 'Country Inhabitants' to Macartney, n.d. (Nov. 1781).
100. B.L. Add. Mss. 22417/1489, Committee of Works to Macartney, 9 Oct. 1781.
101. Ibid.
102. B.L. Add. Mss. 22417/1479, Plumer to Committee of Works, 9 Oct. 1781.
103. B.L. Add. Mss. 22417/1487, Select Committee minute, 6 Nov. 1781.
104. B.L. Add. Mss. 22417/1489, 1490, Petitions to Macartney from Inhabitants of Madras, n.d.
105. B.L. Add. Mss. 22417/1491, H. Maxwell to Macartney, 6 Nov. 1781.
106. B.L. Add. Mss. 22417/1487, 1492, Select Committee minute, 6 Nov. 1781.
107. B.L. Add. Mss. 22415/9, Pearse to C. Smith, 10 June 1781; Add. Mss. 22415/613, Coote to Macartney, 15 Aug. 1781.
108. Bodleian Library, Ms. Eng. Hist. c. 98, Macartney to Benfield, 7 Dec. 1781.
109. P.R.O.N.I. D. 2225/4/8a, Benfield to Macartney, 8 Dec. 1781.
110. B.L. Add. Mss. 22417/1748, Select Committee minute, 13 Dec. 1781.
111. B.L. Add. Mss. 22417/1795, Select Committee minute, 26 Dec. 1781; Add. Mss. 22417/1816, Benfield to Macartney, 28 Dec. 1781.
112. B.L. Add. Mss. 22417/1816, Select Committee minute, 28 Dec. 1781.
113. B.L. Add. Mss. 22418/133, Select Committee minute, 11 Jan. 1782.
114. *Private Correspondence of Lord Macartney,* pp. 180-84, Macartney to L. Sulivan, 28 Jan. 1782.
115. B.L. Add. Mss. 22462, f. 18, Macartney to T. Coutts, 8 Aug. 1782.
116. B.L. Add. Mss. 22418/200, Wheler and Macpherson to Macartney, 26 Dec. 1781.
117. *Private Correspondence of Lord Macartney,* pp. 177-78, Macartney to Robinson, 12 Jan. 1782.
118. Ibid. pp. 180-86, Macartney to Sulivan and others, 28 Jan. 1782.
119. Ibid. pp. 24-27, Macartney to Macpherson, 21 Jan. and 3 Feb. 1782.
120. Ibid. pp. 85-86, Macpherson to Macartney, 7 Feb. 1782.
121. Ibid. pp. 149-50, Staunton to Macartney, 27 Feb. 1782.
122. Ibid. p. 151, same to same, 4 March, 1782.

123. B.L. Add. Mss. 22418/385, Select Committee minute, 8 Feb. 1782.
124. A. T. Mahan, *The Influence of Sea Power upon History* (London, 1890), p. 433.
125. Ibid. p. 456.
126. *Private Correspondence of Lord Macartney,* pp. 29-30, Macartney to Macpherson, 26 Feb. 1782.
127. Ibid. pp. 36-37, same to same, 20 April 1782.
128. Ibid. p. 32, same to same, 2 March 1782.
129. B.L. Add. Mss. 22418/323, Select Committee minute, 6 Feb. 1782.
130. B.L. Add. Mss. 22418/474, Select Committee minute, 21 Feb. 1782.
131. P.R.O.N.I. Mic. 407/4, Macartney to the Nawab, 21 Feb. 1782.
132. B.L. Add. Mss. 22419/773, Nawab to Macartney, 19 March 1782.
133. B.L. Add. Mss. 22419/922, Select Committee minute, 3 April 1782.
134. B.L. Add. Mss. 22419/1084, Memorandum by D. Haliburton, 17 April 1782.
135. B.L. Add. Mss. 22149/1080, Nawab to Select Committee, 17 April 1782.
136. B.L. Add. Mss. 22419/1087, Select Committee minute, 17 April 1782.
137. P.R.O.N.I. T. 3428, Hastings to Macartney, 5 April 1782.
138. Ibid.
139. H. Dodwell, *Warren Hastings' Letters to Sir John Macpherson* (London, 1927), pp. 165, 156, Hastings to Macpherson, 8 Oct. and 'July' 1782.
140. C. H. Philips & B. B. Misra, eds. *Fort William — India House Correspondence,* XV, *Foreign and Secret, 1782-86* (Delhi, 1963), pp.140-48, Hastings to E. India Co., 15 July 1782.
141. *Private Correspondence of Lord Macartney,* pp. 188-94, Macartney to Staunton, 20 March 1782.
142. Ibid. pp. 69-72, Macpherson to Macartney, 3 April 1781.
143. As 141 above.
144. P.R.O.N.I. T. 3428, 'A statement of the several assignments of revenue etc. from the Nabob of Arcot . . .', Appendix.
145. P.R.O.N.I. T. 3428, Hastings to Macartney, 19 Oct. 1782.
146. P.R.O.N.I. T. 3428, 'A statement . . .', statements of Coote and others.
147. P.R.O.N.I. T. 3428, 'A statement . . .'.
148. P.R.O.N.I. T. 3428, Court of Directors to Macartney, 12 July 1782; Committee of Secrecy to Macartney, 15 Sept. 1782.
149. P.R.O.N.I. T. 3428, 'A statement . . .'.
150. P.R.O.N.I. D. 607/B/119, Dunkin to Lord Hillsborough, 29 Sept. 1783.
151. *Private Correspondence of Lord Macartney,* pp. 215-17, Macartney to Dunkin, 30 April 1783.
152. Philips & Misra, eds. op. cit. pp. 188-203, Hastings to E. India Co., 20 Oct. 1783.
153. As 85 above.
154. P.R.O.N.I. D. 2225/4/29, 'Operations of the Army while under the command of Major General James Stuart.'
155. Sir G. T. Staunton, op. cit. pp. 272-77, 'Relation of the arrest of Major General Stuart'.

156. Bodleian Library, Ms. Eng. Hist. c. 77, Macartney to Hastings, 22 Sept. 1783.
157. Bodleian Library, Ms. Eng. Hist. b. 176, Burgoyne to Macartney, 17 Sept. 1783.
158. As 155 above.
159. Bodleian Library, Ms. Eng. Hist. c. 77, Macartney to Hastings, 22 Sept. 1783; Ms. Eng. Hist. c. 101, Macartney to Burgoyne, 20 Sept. 1783.
160. Bodleian Library, Ms. Eng. Hist. b. 176, 'State of charges against Sir John Burgoyne'.
161. Bodleian Library, Ms. Eng. Hist. b. 176, Proceedings of Burgoyne's court martial.
162. Bodleian Library, Ms. Eng. Hist. b. 176, Sir C. Gould, Horse Guards, to Burgoyne, 14 Jan. 1786.
163. Bodleian Library, Ms. Eng. Hist. b. 176, E. India Co. to Lord Sydney, 18 March 1786.
164. B.L. Add. Mss. 22416/1135, Coote to Macartney, 26 Sept. 1781.
165. Bodleian Library, Ms. Eng. Hist. c. 77, Hastings to Macartney, 30 Aug. 1783.
166. Bodleian Library, Ms. Eng. Hist. c. 104, Macartney to Boddam, Bombay, 7 Feb. 1784; Philips & Misra, eds. op. cit. pp. 206-12, Hastings to E. India Co., 30 Nov. 1783.
167. Bodleian Library, Ms. Eng. Hist. c. 77, Hastings to Macartney, 30 Aug. 1783.
168. Bodleian Library, Ms. Eng. Hist. c. 77, Macartney to Hastings, 14 Oct. 1783.
169. Philips & Misra, eds. op. cit. pp. 204-6, Hastings to E. India Co., 25 Nov. 1783.
170. Bodleian Library, Ms. Eng. Hist. c. 104, Macartney to Staunton, 9 Feb. 1784.
171. Bodleian Library, Ms. Eng. Hist. c. 104, same to same, 22 Feb. 1784.
172. B.L. Add. Mss. 22433/747, Treaty of Mangalore.
173. B.L. Add. Mss. 22435/1072, Bengal Council to Macartney, 8 June 1784.
174. B.L. Add. Mss. 22435/2053, Select Committee minute, 15 July 1784.
175. B.L. Add. Mss. 22435/2210, Select Committee minute, 31 July 1784.
176. Bodleian Library, Ms. Eng. Hist. c. 79, Bengal Council to Macartney, 2 Sept. 1784.
177. Sir G. T. Staunton, op. cit. pp. 296-97, Macartney to Fox and others, 28 July 1784.
178. H. Furber, ed. *The Correspondence of Edmund Burke*, V (Cambridge, 1965), pp. 206-12, Burke to Staunton, 21 Jan., 27 Feb. and 15 June 1785.
179. *The Works of the Rt. Hon. Edmund Burke*, Appendix 9, Board of Control to Macartney, 15 Oct. 1784.
180. Ibid. p. 268.
181. Ibid. p. 308.
182. B.L. Add. Mss. 22437/3353, E. India Co. Officers to Macartney, 6 Dec. 1784.

183. *Private Correspondence of Lord Macartney,* pp. 213-14, Macartney to Lord Ossory, 31 Jan. 1783.
184. P.R.O.N.I. D. 572/19/87, Allan to Macartney, 3 July 1782.
185. B.L. Add. Mss. 22461, Macartney to Mercer, 30 March 1785.
186. B.L. Add. Mss. 22438, Select Committee minute, 28 May 1785.
187. B.L. Add. Mss. 22438, Select Committee minute, 1 June 1785; *Private Correspondence of Lord Macartney,* pp. 227-28, Macartney to Dunkin, 14 Oct. 1784.
188. B.L. Add. Mss. 22461, Macartney to Davidson, 7 June 1785.
189. B.L. Add. Mss. 22461, same to same, 21 June 1785.
190. P.R.O.N.I. D. 2225/4/48, Macpherson to Macartney, 15 June 1785; B.L. Add. Mss. 22461, Macartney to Davidson, 21 June 1785.
191. Bodleian Library, Ms. Eng. Hist. c. 81, Macartney to Macpherson, 20 June 1785.
192. Bodleian Library, Ms. Eng. Hist. c. 81, Proceedings of Gov. General's Council, 28 June 1785.
193. Bodleian Library, Ms. Eng. Hist. c. 82, Macartney to Macpherson, 13 Aug. 1785.
194. C. Ross, ed. *Correspondence of Charles, First Marquis Cornwallis,* I (London, 1859), pp. 147-48, 184-85, Cornwallis to Lt. Col. Ross, 26 Oct. 1783, 23 Feb. 1785.
195. P.R.O.N.I. D. 572/19/119, Anon. to Macartney, 24 Dec. 1784.
196. P.R.O.N.I. D. 572/19/129, Anon., letter, n.d.
197. P.R.O.N.I. D. 2225/4/43, E. India Co. Directors to Macartney, 23 March 1785.
198. Bodleian Library, Ms. Eng. Hist. c. 82, Macartney to Macpherson, 13 Aug. 1785.
199. P.R.O.N.I. D. 572/19/133, 'Minutes of conversation between Lord Macartney and the Chairman and Deputy-Chairman of the E. India Co.', 13 Jan. 1786.
200. P.R.O.N.I. D. 572/19/129, Memorandum by anon. n.d.
201. P.R.O.N.I. D. 572/20/19, Macartney to Bute, 27 Feb. 1786.
202. A. Aspinall, ed. *The Later Correspondence of George III,* I (Cambridge, 1962), pp. 206-7, George III to Lord Sydney, 10 Jan. 1786.
203. Ibid. pp. 207-8, George III to Pitt, 14 Jan. 1786.
204. P.R.O.N.I. D. 572/20/19, Macartney to Bute, 27 Feb. 1786.
205. Ibid.
206. See below, pp. 267-277; 'The Letters of John Johnston', *Ulster Genealogical and Historical Guild Newsletter,* I, no. 7 (1981), p. 223, Johnston to H.R. Schoolcraft, 19 Jan. 1828.
207. Bodleian Library, Ms. Eng. Hist. c. 117, 'A statement of the benefits derived from my government of Madras'.

CHAPTER SEVEN   CHINA 1792-94

1. For a translation of the edict, see H. B. Morse, *The Chronicles of the East India Company Trading to China 1635-1834* (Oxford, 1926-9), V, 94-98 (hereafter *Chronicles*). For an account of the formalising of the system between 1750 and 1760, see E. H. Pritchard, *The Crucial Years of Early Anglo-Chinese Relations 1750-1800* (Pullman, 1936)

(hereafter *Crucial Years*). This study provides the best general background account to the Macartney embassy. For an account of the embassy in relation to the overseas expansion of Britain, see V. Harlow, *The Founding of the Second British Empire 1763-93* (London, 1964), II, 527-94.

2. This term is usually applied to the trade which grew up between India, south-east Asia and China. The East India Company took part in this trade indirectly when it granted private merchants in India licences to trade at Canton. See M. Greenberg, *British Trade and the Opening of China 1800-42* (Cambridge, 1951), pp. 10-13 and index.

3. For details of this embassy see Pritchard, *Crucial Years,* pp. 236-71. The preparations made for the Cathcart mission had a direct influence on the preparations for Macartney's subsequent embassy.

4. Sir G. T. Staunton, *Memoir of the Life and Family of the Late Sir G. L. Staunton, Bart.* (London, 1823), pp. 337-38, as quoted in Pritchard, *Crucial Years,* p. 274.

5. Pritchard, *Crucial Years,* p. 275; Macartney Correspondence in the Wason Collection on China and the Chinese, Cornell University, Ithaca, New York (hereafter CMC), No. 22.

6. Pritchard, *Crucial Years,* pp. 277, 282; India Office, China, Lord Macartney's Embassy (hereafter IOCM), vo. 91, 57-59, 87-92.

7. Pritchard, *Crucial Years,* pp. 294-95; CMC, Nos. 40-42, 50, 56, 61, 64, 97-99.

8. Pritchard, *Crucial Years,* pp. 294-95; CMC, Nos. 131, 144; IOCM, vol. 91, 277-78, 281-83.

9. J. L. Cranmer-Byng, *An Embassy to China: being the journal kept by Lord Macartney during his embassy* (London, 1962), pp. 23-24, 307-20 (hereafter Cranmer-Byng, *Embassy*).

10. Pritchard, *Crucial Years,* pp. 295-96; also Cranmer-Byng, *Embassy,* pp. 105, 360 n. 12, 365, n. 25.

11. Cranmer-Byng, *Embassy,* pp. 54, 310, 377, n. 64.

12. J. L. Cranmer-Byng & T. Levere, 'A Case Study in Cultural Collision: Scientific Apparatus in the Macartney Embassy to China, 1793', *Annals of Science,* XXXVIII (1981), 503-25.

13. The full text of the government instructions is printed in Morse, *Chronicles,* II, 232-42. They are summarized in Pritchard, *Crucial Years,* pp. 307-11. For the instructions from the East India Company, see E. H. Pritchard, 'The Instructions of the East India Company to Lord Macartney on his Embassy to China and his Reports to the Company 1792-94', *Journal of the Royal Asiatic Society of Gt. Britain and Ireland,* 1938, Parts 2, 3, 4, 201-4, 375-96, 493-509. For the wider objects of the embassy concerning trade with Japan, Annam and other places, see A. Lamb, 'Lord Macartney in Batavia, March 1793', *Journal of the South Seas Society,* XIV, 57-68.

14. Throughout this chapter I have used the word 'barbarian' to translate the Chinese word *i.* In the Chinese world view, barbarians did not understand 'the way of the sages', though they might learn to do so by being transformed by China's cultural influence. I have deliberately avoided using the word 'foreigner' since it is saturated with modern,

western judgement-values based on a system of national states which is alien to the whole Chinese imperial tradition. On the Chinese terms for 'barbarian', see J. K. Fairbank, ed. *The Chinese World Order : Traditional China's Foreign Relations* (Harvard, 1968), pp. 1-10.

15. These are stock phrases occurring regularly in the official documents of the Macartney embassy and, indeed, in Chinese documents concerning relations with barbarian peoples long before and long after that event. A selection of the more important Chinese documents concerning the Macartney embassy in full or partial translation can be found in J. L. Cranmer-Byng, 'Lord Macartney's Embassy to Peking in 1793, from Official Chinese Documents', *Journal of Oriental Studies*, IV, nos. 1-2 (1957-58), 117-187.

16. This is an oversimplified account of a complex subject and does not indicate that during the eighteenth century a regulated trade took place with European maritime countries through the port of Canton without requiring tribute embassies. See J. K. Fairbank and S. Y. Teng, 'On the Ch'ing Tributary System' in their *Ch'ing Administration : Three Studies* (Harvard, 1960), pp. 107-218. Also J. L. Cranmer-Byng and J. E. Wills, Jr. 'Trade and Diplomacy with Maritime Europe, 1644-1800', in *The Cambridge History of China*, Vol. IX, Pt. 1 (in press), where a modified interpretation of the interrelation of trade and diplomacy in this period is put forward.

17. Cranmer-Byng, *Embassy*, p. 278. From indications scattered through the Macartney papers concerning the China embassy, and in the journal, it seems likely that Macartney read, among other works, the following: *Lettres édifiantes et curieuses écrites des missions étrangères*, 26 vols. (Paris, 1780-83); *Mémoires concernant l'Histoire, les Sciences, les Moeurs, les Usages etc., des Chinois, par les missionaires de Pékin*, 15 vols. (Paris, 1776-91); du Halde, *Description Géographique, Historique, Chronologique, Politique et Physique de l'Empire de la Chine et de la Tartarie Chinoise*, 4 vols. (Paris, 1735); J. de Mialla, *Histoire Générale de la Chine*, 12 vols. (Paris, 1777-83); Abbé Grosier, *Description Générale de la Chine* (Paris, 1785); J. Bell, *Travels from St. Petersburg in Russia to Diverse Parts of Asia*, 2 vols. (Glasgow, 1763).

18. Now known as Danang Bay. It is situated on the coast of Vietnam, a little south of Hué. Cranmer-Byng, *Embassy*, pp. 208-9.

19. The manuscript of the journal of the outward voyage is preserved in the Wellcome Historical Medical Library in London. The manuscript of the China journal is preserved in the Tōyō Bunko (The Oriental Library) in Tokyo. It contains two copies of the 'Observations'. In November 1962 a second copy of the China journal, on paper watermarked 1803, was sold at Hodgson's, and is now in the collection of Mr. James M. Osborn in the Beinecke Rare Book and Manuscript Library at Yale University. For a note on the transmission of the MS of the journal, see Cranmer-Byng, *Embassy*, pp. 332-34.

20. Ibid. p. 86.

21. Ibid. p. 199, footnote. For further comment on the composition, content and value of Macartney's China journal, see 'Introduction' to

Cranmer-Byng, *Embassy*, pp. 38-58. My reasons for modernising the spelling throughout the journal are given in the 'Preface' to ibid. p. xii.

22. While at Macao one of the interpreters, Paolo Cho, 'suddenly took fright, and was so impressed with an apprehension of the government at Peking that he could not be persuaded to proceed with us'. Cranmer-Byng, *Embassy*, p. 64

23. Safe navigation through the Yellow Sea was the main problem which now faced Capt. Gower in the *Lion*. European navigational experience of the coast of China from the Bay of Hangchow to the Gulf of Chihli was non-existent at that time, and Capt. Gower and his officers kept detailed observations which were of value to later ships sailing in that area. Macartney, in his journal for 9 December, stated that the Emperor disapproved of his sailing direct to the Gulf of Chihli, but added: 'nevertheless, I would not for any consideration that we had not, as by these means we are now masters of the geography of the north-east coasts of China, and have acquired a knowledge of the Yellow Sea, which was never before navigated by European ships'.

24. For my reasons for making these identifications, see Cranmer-Byng, *Embassy*, pp. 325-31, where I have given brief biographies of both these officials.

25. For Alexander's drawings and MS. journal, see ibid. pp. 314-16, 342-43; also M. Archer, 'From Cathay to China: the Drawings of William Alexander 1792-94', *History Today*, XII, no. 12 (Dec. 1962), 864-71.

26. Cranmer-Byng, *Embassy*, p. 74.

27. Ibid. pp. 74-76; for Liang's career, see p. 356, n. 4.

28. Ibid. p. 77.

29. Ibid. p. 78.

30. See ibid. pp. 322-25 for a brief biography.

31. Cranmer-Byng, 'Macartney's Embassy from Official Chinese Documents', p. 155.

32. For a detailed description of the presents, see Cranmer-Byng, *Embassy*, pp. 360-61, n. 12.

33. Macartney had, in fact, been made a Privy Councillor in May 1792. See below, pp. 291-92.

34. Cranmer-Byng, 'Macartney's Embassy from Official Chinese Documents', pp. 140-41.

35. Ibid. pp. 144-45.

36. The full kotow ceremony consisted of kneeling down and then falling prostrate on the ground, followed by knocking the ground three times with the forehead, then rising up onto the knees and feet, the whole performance being repeated until one had completed three kneelings and nine knockings of the head. The ceremony was normally carried out to the commands of a court usher in company with others performing the kotow. It therefore required rehearsing. See E. H. Pritchard, 'The Kotow in the Macartney Embassy to China in 1793', *Far Eastern Quarterly*, II, no. 2 (1943), 163-203.

37. Cranmer-Byng, *Embassy*, p. 82.

38. Ibid. p. 85.

39. Ibid. p. 87. This passage was quoted by Charles Taylor, correspondent of the *Toronto Globe and Mail* in Peking (1964-65), in his book *Reporter in Red China* (Toronto, 1966), p. 22 to describe the way in which the authorities in China in 1965 dealt with requests from foreign diplomats, reporters, businessmen and visitors which they had no intention of granting. For Macartney's remarks on Chinese ideas of truthfulness, see Cranmer-Byng, *Embassy,* pp. 90, 223.
40. Ibid. pp. 87-88.
41. Ibid. pp. 86-87. For the Chinese campaign against the invading Gurkhas in Tibet during the years 1791-92, see ibid. pp. 362-63, n. 18.
42. Ibid. p. 88.
43. Ibid. p. 194; see also p. 82.
44. For the Summer Palace, see Cranmer-Byng, *Embassy,* p. 359, n. 11.
45. Ibid. p. 98.
46. Cranmer-Byng, 'Macartney's Embassy from Official Chinese Documents', p. 149.
47. Ibid. p. 149.
48. Cranmer-Byng, *Embassy,* pp. 104-5. But the mandarins appear to have attended more out of curiosity than genuine interest, and most of them viewed scientific and technical objects with stolid indifference. See the remarks by Dr. Dinwiddie quoted in ibid. p. 54.
49. Ibid. p. 106.
50. The quotation is given in ibid. pp. 40-41. See also William Alexander's regret at not being included in the party going to Jehol and that he would, therefore, miss seeing the Great Wall. Ibid. p. 342.
51. Ibid. p. 113. On the return journey Macartney recorded that the gap in the wall had been closed and that they were unable to climb onto it.
52. Ibid. pp. 115-16. Macartney's escort consisted of a military guard of forty-three, ten servants, four musicians, six gentlemen, with Sir George Staunton, his son and Macartney riding in a chariot.
53. Ibid. p. 117.
54. Cranmer-Byng, 'Macartney's Embassy from Official Chinese Documents', p. 133. The final version was promulgated on 23 September and handed to Macartney on 3 October.
55. Cranmer-Byng, *Embassy,* p. 119. This episode also gives an insight into the attitude of the English Court at that time and of the ambassador who represented it. However, the question of the kotow ceremony in the Macartney embassy was not to end so easily. It was revived again in 1816 when Lord Amherst went to Peking and was firmly told by the Chinese officials that Macartney had performed the full kotow in spite of the fact that Sir George Thomas Staunton, who had been present at the audience in 1793 as Macartney's page, was a member of Lord Amherst's embassy. For a very careful weighing of the historical evidence, see Pritchard, 'The Kotow', pp. 163-203.
56. Cranmer-Byng, 'Macartney's Embassy from Official Chinese Documents', pp. 158-59.
57. Cranmer-Byng, *Embassy,* pp. 120-21.
58. Ibid. pp. 122-24.
59. In fact he celebrated his eighty-third birthday four days after the

audience. He was born on 25 September 1711 and died in 1799. He reigned from 1736 to 1796, abdicating in that year rather than exceeding sixty years in office, which was the length of the reign of his eminent grandfather, K'ang-hsi.

60. Cranmer-Byng, 'Macartney's Embassy from Official Chinese Documents', p. 163. Ch'ien-lung's 'poem', which is of no great literary merit, is translated in Cranmer-Byng, *Embassy*, p. x.

61. Cranmer-Byng, *Embassy*, pp. 124-29.

62. Ibid. p. 128. This explanation is not very convincing. Fu-k'ang-an had been Governor General of the provinces of Kwangtung and Kwangsi from 1789 until 1791, but in this exalted position he is unlikely to have had any direct dealings with the East India Company's representatives at Canton. At this time the Governor General of the two Kwangs had his official office at Chao-ch'ing, only maintained a 'flying office' at Canton, and in any case barbarian merchants and ships' captains were not allowed inside the city of Canton and could only petition through the Hong merchants. His hostility is more likely to have arisen from his experiences in Tibet. Ibid. pp. 362-63, n. 18.

63. Ibid. p. 129.

64. Ibid. p. 283.

65. Ibid. p. 131.

66. See E. de Selincourt, ed. *The Prelude* (Oxford, 1926), Book 8, p. 266 (1805-6 edn.), p. 267 (1850 edn.), and editor's note on p. 550. Here Wordsworth was drawing on Macartney's description of both the eastern and western parts of the gardens at Jehol, as quoted by J. Barrow, *Travels in China* (London, 1804), pp. 127-33. Barrow did not always quote accurately from Macartney's journal.

67. Cranmer-Byng, *Embassy*, pp. 136-40.

68. Ibid. pp. 144-45.

69. Ibid. pp. 147-48.

70. Ibid. pp. 149-50.

71. Ibid. p. 150.

72. Ibid. The full text of the requests is given in enclosure 12 to Macartney's despatch to Dundas of 9 Nov. 1793, and can be found in E. H. Pritchard, 'Letters from Missionaries at Peking relating to the Macartney Embassy, 1793-1803', *T'oung Pao*, XXXI(1934), 25-27.

73. Cranmer-Byng, *Embassy*, p. 154.

74. Ch'ang-lin, a Manchu of the Imperial clan, at this time Governor of Chekiang. See ibid. p. 373, n. 51 and p. 374, n. 56.

75. Cranmer-Byng, 'Macartney's Embassy from Official Chinese Documents', pp. 167-68.

76. Cranmer-Byng, *Embassy*, pp. 155-56.

77. See D. S. Nivison, 'Ho-shen and His Accusers' in Nivison & A. F. Wright, eds. *Confucianism in Action* (Stanford, 1959), pp. 209-43. The relevant Chinese documents are given in translation in Sir G. T. Staunton, *Ta Tsing Leu Lee* (London, 1810), pp. 498-502.

78. Cranmer-Byng, *Embassy*, pp. 197-200, 378 n. 68.

79. Ibid. p. 187, entry for 24 Nov. 1793.

80. Ibid. p. 181. There were eleven articles in all. See Pritchard, *Crucial Years*, p. 357, and Morse, *Chronicles*, II, 252-53.

81. Cranmer-Byng, *Embassy,* pp. 190-91, 376 n. 63.
82. Ibid. p. 210, beginning eight lines from the end of the page to the middle of p. 215.
83. Ibid. pp. 212-13. China was very nearly dashed to pieces during the Taiping Rebellion (1851-64), which climaxed more than fifty years of unrest and sporadic rebellion. An attempt to rebuild her on the old foundations, known as the T'ung-chih Restoration (1861-74), and the subsequent attempts at 'self-strengthening', both failed and the dynasty succumbed in the Revolution of 1911, and was succeeded by a Republic.
84. Ibid. pp. 219-20.
85. Ibid. pp. 336-41, where it is printed in full; also Cranmer-Byng, 'Macartney's Embassy from Official Chinese Documents', pp. 133-37.
86. For Macartney's description of precious articles of European manufacture, especially clockwork articles, 'singsongs' as they were called in the Canton trade, see Cranmer-Byng, *Embassy,* pp. 125-26, 355 n. 1.
87. Tin was widely used. Macartney mentions some of its uses in the 'Observations' to his journal and states that it was chiefly used in offerings at altars and in funeral ceremonies. Paper money containing thin strips of tin is still scattered at Chinese funerals in Hong Kong and Singapore for the use of the deceased in the next world.
88. E. Backhouse & J. O. P. Bland, *Annals and Memoirs of the Court of Peking from the 16th to the 20th Century* (London, 1913), pp. 322-34. The authors do not state from which collection of Chinese documents they made their version. It is more in the nature of a paraphrase than a close translation, so that Chinese ideas are sometimes made to fit too neatly into English conceptions and phrases. Sir Edmund Backhouse had considerable ability as a translator of Chinese documents. How ever, his creative abilities as a forger of English translations of spurious Chinese documents should alert scholars to examine carefully the accuracy of his translations from genuine Chinese documents. For a sustained piece of literary detective work, see his biography by H. Trevor-Roper, *Hermit of Peking : the Enigma of Sir Edmund Backhouse* (London, 1976).
89. Morse, *Chronicles,* II, 247-52 prints a version translated from the Latin translation which had been made from the Chinese by Fr. Nicholas-Joseph Raux and Fr. Louis de Poirot. However, as Poirot admitted in a letter to Macartney, they were accustomed to modify certain expressions while translating from the Chinese so as not to offend European feelings. The text of his letter is in Pritchard, 'Letters from Missionaries', pp. 39-43.
90. What follows is based on my own unpublished translation of the full text of the Chinese original.

CHAPTER EIGHT   VERONA 1795-96

1. I gratefully acknowledge the agreement of the Editor, *Bulletin of the John Rylands University Library of Manchester* (Dr. Frank Taylor, F.S.A.) that I should publish here in shorter form the substance of my article, 'The Mirage of Restoration: Louis XVIII and Lord Macartney, 1795-6', *Bulletin,* Autumn 1979, pp. 87-114 and Spring 1980, pp. 388-422.
2. H. H. Robbins, *Our First Ambassador to China* (London, 1908), pp. 413-14.
3. P.R.O. F.O. 27/45, Macartney to Grenville, 12 Aug. 1795; cf. H. H.

Robbins, op. cit. p. 417.
4. B.L. Add. Mss. 36811, f. 41, Macartney to Lord Bute, 6 Aug. 1795; cf. W. L. Clements Library, Ann Arbor, Michigan, Macartney Papers, Macartney to Dundas, 14 July 1795. I gratefully acknowledge the assistance of the Curator of Manuscripts, W. L. Clements Library.
5. W. L. Clements Library, Macartney to Dundas, 14 July 1795. In regard to the question of a British peerage, see P.R.O.N.I. D. 572/19/129, Friends of Macartney to Pitt, Dec. 1785. On his 'private' mission to Verona as not 'lucrative', see Yale University, J. M. Osborn Collection, Macartney Papers, no. 124, Macartney to Sir G. Staunton, 20 Dec. 1795. What, at all events, *was* Macartney's remuneration at Verona? The Editor rightly urged this question; but I am advised by the Search Department, P.R.O., after their thorough investigation, that an early 'taking out' of Treasury Paper 2569, 29 June 1796, has removed their only means of answering it.
6. P.R.O.N.I. D. 572/6/1, 2, 4, Alberto Albertini to Macartney, 23 June and 12 May 1796, 1 June 1797.
7. W. L. Clements Library, Macartney to Dundas, 14 July 1795; P.R.O. F.O. 27/45, Macartney to Grenville, 29 July and 10 Aug. 1795; B.L. Add. Mss. 36811, f. 41, Macartney to Bute, 6 Aug. 1795.
8. J. Godechot, *La Contre-Révolution* (Paris, 1961); E. Daudet, *Histoire de l'Emigration* (3rd edn. Paris, 1907); P. de la Gorce, *Louis XVIII* (Paris, 1926); A. Righi, *Il Conte de Lilla* (Comte de Lille = Louis XVIII) *e l'emigrazione francese a Verona, 1794-6* (1909). Louis was eighteen years younger than Macartney.
9. Royal *Declaration, London Gazette,* 29 Oct. 1793; Foreign Secretary's Instructions to William Wickham, for special mission to the Swiss Cantons (really to do with French affairs), 1794, W. Wickham, *Correspondence of William Wickham,* (London, 1870), I, 9f. P.R.O. F.O. 27/44, Grenville to Harcourt, 22 June 1795.
10. Sir A. Ward & G. P. Gooch, eds. *Cambridge History of British Foreign Policy,* I (Cambridge, 1922), 260ff; P.R.O. F.O. 27/44, Grenville to Harcourt, 18 Dec. 1795.
11. B.L. Add. Mss. 37846, Grenville to Windham, 5 Feb. 1797.
12. Instructions to Wickham, as in 9 above.
13. P.R.O. F.O. 27/45, Grenville to Macartney, 8 Sept. 1795.
14. W. R. Fryer, *Republic or Restoration in France? 1794-97* (Manchester, 1965); 'The Mirage of Restoration', pp. 90-91.
15. Instructions to Wickham, as in 9 above; P.R.O. F.O. 27/45, Instructions to Macartney, 10 July, 1795; cf. Yale University, J. M. Osborn Collection, Macartney Papers, no. 125, Macartney to Sir G. Staunton, 10 Jan. 1796 (with acknowledgements to the Curators of the Collection).
16. W. R. Fryer, *Republic or Restoration?*, Chapt. 1; 'The Mirage of Restoration', pp. 92-94.
17. W. R. Fryer, 'The Mirage of Restoration', pp. 94-95.
18. See P.R.O. F.O. 27/45, Macartney to Grenville, 27 Sept. 1795.
19. P.R.O. F.O. 27/45, Macartney to Grenville, 12 Aug. 1795.
20. Ibid. same to same, 27 Sept. 1795.
21. Ibid. same to same, 27 Sept. and 10 Dec. 1795.
22. Ibid. same to same, 8 Feb. 1796, 12 Aug. 1795.
23. Ibid. same to same, 27 Sept. 1795.
24. Ibid. same to same, 8 Feb. 1796.

25. Ibid. same to same, 27 Sept. 1795, 8 Feb. 1796.
26. Yale University, J. M. Osborn Collection, Macartney Papers, no. 125, Macartney to Sir G. Staunton, 10 Jan. 1796.
27. P.R.O.N.I. D. 572/21/72, 83 Louis XVIII to Macartney, 18 June 1796, 19 Dec. 1799; A. de Barante, *Lettres et Instructions de Louis XVIII au Cte. de St-Priest* (Paris, 1845), p. 91.
28. P.R.O. F.O. 27/45, Macartney to Grenville, 12 Aug. 1795.
29. Ibid. same to same, 27 and 30 Sept. and 9 Dec. 1795; further on the French Royal debts, see P.R.O. F.O. 27/44, especially Artois to Harcourt, 3 May 1795, and F.O. 27/45, Macartney to Grenville, 12 Aug. 1795; on the Army of Condé, see R. Bittard des Portes, *Histoire de l'Armée de Condé* (Paris, 1896).
30. B.L. Add. Mss. 37876, XXXV, f. 100, Memorandum, n.d.; H. Mitchell, *The Underground War against Revolutionary France* (Oxford, 1965), pp.53-58.
31. P.R.O. F.O. 27/45, Macartney to Grenville, 27 Sept. 1795.
32. Ibid. same to same, 12 Aug. 1795; F.O. 27/44, Louis XVIII to George III, 14 Aug. 1795. Macartney had been instructed to proffer not more than £10,000; he held back the remaining £2,000, in case the exiled Court later needed this small 'uncovenanted mercy' — as it did, when abruptly ejected from Verona in April 1796. See below, pp. 264-65.
33. P.R.O.N.I. D. 572/17/3, Col. Charles (Gregan-) Crauford, British representative with Condé, to Macartney, 24 Aug. 1795; for the effect of this on Marshal de Castries, see Daudet, *Histoire de l'Emigration,* I, 288-89.
34. P.R.O. F.O. 27/45, Macartney to Grenville, 8 Feb. 1796. *Cordons bleus,* chevaliers du Saint- Esprit (1578-); *cordon rouge,* grand' croix (or commandeur) de Saint-Louis (1693-); *Mont-Carmel* and *St.-Lazare,* grand' croix de ces Ordres de chevalerie militaire et religieuse; *Croix de St.-Louis,* simples chevaliers de St.-Louis. See M. Marion, *Dictionaire des Institutions de la France* (Paris, 1923), pp. 410-11.
35. On these, see *Dict. de biographie française,* or Robinet and others, *Dict. hist. et biograph. de la Révolution et de l'Empire* (Paris, 1899).
36. P.R.O. F.O. 27/45, Macartney to Grenville, 12 Aug., 28 Sept. and 8 Nov. 1795 — the Earl did not mention the Marshal's disagreement with Louis about the *Gardes du Corps,* the main reason for the Marshal's resignation; on Arras, see ibid. same to same, 16 Nov. 1795 (but cf. 9 Dec. 1795); cf. again however P.R.O.N.I. D. 572/17/95, T. Jackson, Turin, to Macartney, 31 Aug. 1795, which cannot have improved Macartney's opinion of the Bishop.
37. P.R.O. F.O. 27/45, Macartney to Grenville, 8 Nov. and 9 Dec. 1795. La Vauguyon and St.-Priest were very different men, but were both prominent in (inevitably) anti-English diplomatic developments after the War of American Independence.
38. W. R. Fryer, *Republic or Restoration?*, pp. 171-85.
39. Louis had indeed summoned St.-Priest; but the latter turned aside en route to solicit more strenuous aid from St. Petersburg and Vienna. See Barante, op. cit. pp. clxxv-cxv and 2-18.
40. P.R.O. F.O. 27/45, Macartney to Grenville, 12 Aug., 27 Sept. and 15 Nov. 1795.
41. Ibid. same to same, 22 April 1796; P.R.O.N.I. D. 572/13/15, A. Carlotti to Macartney, 11 May 1796; D. 572/21/73, Comte

d'Avaray to Macartney, 20 June 1796; D. 572/21/79, Macartney to Comte d'Avaray, 25 July 1796.

42. Sir N. Henderson, *Failure of a Mission : Berlin, 1937-39* (London, 1940).
43. P.R.O. F.O. 27/45, Grenville to Macartney, 8 Sept. 1795.
44. Ibid. Macartney to Grenville, 12 Aug. 1795. Louis thought the draft declaration from Grenville 'pitoyable' — Barante, op. cit. p. 91. For his masterly defence of his own declaration, see ibid. pp. 78-87.
45. W. R. Fryer, *Republic or Restoration?*, pp. 15-16, 25; P.R.O. F.O. 27/45, Macartney to Grenville, 18 Oct. 1795.
46. P.R.O. F.O. 27/45, Macartney to Grenville, 27 Sept. 1795; Macartney to Wickham, in W. Wickham, op. cit. I, 195-96; W. R. Fryer, 'The Mirage of Restoration', pp. 391-92; F.O. 27/45, Macartney to Grenville, 15 and 16 Nov. 1795.
47. P.R.O. F.O. 27/45, Macartney to Grenville, 18 Oct. 1795.
48. Ibid. Grenville to Macartney, 8 Sept. 1795.
49. Ibid. Macartney to Grenville, 12 Aug. 1795; cf. same to same, 15 Nov. 1795.
50. P.R.O. F.O. 27/44, Harcourt to Grenville, endorsed by Grenville 'June 26' 1795.
51. P.R.O. F.O. 27/45, Macartney to Grenville, 12 Aug. 1795. Field-Marshal Count Clerfayt, Commander-in-Chief, Austrian forces, Upper Rhine.
52. Ibid. same to same, 23 Aug. and 15 Nov. 1795.
53. Ibid. same to same, 12 Aug. 1795.
54. Ibid. Grenville to Macartney, 8 Sept. 1795; cf. F.O. 27/44, Louis XVIII to George III, 14 Aug. 1795.
55. P.R.O. F.O. 27/45, Macartney to Grenville, 10 and 28 Sept. 1795.
56. Ibid. same to same, 7 Oct. 1795. Was Louis jealous of his brother? Cf. F.O. 27/44, Louis to Harcourt, 28 Sept. 1795; but for their *entourages*, see W. R. Fryer, *Republic or Restoration?*, pp. 70-71.
57. P.R.O. F.O. 27/44, Grenville to Harcourt, 14 Aug. 1795; Grenville's exchanges with Artois, 15 and 16 Aug., 25 Oct. and 19 Nov. 1795; F.O. 27/45, Grenville to Macartney, 17 Nov. and 29 Dec. 1795.
58. J. Godechot, op. cit. pp. 282ff., 292; P.R.O. F.O. 27/45, Macartney to Grenville, 10 Dec. 1795 (adverting to signs, mid-November, of Austro-Royalist offensive against Eastern France).
59. P.R.O. F.O. 27/45, Macartney to Grenville, 28 Nov. 1795; cf. same to same, 10 Dec. 1795.
60. Ibid. 10 Dec. 1795.
61. Ibid. Macartney to Grenville, 13 Dec. 1795, 31 Jan. 1796.
62. Ibid. same to same, 15 Nov. 1795.
63. Ibid. same to same, 27 Sept. 1795: British 'right' to 'portions of the French West Indies', opportunity to claim the remainder of French India, to keep Corsica and to take Sardinia, too — from Louis's father-in-law, one of the *Allies*.
64. Ibid. same to same, 27 Sept. and 28 Nov. 1795.
65. Macartney on conversation with Arras, with the Marshal, ibid, same to same, 15 Nov. and 27 Sept. 1795.
66. W. R. Fryer, 'The Mirage of Restoration', pp. 410-11 and note.
67. Ibid. pp. 411-12.
68. P.R.O. F.O. 27/45, Macartney to Grenville, 8 Feb. 1796; Grenville to

Macartney, 26 Feb. 1796.
69. W. R. Fryer, 'The Mirage of Restoration', pp. 413-14.
70. P.R.O. F.O. 27/45, Macartney to Grenville, 8 Feb. 1796.
71. Ibid. same to same, 22 April 1796; B.L. Add. Mss. 36811, f. 178, Copy, Macartney to Sir R. Worsley, British Minister to Venice, 14 April 1796.
72. P.R.O. F.O. 27/45, Macartney to Grenville, 22 April 1796.
73. Ibid, same to same, 19 April 1796; F.O. 74/17, Wickham to Grenville, 29 April 1796, describing the arrival of Louis at Condé's camp, and his appreciation of Macartney.
74. P.R.O. F.O. 27/45, Macartney to Grenville, 22 April 1796; B.L. Add. Mss. 36811, f. 182, Macartney to Bute, 21 April 1796.
75. W. R. Fryer, 'The Mirage of Restoration', p. 420.

CHAPTER NINE   THE CAPE OF GOOD HOPE 1796-98
1. F. Bickley, ed. *The Diaries of Sylvester Douglas (Lord Glenbervie)* (London, 1928), I, 80.
2. H. Furber, *Henry Dundas, 1st Viscount Melville, 1742-1811* (London, 1931), p. 104.
3. *Fortescue (Grenville) Mss.* II (H.M.C. 1894), pp. 645-46, Dundas to Grenville, 16 Nov. 1794.
4. J. S. Corbett, ed. *The Spencer Papers, 1794-1801* (Navy Records Society, 1913), I, 239-41, Dundas to Spencer, 24 March 1796.
5. Sir J. Barrow, *Some Account of the Public Life and a Selection from the Unpublished Writings of the Earl of Macartney* (London, 1807), I, 357-58.
6. C. McC. Theal, ed. *Records of the Cape Colony* (Cape Town, 1898), II, 34-37; Sir J. Barrow, op. cit. I, 358; P.R.O.N.I. Mic. 221 (Bodleian Library, MSS Afr. T2), p. 3, Macartney to Col. Brooke, 29 March 1797.
7. P.R.O.N.I. Mic. 221, p. 1, Macartney to Dundas, 9 Feb. 1797.
8. A. M. Lewin Robinson, ed. *The Letters of Lady Anne Barnard to Henry Dundas* (Cape Town, 1973), p. 260, Lady Barnard to Dundas, 16 Feb. 1801.
9. P.R.O.N.I. Mic. 221, p. 89, Macartney to Christian, 7 May 1798.
10. A. M. Lewin Robinson, ed. op. cit. pp. 98-99, Lady Barnard to Dundas, 3 Feb. 1798.
11. P.R.O.N.I. Mic. 177, Page from diary, n.d. (c. 1797).
12. A. M. Lewin Robinson, ed. op. cit. p. 70, Lady Barnard to Dundas, 15 Oct. 1797.
13. Ibid. p. 42, same to same, 10 July 1797.
14. Ibid. p. 99, same to same, 3 Feb. 1798.
15. G. McC. Theal, op. cit. II, 3-19.
16. Ibid. pp. 83-84, 94, 188-95, 205-6, 239, 265.
17. Ibid. pp. 92-94, 108-9; P.R.O. C.O. 49/1, f. 110, Macartney to Dundas, 13 July 1797.
18. P.R.O. C.O. 49/1, ff. 104-110, Macartney to Dundas, 10 July 1797.
19. A. M. Lewin Robinson, ed. op. cit. pp. 58, 65, Lady Barnard to Dundas, 16 and 23 Aug. 1797.
20. Ibid. pp. 75-81, Lady Barnard to Dundas, 29 Nov. 1797; H. Giliomee, *Die Kaap tydens die Eerste Britse Bewind, 1795-1803* (Cape Town, 1975), pp. 64-65.

21. P.R.O. C.O. 49/1, f. 145, Macartney to Dundas, 9 July, 1798.
22. A. M. Lewin Robinson, ed. op. cit. p. 175, Lady Barnard to Dundas, Sept. 1798; W. H. Wilkins, ed. *South Africa a Century Ago : Letters Written from the Cape of Good Hope by Lady Anne Barnard* (London, 1901), p. 196; R. Giliomee, op. cit. p. 67.
23. G. McC. Theal, *History of South Africa since 1795* (London, 1908), I, 28.
24. P.R.O.N.I. Mic. 221, p. 315, Barnard to Burgher Senate, 3 June 1798; H. Giliomee, op. cit. pp. 67, 108-9.
25. D. Fairbridge, *Lady Anne Barnard at the Cape of Good Hope, 1797-1802* (Oxford, 1924), p. 34.
26. G. McC. Theal. ed. *Records of the Cape Colony,* II, 105.
27. P.R.O.N.I. Mic. 221, P. 74, Macartney to *Landdrost* and College of Heemraden at Stellenbosch, 30 June 1797.
28. A. M. Lewin Robinson, ed. op. cit. pp. 73, 75, Lady Barnard to Dundas, 30 Oct. and 29 Nov. 1797.
29. P.R.O. C.O. 49/1, ff. 103, 121, 126, Macartney to Dundas, 9 May, 13 Oct. and 26 Nov. 1797; P.R.O.N.I. Mic. 221, p. 27, Macartney to W. Huskisson, 23 Aug. 1797.
30. A. M. Lewin Robinson, ed. op. cit. p. 169, Lady Barnard to Dundas, 13 Aug. 1798.
31. H. Giliomee, op. cit. p. 68.
32. P.R.O.N.I. Mic. 221, pp. 75-77, Macartney to Dundas, 7 May 1798.
33. A. M. Lewin Robinson, ed. op. cit. p. 187, Lady Barnard to Dundas, 4 May 1799.
34. Ibid. p. 194, same to same, 12 Sept. 1799.
35. G. McC. Theal, ed. *Records of the Cape Colony,* II, 110-11; C. Lloyd, *Mr. Barrow of the Admiralty: A Life of Sir John Barrow, 1764-1848* (London, 1970), p. 53.
36. P.R.O.N.I. Mic. 221, pp. 65-66, 72, 102-4, 232-34, Macartney to Dundas, 4 Feb., 5 and 9 March, 25 April 1801.
37. P.R.O.N.I. Mic. 221, p. 6, Macartney to Col. R. Brooke, 9 May 1797; ibid. p. 33, Macartney to Major-General Sydenham, 12 Sept. 1797; ibid. pp. 45-46, 50, 65, Macartney to Dundas, 29 Nov. and 29 Dec. 1797, 9 March 1798; ibid. p. 72, Macartney to Sir F. Baring, 5 March 1798; ibid. p. 97, Macartney to Lord Mornington, 22 May 1798; G. McC. Theal, ed. *Records of the Cape Colony,* II, 223, A. Maxwell to W. Huskisson, 6 Jan. 1798; A. M. Lewin Robinson, ed. op. cit. p. 64, Andrew Barnard to Dundas, 23 Aug. 1797; ibid. pp. 71, 116, 177, 180, Lady Barnard to Dundas, 30 Oct. 1797, 13 Aug., Sept., and 10 Nov. 1798.
38. G. McC. Theal, ed. *Records of the Cape Colony,* II, 298-99; Sir J. Barrow, op. cit. I, 365-67.

CHAPTER TEN   LATER YEARS 1780-1806

1. P.R.O.N.I. T. 3169/5, Macartney to Coutts, 15 Dec. 1797.
2. Sir J. Barrow, *Some Account of the Public Life and a Selection from the Unpublished Writings of the Earl of Macartney* (London, 1807), I., 371.
3. Lady Portarlington to Lady L. Stuart, 8 Sept. 1786, quoted in H. H. Robbins, *Our First Ambassador to China* (London, 1908), p. 165.
4. For examples, see P.R.O.N.I. D. 572/14/44, T. Coutts to Lady Macartney, 16 Jan. 1784 and B.L. Add. Mss. 22462, ff. 35-36, Macartney to T. Coutts, 28 July 1784.

5. H. H. Robbins, op. cit. pp. 156-59.
6. Ibid. p. 51.
7. See B.L. Add. Mss. 22462, ff. 1-2, 10-12, Macartney to Lady Macartney, 27 March and 13 Aug. 1782; also, see above, pp. 131-32, and below, pp. 306-7.
8. G. B. Hill, *Boswell's Life of Johnson,* rev. & enlarged L. F. Powell (2nd ed. Oxford, 1964), I, 13, 367, 380, 418, 477, 479; IV, 465; C. N. Fifer, ed. *The Correspondence of James Boswell with Certain Members of the Club* (London, 1976), pp. xx, lxiii, lxxvi-lxxvii, 361, 372; W. Jackson Bate, *Samuel Johnson* (London, 1978), pp. 367, 504-5. Macartney became an F.R.S. on 7 June 1792. G. E. C[ockayne], *The Complete Peerage,* ed. V. Gibbs and others (London, 1910-40), VIII, 324.
9. B.L. Add. Mss. 22462, f. 31, Macartney to T. Coutts, 5 Jan. 1784. See also P.R.O.N.I. D. 572/14/14, T. Coutts to Lady Macartney, 16 Jan. 1784.
10. Coutts Bank, London, Ledgers 75, 77, 79, 81, 83, 86.
11. B.L. Add. Mss. 22462, f. 18, Macartney to T. Coutts, 8 Aug. 1782; see also ff. 1-5, Macartney to Lady Macartney, and to T. Coutts, both 27 March 1782.
12. Ibid. ff. 1-2, Macartney to Lady Macartney, 27 March 1782; ff. 16-17, Macartney to T. Coutts, 24 Oct. 1782.
13. Ibid. ff. 10-12, Macartney to Lady Macartney, 13 Aug. 1782; see below, p. 287.
14. Ibid. f. 7, Macartney to R. & H. Drummond, 28 March 1782.
15. Coutts Bank, Ledger 75, f. 440B, 16 Feb. 1781. See C. Clay, 'The Price of Freehold Land in the Later 17th and 18th Centuries', *Ec. Hist. Rev.* 2nd ser. XXVII, no. 2 (May, 1974), p. 185 and *passim.*
16. B.L. Add. Mss. 22462, ff. 1-2, 10-12, Macartney to Lady Macartney, 27 March and 13 Aug. 1782; ff. 3-5, 8-9, 18, Macartney to T. Coutts, 27 March, 8 and 10 Aug. 1782; f. 6, Macartney to J. Powell, 28 March 1782; f. 7, Macartney to R. & H. Drummond, 28 March 1782.
17. Ibid. f. 1, Macartney to Lady Macartney, 27 March 1782.
18. Coutts Bank, Ledgers 79, 81, 83.
19. H. Furber, ed. *The Correspondence of Edmund Burke,* V (Chicago, 1965), p. 126, Macartney to Burke, 31 Jan. 1784.
20. B.L. Add. Mss. 22462, f. 34, Macartney to T. Coutts, 5 June 1784; Coutts Bank, Ledger 86, ff. 615B, 616A; Bodleian Library, Ms. Eng. Hist. c. 117, 'A statement of the benefits derived from my government of Madras'.
21. P.R.O.N.I. D. 572/9/1, R. Marley to Macartney, 7 Feb. 1786.
22. *Complete Peerage,* VIII, 324 (d); Coutts Bank, Ledger 89, f.672, e Aug. 1786.
23. P.R.O.N.I. D. 572/9/5, 6, R. Jackson to Macartney, 4 and 24 March 1786; D. 1062/2/1/42, Revocation of Trust, 16 April 1786; 43, Redemption of Mortgage, 26 July 1786; Registry of Deeds, Dublin, Book 380, p. 385, no. 256654; Book 383, p. 16, no. 252852.
24. H. H. Robbins, op. cit. p. 165, Lady L. Stuart to Lady Portarlington, 1786-87; P.R.O.N.I. D. 557, Macartney's Memorandum Book, [from] 1790, f. 121.
25. H. H. Robbins, loc. cit.; Surrey Co. Record Office, Guildford Muniment Room, Abstract of Title relating to Parkhurst, c. 1827. I am indebted to Mrs. S. Corke of the Guildford Muniment Room for

providing me with details from this document.

26. M. Bence-Jones, *Burke's Guide to Country Houses*, I, *Ireland* (London, 1978), p. 188. I am indebted to Mr. J. Mackie, the present owner of Lisanoure, for allowing me to inspect the architect's plan of the alterations in the Classical style in his possession, and for conducting me around the demesne.

27. P.R.O.N.I. D. 572/9/14, R. Jackson to Macartney, 1 Aug. 1787.

28. Ibid. and D. 572/9/16, 33, same to same, 30 Oct. 1787 and 19 Oct. 1789; D. 2225/7/48, 'Directions for work to be done in the garden', n.d. (c. 1790).

29. P.R.O.N.I. D. 1062/2/6, Copy, Macartney to T. Mercer, 10 Sept. 1788; D. 572/9/14, 16, 33, 34, R. Jackson to Macartney, 1 Aug. 1787, 30 Oct. 1787, 4 Nov. 1788, 19 Oct. 1789. Between 1788 and Feb. 1791 some 122,055 trees, 'cuttings' and shrubs were planted at Lisanoure. D. 557, ff. 32-33.

30. P.R.O.N.I. D. 557, ff. 46-47, 50-59, 64-78; D. 572/9/33, R. Jackson to Macartney, 19 Oct. 1789. D. 1062/2/4, Volume of Estate Maps, [mainly] 1772, contains the 1788 map of the demesne.

31. P.R.O.N.I. D. 1062/2/6, Copy, Macartney to T. Mercer, 10 Sept. 1788; D. 557, f. 4.

32. P.R.O.N.I. D. 572/9/14, 15, 16, 33, R. Jackson to Macartney, 1 Aug., 25 Sept., 30 Oct. 1787, 19 Oct. 1789; D. 572/9/62, J. Leslie to Macartney, 2 Nov. 1789; D. 2225/7/80, Revd. G. Macartney to Macartney, 8 July 1802.

33. P.R.O.N.I. D. 426/5, Estate Rental (including tenurial details), 1789.

34. P.R.O.N.I. T. 2408/32, Case and Opinion by C. O'Neill, 1 Dec. 1790; T. 2408/33, Draft Advertisement, c. 1790; D. 572/18/26, 27, 31, J. Arbuckle to Macartney, 15 and 24 July, 3 Aug. 1790; D. 572/18/28, 32, 33, D. Ker to Macartney, 26 July, 22 Aug. and 25 Sept. 1790; D. 572/18/30, Copy, Macartney to Ker, n.d.

35. P.R.O.N.I. D. 2225/7/38P, S, T. Mercer to Macartney, 31 July 1788, 4 June 1789; Registry of Deeds, Book 407, p. 462, no. 271995; Book 411, p. 369, no. 271996.

36. P.R.O.N.I. D. 572/18/36, 'Note for Lady Macartney', Sept. 1792, mentioning the debt to Mercer. See above, p. 137.

37. J. O. Laverty, *An Historical Account of the Diocese of Down and Connor, Ancient and Modern*, IV (Dublin, 1887), pp. 109-10.

38. P.R.O.N.I. D. 572/9/33, R. Jackson to Macartney, 19 Oct. 1789.

39 P.R.O.N.I. D. 2225/7/51A-K, Lisanoure Accounts, May - June 1791; D. 557, Macartney's Memorandum Book, ff. 5-7, 24, 138, 142.

40. P.R.O.N.I. D. 557, ff. 4, 6, 8-9, 11, 14, 20-21, 29, 40, 84; for a further list of prices, see D. 572/18/25, 1 May 1788.

41. P.R.O.N.I. D. 2225/7/44, N. MaGawley to J. Wray, 14 Aug. 1790; 7/46, Mr. Bristow to Macartney, 10 Dec. 1790.

42. P.R.O.N.I. D. 557, f. 154, 'List of Co. of Antrim Papers lent to Dr. MacDonnel, 1802'.

43. P. Roebuck, 'Rent Movement, Proprietorial Incomes and Agricultural Development, 1730-1830' in Roebuck, ed. *Plantation to Partition : Essays in Ulster History in Honour of J. L. McCracken* (Belfast, 1981), p. 94 and *passim.*

44. P.R.O.N.I. D. 426/5, Estate Rental, 1789; D. 572/21/98, Estate Rental, 1796. Both contain full tenurial details.

45. Coutts Bank, Ledgers 89, 92, 95, 98, 101, 104, 107.
46. P.R.O.N.I. D. 572/18/36, 'Note for Lady Macartney', Sept. 1792, including a list of current debts.
47. H. H. Robbins, op. cit. p. 170, quoting Jackson to Lady L. Stuart, 'autumn' 1789.
48. P.R.O.N.I. D. 2225/7/38H, T. Mercer to Macartney, 12 April 1788.
49. P.R.O.N.I. D. 572/9/71, Lady Bute to Lady Macartney, 22 July 1790.
50. P.R.O.N.I. T. 3169/4, Macartney to T. Coutts, 3 Jan. 1791.
51. Macartney was appointed to the Privy Council on 2 May 1792. *Complete Peerage*, VIII, 324.
52. P.R.O.N.I. D. 572/18/36, 'Note for Lady Macartney', Sept. 1792.
53. Ibid.; Coutts Bank, Ledgers, 110, f. 840; 114, ff. 998-99; C. Clay, op. cit. p. 185.
54. See above, pp. 244, 246.
55. Coutts Bank, Ledgers, 107, 110, 114, 118, 122, 126, 131, 136, L-M 1800-1.
56. Ibid. Ledger 118, ff. 1068-69.
57. Ibid. 31 May 'for value of his bond'.
58. Ibid. 21 Nov.
59. P.R.O.N.I. D. 572/18/36, 'Note for Lady Macartney', Sept. 1792.
60. Registry of Deeds, Book 481, p. 388, no. 318271; P.R.O.N.I. D. 572/21/101, Estate Rental, 1801, f. 16.
61. P.R.O.N.I. D. 572/21/98, Estate Rental, 1796.
62. P.R.O.N.I. D. 572/18/37, J. Wray to Macartney, 27 March 1795; D. 572/21/98, same to same, 28 June 1796, sent with estate rental and a list of 'sundry works' completed between July 1792 and June 1796.
63. See above, p. 267.
64. Coutts Bank, Ledger 122, ff. 1026-28; 126, ff. 1058-59; 131, ff. 1173-75; 136, ff. 1352, 1354-55.
65. Surrey Co. Record Office, Guildford Muniment Room, Abstract of Title relating to Parkhurst, c. 1827; P.R.O.N.I. D. 557, Macartney's Memorandum Book, ff. 100-101.
66. P.R.O.N.I. D. 572/21/82, Schedule of Macartney's Income from 5 Feb. 1798 to 5 Feb. 1799, 29 March 1799; D. 572/18/148, Ditto from 5 Feb. 1799 to 5 Feb. 1800, 8 July 1800.
67. P.R.O.N.I. D. 572/21/101, Estate Rental, 1801.
68. P.R.O.N.I. D. 557, ff. 102-103.
69. *Complete Peerage*, VIII, 325.
70. P.R.O.N.I. D. 572/18/43, Lady Macartney to Lady Staunton, 10 July 1801.
71. B.L. Add. Mss. 51389 (P.R.O.N.I. Mic. 227/1), Copy, Macartney to Lady Spencer, 30 Oct. 1801.
72. P.R.O.N.I. D. 572/18/41, Rental of Mountjoy's Estate in Co. Antrim, 1800; D. 572/18/40, Revd. G. Macartney to Macartney, 4 Dec. 1800; D. 572/18/57, H. Montgomery to Macartney, 4 May 1802.
73. P.R.O.N.I. D. 1062/2/1/59, Deed of Assignment, 10 Nov. 1800; 1/60, Bond, same date; D. 572/21/101, Estate Rental, 1801, f. 6.
74. P.R.O.N.I. D. 2225/7/84B, Account, 25 July 1804; 7/84A, Estimate for steeple, 26 April 1802; D. 572/18/70, J. Wray Jnr. to Macartney, 9 Jan. 1805; D. 572/18/80, 84, Revd. G. Macartney to Macartney, 25 March and 27 April 1805.
75. P.R.O.N.I. D. 572/18/43, Lady Macartney to Lady Staunton, 10 July

1801. For a list of prices at Lisanoure and Coleraine, 1801 and 1802, see D. 557, f. 84.

76. P.R.O.N.I. D. 557, f. 36; D. 572/18/11, F. Laverty's Account of Timber Felling, 10 Dec. 1805.

77. P.R.O.N.I. D. 572/18/75, 90, J. Wray Jnr. to Macartney, 24 Feb. and 13 June 1805; D. 1062/2/6, same to same, 3 Nov. 1805; D. 572/18/76, 80, 42, 101, 106, Revd. G. Macartney to Macartney, 1/2 March, 28 March, 22 June, 30 Aug. and 29 Oct. 1805.

78. P.R.O.N.I. D. 1062/2/1/64, Deed of Sale, 15 July 1802; D. 572/18/44, J. Stirling to Macartney, 24 July 1801; 18/49, N. McPeak to Macartney, 11 Dec. 1801; 18/61, J. Wray Jnr. to Macartney, 31 July 1802; T. 2408/34, Case and Opinion regarding Pharis, 15 June 1802.

79. See for example P.R.O.N.I. D. 572/18/83, Revd. G. Macartney to Macartney,. 17 April 1805.

80. P.R.O.N.I. D. 572/9/6, R. Jackson to Macartney, 24 March 1786.

81. Revd. Macartney was descended from 'Brown George' Macartney of Belfast, a contemporary of Macartney's great-grandfather, 'Black George'. He was B.A., M.A., LL.B. and LL.D. of Trinity College, Dublin, ordained in the Church of Ireland in 1766, and Vicar of Antrim from 1773 till his death in 1824. For full details, see 'Biographical Succession List of the Clergy of Connor Diocese', a typescript by J. B. Leslie in the Representative Church Body Library, Dublin. I am indebted to Miss G. Willis, once Librarian of this institution, for providing me with a summary of the entry on Revd. Macartney.

82. B.L. Add. Mss. 37535, f. 198, Macartney to Lord Hardwicke, 17 July 1802.

83. P.R.O.N.I. D. 572/18/94, Draft, Macartney to Revd. Macartney, 7 Aug. 1805; 18/110, Draft, Macartney to J. Wray Jnr. 1 Dec. 1805.

84. See the map and survey of the Dervock townlands, 1772, in P.R.O.N.I. D. 1062/2/4, and the estate rentals (containing tenurial details) of 1789 and 1796 (D. 426/5 and 527/21/98).

85. P.R.O.N.I. D. 572/21/96, Estate Survey and 'Observations', 1767, ff. 1-2.

86. P.R.O.N.I. D. 557, f. 29; T. 925/1, J. Macky's Diary, entry for 1 Oct. 1792.

87. See above, p. 138.

88. H. McNeill, *Annals of Derrykeighan* (Belfast, 1910), p. 41. I am indebted to Mr. H. A. Boyd for this reference.

89. P.R.O.N.I. D. 572/21/101, Estate Rental, 1801.

90. P.R.O.N.I. D. 572/6/82, 122, C. Gardner to Macartney, 5 Dec. 1801, 2 Oct. 1802.

91. P.R.O.N.I. D. 1062/2/4, Volume of Estate Maps, [mainly] 1772, Plan for Dervock, c. 1801.

92. Ibid.; P.R.O.N.I. D. 572/18/81, J. Wray Jnr. to Macartney, 12 April 1805

93. P.R.O.N.I. D. 572/18/89, same to same, 12 May 1805.

94. P.R.O.N.I. D. 572/18/67, Draft Agreement, 24 Aug. 1804; 18/106, 88, Revd. G. Macartney to Macartney, 29 Oct. and 29 April 1805.

95. P.R.O.N.I. D. 572/18/116, J. Wray Jnr. to Macartney, 29 Dec. 1805.

96. P.R.O.N.I. D. 572/18/113, 114, Revd. G. Macartney to Macartney, 14 and 17 Dec. 1805.

97. P.R.O.N.I. D. 572/18/116, J. Wray Jnr. to Macartney, 29 Dec. 1805.
98. P.R.O.N.I. D. 572/18/71, Revd. G. Macartney to Macartney, 11 Jan. 1806.
99. P.R.O.N.I. D. 572/18/124, same to same, 8 Feb. 1806.
100. P.R.O.N.I. D. 572/18/89, J. Wray Jnr. to Macartney, 12 May 1805; D. 572/18/120, Revd. G. Macartney to Macartney, 22 Jan. 1806.
101. P.R.O.N.I. T. 2408/7, Abstract of Title, together with a summary rental and notes, *c.* 1804; P. Roebuck, 'The Lives Lease System and Emigration from Ulster : An Example from Montgomery County, Pennsylvania', *Ulster Genealogical and Historical Guild Newsletter,* I, no. 7 (1981), 217-19.
102. Roebuck, 'Rent Movement, Proprietorial Incomes . . .', p. 88 and *passim.*
103. P.R.O.N.I. D. 572/21/102, Estate Rental, 1816, which provides details of earlier lettings.
104. P.R.O.N.I. D. 572/18/105, 108, Sir W. Kirk to Macartney, 26 Oct. and 16 Nov. 1805; 18/104, 130, Macartney to Kirk, 28 Nov. 1805, 11 March 1806.
105. Coutts Bank, Ledgers L-M 1800-1, M 1801-2, M 1802-3, M 1803-4, M 1804-5, M 1805-6.
106. P.R.O.N.I. D. 572/18/147, Draft, Macartney to Coutts Bank, 20 Oct. 1803.
107. B.L. Add. Mss. 51389, Copy, Macartney to Lady Spencer, 30 Oct. 1801.
108. B.L. Add. Mss. 35736, f. 202, Macartney to Lord Hardwicke, 9 Oct. 1802; Add. Mss. 35744, f. 47, same to same, 30 Nov. 1803.
109. P.R.O.N.I. D. 572/21/91, Copy, Macartney, Lisanoure, to N. McPeak, 18 Aug. 1804.
110. P.R.O.N.I. D. 572/18/74, Revd. G. Macartney to Macartney, 21 Feb. 1805.
111. P.R.O.N.I. D. 572/18/104, Macartney to Sir W. Kirk, 28 Nov. 1805.
112. P.R.O.N.I. D. 572/18/130, same to same, 11 March 1806.
113. *Belfast News Letter,* 15 April 1806. For the death notice, see 8 April 1806. I am indebted to Mr. B. Trainor for these references.
114. P.R.O.N.I. D. 1905/2/29/2.
115. P.R.O.N.I. D. 572/19/114, Lady Macartney to Macartney, 18 Aug. 1784; 9/17, R. Jackson to Macartney, 12 Dec. 1787.
116. H. H. Robbins, op. cit. p. 456.
117. P.R.O.N.I. D. 1905/2/29/2; *Complete Peerage,* VIII, 325.

CHAPTER ELEVEN   CONCLUSION

1. Earl of Ilchester, ed. *The Journal of Elizabeth, Lady Holland, (1791-1811)* (London, 1908), I, 240-41, 21 April 1799.
2. B.L. Add. Mss. 51388 (P.R.O.N.I. Mic. 227/1), Macartney to Lord Holland, 7/18 June 1765.
3. G. Benn, *A History of the Town of Belfast* (2nd ed. London, 1877), I, 256-58.

BIBLIOGRAPHY

PRIMARY SOURCES: MANUSCRIPT
(Arranged alphabetically according to Repository.)

British Library, London
Governorship of Grenada: Additional MS 12438.
Madras Presidency: Additional MSS 22415, 22416-19, 22433, 22435, 22437-38,
          22461-62.
Mission to Verona: Additional MSS 36811, 37846, 37876.
Correspondence with Lord Hardwicke: Additional MSS 37535-36.
Correspondence with the Holland Family: Additional MSS 51388-89.

Bodleian Library, Oxford
Madras Presidency: MSS Eng. Hist. b. 176.
                    MSS Eng. Hist. c. 77, 79, 81-82, 98, 101, 104, 117.

Cornell University, Ithaca, New York
Wason Collection on China and the Chinese: Macartney Correspondence.

Coutts Bank, London
Accounts of Macartney and his wife, 1768-1806.

Borough Library, Derby
Catton Collection (Ireland): Wilmot Papers.

Huntington Library, Los Angeles
Macartney's Commonplace Book, 1767-77: HM 686.

India Office Library and Records, London
East India Company: Court Books, 1780-86.
                   Political and Secret Department Records, 1780-86.
                   The China Embassy, 1792-94.

National Library of Ireland, Dublin
Ballitore MSS: Mic. P.1089.
'A Sketch of the Revenue of Ireland in 1773' (by Macartney): MS 11, 967.

Public Record Office, London
State Papers.
Colonial Office Papers.
Foreign Office Papers.
Treasury Papers.

Public Record Office of Ireland, Dublin
Townshend Correspondence: M.733.

Public Record Office of Northern Ireland, Belfast
Macartney Papers: D. 426, 557, 572, 1062, 1184, 2731.
                T. 2408, 2480, 3169, 3428.
                Mic. 177, 221, 227, 395, 405, 407.
                T.D. 4779.

Macartney of Lisanoure 1737-1806

Public Record Office of Northern Ireland, Belfast
Macartney/Filgate Papers: D. 2225.
Foster/Massereene Papers: D. 562.
McGildowney Papers: D. 1375.
Gosford Papers: D. 1606.
Downshire Papers: D. 607.
L'Estrange & Brett Papers: D. 1905.
J. Macky's Diary, 1791-1809: T. 925.

Registry of Deeds, Dublin
Various Entries of Memorials, 1733-1806.

Representative Church Body Library, Dublin
Typescript: J. B. Leslie, 'Biographical Succession List of the Clergy of Connor
  Diocese'.

Surrey County Record Office, Guildford Muniment Room
Abstract of Title relating to Parkhurst, *c.* 1827.

Trinity College, Dublin
Entrance Book, 1725-58.
Examination Returns, 1750-54.
Bursar's Books, 1750-55.
Degrees Conferred, 1743-1834.

W. L. Clements Library, Ann Arbor, Michigan
Macartney Papers.
Townshend Letter Books.
List of Offices in N. America and the W. Indian Colonies, *c.* 1775: A.M. 21.

Yale University
J. M. Osborn Collection: Macartney Papers.

PRIMARY SOURCES: PRINTED

Anon.	*Some observations which may contribute to afford a just idea of the nature, importance and settlement of our new West Indian colonies* (London, 1764).
Anson, W. ed.	*The Autobiography and Political Correspondence of Augustus Henry, Third Duke of Grafton* (London, 1898).
Aspinall, A. ed.	*The Later Correspondence of George III* (5 vols. Cambridge, 1962).
Backhouse, E. and Bland, J. O. P.	*Annals and Memoirs of the Court of Peking from the 16th to the 20th Century* (London, 1913).
Barrow, Sir J.	*Travels in China* (London, 1804).
— —	*Some Account of the Public Life and a Selection from the Unpublished Writings of the Earl of Macartney* (2 vols. London, 1807).
Bartlett, T. ed.	*Macartney in Ireland 1768-72: A Calendar of the Chief Secretaryship Papers of Sir George Macartney* (P.R.O.N.I. 1979).

Belfast News Letter

Bell, J.   *Travels from St. Petersburg in Russia to Diverse Parts of Asia* (2 vols. Glasgow, 1763).

Bickley, F. ed.   *The Diaries of Sylvester Douglas (Lord Glenbervie)* (London, 1928).

Bland, J. O. P.   *See* Backhouse, E.

[Burke, E.]   *The Works of the Rt. Hon. Edmund Burke* (8 vols. London, 1803).

C[ockayne], G. E.   *The Complete Peerage*, ed. V. Gibbs & others (13 vols. London, 1910-40).

[Coke, Lady M.]   *The Letters and Journals of Lady Mary Coke* (4 vols. priv. pr. 1889-96, fac. edn. London, 1970).

Corbett, J. S. ed.   *The Spencer Papers, 1794-1801* (Navy Records Society, 1913).

Cranmer-Byng, J. L. ed.   *An Embassy to China: being the Journal kept by Lord Macartney during his Embassy to the Emperor Ch'ien-lung, 1793-94* (London, 1962; Hamden, Conn. 1963; repr. Michigan, 1972).

Davies, C. C. ed.   *The Private Correspondence of Lord Macartney, Governor of Madras (1781-85)*, Roy. Hist. Soc. Camden Third Series, LXXVII (London, 1950).

de Barante, A.   *Lettres et Instructions de Louis XVIII au Cte. de St-Priest* (Paris, 1845).

de Mialla, J.   *Histoire Générale de la Chine* (12 vols. Paris, 1777-83).

Dodwell, H.   *Warren Hastings' Letters to Sir John Macpherson* (London, 1927).

du Halde, P.   *Description Géographique, Historique, Chronologique, Politique et Physique de l'Empire de la Chine et de la Tartarie Chinoise* (4 vols. Paris, 1735).

Edwards, B.   *History of the British Colonies in the West Indies* (4 vols. London, 1806).

Fifer, C. N. ed   *The Correspondence of James Boswell with Certain Members of the Club* (London, 1976).

Fitzgerald, B. ed.   *The Correspondence of Emily, Duchess of Leinster* (3 vols. I.M.C. 1949-57).

Fortescue, J. ed.   *The Correspondence of George III* (6 vols. London 1927).

Freeman's Journal (Dublin).

Furber, H. ed.   *The Correspondence of Edmund Burke, V 1782-89* (Cambridge, 1965).

Garlick, K. and MacIntyre, A. eds.   *The Diary of Joseph Farington* (8 vols. fac. edn. London, 1978).

Grosier, Abbé.   *Description Générale de la Chine* (Paris, 1785).

Hill, G. B.   *Boswell's Life of Johnson*, rev. & enlarged L. F. Powell (6 vols. Oxford, 1934-64).

H.M.C.	*Donoughmore Mss.* (1891).
— —	*Fortescue (Grenville) Mss.* II (1894).
— —	*Fortescue Mss.* III (1899).
— —	*Various Collections,* VI (1909).
— —	*Ormonde Mss.* new ser. VIII (1920).
Hoffman, R. ed.	*Edmund Burke, New York Agent* (Philadelphia, 1956).
Howard, G. E.	*History of the Exchequer and Revenue of Ireland* (Dublin, 1776).
Ilchester, Earl of, ed.	*The Journal of Elizabeth, Lady Holland, 1791-1811* (2 vols. London, 1908).
[Jackson, R.]	*See* [Macartney, Sir G.].
[Johnston, J.]	'The Letters of John Johnston', *Ulster Genealogical and Historical Guild Newsletter,* I, no. 7 (1981).

Lettres édifiantes et curieuses écrites des missions étrangères (26 vols. Paris, 1780-83).

Lewin Robinson, A.M. ed.	*The Letters of Lady Anne Barnard to Henry Dundas* (Cape Town, 1973).
Lewis, W. S. ed	*Horace Walpole's Correspondence* (39 vols. London, 1937-).
Lodge, J.	*Peerage of Ireland,* rev. M. Archdall (7 vols. Dublin, 1789).
London Gazette.	
Londonderry Journal.	
Long, E.	*History of Jamaica* (3 vols. London, 1774).
[Macartney, Sir G. and Jackson, R.]	*A Comparative State of the Two Rejected Money Bills in 1692 and 1769, by a Barrister* (Dublin, 1770).
[Macartney, Sir G.]	*An Account of Ireland in 1773, by a late Chief Secretary of that Kingdom* (priv. pr. 1773).
MacIntyre, A.	*See* Garlick, K.
Marshall, P. J. ed.	*The Writing and Speeches of Edmund Burke,* V *1774-85* (Oxford, 1981).

Mémoires concernant l'Histoire, les Sciences, les Moeurs, les Usages etc. des Chinois, par les missionaires de Pékin (15 vols. Paris, 1776-91).

Misra, B. B.	*See* Philips, C. H.
Philips, C. H. and Misra, B. B. eds.	*Fort William-India House Correspondence,* XV *Foreign and Secret, 1782-86* (Delhi, 1963).
[P.R.O.I.]	*Twenty-Sixth Report of the Deputy-Keeper of the Public Records of Ireland* (Dublin, 1894).
Redding, J. ed.	*Calendar of Home Office Papers 1766-69* (London, 1879).
Ross, C. ed.	*Correspondence of Charles, First Marquis Cornwallis* (3 vols. London, 1859).
Smith, W. J. ed.	*The Grenville Papers* (4 vols. London, 1853).
Theal, G. McC. ed.	*Records of the Cape Colony* (36 vols. Cape Town, 1897-1905).
Wickham, W.	*Correspondence of William Wickham* (2 vols. London, 1870).

Wilkins, W. H. ed.	*South Africa a Century Ago: Letters Written from the Cape of Good Hope by Lady Anne Barnard* (London, 1901).
Woods, J. A. ed.	*The Correspondence of Edmund Burke,* IV *1778-82* (Cambridge, 1963).
Wraxall, N.	*Historical Memoirs of My Own Time* (2 vols. London, 1815).

SECONDARY SOURCES

Archer, M.	'From Cathay to China: the Drawings of William Alexander 1792-94', *History Today,* XII, no. 12 (December, 1962).
Armytage, F.	*The Freeport System in the British West Indies 1766-1822* (London, 1954).
Bartlett, T.	'The Townshend Viceroyalty 1767-72' in Bartlett & D. W. Hayton, eds. *Penal Era and Golden Age: Essays in Irish History 1690-1800* (Belfast, 1979).
— —	'Viscount Townshend and the Irish Revenue Board 1767-73', *Proc.* R.I.A. LXXXIX, section C, no. 6 (1979).
— —	'The Irish House of Commons' Rejection of the Privy Council Money Bill in 1769', *Studia Hibernica,* no. 19 (1979).
Bence-Jones, M.	*Burke's Guide to Country Houses,* I *Ireland* (London, 1978).
Benn, G.	*A History of the Town of Belfast* (2 vols. 2nd edn. London, 1877).
Besterman, T. ed.	*Studies in Voltaire and the 18th Century,* XLIV, Sir G. de Beer & A-M. Rousseau, eds. *Voltaire's British Visitors* (Geneva, 1967).
— —	*The Complete Works of Voltaire: Correspondence and Related Documents,* XXVI (Banbury, 1973).
Bittard des Fortes, R.	*Histoire de l'Armée de Condé* (Paris, 1896).
Brooke, J.	*See* Namier, Sir L.
Burtchaell, G. D. and Sadleir, T. U. eds.	*Alumni Dublinenses* (London, 1924).
Checkland, S. G.	'Finance for the West Indies 1780-1815', *Ec. Hist. Rev.* 2nd ser. X (1957-58).
Clay, C.	'The Price of Freehold Land in the Later 17th and 18th Centuries', *Ec. Hist. Rev.* 2nd ser. XXVII (1974).
Cranmer-Byng, J. L.	'Lord Macartney's Embassy to Peking in 1793, from Official Chinese Documents', *Journal of Oriental Studies,* IV, nos. 1 & 2 (1957-58).
Cranmer-Byng, J. L. and Levere, T.	'A Case Study in Cultural Collision: Scientific Apparatus in the Macartney Embassy to China, 1793', *Annals of Science,* XXXVIII (1981).

Cranmer-Byng, J. L. and Wills, J. E. Jr. — 'Trade and Diplomacy with Maritime Europe, 1644-1800' in *The Cambridge History of China*, IX, pt. 1 (forthcoming).

Daudet, E. — *Histoire de l'Emigration* (3 vols. 3rd edn. Paris, 1907).

Davies, J. — *Cardiff and the Marquesses of Bute* (Cardiff, 1981).

de la Gorce, P. — *Louis XVIII* (Paris, 1926).

de Selincourt, E. ed. — *The Prelude* (Oxford, 1926).

Dictionaire de Biographie Française

Dictionary of National Biography

Drake, M. — 'The Irish Demographic Crisis of 1740-41' in T. W. Moody, ed. *Historical Studies VI* (London, 1968).

Fairbank, J. K. and Yeng, S. Y. — *Ch'ing Administration: Three Studies* (Harvard, 1960).

Fairbank, J. K. ed. — *The Chinese World Order: Traditional China's Foreign Relations* (Harvard, 1968).

Fairbridge, D. — *Lady Anne Barnard at the Cape of Good Hope, 1797-1802* (Oxford, 1924).

Fryer, W. R. — *Republic or Restoration in France? 1794-97* (Manchester, 1965).

— — 'The Mirage of Restoration: Louis XVIII and Lord Macartney 1795-96', *Bulletin of the John Rylands University Library of Manchester,* Autumn 1979, Spring 1980.

Furber, H. — *Henry Dundas, First Viscount Melville, 1742-1811* (London, 1931).

Giliomee, H. — *Die Kaap tydens die Eerste Britse Bewind, 1795-1803* (Cape Town, 1975).

Godechot, J. — *La Contre-Révolution* (Paris, 1961).

Gooch, G. P. — *See* Ward, Sir A.

Goveia, E. — *Slave Society in the British Leeward Islands at the end of the 18th Century* (Yale, 1965).

Grattan, H. ed. — *Memoirs of the Life and Times of the Rt. Hon. Henry Grattan* (5 vols. Dublin, 1839-46).

Greenberg, M. — *British Trade and the Opening of China 1800-42* (Cambridge, 1951).

Harlow, V. T. — *The Founding of the Second British Empire 1763-93* (2 vols. London, 1952-64).

Henderson, Sir N. — *Failure of a Mission: Berlin, 1937-39* (London, 1940).

Higman, B. W. — *Slave Population and Economy in Jamaica, 1807-34* (Cambridge, 1976).

Ilchester, Earl of — *Henry Fox, First Lord Holland: His Family and Relations* (2 vols. London, 1920).

Jackson Bate, W. — *Samuel Johnson* (London, 1978).

Jameson, J. F. — 'St. Eustasius and the American Revolution', *American Historical Review,* VIII (1902-3).

Johnston, E. M.	*Great Britain and Ireland 1760-1800* (Edinburgh, 1963).
Lamb, A.	'Lord Macartney in Batavia, March 1793', *Journal of the South Seas Society,* XIV.
Levere, T.	*See* Cranmer-Byng, J. L.
Lewis, S.	*A Topographical Dictionary of Ireland* (2 vols. London, 1837).
Lloyd, C.	*Mr. Barrow of the Admiralty: A Life of Sir John Barrow, 1764-1848* (London, 1970).
Mahan, A. T.	*The Influence of Sea Power upon History* (London, 1890).
McCourt, D.	'The Decline of Rundale 1750-1850' in P. Roebuck, ed. *Plantation to Partition: Essays in Ulster History in Honour of J. L. McCracken* (Belfast, 1981).
McDowell, R. B. and Webb, D. A.	'Courses and Teaching in Trinity College, Dublin, during the First Two Hundred Years', *Hermathena,* LXIX (1947).
— —	*Trinity College, Dublin 1592-1952: An Academic History* (Cambridge, 1982).
McNeill, H.	*Annals of Derrykeighan* (Belfast, 1910).
Maguire, W. A.	'Lord Donegall and the Hearts of Steel', *Irish Historical Studies,* XXI, no. 84 (1981).
Maroon, M.	*Dictionaire des Institutions de la France* (Paris, 1923).
Marshall, P. J.	*Problems of Empire: Britain and India 1757-1813* (London, 1968).
Mason, P.	*A Matter of Honour* (London, 1974).
Melvin, P.	'Colonel Maurice Griffin Dennis, 1805-63', *The Irish Sword,* XIII (1977).
Metcalf, G.	*Royal Government and Political Conflict in Jamaica, 1729-83* (London, 1965).
Mitchell, H.	*The Underground War against Revolutionary France* (Oxford, 1965).
Morse, H. B.	*The Chronicles of the East India Company Trading to China 1635-1834* (2 vols. Oxford, 1926-29).
Mullin, T. H.	*Coleraine in By-Gone Centuries* (Belfast, 1976).
Murray, D. J.	*The West Indies and the Development of Colonial Government* (London, 1965).
Namier, Sir L. and Brooke, J.	*The House of Commons 1754-90* (3 vols. London, 1964).
Nivison, D.	'Ho-shen and His Accusers' in Nivison & A. F. Wright, eds. *Confucianism in Action* (Stanford, 1959).
O'Laverty, J.	*An Historical Account of the Diocese of Down and Connor, Ancient and Modern* (5 vols. Dublin, 1878-95).

Pares, R.	*War and Trade in the West Indies 1739-63* (Oxford, 1936).
— —	*A West India Fortune* (London, 1950).
— —	*Yankees and Creoles* (London, 1956).
— —	'The London Sugar Market, 1740-69', *Ec. Hist. Rev.* 2nd serv. IX (1956).
Penson, L. M.	'The London West India Interest in the 18th Century', *English Historical Review,* XXXVI(1921), reprinted in R. Mitchison, ed. *Essays in 18th-Century History* (London, 1966).
— —	*The Colonial Agents of the British West Indies* (London, 1924).
Pitman, F. W.	*The Development of the British West Indies* (New Haven, 1917).
Pritchard, E. H.	'Letters from Missionaries at Peking relating to the Macartney Embassy, 1793-1803', *T'oung Pao,* XXXI (1934).
— —	*The Crucial Years of Early Anglo-Chinese Relations 1750-1800* (Pullman, 1936).
— —	'The Instructions of the East India Company to Lord Macartney on his Embassy to China and his Reports to the Company 1792-94', *Journal of the Royal Asiatic Society of Gt. Britain and Ireland,* 1938, parts 2, 3, 4.
— —	'The Kotow in the Macartney Embassy to China in 1793', *Far Eastern Quarterly,* II, no. 2 (1943).
[P.R.O.N.I.]	*Report of the Deputy-Keeper of the Records for 1960-65* (Belfast, 1966).
Ragatz, L. J.	*The Fall of the Planter Class in the British Caribbean* (American Historical Association, 1928).
— —	*Statistics for the Study of British Caribbean Economic History 1763-1833* (London, 1928).
— —	'Absentee Landlordism in the British Caribbean 1750-1833', *Agricultural History,* V (1931).
Righi, A.	*Il Conte de Lilla e l'émigrazione francese a Verona, 1794-96* (n.p.p. 1909).
Robbins, H. H.	*Our First Ambassador to China* (London, 1908).
Roberts, M.	*Macartney in Russia, English Historical Review,* Special Supplement no. 7 (1974).
Robinet and others	*Dictionaire Historique et Biographique de la Revolution et de l'Empire* (Paris, 1899).
Roebuck, P.	'The Making of an Ulster Great Estate: the Chichesters, Barons of Belfast and Viscounts of Carrickfergus, 1599-1648', *Proc. R.I.A.* section C, no. 1 (1979).
— —	*Yorkshire Baronets, 1640-1760: Families, Estates and Fortunes* (Oxford, 1980).

Roebuck, P.   'Rent Movement, Proprietorial Incomes and Agricultural Development, 1730-1830' in Roebuck, ed. *Plantation to Partition: Essays in Ulster History in Honour of J. L. McCracken* (Belfast, 1981).

— — 'Landlord Indebtedness in Ulster in the 17th and 18th Centuries' in J. M. Goldstrom & L. A. Clarkson, eds. *Irish Population, Economy and Society: Essays in Honour of the Late K. H. Connell* (Oxford, 1981).

— — 'The Lives Lease System and Emigration from Ulster: An Example from Montgomery County, Pennsylvania', *Ulster Genealogical and Historical Guild Newsletter*, I, no. 7 (1981).

Sadleir, T. U.   *See* Burtchaell, G. D.

Sheridan, R. B.   'The Rise of a Colonial Gentry: A Case Study of Antigua, 1730-75', *Ec. Hist. Rev.* 2nd ser. XIII (1960-61).

Simms, J. G.   *The Williamite Confiscation in Ireland 1690-1703* (London, 1964).

— — *Jacobite Ireland 1685-91* (London, 1969).

Staunton, Sir G. T.   *Ta Tsing Leu Lee* (London, 1810).

— — *Memoir of the Life and Family of the Late Sir G. L. Staunton* (London, 1823).

Stubbs, J. W.   *The History of the University of Dublin from Its Foundation to the End of the 18th Century* (London, 1889).

Sutherland, L. S.   *The East India Company in Eighteenth-Century Politics* (Oxford, 1952).

— — 'Lord Macartney's Appointment as Governor of Madras, 1780: the Treasury in East India Company Elections', *English Historical Review*, XC (1975).

Taylor, C.   *Reporter in Red China* (Toronto, 1966).

Theal, G. McC.   *History of South Africa 1795-1872* (5 vols. London, 1919-27).

Trench, C. V.   *The Wrays of Donegal, Londonderry, Antrim* (Oxford, 1945).

Trevor-Roper, H.   *Hermit of Peking: the Enigma of Sir Edmund Backhouse* (London, 1976).

Ward, Sir A. and Gooch, G. P. eds.   *Cambridge History of British Foreign Policy* I (Cambridge, 1922).

Webb, D. A.   *See* McDowell, R. B.

Wills, J. E. Jr.   *See* Cranmer-Byng, J. L.

Yeng, S. Y.   *See* Fairbank, J. K.

INDEX

Index

Index

369

Index

Index